Exporting
and
Importing

Exporting and Importing

Negotiating Global Markets

Amy Zuckerman
and
David Biederman

AMACOM
American Management Association

New York • Atlanta • Boston • Chicago • Kansas City • San Francisco • Washington, D.C.
Brussels • Mexico City • Tokyo • Toronto

This book is available at a special discount when ordered in
bulk quantities. For information, contact Special Sales
Department, AMACOM, a division of American Management
Association, 1601 Broadway, New York, NY 10019.

This publication is designed to provide accurate and authoritative
information in regard to the subject matter covered. It is sold with
the understanding that the publisher is not engaged in rendering
legal, accounting, or other professional service. If legal advice or
other expert assistance is required, the services of a competent
professional person should be sought.

Library of Congress Cataloging-in-Publication Data

Zuckerman, Amy.
    Exporting and importing : negotiating global markets / Amy
Zuckerman and David Biederman.
        p.   cm.
    Includes bibliographical references and index.
    ISBN 0-8144-0391-3
    1. Export marketing—United States.   2. Foreign trade regulation—
United States.   3. Exports—United States.   4. Imports—United
States.   5. Export marketing—United States—Information services.
I. Biederman, David.   II. Title.
HF1416.5.U6Z83   1998
382'.0973—dc21   98-24142
                                                          CIP

A previous edition of this book was published as Importing &
Exporting by Warren Gorham & Lamont in 1995.

Printing number

10   9   8   7   6   5   4   3   2   1

To Julia

Contents

Government Forms

To meet the fast-paced demands of the international trade community in a booming global economy, the United States government has undergone massive reorganizations of both the Bureau of Export Administration (BXA) and the U.S. Customs Service. Changes are taking place constantly, which makes it impossible to provide entirely up-to-date forms in a book context.

However, exporters and importers who want quick access to government forms have a new service at their fingertips. The BXA and Customs both provide many forms online through their web sites. Here are the URLs to use to access government forms:

Bureau of Export Administration

Web site: www.bxa.doc.gov
BXA issues: www.bxa.doc.gov/bxaissues.htm
Denied parties: www.bxa.doc.gov/2_denial.htm
Regulations (Ear Marketplace): www.bxa.doc.gov/EARwebpg.htm
Locations: www.bxa.doc.gov/wherwe.htm
Call us: www.bxa.doc.gov/bxahelp.htm
Mission: www.bxa.doc.gov/whoarewe.htm

U.S. Customs Service

Web site: www.customs.ustreas.gov
Importing and exporting: www.customs.ustreas.gov/imp-exp/
Import quotas: www.customs.ustreas.gov/imp-exp/quotas/reports.htm
Customs regulations: www.customs.ustreas.gov/imp-exp/rulings/t19custm/index.htm
Rulings: www.customs.ustreas.gov/imp-exp/rulings/rulclist.htm
Commercial importing procedures and requirements: www.customs.ustreas.gov/imp-exp/comm-imp/index.htm
Harmonized coding system: www.customs.ustreas.gov/imp-exp/rulings/harmoniz/index.htm
Traveler information: www.customs.ustreas.gov/travel/index.htm

Acknowledgments

Many importing and exporting professionals offered their expertise during the writing of this book. The authors offer very special thanks to Ed Kaplan, Mike McCarthy, and Harvey Waite, members of the staff of OCEANAIR, who made this publication possible. Special thanks also goes to Paul DiVecchio of DiVecchio and Associates; Thomas Johnson of Baker & McKenzie, author of *Export/Import Procedures and Documentation;* Doreen Trottier of Waters Corporation; Mike Davis of the Reference Department of the University of Massachusetts library; Jerry Dooner of the Roanoke Insurance Companies; and Jeff Pomeroy of BXA West.

Transport professionals who lent assistance to this book include Henk Benjamins, Bob Bullock, Rob Casey, Tom Cantwell, Doug Fisher, Cosmos Hoefnagels, Greg Howard, Jim Justice, Art Litman, Ernie Mahassey, Greg Pitkoff and Harold Zassenhaus. Insurance professionals who assisted include Greg Kritz and Frank Reynolds.

Many U.S. government professionals also provided assistance. We offer special thanks to Larry Christensen and Eugene Cotilli of the Bureau of Export Administration (BXA), Cecile Ablack, Iain Baird, Joel Barkin, Bill Buck, Kurt Coltiss, Steve Copeland, Pat Cross, Bob Dix, Steven Duchesne, Lorna Finley, Sandra Gethers, Darryl Griffin, John Hammond, Paul Hegland, Mark Laria, Joyce Loebig, Joyce Metzger, Ann Ngo, Bill Rosoff, Peter Ruzicka, Dale Snell, Bill Spiltzez, Curt Steinberg, Becky Trafton, Julia Walker, and Iscella Wittich.

Thanks also go to members of the Export Company, the Port of New York, and the World Trade Institute of the Port Authority of New York, particularly Fritz McLymont, Barry Watkins, and Dick Haran.

Finally, the authors thank the following individuals who provided editorial and research support: Seka Berger, Randy Bernard, Amanda Birmingham, Dan Goitein, Jeremy Pierce, Elise Sealy, Sean Sullivan, Laura Sylvester, and Jordan Wine. Thanks also to former AMACOM acquisitions editor Tony Vlamis and to AMACOM editors Jackie Flynn, Ray O'Connell, and Richard Gatjens for the efforts they put into revising this manuscript.

Exporting
and
Importing

1

Export Markets

Key Questions Answered in This Chapter

Introduction

With respect to exporting, U.S. companies are novices in a world full of international trade experts. European nations trade with one another. Japan needs imports to survive. Nations in the Middle East and Asia have trade routes going back thousands of years. By contrast, in part because of the size of the domestic market, most American manufacturers have not had to move into the global marketplace until recently. Commerce Department statistics reveal that a relatively small number of multinational corporations account for 85 percent of U.S. trade overseas; in 1987, only 13 percent of U.S. manufacturers exported products.

But change is occurring rapidly. U.S. Customs Service, Commerce Department, and Census Bureau officials all report more and more small and midsize companies venturing overseas in the last decade. In 1990, 36 percent of firms with less than $100 million in annual revenue exported their products; in 1993, that figure increased to 50 percent.

And it seems certain that sometime before the year 2000, legislation will be passed authorizing the president and/or Congress authority to "fast track" trade agreements when speed is of the essence in the world marketplace. President Clinton tabled his fast-track package in the fall of 1997 in the face of a united labor campaign to defeat the legislation. U.S. industry, in the meantime, supports the fast-track concept and the president has vowed to pursue this course. Future fast-track proposals will likely seek presidential authority to negotiate sectoral agreements affecting specific industries, a reduced emphasis on regional trade zones such as the North America Free Trade Agreement, and stepped-up efforts to enforce existing trade pacts.

No matter what form fast-track legislation eventually takes, this issue is just one of many indicators that the United States is now part of a global economy and that international trade has become a top priority for government, business, and labor. However, even as more U.S. companies engage in international trade, they are, at the same time, often confused about foreign cultures, business practices, and increasingly complex procedural requirements. Many American firms conduct business overseas in a slipshod, even careless, fashion. Many U.S. companies appear lost in an international "gold rush" mentality, racing to capitalize on huge new potential markets without taking the time to research and plan. When it comes to foreign trade, some technical knowledge is required; but mastery of international trade regulations will not matter if a product is unsuited to a foreign market. And that product will not sell if American companies lack awareness of the demands of international business and foreign cultures and therefore cannot maintain long-term relationships with their foreign sales force or customer base.

American businesses can avoid pitfalls and misunderstandings (and the potential losses they bring) by carefully assessing their ability to conduct business abroad and evaluating products and markets. This chapter addresses these two tasks in detail. Topics covered include conducting international market research; identifying overseas markets for products; selecting products suitable for international trade; finding international business contacts; and gaining insight into foreign cultures as they affect business.

1.1 VENTURING ABROAD

There are a number of reasons why Americans have not worked overseas. Here are some of the main concerns reflected in interviews with hundreds of U.S. companies from all sectors:

- Lack of market demand
- Fear of the unknown
- Unfamiliarity with foreign cultures
- Cost factors
- Lack of knowledge on how to break into foreign markets
- Misinformation about foreign markets

The emergence of multilateral trade pacts such as the General Agreement on Tariffs and Trade (GATT) and the North American Free Trade Agreement (NAFTA), the shifting value of the dollar, and an unpredictable economy at home are having a profound impact on Americans' willingness to work abroad. For large and small companies alike, expanding into world markets can equal survival. The costs of starting up in a foreign market can be greater in the short term, but the financial rewards can also be enormous. And even the smallest company can make a profit in foreign trade if that company uses common sense in its approach to a foreign market.

Assessing the Ability to Venture Abroad

U.S. businesses need to do some preliminary assessment to determine whether they are willing and ready to do business abroad. Do management personnel have the curiosity, determination, and patience required to work with foreign businesses? Does the business have the resources to withstand what may be a longer lag time before receiving a payoff on their investment?

The following example illustrates situations a business might expect to confront when trading internationally and highlights the characteristics businesses must possess before venturing abroad.

EXAMPLE

Luxury goods were in high demand during the boom years of the 1980s. An American import/export firm formed a joint venture with a group of Dutch yacht brokers to import European-built yachts into the United States. They successfully sold a number of yachts using nontraditional marketing efforts. Their main tools were:

- Media placement (i.e., news stories written about their efforts)
- Targeted direct sales

The business was growing when the stock market crash of 1987 reduced U.S. demand for expensive yachts. Recognizing that the market was changing, the American-Dutch joint venture team sought new markets and new products.

Market Switch

While the U.S. marine market was in decline, the market in Western Europe remained strong. In particular, there was a growing demand for American brands of marine electronics, notably VHF radios, radar, loran, outboard mo-

tors, and Global Positioning Systems (GPS). The Dutch yacht brokers had a
ready network of buyers, and for several years the American import/export
firm sourced and supplied products for sale in Germany, Belgium, and the
Netherlands.

By the early 1990s, the business was again growing. The American partners increased sales by contacting wholesalers and retailers directly through
fax notices and telephone calls. By using international directories, Chamber of
Commerce resources, and association and trade show lists, they were able to
locate almost all of the important marine sales outlets in their target countries.

More Hurdles

The next hurdles were as unexpected as the stock market crash of 1987. Changing licensing regulations for handheld VHF radios made many potential buyers switch to console units, which were readily available from other sources. In
addition, the Dutch partners faced a zoning change due to new development in
the harbor where their marina was located, throwing the operation into temporary disarray.

Going It Alone

For several years, the American firm continued the business alone, shipping
the electronics directly to the buyers. At one point, the firm expanded its territory to include outlets in the U.K. Although this decision was profitable in the
short term, the business was put on hold when more lucrative opportunities
presented themselves. Moreover, direct sales required the use of letters of
credit (see Chapter 5) to ensure payment from the European buyers, which
was risky for a small firm.

Guidance

As the Americans and Dutch partners learned, it is more than feasible for a small
company with limited resources to market products overseas. Over the course of
several years and several import/export ventures, these businesspeople were able
to:

1. Correctly determine market demand
2. Design creative market strategies that made the best use of their talents
   and abilities with the least financial expenditure
3. Exit the market when it became apparent that the time/cost ratio required
   to stay in business was too great

They learned the following lessons from their import/export experiences:

1. *Speed is of the essence.* Markets are fickle and can change. Succeeding in
   international trade means "turning on a dime."
2. *Relying on one partner, agent, or distributor is risky.* Personal factors and the
   normal vicissitudes of business can create havoc for a growing company.
3. *Culture plays a major role in business success.* Misreading a foreign partner
   can mean disaster for the company.
4. *Working overseas introduces many unknowns and uncertainties.* It is necessary

to keep constant tabs on world events—and local events in target countries—and to be able to size up their impact on the business.

5. *Getting paid for goods or services is a major problem in international business.* For smaller companies, in particular, this lesson learned may be especially important.

6. *Sound market research is the cornerstone of an international business venture, just as in any business venture.* The ability to "turn on a dime" depends on being attuned to market trends and being able to correctly analyze those trends.

It cannot be emphasized enough that speed and flexibility are crucial factors when selling overseas. The best market research is worth little if the time expended on the work causes so many delays that a competitor reaches the overseas market first. And with political and economic factors in constant flux internationally, exporters must be willing to jettison a product, perhaps an entire product line, to make the best possible overseas sale.

1.2 SELECTING PRODUCTS AND MARKETS

Choosing the right product to market overseas is similar to selecting a product for sale in the United States. It requires the right mixture of research and intuition, coupled with proper timing and luck. All of these factors and more make up a product's marketability.

Apart from these basics, an exporter must consider some additional parameters:

1. What is the foreign competition for the product?

2. What is the U.S. competition in the same market?

3. Is the product compatible with foreign culture and tastes? For example, the Dutch like to buy baked goods with see-through cellophane covers so they know what they are purchasing. The British, on the other hand, relish fancy packaging more than being able to actually see the product.

4. How do foreign packaging, labeling, and product safety requirements vary from product to product and country to country? Just as in the United States, many countries have strict packaging and labeling regulations and may require ingredients to be listed in a certain fashion. (For more on packaging and labeling, see Chapter 6, sections 6.1 and 6.4.)

5. How do foreign government health, safety, and product standards vary from country to country? (For more on these standards, see section 6.4.)

6. What are the costs of doing business in the selected market? (For more information on assessing costs, see Chapter 4's discussion on Export Costs and Pricing.) Costs may include:

- Customs duties
- Taxes and tariffs
- Shipping charges
- Sales and distribution
- Marketing and advertising
- Nontariffed trade barriers

7. At what price will the product be sold? What is the expected profit margin?

8. Is the foreign country's currency relatively stable, or is it subject to frequent fluctuations?

9. Are there any anticipated shipping problems? This is an especially important, and often overlooked, consideration, especially if the product is being sold in less developed nations. (For more information, see Chapter 6's discussion of Export Shipping and Distribution.)

10. Is the foreign market's government stable? Is it in a war or other conflict?

Often, the selection of a product depends on market conditions, which are almost always variable. The Dutch and American parties mentioned in the example in section 1.1 began to sell marine radios because the market for their earlier product disappeared. Moreover, they had a ready market for the radios and the markup potential was high.

Markets present opportunities for those who are aware of trends and developments. A group of recent immigrants from India to the U.S. learned from contacts in their home country that there was a demand for wastepaper. The United States has a plentiful supply of wastepaper; the new immigrants began exporting wastepaper to India. Demand was so great that they eventually created a large-scale export operation.

Note. It is almost impossible to overstate the ways in which the use of computers and the Internet are changing the face of the global marketplace. All of the steps outlined in sections 1.1 and 1.2 can now be facilitated through the use of online services and data. However, E-mail and online data are no substitutes for sound business sense or a successful person-to-person telephone call or meeting.

Product and market selection also depends heavily on market research. As section 1.3 explains, there are many resources available to assist exporters in making crucial product and market choices.

1.3   INTERNATIONAL MARKET RESEARCH

Prospective exporters face three important tasks at the outset:

1. Product selection
2. Market selection
3. Development of an international business network

International market research is the first step in accomplishing these tasks. The main tools of international marketing are human-based research using the myriad of publications designed for exporter use.

This section will assist those exporters, especially novices, in determining an international niche for their market and creating their own network of overseas contacts. These contacts will be invaluable for purposes of researching the market and keeping abreast of developments in the foreign country of choice.

Note. Chapter 2, "Export Distribution Channels," examines more fully the kinds of professional assistance that can be used to enter that foreign market. Also, one of the best online sites for export marketing and related information is International Business Resources (http://ciber.bus.msu.edu/busres.htm) on the World Wide Web, which provides links to hundreds of useful sites. Other useful web sites can be found in sections 1.3.3 and 1.3.7 of this chapter.

1.3.1 Assessing International Market Trends

The first place for a novice to start analyzing overseas market potential is in the international business sections of major newspapers and magazines. *The Wall Street Journal* and *The Financial Times* (of London) are two examples of major publications that focus extensively on international business trends and analysis.

If a product is related to the automobile industry, for instance, it would be prudent to keep up on overseas developments in that area by doing target reading. Within a matter of weeks, it should be easy to gain at least a superficial assessment of auto industry trends that could affect sales of a product in a given market.

EXAMPLE

An American auto dealer observes news articles that indicate there is a growing demand in Europe for slightly used American cars. An overseas source verifies the demand and is willing to facilitate sales. Being "slightly used" means there will be potential discounts on foreign custom duties, not to mention attractive prices for European buyers. But news reports also indicate that gasoline prices are on the rise in Europe. Although the U.S.-made cars may be priced well for sale overseas, they are not equipped for propane use and may prove too expensive to operate. The auto dealer decides against exporting American cars for the present.

1.3.2 Publications and Other International Resources

Newspapers are good means of assessing overall trends, and they provide some market leads. But they are not geared to helping exporters make the human contacts needed to conduct business over the long term.

U.S. government agencies—especially the U.S. Customs Service and the Commerce Department—offer several publications to assist U.S. exporters in entering foreign markets. There are numerous private-sector publications as well to aid exporters wishing to create an international network.

The publications discussed in the following sections provide market trends as well as actual names and addresses of possible foreign contacts in a given country and a given field.

International Business Magazines

International business magazines provide important information on assessing market trends and locating export customers. They can be located in international periodical guides at most major libraries. The examples listed here are English-language publications; telephone numbers for subscriptions are in parentheses:

⊛ *Business Central Europe.* This magazine offers an overview of business trends and practices in central European countries. Published by the Economist Newspapers, 20 Newton Road, Wimbledon, London, SW19 3PJ, U.K. Subscriptions cost $45 per year.

⊛ *China Business Review.* This highly regarded magazine covers trade and investment in China and Hong Kong, with a focus on identifying opportunities for U.S. companies. Published by the China Business Forum, 1818 N Street, N.W., Suite 500, Washington, D.C. 20036 (202-429-0340). Subscriptions cost $99 per year.

⊛ *East Asian Executive Reports* and *Middle East Executive Reports.* These periodicals provide in-depth information on import/export, contract, licensing and labor laws, joint venturing, taxation, marketing, and advertising. Also available are twice-monthly newsletters with business leads and investment opportunities from government and private sources. Published by International Executive Reports, 717 D Street, N.W., Suite 300, Washington, D.C. 20004-2805 (202-628-6900). Subscriptions cost $455 per year.

⊛ *Daily Trade News.* Covers aspects of doing business in Korea. Published by the Korean Foreign Trade Association.

Industry-Specific Foreign Trade Journals

Foreign trade journals offer detailed information on markets, products, and technical developments in specific industry segments. The examples provided here are in English. However, if an exporter speaks a foreign language or has access to translation services, trade magazines in the language of the target country could provide valuable inside information on a market that is not readily available to competing exporters.

Foreign trade journals are sometimes difficult to obtain. Trade offices of the consulate of the country in question or a specific country's trade desk at the Department of Commerce are good starting places. (The Export Assistance Center Network can be reached at 800-872-8723.) Also, most major libraries have directories of international trade publications such as the following:

⊛ *The International Journal of Biotechnology.* This magazine offers information on the latest products, company news, and regulatory information in the biotechnology field. Published in English by the Biotech Forum Europe in Heidelberg, Germany.

    ● *Misset Poultry News.* Published in the Netherlands, this English-language journal covers all aspects of the poultry industry throughout the world.

International Professional Association Guides

Professional associations exist in virtually every industry and service group and country. International business and trade associations often publish membership lists with telephone numbers and names of contact persons. These directories are usually available for a fee or for the price of membership. As noted, there are many international and domestic industry associations with information on the international marketplace. Their publications often provide targeted information on the exact industry sector sought by the exporter.

The *Encyclopedia of Associations* and the *Encyclopedia of International Associations* contain listings of trade and industry associations, including telephone numbers, membership information, and relevant publications. Examples of these associations include:

    ● *Japan Medical Products International Trade Association.* A membership directory published in English lists more than 160 distributors and manufacturers of medical instruments and supplies in Japan.

    ● *Importers and Exporters Association of Taipei.* This organization promotes foreign trade among its 10,000 members, organizes gatherings for foreign exporters, and publishes an English-language monthly called *Taiwan International Trade.*

    ● *South East Asia Iron and Steel Institute (SEAISI).* More than 650 steel-producing and related enterprises are members of this organization. SEAISI compiles statistics on steel consumption, trade, and production in Australia, Indonesia, Japan, Malaysia, Philippines, Singapore, Taiwan, Thailand, and the Republic of Korea. In addition, the organization publishes a membership directory and quarterly journal, both in English.

International Directories

International directories are available for a huge range of industry segments and markets in most countries around the world. These publications are invaluable for the exporter who has chosen a specific product, target market, and country. Most major libraries have a number of different "directories of directories" that are extremely useful. Examples of specific directories include the following (telephone numbers for ordering subscriptions are in parentheses):

    ● *Sell's Marine Market International.* This comprehensive 650-page guide to the boating and boating equipment industries lists all manufacturers and distributors in each product category. Service providers, wholesalers, and retailers are also listed in alphabetical order and according to product type. Available through

Miller Freeman plc, Riverbank House, Angel Lane, Tonbridge, Kent TN9 15E, U.K. (Telephone: 44-1732-377294.) The cost is approximately $75.

    • *International Directory of the Perfume and Cosmetics Industry.* Almost 3,000 distributors, wholesalers, and manufacturers in the perfume and cosmetics industry are listed in this 900-page guide. Published in both English and French, the guide costs approximately $40. (Telephone: 33-1643-00561.)

    • *Africa's Import/Export Trade Opportunities Directory.* This 350-page directory lists African business organizations, firms and individuals involved in foreign trade operations. Each entry includes company name, address, telephone number, names and titles of top personnel, type of product or service, and banking references. Also included are lists of trade associations, trade shows, and U.S. and Canadian trade representatives in Africa. The cost is $50. (Telephone: 416-433-7493.)

    • *Directory of Argentine Exporters and Importers.* Over 3,200 manufacturers, importers, exporters, and companies that provide service to international traders are listed with addresses, phone numbers, and fax numbers. Each listing is classified according to the type of product or service.

    • *The North American Export Pages.* Over 50,000 product and service suppliers in the United States, Mexico, and Canada are categorized by six major industry sectors. Both text and CD-ROM versions are available.(Telephone: 800-422-8793.) The directory can also be accessed via the Internet (http://export.uswest.com).

U.S. Government Publications

The U.S. Government Printing Office publishes several export-related guides that are available to the public at relatively low cost. Publications include:

    • *Basic Guide to Exporting*, 173 pages, $9.50.
    • *Destination Japan: A Business Guide for the 90s*, 73 pages, $4.
    • *Export Trading Company Guidebook*, 159 pages, $8.50.
    • *Exporter's Guide to Federal Resources for Small Businesses*, 132 pages, $4.75.
    • *North American Free Trade Agreement: Opportunities for United States Industries, NAFTA Industry Sector Reports*, 395 pages, $24. This book gives statistical data on exports of thirty-six manufacturing sectors to NAFTA countries and the world.
    • *The China Business Guide*, 52 pages, $4.50.

A comprehensive list of government publications can be found at the vast Department of Commerce World Wide Web site known as Stat-USA (http://www.stat-usa.gov/). Government publications can also be ordered by writing the Superintendent of Documents at the U.S. Government Printing Office by calling 202-512-1800. For lists of documents and information on subscriptions, call 202-512-1806; to set up an account with the Superintendent of Documents, call 202-512-0822.

The Trade Information Center is a central resource for the trade and export promotion activities of eighteen government agencies. The Center provides information on how to locate and use government programs and market information; it also furnishes export assistance and counseling.

The Center publishes a useful booklet entitled "Export Programs: A Business Guide to Federal Export Assistance Programs," which contains more than ninety-five pages of import/export-related programs. To order the booklet or for other questions, contact the Trade Information Center by phone (800-872-8723); a special line for the hearing-impaired is also available (800-833-8723). The Center can also be reached by fax (202-482-0543), E-mail (tic@ita.doc.gov), and via the Web (http://www.ita.gov).

1.3.3 U.S. Department of Commerce Resources

The U.S. Department of Commerce offers a variety of resources and services to assist exporters.

Amerifax

Amerifax provides a wide range of information on regional export markets in Central and South America. Although general in nature, these services are an excellent place to start researching a market. The services are free by calling 202-482-2521; a recording provides a list of options. Using a touch-tone phone, callers can key in the documents they want so they can be sent to the callers' fax machine. Amerifax includes information on:

- NAFTA and NAFTA countries
- Central American countries
- Southern cone countries (Argentina, Paraguay, Chile, and Uruguay)
- Andean countries (Colombia, Ecuador, Peru, and Venezuela)
- Caribbean Basin countries
- Summit of the Americas

Export Yellow Pages

The Export Yellow Pages is a comprehensive directory, published by the U.S. Department of Commerce, that includes telephone numbers and addresses of export-related:

- U.S. manufacturers
- Banks
- Service organizations
- Export trading companies
- To order a free copy of the Export Yellow Pages, call 800-872-8723 for the nearest Department of Commerce office.

Stat-USA/Internet

A vast amount of trade, economic, and business information is available at this World Wide Web site (http://www.stat-usa.gov/). Subscriptions are $50 per quarter or $150 per year for unlimited access. For information, contact the Stat-USA Helpline by telephone (800-782-8872) or by fax (202-482-2164).

Stat-USA has five main components. They are:

1. *The National Trade Data Bank.* The NTDB is the U.S. government's most comprehensive source of international trade data. Much of it is current and extremely useful. The NTDB contains more than 90,000 documents culled from fifteen government agencies and is available through the Internet or on CD-ROM. Users of the NTDB can key into individual country names to yield country-specific information. The NTDB covers the entire spectrum of the exporting process, including:

* Export promotion activities and prospects for U.S. exporters
* Detailed commercial, demographic, political, and socioeconomic overviews of hundreds of countries
* Economic trends, financing, and investment outlooks
* Pricing information
* Marketing of U.S. products and services and market research reports for hundreds of product and service categories
* Trade regulations and standards, including customs laws
* Tax, duty, tariff, and documentation requirements
* Schedules of trade events

EXAMPLE

One market research report analyzed the emerging Dutch market for southwestern-style jewelry. The report discussed opportunities for U.S. exporters in terms of retail and wholesale outlets. Included was a price range that Dutch consumers would be willing to pay and a list of styles thought appropriate for the market. The report concluded that although this jewelry was not sought as a collectible by Dutch consumers, they would be willing to pay for quality, as with other jewelry.

Another report discussed the market for security and safety equipment in Brazil, detailing the limited growth of domestic competition and the economic and political factors that contribute to a favorable export climate.

By keying in on the Dominican Republic, exporters would learn that Dominican Customs officials often extract arbitrary and excessive duty amounts, and goods can be retained in Customs' custody for over a year.

The NTDB can be purchased on CD-ROM for $59 per monthly issue or $575 for an annual subscription. Interested parties can call the Stat-USA numbers listed previously. Please note that the cost of unlimited Internet access is considerably less than that of the CD-ROM version.

2. *The Economic Bulletin Board.* The Economic Bulletin Board component of Stat-USA is a comprehensive source for U.S. government economic releases; business leads; individual sector analysis; and daily economic, business, and trade news.

3. *Global Business Procurement Opportunities.* This section of Stat-USA includes both large and small procurement opportunities for U.S. businesses from around the world.

4. *Bureau of Economic Analysis.* The BEA furnishes news releases, surveys of current business issues, and detailed data files from BEA regional, national, and international accounts.

5. *The Electronic Bulletin Board.* In addition to trade leads, the Electronic Bulletin Board (EBB) offers information on exchange rates, money supplies, and statistical releases from various government agencies, including the Bureau of Economic Analysis, the Bureau of Census, the Bureau of Labor Statistics, the Federal Reserve Board, and the Department of the Treasury.

The United States and Foreign Commercial Service (US&FCS)

An agency of the U.S. Department of Commerce, US&FCS offers a wide range of customized services to exporters through over 60 branch offices throughout the country and a network of trade specialists worldwide. Information can be obtained by phone (800-872-8723). Services provided include:

- *Agent/Distributor Service (ADS).* A U.S. firm's own product literature can be sent abroad to help identify potential agents, distributors, and foreign representatives. The fee is $250.

- *Customized Sales Survey (CSS).* US&FCS specialists can conduct surveys in selected countries to help determine the marketability of a product. Information can also be provided on key competitors, pricing of comparable products, distribution and promotion practices, trade barriers, potential business partners, and related trade events. Fees run between $600 and $3,500.

- *World Trade Data Report (WTDR).* This service provides a confidential report with information on the financial status, reputation, and reliability of a potential trading partner. The fee is $100.

- *Gold Key Service.* For representatives of U.S. firms planning to visit a foreign country, this service offers market research assistance, introductions to potential partners, orientations, briefings, interpreter services, and follow-up planning. The fee is variable.

- *Trade Opportunities Program (TOP).* Current sales leads are provided from foreign firms seeking to buy or represent U.S. products or services. The leads are printed in some newspapers and are also available through the U.S. Department of Commerce Electronic Bulletin Board. There is a nominal annual fee and connect charge.

⊕ *Export Contact List Service (ECLS).* This is a database retrieval service that provides detailed information on foreign firms seeking U.S. goods and services.

See Appendix A for a directory of US&FCS branch offices.

International Trade Administration Commercial Offices

The International Trade Administration (ITA) of the U.S. Department of Commerce has several offices that offer export assistance for specific countries or regions:

⊕ *Western Europe Office.* Exporters can access marketing information and potential agents or distributors in the U.K. and other Western European countries by phone (202-482-3748).

⊕ *Asia Pacific Office.* The Asia Pacific Office offers a service similar to Amerifax. Exporters can call a telephone number (202-482-3875) for a menu of documents that can be sent to their fax machines. In addition, trade specialists are available for telephone consultations. The telephone numbers are:

Southeast Asia countries (202-482-2522)
Korea and Taiwan (202-482-4390)
Hong Kong and China (202-482-4681)
Australia and New Zealand (202-482-2954)
Or for all of the above (800-872-8723 or 800-USA-TRADE)

U.S. Department of Commerce Publications

Numerous publications are available that provide information on specific countries, regions, or markets. One of the best is *Business America,* a magazine that culls information from the Commerce Department and Foreign Commercial Service offices around the world to assist American firms in identifying export markets and opportunities. An annual subscription to this monthly magazine, which costs $43, can be ordered by phone(202-482-3251) or fax (202-482-5819).

1.3.4   *Small Business Development Centers (SBDC)*

Small Business Development Centers, a partnership of the U.S. Small Business Administration (SBA), provide business owners with services and resources to help identify export opportunities. Most states have at least one SBDC office, usually at a state university or community college. Assistance is available by phone, fax, or appointment. The Office of Small Business Development Centers can be reached by phone (202-205-6766).

Services provided by the SBDC include:

⊕ *Outreach counseling.* International trade counselors can help companies prepare export strategies. They often work as liaisons with other state and federal agencies offering export assistance.

⊛ *Market research information.* Most centers provide free reports taken from the Department of Commerce's National Trade Data Bank, which contains over 100,000 files on market research, export promotion, country profiles, documentation requirements, trade contacts, and statistical export data.

⊛ *International Trade Data Network.* This valuable service provides trade leads to exporters. The leads identify contact persons, as well as telephone and fax numbers of companies that are sourcing U.S. products or services. Compiled from U.S. government and private sources, the service also matches client profiles with trade opportunities and provides lists of potential distributors.

⊛ *Customized research projects.* Some Small Business Development Centers offer clients customized market research, often provided by graduate students in business and management programs.

⊛ *Libraries.* Many centers have libraries with international directories, foreign yellow pages, marketing books, business magazines, and other resources.

⊛ *Workshops and seminars.* Most centers work with local business development organizations and other state and federal agencies to provide seminars, workshops, and training programs on various international trade issues.

See Appendix B for a directory of Small Business Development Centers.

The SBA also has an Internet home page (http://www.sbaonline.sba.gov) or can be reached by phone (800-697-4636). For information on newsgroups, data banks, downloadable files, and software, small business owners can call 202-401-9600).

An adjunct to the SBA is the Service Corps of Retired Executives (SCORE). Comprised of approximately 500 retired business executives, most of whom are experienced in foreign trade, SCORE can assist businesses in devising successful exporting strategies. The organization has approximately 370 chapters with at least one in each state. SCORE can be contacted by phone (800-634-0245) or fax (202-205-7636).

1.3.5 State and Regional Export Services

In addition to the SBDC and other export-related services provided by the U.S. Department of Commerce, most states provide trade information through their offices of economic development or regional trade associations. (See Appendix C for a directory of state international trade contacts.) Following are examples of the types of export services provided by individual states:

⊛ *Ohio.* The Department of Development of the Ohio International Trade Division publishes the Ohio Export Services Directory, which assists small to midsize manufacturers in identifying export opportunities. Information is provided on international business leads, trade consultants, export management companies, and export trading companies; translation services; Ohio-based international law firms; and freight forwarders and shipping companies.

    • *California.* California has a network of nine International Trade Development Centers. Based at community colleges throughout the state and operated in conjunction with the Export Managers Association of California, these centers offer one-on-one export counseling; technical assistance in management, marketing, financing, regulations, and taxation; referral services and trade leads; and workshops and seminars.

    • *New York.* The New York District Export Council publishes the *Internationalist* magazine. A tristate edition lists all government and private export-related resources for New York, New Jersey, and Connecticut. Published three times a year, the tristate *Internationalist* is available for $15. The magazine contains contacts and calendars of events listings for the National Association of Export Companies (212-725-3311). There are also listings for all regional international trade organizations, international educational organizations, trade missions, and trade shows.

1.3.6   *Foreign Embassies and Chambers of Commerce*

Foreign embassies and consulates located in the United States often furnish information on export markets through commercial or trade offices. Similar services are available through chambers of commerce operated jointly by the U.S. and foreign trading partners. Begin by calling a foreign country's embassy in Washington, D.C. and asking for a trade office. The U.S. Chamber of Commerce can provide leads to other chambers.

    Especially useful are foreign Chamber of Commerce service guides. These guides are categorized by industry and list all pertinent information needed to contact a foreign company, including names, addresses, and telephone and fax numbers of overseas companies. For instance, the Netherlands Chamber of Commerce sells bound service guides that cover almost all industries. To reach Dutch counterparts in specialty foods, for example, all that is needed is the service guide for that sector. Complete contact information is listed for each subscribing company. A few random phone calls may produce just the lead required or at least some information on how to proceed to enter a market in that region.

1.3.7   *Online International Trade Services*

Changes are made almost daily in cyberspace, leaving many users confused about how to take best and most efficient advantage of the vast amount of available international trade information. Make no mistake: The era of conducting import/export transactions online has arrived. Though much of the buzz around the Internet and World Wide Web is hype, and most online information can be procured through other sources, computer-literate exporters have a distinct advantage and can save a great deal of time.

    A growing number of online services and sites cater to international trade and business. Access to these resources depends in large measure on the capabilities of the user's hardware and software. Also, most businesses require the use of a third party to provide access to the Internet. Many regional yellow pages now have "Internet Services" headings; readers should contact Internet access and service providers directly for more information. Additionally, many universities and private companies offer courses, both online and in the classroom, on Internet uses and applications.

The examples of World Wide Web sites described here are intended as a primer on the vast amount of international trade information available online. Most of the sites link to dozens of other sites. Being able to zero in on the most relevant and worthwhile information is important; surfing the Internet and navigating through tens of thousands of web sites is fun but can be time-consuming. There are a number of private companies that offer consulting services on how to use the Internet to meet specific business needs.

Note. It is important to remember that the accuracy and currency of online information vary tremendously. There are no standards or guidelines for posting information online; anyone can do it. There is often no clear distinction between information and advertising. Moreover, online information is subject to intentional or accidental alteration. Software limitations or other technical glitches may cause graphics and other information to be downloaded incompletely or out of context. Online sites can also disappear without notice, and many are simply advertisements for fee-based services. Information gathered online should always be checked against other sources.

The Internet

The Internet refers to the interconnected set of computer sites worldwide. There is no central headquarters; users themselves comprise the Internet and the standards under which it operates. Companies and universities generally pay a monthly or yearly fee to join a regional network that gives them access to the Internet. Small firms and individuals can pay a fee to networks such as America Online and CompuServe to gain access to "the Net."

Many reference books are available about the Internet and its various business applications. Some of the best are:

- *Navigating the Internet* by Richard J. Smith and Mark Gibbs (Indianapolis: Sams Publishing, 1994)
- *Marketing on the Internet* by Jill and Matthew Ellsworth (New York: John Wiley & Sons, Inc., 1995)
- *The Internet Business Guide: Riding the Information Superhighway to Profit* by Rosalind Resnick and Dave Taylor (Indianapolis: Sams Publishing, 1994)
- *Internet Business to Business Directory* by Sandra Eddy (Alameda, CA: Sybex Publishing, 1996)
- *Small Business Resource Guide to the Web 1997* by David Peal, Robert McNamara, Suzanne V. Cross, and Kathleen Mims (Emeryville, CA: Lycos Press, 1997)

The three most popular Internet applications for information on global trade are:

- Electronic mail (E-mail)
- Remote log-in (Telnet)
- World Wide Web

Electronic Mail

Probably the most important function of E-mail is that it enables users to contact foreign firms directly. E-mail is a great way to make an introduction. Numerous web sites list the E-mail addresses of such firms, including the World Wide Yellow Pages (http://www.yellow.com). Any web site that deals with international trade, whether it is industry or country specific, is likely to contain E-mail addresses of any company that is mentioned.

With E-mail, computer users can also "talk" with other individuals or discussion groups—called special interest groups (SIGs) or Usenet groups—around the world. SIGS exist under a number of trade-related headings, including:

- International trade
- The Eastern European Business Network
- The Caribbean economy

Telnet

Telnet refers to a type of computer software that allows a user to access the database of another Internet computer. The database may be anything from a journal index to an online library catalog. To access telnet sites, users need a telnet helper application such as TrumpTel. Many Internet services provide users with the appropriate telnet site software. Telnet sites include:

- Fedworld gateway
- European Commission Host Organization
- U.S. State Department Travel Advisories

World Wide Web

The World Wide Web is the fast-growing hypermedia component of the Internet, containing a host of interactive and multimedia features. Tens of thousands of companies currently market themselves on World Wide Web "home pages," with many more going online daily. The hypertext component of the Web allows these companies to go beyond the constraints of the gopher menu format by using audio, movies, and an array of graphics capabilities. The 3.5 million users of the Web can scan these commercial and marketing pitches with the appropriate online service provider and software.

The "open market" is where companies advertise and present their home pages. Companies such as Federal Express, Chrysler, Sony Music, Volvo, MCI Communications, Time Warner, Boeing, and Monsanto all have home pages in the open market. Small businesses also advertise on the Web.

Since the Web is expected to have 25 million users by the year 2000, home page presentations can be expected to reach a wide international audience. As security systems, software, and phone lines become more sophisticated, online ordering and payment for products and services may become more commonplace.

Note. To view web sites and related links—other web sites and documents containing potentially relevant information—users need software known as a web browser. Most Internet access providers include a selection of web browsers as a standard part of their service. Information on browser software can be found in many computer periodicals and books.

The following is a list of World Wide Web sites of particular interest to those involved with international trade:

Useful Web Sites on Global Trade

- World Wide Yellow Pages (http://www.yellow.com). A list of all the businesses on the Web, with daily updates.
- International Business Resources on the World Wide Web (http://ciber.bus.msu.edu/busres.htm). Includes links to a vast amount of international trade-related sites.
- Quotecom (http://www.quote.com). International financial news and information, as well as stock quotes.
- U.S. Patent and Trade Office (http://www.uspto.gov/). Contains information about patents, trademarks, and copyrights, although online patent searches are not yet available.
- The Embassy Page (http://www.globescope.com/).
- Trade Point USA (http://www.i-trade.com/dir09/). This site offers the full text of many government documents on exporting, NAFTA, INCOTERMS, international trade law, and other import/export related topics.
- Global Export Market Information (http://www.itaiep.doc.gov/).
- Virtual Africa (http://www.africa.com/).
- Southeast Asia Information (http://sunsite.nus.sg/asiasvc.html).
- Latin American Network Information Center, or LANIC (http://lanic.utexas.edu/).
- KPMG Online, Canada (http://www.kpmg.ca/).
- Trade Information Center (http://www.ita.doc.gov). This comprehensive International Trade Administration site offers a vast amount of import/export information as well as numerous links to other U.S. Government agency sites.

Online Commercial Services

Online commercial services offer a wide range of targeted, up-to-date information. Many of these services charge hourly or subscription-rate user fees. These services are especially useful to importers or exporters who have a clear idea of the specific type of information they need and a solid working knowledge of computers. Accessing the right database can save hours of travel and research time. Several online commercial services are described here:

1. LEXIS/NEXIS is the world's largest database of business and legal information with almost 200 million documents available online. LEXIS contains legal information; NEXIS offers business news and company reports. For example:

- Company Library has foreign and domestic company profiles, market reports, bankruptcy reports, stock reports, mergers and acquisitions information, and business opportunities.
- Asia/Pacific Rim Library has detailed information about every country in Asia and the Pacific Rim, including business analysis, business ventures, and legal information.
- News and Business Library has 2,300 full-text U.S. and foreign newspapers, magazines, journals, and newsletters listed according to business news, financial news, trade/technology news, and legal news.

1. Investext has more than 320,000 full-text reports that examine 14,000 companies worldwide in 53 different industry groups. Written by 180 top investment and research firms, the reports are intended to assist firms in all phases of strategic planning, market research, acquisition strategies, and competitive analysis.
2. Japan Economic Newswire Plus includes the complete English-language texts of the *Japan Economic Daily, Kyoto English-Language News,* and other international coverage relating to business developments in Japan. Updated daily, the service offers information gathered from over 2,000 correspondents in 43 news bureaus around the world.
3. Marketfull offers over 30,000 market research reports averaging 200 to 300 pages each, on topics such as products, industries, market share, pricing, consumer attitudes, and sources of supply.

There are products available on CD-ROM as well with valuable import/export related information. An example is the Thomas Register of European Manufacturers, which lists 130,000 European companies under 9,500 product and service headings. The product can be ordered by phone (800-699-9822).

1.4   Creating an International Network

1.4.1   Introduction

Publications are good starting points for overseas contact-building, but at some point, it is necessary to communicate with foreign businesses directly. A U.S. business that is considering getting involved in international trade should begin seeking out foreign counterparts who can later play a role in driving sales of the product. These sources can offer market tips and information on distribution, or even act as joint-venture partners. These leads can come from several sources, such as:

- Personal visits to foreign markets
- Trade shows
- Foreign embassies/consulates
- Local, regional, national, and international chambers of commerce
- State export or international trade offices
- World trade centers
- International trade associations
- Commerce Department Export Assistance Centers
- Small Business Administration (SBA) export assistance leads offered through their Small Business Development Centers

EXAMPLE

A U.S. manufacturer of equipment to recycle refrigerant gases wants to sell its product in Germany and Holland, where environmental regulations are creating a large demand. The vice president of sales has never been overseas. Where to begin? He attends trade shows in Germany and Holland and starts to collect names of potential sales distributors and agents. He then hires an international market research company to investigate these leads more thoroughly and come up with alternatives. Within six months, the VP has hired a foreign agent to set up a distribution network and within a year is making brisk sales in these markets.

Once an exporter has selected a target market, there are various country-specific services available to help determine market trends and develop networks.

EXAMPLE

If an exporter has targeted China, the U.S. and Foreign Commercial Service of the Department of Commerce's International Trade Administration (ITA) offers, for a small fee, a customized assessment of the Chinese market for a particular product. It also offers Gold Key Service, where for a modest fee, U.S. Embassy personnel can arrange appointments, transportation, and interpreter services.

The ITA also maintains offices in China, Hong Kong, and Mongolia that furnish specific information on Chinese market trends, trade shows, and trade missions. The Chinese government maintains commercial consuls in six major U.S. cities (Washington, D.C., Chicago, New York, Houston, Los Angeles, and San Francisco) that can put exporters in touch with Chinese purchasing agents with offices in the United States.

1.4.2 Networking Methods

As noted, there are many ways to make valuable overseas contacts. The method an exporter chooses to break into a market—and eventually establish an overseas distribution system—depends on personality and resources. Although it is ideal to make an overseas visit, today's high technology allows exporters to start breaking into markets from a home office. Distant regions are easily reached by phone or fax.

Phone/Fax/E-Mail

Once the novice exporter develops a list of leads for overseas business, the next step is reaching out to potential contacts to see what activity may be generated. Here are the best steps to take for the most efficient use of this methodology using a combination of phone, fax, or E-mail techniques:

1. *Cold calling.* If there is no contact name listed or available, the first step is to call the company or individual to determine who should receive the exporter's inquiry, sales pitch, or other information being imparted. Calling first may allow for an initial conversation that will either initiate further discussion or eliminate the lead from consideration. In many cases, there will be interest on the part of the foreign company or businessperson simply because the exporter is American. This may be idle curiosity or genuine interest. Only time and further contact will tell.

2. *Proper pitching.* Prospective exporters must make sure to design the inquiry and sales presentation to meet the market in question.

3. *E-mailing.* Sending an E-mail message is a fast and easy way to make initial contact with a target company. Numerous directories, both in text and online, contain E-mail addresses of companies throughout the world.

4. *Fax modeming.* With the advent of fax modems, it is possible to transmit information directly over the phone lines and to have that information reach the targeted lead in the form of a fax. Depending on staffing, a businessperson could reach as many as a hundred or more contacts in the course of a day or a week using this approach.

5. *Faxing.* For those with less-advanced technology—a standalone fax machine, for example—it is still possible to conduct targeted outreach. In fact, the less costly approach—yet an approach that allows for correcting misdirections without much waste of time or money—is to send 15–20 trial faxes and wait to see the response rate. Even one or two replies, especially if generated without follow-up calling, can indicate a potential market.

EXAMPLE

When the American team discussed in section 1.1 decided to expand marine electronic sales into both Great Britain and Germany, they were seeking readily available contact information. A metropolitan-area library proved to have quite a few foreign yellow pages. Many ads listed phone and fax numbers, making outreach quick and easy. Advertising sheets were produced on a home computer and trial faxes were made in batches of fifteen each to both Germany and Great Britain. Several responses came back via fax from each country without the need for follow-up calls. The Americans discerned from this response that there was a market for the goods in question and eventually made a number of sales, thanks to this quick and inexpensive marketing approach.

Follow-up Calls

Prospective exporters should not become concerned if there are no responses generated without follow-up calls. Faxes are often lost in the shuffle in a large company; E-mail messages are often ignored. For this reason, it is always best to follow up a fax or E-mail message with a phone call. These additional calls also give the exporter an "in," allowing the exporter to check up on the arrival of a fax or E-mail message without giving the appearance of being overly aggressive.

Note. Once it is determined a message has been received, it is best to wait a week before attempting to reach the party to whom it has been addressed. That allows for the potential overseas contact to read and process the information.

Guidance

The one exception to these rules of thumb about phoning and faxing is when target marketing—as opposed to mass marketing—approaches are being used. Consider these preliminary 15–20 calls a form of polling. If they do not generate interest, then consider the following factors:

- Whether the sales pitch is off-putting
- Whether the product is right for the market intended
- Whether the audience queried is right for the product

1.4.3 Trade Shows

Trade shows are excellent venues for both showing products and picking up international market leads. The issue for small companies especially will be deciding which shows to attend, as there are literally hundreds scheduled each year for every imaginable product and market.

EXAMPLE

Every spring the Jacob Javits Center in New York City hosts a major international specialty foods show. Booths are organized by country for quick and easy access to a region of choice. Exhibitors comprise a full spectrum of the market, from manufacturers to manufacturers/distributors and distributors/wholesalers. By walking the aisles it is possible for an exporter to assess market trends, learn about foreign packaging requirements, and meet potential contacts in person.

In three hours at this show, a marketing team was able to connect with both American and European manufacturers of specialty food items, with the possibility of acting as a link between those parties. Contacts made on this one occasion became useful in terms of market research and helped spawn a business trip to Holland on behalf of an American manufacturer of soup bases.

When contemplating trade shows as a means of making international contacts, exporters must consider whether to take a booth at a show, attend as a visitor, or decide on a focus (i.e., is the purpose to make international contacts, glean market information, or both?). Cost is usually the deciding factor under these circumstances. To put together a booth or display for a show may be cost-prohibitive for many small companies.

Selecting the Right Shows to Attend

Trade shows run the gamut in size and cost. A regional wooden boat show in Minnesota might charge the seller of a used boat $50 to dock in a pristine lake. At the giant Comdex show, the premier marketing forum for the computer industry, many of the more than 2,000 exhibitors paid well into six figures to be seen by 225,000 industry insiders and attendees in Las Vegas in November 1996. At the Baltimore boat show, vendors of marine insurance, vacuum cleaners, and nautical trinkets have been known to place tabletops across stacks of cinder blocks, cover them with tablecloths, and put out literature and samples. At some of the major electronics shows, exhibits are elaborate stage sets, with light shows, lasers, and robots.

There is no guarantee, however, that Comdex is more effective than the boat show in terms of exhibitors selling their goods or making important contacts. It is up to the exhibitor and/or attendee to determine company needs and consider the cost and time of attending a show.

Several comprehensive guides list trade shows and exhibitions. For example:

⊛ Bill Communications in New York City publishes *The Trade Show and Exhibition Schedule,* which includes over 11,000 entries covering trade shows in all industries in the United States and Canada. The book costs $195 and is available through Bill Communications (800-266-4712).

⊛ The U.S. Government Printing Office offers a publication titled *European Trade Fairs: A Key to the World for U.S. Exporters.* The book is a comprehensive overview of European trade fairs and includes a step-by-step review of procedures to be followed before, during, and after each exhibition. The cost is $5.50.

There are also several programs sponsored by the International Trade Administration (ITA) and the U.S. Department of Commerce to assist exporters with trade exhibitions. These include:

⊛ *International Buyer Program (IBP).* In seeking to attract foreign buyers to domestic trade shows that feature U.S. products and services with high export potential, the IBP publicizes its shows through embassy newsletters, foreign trade associations, import agents, corporations, and equipment distributors. Contact the Office of Export Promotion Services by phone (202-482-0481) or fax (202-482-0115).

⊛ *Multi-State/Catalog Exhibitions Program.* This program distributes company and product literature at international exhibitions and sends the trade leads directly to participating U.S. firms. Contact the Office of Export Promotion services by phone (202-482-0481) or fax (202-482-0115).

• *Trade Fairs and Exhibitions.* The Commerce Department selects nearly 100 international trade fairs annually at which to establish its USA pavilion. Exhibitors chosen to participate receive pre- and post-event logistical and transportation support and overseas market promotional campaigns. For a list of recruited trade shows and trade events, contact the Trade Information Center (800-USA-TRADE) or on the World Wide Web at http://www.ita.doc.gov.

• *Trade Fair Certification.* For a list of Commerce Department–certified international trade fairs and related services, contact Trade Fair Certification (202-482-2525).

Narrowing down the selection is fairly easy for manufacturers. Most industries schedule big shows each year that are well known. There are also association shows and conferences that focus on given topics of concern within a basic industry. For exporters, show selection should be based on the ability to gather as much specific market information possible in support of overseas product sales and to make contacts in preselected foreign markets.

Getting the Most From the Experience

Given the sheer numbers of attendees at most trade shows, exporters would do well to do some preparatory work before entering the hall. If possible, exporters should obtain a list of exhibitors beforehand and consider the following approach:

1. Target the products, markets, and international regions that suit current export efforts.
2. Decide how many days to attend a given show.
3. Divide the prospective contact list by the number of days planned for attendance and make a priority list for calling on those booths in question.
4. If possible, contact the best prospects by phone or fax before the show and set up appointments.

If staffing allows, management should attend to the sales appointments. Other personnel can be designated to cold-call exhibitors lower down on the priority list. Most trade show exhibitors provide bowls at their booths for collecting business cards and maintain high staffing levels to allow for this sort of informal networking.

Any major industry show in the United States attracts many foreign visitors and exhibitors. Given the cost of exhibiting in this country, exporters can be certain of a fairly warm reception from prospective foreign customers and clients. They have usually made a tremendous effort to show their products in this country and are generally eager to meet Americans who can create business for them.

Foreign Trade Shows

If financially feasible, an American exporter should always attend major industry shows taking place in foreign countries. Going abroad allows American businesses to meet far more foreign manufacturers, to meet them on their own territory, and to better assess overseas market trends.

1.5   INTERNATIONAL FIELD RESEARCH

1.5.1   Introduction

Too often exporters, even experienced ones, take shortcuts on field research and rush into manufacturing a product to meet client demand. Although potentially lucrative in the short run, this approach can prove disastrous over time because the exporter:

- May not learn the market as a totality
- May miss ongoing trends that could make a product obsolete
- May miss out on better opportunities for growth

The following are three examples of companies that suffered because they ignored the field research stage.

EXAMPLE 1

A Dutch manufacturer of specialty nut products did not succeed in selling its products in Thailand despite interest expressed by Thai brokers at an international food show and a great deal of export experience in Europe. The Thai population found the Dutch-manufactured products unfamiliar and foreign. A manager in this company's export department attributed the failure to inadequate market research and inadequate marketing in Thailand.

EXAMPLE 2

A manufacturer of fine French soaps had only passing interest in entering the U.S. market; the product sold well in Europe. There was some interest in a U.S. start-up, but no specific funds were set aside for this purpose. Someone in the marketing department had a single contact in North Carolina who was willing to do some trial selling. That effort was derailed when the shipment was stolen at the docks. Then a New York agent was hired whose sole contact was Bloomingdale's. The department store showed interest and sales were under way when Bloomingdale's was bought out. Rather than undertake a proper marketing campaign, the company gave up on the U.S. market.

EXAMPLE 3

Two enterprising business partners joined to market their pasta sauce overseas. The product was well received in the United States; one of the partners had worked internationally. They exhibited their wares at an international trade show and received interest from a Malaysian distributor. Rather than conduct any further research, they procured a loan to manufacture the product based on several orders and went into business. Although a few shipments were made, there were no follow-up orders; the product failed to make a splash with Malaysian consumers. Burdened with overcapacity, the new business nearly failed.

Note. This last example typifies a common problem among first-time exporters; the tendency to put all of their eggs in one basket. Generally one order or one distributor does not make a successful exporting venture. The international market is an exciting place to be; exporters large and small, from the pasta sauce partners to multinational corporations, often get stars in their eyes from the adventure and the romance of making contact with foreign cultures. The best guidance is to adhere to sound business practices. In that respect, global is the same as local.

1.5.2 *Effective Field Research*

Solid field research can save tremendous time and money, as well as ensure against false leads. This is particularly important in international markets, where the cost of doing business is incrementally higher than in domestic markets.

The following are some examples illustrating how solid field research either created a direction and focus, or literally paid off in sales.

EXAMPLE: DOING PROPER MARKET ANALYSIS

A manufacturer of Christmas tree stands wanted to do business in Europe. Rather than randomly picking a country for a market focus and concluding a hasty deal at a trade show, this exporter carefully considered where the product might sell best. After some field research, the decision was made to target countries with a tradition of Christmas. The international trade counselor who assisted this manufacturer found this to be one of the more astute marketing approaches she had encountered, given the gold-rush mentality that often surrounds international trade.

EXAMPLE: AVOIDING FALSE LEADS

An industrial park attached to a major U.S. Air Force base was seeking European manufacturers. The original premise was to entice aircraft maintenance companies to locate there. But it turned out that these companies were suffering from an economic downturn and were not interested in establishing a U.S. base. Further field research indicated strong potentials with European producers of fresh flowers, fish, and other perishables, which would benefit from the easy air and highway access the site provided.

EXAMPLE: MAKING A SUCCESSFUL MARKET ENTRANCE

A major European temporary agency decided to enter the U.S. market through acquisition of American-based companies. A tremendous amount of thought and research went into selecting possible locations for a headquarters, with

Boston, Atlanta, and Chicago heading the list. Before entering the U.S. market, the company conducted research on the social and political climate in the United States. Specifically, the company wanted to know:

- The effect of trade unions on their industry
- U.S. attitudes toward foreign-owned firms
- Whether the growing trend toward temporary employment was a politically charged issue or a source of resentment
- The economic climate and living conditions in these cities

The company then hired a small American market research firm to further explore employment trends, as well as to report in detail on these locations. Atlanta was chosen, a headquarters was established, and several years later this company won a major sporting-events contract. The company also hired a person with extensive experience in the U.S. banking industry to head its fledgling American operation. This individual was well versed in American cultural and business trends.

1.5.3   Penetrating Retail Markets

In developed regions such as Europe, an American manufacturer is competing heavily, especially when the product is retailed. Looking at specialty foods again, European wholesalers report store shelves already packed with hundreds of indigenous products. The best way for an American company to enter a heavily saturated market without a large infusion of advertising is to find an already-established joint venture partner.

Because of the proximity of many European countries, it is still possible to generate many sales through word of mouth. A Dutch company, Sunshine Foods, was able to make its cone-shaped taco shell and other Tex-Mex food items sell well by personally introducing products to European restaurateurs and caterers. Doing business with an innovative company such as Sunshine could mean easy market entry for an American manufacturer.

1.5.4   Productive Overseas Visits

There are many reasons that exporters should travel and conduct market research in the overseas market of choice. The most obvious are:

- To attain personal awareness of the market
- To learn the culture first-hand
- To observe industry trends
- To retain more control in the event a foreign agent or distributor is hired to break into the market (see Chapter 2)

Researching the Market in Person

Exporters do not need to attend trade shows to make personal contacts. As already noted, contacts can be made by phone and fax machine. Meeting these same contacts in person becomes a natural extension of that method.

Other means of locating potential contacts and setting up in-person meetings include using resources available from:

- The U.S. Commerce Department
- International chambers of commerce
- International trade associations

Exporters should consider calls made to foreign business counterparts educational at the very least. They should be prepared to make several visits and conduct a good deal of correspondence before the first transaction is concluded. Exporters of American goods may find they have a ready audience when they travel abroad, but they should not mistake curiosity for willingness to conduct business, at least on American terms. Rather, they should expect to encounter shrewd, seasoned businesspeople and traders and, when overseas, to conduct business on the terms of the foreign country.

EXAMPLE: ANOTHER SUCCESSFUL MARKET ENTRANCE

A good example of a successful market entrance—and of the types of issues that small exporters face—is the experience of Amerinx Artificial Intelligence (AAI), an Amherst, Massachusetts, manufacturer of imaging software. The fifty-three employee company and its president, Richard Kretchsmann, did all of their homework. They understood their markets and were patient, and so were able to avoid many of the pitfalls that are common to small exporters.

Kretchsmann's decision to start exporting software in 1991 was based on an educated hunch. "We attended computer imaging shows all over the country and there were always a significant number of potential foreign purchasers," he said. That was enough for the fledgling exporting efforts.

Amerinex produces highly specialized software for users who require imaging components in engineering, research, and design applications. The imaging software provides a visual field or context for such applications. Imaging is used in tasks that are too dangerous for direct human involvement—such as designing target seekers for missiles—or where the results may suffer as a result of operator fatigue, such as Pap-smear analysis or medical screening for tumors.

Kretchsmann met a consultant at a trade show who already had information about specific companies in Europe that were looking to distribute U.S. products. First, Kretchsmann screened the consultant. "We treated him as we would a new employee," he said. "We talked with him at length, checked his credentials and his references, and asked him to submit a plan as to how he would go about finding European distribution. That plan included a specific budget."

Satisfied that he had found a suitable person—finding the *best* person Kretchsmann said would have cost considerably more—the consultant was authorized to go to Europe on behalf of the company. They agreed that he would approach targeted distributors and would put the deals together but not actually close them.

The initial effort was successful and for the first time AAI products were being sold in Europe through a French distributor. The consultant then traveled to Spain and Italy on the company's behalf as part of a trade mission organized by a Massachusetts state agency. Unfortunately, the consultant passed away a few months after the trade mission, and the Spanish and Italian connections, said Kretchsmann, "did not come to a successful conclusion."

Following up on those first contacts, AAI's first French distributor made inroads into Italy, but nothing came of it either. "For Italy," said Kretchsmann, "you need an Italian distributor."

It wasn't just the death of the consultant that set back AAI's initial exporting efforts. There were other difficulties. The company had no employee in Europe to oversee the sales and marketing in the critical early stages.

"When you are using a distributor you are competing with the other product lines that the distributor represents," said Kretchsmann. "He will focus his time and resources on those products which bring him the best return, and often that means the quickest return."

AAI's complex software is not the type of product on which anyone can make a quick buck. It is a specialized niche product that requires a great deal of backup support and customer service. "We always had to pay attention to make sure they were providing enough information and training," said Kretchsmann. "It was not a panacea by any stretch of the imagination."

As a result, Amerinex did not do very well in its first few years in the export market. At first they had a company employee go overseas several times each year, but as soon as they stopped doing that their orders decreased. It wasn't until they had someone over there on a regular basis that the orders began to pick up again.

That crucial overseas presence in 1995 led to the formation of a strategic alliance with a French company, ADCIS, or Advanced Concepts in Imaging Software. Amerinex owns one third of the joint partnership, which is a corporation under French law. A French national who is now an employee of AAI was in charge of the formation of the partnership. In addition, "as a sort of crisis check," according to Kretchsmann, the foreign offices of consulting giant Arthur Andersen were employed to make sure all the *i*'s were dotted and all the *t*'s were crossed. Since most of the legal work was done up front, the role of Andersen was "constrained," according to Kretchsmann, so that it was not a huge expense.

The benefits of having a reliable overseas presence to look over the company's interests were huge. The two companies have since combined their technologies to undertake innovative product development work, and the result of that collaboration—Apehlion, a state-of-the-art imaging software—is the focus of a joint international marketing effort.

For his part, Kretchsmann couldn't be happier. "The strategic alliance gives us a corporate presence in the European Community," he said. "Technical support, warranties, sales and service are now handled by the French."

Not that his worries are over. There are still matters like getting paid to contend with. "In the U.S. the standard practice is for companies to be paid in 30 days," said Kretchsmann, "but in Europe, 45 to 60 days is the norm, and in Italy it can be as long as 90 days." He credits his consultant with bringing the payment issue to his attention; current distribution agreements set payment terms at 30 days or less. Moreover, payment is done through wire transfers, thereby avoiding complex letters of credit, a bane in the existence of small exporting firms.

"Prior to working at Amerinex I worked at a larger company where there were frequent problems with letters of credit, such as wrong numbers, missing paperwork, and bad timing," said Kretchsmann.

Another major concern of the U.S. software industry is pirating and copyright violations of intellectual properties. The problem is so widespread in countries like China and India that in May 1996 the United States and China came to the brink of a major trade war when the United States demanded that thirty factories that were allegedly producing counterfeit compact disks and videos in Southern China be shut down.

Kretchsmann says that for AAI the problem is somewhat mitigated by the specialized nature of the product. The problem is not so much counterfeiters who duplicate and resell bootlegged copies of popular products like Microsoft's Windows 95, he said, but rather customers who buy one copy and want to install it in two or three work stations. "They can circumvent the security features," he said. "They can say that one computer died and they need to have another copy for a new computer."

There are other built-in security features that help. "There are places in the code," he said, "that check certain data to see if it is a valid installation. We also use dongles. These are hardware devices with logic components that attach to parallel ports on computers. The CD-ROM knows what the code is and will only run software that matches the dongle."

Other areas of concern are trade barriers and government regulations, though they can be thought of as two sides of the same coin. As multilateral treaties such as GATT and NAFTA lower duties and tariffs that are assessed and collected by the customs services of target countries, other non-tariff trade barriers are springing up as governments move to protect their domestic industries. These non-tariff barriers often take the form of increased regulatory scrutiny and government-mandated standards with which imported products must comply.

For example, in 1996 Japan proposed the establishment of a "voluntary" system under which foreign software producers would have third party auditors confirm the quality of the processes involved in their software production. The American National Standards Institute objected, saying the process would be cumbersome and would allow Japanese auditing firms to inspect and approve American products.

Ironically, it is U.S. government regulators who have caused the most headaches for Kretchsmann and members of the WMSA. The Bureau of Export Administration (BXA) is the U.S. agency charged with export licensing. Under its proliferation controls program, it scrutinized any technology with a potential military application. Unfortunately for software producers, that includes virtually any computer or software technology.

"Dealing with government agencies has been a bit of an impediment," said Kretchsmann. "In some cases we have to get approval from the Commerce Department and the Department of Defense. There is paperwork and there are delays in the approval process. On some of our earlier products, we had to get the foreign buyer to provide written assurance that they would not transship the product to other countries."

To expand the company's overseas presence, Kretchsmann attended CeBit 97, the world's largest information technology show, which was held in March 1997, in Hanover, Germany. Foreign trade shows are crucial for promoting export products, but it is important to select the right show. For Kretchsmann, CeBit was a mixed bag. "On the one hand, it was overwhelming," he said. "The halls are filled with all kinds of music, and the exhibits themselves can be quite spectacular. Musicians, robots, and comedians are used to attract people to the booths."

One of his goals at CeBit was to introduce Amerinex products in Germany and, hopefully, to generate sales. To that end, AAI's German distributor provided both funds and staff for the exhibition booth. But with such a specialized product, Kretchsmann felt a little lost in the crowd, which was so large and had such momentum that to check out a booth you literally had to leap out of the massed streams of humanity.

"Our product is so specialized," said Kretchsmann, "in general, it is not as effective for us. Usually we go to imaging shows."

1.6 CULTURAL ISSUES

On the surface, the world and its people are becoming more homogenized. Mass media and communications are creating a global culture of sorts. But without a doubt, exporters will run into both national and/or corporate cultural barriers. Routine occurrences at home—getting cash, renting a car, shopping for clothes, extending hospitality—can present formidable obstacles overseas. An exporter who does not take the time to learn about the culture of a target country or company, or work with a foreign partner, agent, distributor, or customer on his or her terms, will likely encounter problems later on. The following examples illustrate the need for awareness of cultural differences.

Class Issues

A Dutch national agrees to act as a liaison for an American export management company. A monthly fee is set and the Americans begin to make assignments. One of the tasks is to contact the president of a midsize Dutch company to request payment long overdue for a previous project. The liaison—a midlevel manager in a publishing concern—agrees to handle the task but continually puts off reaching the company president. Eventually he explains that the president in question is from a well-known, "old money" family; he owns airplanes, several Mercedes, and a large country estate. The liaison is uncomfortable approaching him in a way that might be construed as demeaning. The manager of the export management company selects someone else for the job.

Corporate Issues

In the United States alone there are huge cultural differences among corporations; those differences are magnified when dealing with foreign corporations.

In 1995, executives of Upjohn Co. of Kalamazoo, Michigan, and Pharmacia AB of Sweden were delighted with the merger of their two pharmaceutical companies. They anticipated streamlined operations, reduced costs, and additions to aging product lines.

What they failed to anticipate were cultural differences that sent both partners reeling. Scheduled meetings were repeatedly canceled because the Americans were unaware that almost everyone in Sweden spends the month of July on vacation. The Swedish workers, accustomed to work teams and a large measure of independence, were frustrated by the hard-charging, "in your face" style of the American managers. Several top European executives and research specialists left the company when they were required to file detailed monthly reports rather than make informal presentations several times a year.

Pharmacia, with headquarters in Stockholm and Milan, opposed a shift to

Kalamazoo. To placate both sides, an additional headquarters was established in London. Communication became even more difficult; differences in the new partners' computer systems delayed timely production of a new-drug application process.

Upjohn required all of its workers, even top management, to submit to drug and alcohol testing; in Italy wine was served every day in the company dining room. Smoking was not permitted in Upjohn's headquarters; Pharmacia provided humidors to cigar-smoking executives.

The Americans became frustrated with Italian accounting methods, labor laws, and trade unions; a climate of mistrust developed. The Italians, in turn, comfortable with a business hierarchy, were put off by the Swedes' informal style. When Italians workers left work to attend to sick relatives or children the Swedes saw it as a lack of commitment to the company. (*The Wall Street Journal*, 2/4/97)

Language Barriers

A high-level Russian delegation from the region of Pushkin visits Massachusetts to attempt to build trade relations between the two regions. Only one of the seven-member task force members speaks English and even his ability is limited. The issue of hard currency arises during the discussion and it becomes clear that it will be difficult to conduct business with the small amount of cash the Russians have available.

More important, the language barriers create a tremendous impediment. Three hours into the discussion, it is unclear if all sides understand each other. Talks break off with no business concluded at the end of the day. The American team decides not to pursue the matter. The communication gap is so great that the small amount of business in question does not seem worth the effort.

Establishing Timeframes

In general, Americans have a forthright approach to business. One or two meetings with total strangers may be all that is needed to conclude a deal. But in many Asian cultures, it is customary to develop long-term relationships before any business is conducted. A major American manufacturer of machine tools reports attending many sessions with a prospective Japanese customer—including lunches and dinners—before the first deal is made. He also reports that the Japanese customer has continued to increase orders since that trusting relationship evolved.

Bribes and Kickbacks

The issue of bribes and kickbacks is a very real one. In some countries, these payments to government officials are simply part of doing business (Chapter 9 has more information on this subject).

1.7 PROFESSIONAL ASSISTANCE: EXPORT MANAGEMENT COMPANIES AND EXPORT TRADING COMPANIES

For small and midsize companies, an export management company (EMC) or export trading company (ETC) may be the most cost-effective route to overseas markets. Both EMCs and ETCs are usually small firms; 60 percent of these types of companies have six or fewer employees. They are entrepreneurial in style and maintain active networks of international agents and distributors. Both are able to link buyers with sellers and can represent a client company at international trade shows. Most specialize in a specific product category, but among the companies themselves, there is a tremendous diversity of specialization. Some are regional while others have a worldwide focus.

As more exporters get involved with countertrade—where the exporter accepts payment in goods or services—the use of export intermediaries has increased. Exporters interested in learning more about the services of EMCs and ETCs can check the following sources:

* The Office of Export Trading Companies (201-482-5131)
* The Export Yellow Pages
* Directory of Leading U.S. Export Management Companies

Export Management Companies

Export management companies offer specific expertise in a given industry and product line, and can be hired on as a company's overseas selling/distribution arm. The EMC:

* Acts as the export department for one or several producers of goods or services.
* Solicits and transacts business in the name of the producers.
* Works on a commission, salary, or retainer-plus basis.
* Usually specializes either by product, by foreign market, or both. Because of their specialization, the best EMCs know their products and the markets they serve very well and usually have well-established networks of foreign distributors already in place.

The immediate access to foreign markets is one of the principal reasons for using an EMC. Establishing a productive relationship with a foreign representative may be a costly and lengthy process. EMCs pose a threat to manufacturers in the sense that, as third parties, they deal directly with foreign sources. This means that the American company risks losing control over foreign sales.

Export Trading Companies

In contrast to the specialized export management company, export trading companies are more demand driven and transaction oriented. They often act as independent distributors who will often buy goods for resale at a higher profit or source goods in answer to the lead of an overseas buyer. For example, an ETC may trade in food products one day and computer components the next. An ETC facilitates the export of U.S. goods and services by acting as the export department for producers and by taking title to the product for direct export.

EXAMPLE

A Small Business Development Center database lists a government tender from Malaysia. The Malaysian seller is looking for buyers for 200 pounds of dried shrimp. Knowing potential buyers in the U.S. restaurant business, the ETC representative makes contact with the Malaysian seller to verify the lead. The ETC representative then contacts restaurant owners in the United States and secures a buyer. The ETC may broker the deal or buy up the shrimp for resale.

Note. As will be discussed in Chapter 2, ETCs are just one of several ways that exporters can maneuver in foreign markets.

Summary of Key Points Raised in This Chapter

1. American companies have historically avoided international trade because of lack of knowledge of foreign markets and cultures.

2. Companies seeking to do business abroad must be patient and flexible, and should have the financial resources to withstand longer payment times.

3. Sound market research can help American businesses avoid conflicts and is an effective tool for cost savings.

4. In selecting a product to market overseas, companies should consider existing foreign and U.S. competition, the product's compatibility with foreign cultures, foreign legal and regulatory requirements, costs of doing business abroad, and the foreign market's political and fiscal stability.

5. General business periodicals, as well as specific industry publications, can help prospective overseas traders make a preliminary assessment of the target market.

6. The Commerce Department and the U.S. Customs Service offer publications and other assistance for U.S. businesses venturing abroad.

7. Foreign chambers of commerce produce guides to assist U.S. businesses in obtaining contacts.

8. U.S. businesses must be aware of the cultural issues that affect doing business abroad; these include class issues, language barriers, and attitudes toward business relationships.

9. Export management companies and export trading companies can assist U.S. businesses in doing market research.

Appendix A   Directory of U.S. and Foreign Commercial Service Domestic District Offices

For a comprehensive listing of Export Assistance Centers, readers should access the International Trade Administration/U.S. Department of Commerce web site at (http://www.ita.doc.gov). Addresses and phone numbers of the Commerce Department and Small Business Administration Export Assistance Centers are provided for every state.

Listings of local and regional offices are also provided for the following U.S. government agencies that offer a wide range of export assistance:

U.S. Department of Commerce
Export-Import Bank of the United States
Small Business Administration
U.S. Agency for International Development
U.S. Department of Agriculture

The web site also provides listings of trade events, programs, and seminars, as well as trade statistics, on a state-by-state basis. There is also information on specific industry sectors and foreign countries, and there are links to numerous other useful sites.

ALABAMA
Berry Building
Room 302, 2015 2nd Avenue North
Birmingham, AL 35203
(205) 731-1331

ALASKA
World Trade Center Alaska
Suite 319
4201 Tudor Center Drive
Anchorage, AK 99508-5916
(907) 271-6237

ARIZONA
Phoenix Plaza
Suite 970
2901 North Central Avenue
Phoenix, AZ 85012
(602) 640-2513

ARKANSAS
TCBY Building
Suite 700
425 West Capitol Avenue
Little Rock, AR 72201
(501) 324-5794

CALIFORNIA
Room 9200
11000 Wilshire Blvd.

Los Angeles, CA 90024
(310) 575-7104

Suite 1670
One World Center
Long Beach, CA 90031
(310) 980-4550

Suite 305
3300 Irvine Avenue
Newport Beach, CA 92660
(714) 660-1688

Suite 230
6363 Greenwich Drive
San Diego, CA 92122
(619) 557-5395

250 Montgomery Street
14th Floor
San Francisco, CA 94101
(415) 705-2300

Techmart Building
Suite 456
5201 Great American Parkway
Santa Clara, CA 95054
(408) 291-7625

COLORADO
Suite 680
1625 Broadway
Denver, CO 80202
(303) 844-6622

CONNECTICUT
Federal Building
Room 610-B
450 Main Street
Hartford, CT 07103
(203) 240-3530

DELAWARE
Served by Baltimore, MD, Export Assistance Center

DISTRICT OF COLUMBIA
Served by Baltimore, MD, Export Assistance Center

FLORIDA
P.O. Box 590570
Trade Port Building

6th Floor
5600 NW 36th Avenue
Miami, FL 33159-0570
(305) 526-7425

120 Osceola Avenue
Clearwater, FL 34615
(813) 461-0011

Eola Park Center
Suite 695
200 East Robinson Street
Orlando, FL 32801
(407) 648-6235

Collins Building
Room 366G
107 West Gaines Street
Tallahassee, FL 32399-2000
(904) 488-6469

GEORGIA
Plaza Square North
Suite 310
4360 Chamblee-Dunwoody Road
Atlanta, GA 30341

Room A-107
120 Barnard Street
Savannah, GA 31401
(912) 652-4204

HAWAII
P.O. Box 50026
Room 4106
300 Ala Moana Blvd.
Honolulu, HI 96850
(808) 541-1782

IDAHO
Joe R. Williams Building
2nd Floor
700 West State Street
Boise, ID 83720
(208) 334-3757

ILLINOIS
Xerox Center
Suite 2440

55 West Monroe
Chicago, IL 60603
(312) 353-8040

Illinois Institute of Technology
Rice Campus
201 East Look Road
Wheaton, IL 60187
(815) 353-4332

P.O. Box 1747
515 North Court Street
Rockford, IL 61110-0247
(815) 987-4347

INDIANA
Penwood One
Suite 106
11405 North Pennsylvania Street
Carmel, IN 46032
(317) 582-2300

IOWA
Federal Building
Room 817
210 Walnut Street
Des Moines, IA 50309
(515) 284-4222

KANSAS
151 North Volutsia
Wichita, KS 67214-4695
(316) 269-6160

Marmaduke Building
3rd Floor
520 South Fourth Street
Louisville, KY 40202
(502) 582-5066

LOUISIANA
Hale Boggs Federal Building
Room 1043
501 Magazine Street
New Orleans, LA 70130
(504) 589-6546

MAINE
Suite 59
187 State Street

Augusta, ME 04333
(207) 622-8249

MARYLAND
World Trade Center
Suite 2432
401 East Pratt Street
Baltimore, MD 21202
(410) 962-4359

MASSACHUSETTS
World Trade Center
Suite 307
164 Northern Avenue
Boston, MA 02210
(617) 565-8563

MICHIGAN
1140 Michigan Avenue
Detroit, MI 48226
(313) 226-3650

Room 408
3000 Monroe NW
Grand Rapids, MI 49503
(616) 456-2411

MINNESOTA
108 Federal Building
110 South 4th Street
Minneapolis, MN 55401
(612) 348-1638

MISSISSIPPI
Suite 310
201 West Capitol Street
Jackson, MS 39201-2005
(601) 965-4388

MISSOURI
Suite 303
8182 Maryland Avenue
St. Louis, MO 63105
(314) 425-3302

Room 635
601 East 12th Street

Kansas City, MO 64106
(816) 426-3141

MONTANA
Served by Boise, ID, Branch Office

NEBRASKA
11133 O Street
Omaha, NE 68137
(402) 221-3664

NEVADA
Suite 152
1755 East Plumb Lane
Reno, NV 89502
(702) 784-5203

NEW HAMPSHIRE
Suite 29
601 Spaulding Turnpike
Portsmouth, NH 03801-2833
(603) 334-6074

NEW JERSEY
Building 6
Suite 100
3131 Princeton Pike
Trenton, NJ 08648
(609) 989-2100

NEW MEXICO
c/o New Mexico Department of Economic Development
1100 St. Francis Drive
Santa Fe, NM 87503
(505) 827-0350

NEW YORK
1312 Federal Building
111 West Huron Street
Buffalo, NY 14202
(716) 846-4191

Suite 220
111 East Avenue
Rochester, NY 14604
(716) 263-6480

Room 3718
26 Federal Plaza
New York, NY 10278
(212) 264-0634

NORTH CAROLINA
Room 400
400 West Market Street
Greensboro, NC 27401
(910) 333-5345

NORTH DAKOTA
Served by the Minneapolis, MN, district office.

OHIO
9504 Federal Building
550 Main Street
Cincinnati, OH 45202
(513) 522-4750

Bank One Center
Suite 700
600 Superior Avenue
Cleveland, OH 44114-2650
(216) 522-4750

OKLAHOMA
Room 200
6601 Broadway Extension
Oklahoma City, OK 73116
(405) 231-5302

440 South Houston Street
Tulsa, OK 74127
(918) 581-5302

OREGON
One World Trade Center
Suite 242
121 SW Salmon
Portland, OR 97204
(503) 326-3001

PENNSYLVANIA
660 American Avenue
Suite 201
King of Prussia, PA 19406
(215) 962-4980

2002 Federal Building
1000 Liberty Avenue
Pittsburgh, PA 15222
(412) 644-2850

PUERTO RICO
Federal Building
Room G-55
Chardon Avenue
San Juan, PR 00918
(809) 766-5555

RHODE ISLAND
7 Jackson Walkway
Providence, RI 02903
(803) 765-4051

SOUTH CAROLINA
Strom Thurmond Federal Building
Suite 172
1835 Assembly Street
Columbia, SC 29201
(803) 765-5345

c/o Trident Technical College
P.O. Box 118607 CE-P
66 Columbus Street
Charleston, SC 29423
(803) 727-4051

SOUTH DAKOTA
Served by Omaha, NE, district office

TENNESSEE
Parkway Towers
Suite 114
404 James Robertson Parkway
Nashville, TN 37219-1505
(615) 736-5161

The Falls Building
Suite 200
22 North Front Street
Memphis, TN 38103
(901) 544-4137

301 East Church Avenue
Knoxville, TN 37915
(615) 545-4637

TEXAS
Suite 170
2050 North Stemmons Freeway
P.O. Box 58130
Dallas, TX 75258
(214) 767-0542

Suite 414-A
410 East 5th Street
P.O. Box 12728
Austin, TX 78711
(512) 482-5939

Suite 1160
1 Allen Center
Houston, TX 77002
(713) 229-2578

UTAH
Suite 105
324 South State Street
Salt Lake City, UT 84111
(801) 524-5116

VERMONT
4th Floor
109 State Street
Montpelier, VT 05609
(802) 771-2246

VIRGINIA
700 Center
Suite 550
704 East Franklin Street
Richmond, VA 23219
(804) 771-2246

WASHINGTON
Suite 290
3131 Elliott Avenue
Seattle, WA 98121
(206) 553-5615

Suite 350
320 North Jackson Street
Kennewick, WA 99336
(509) 735-2751

WEST VIRGINIA
Suite 807
405 Capitol Street
Charleston, WV 25301
(304) 347-5123

WISCONSIN
Room 596
517 East Wisconsin Avenue
Milwaukee, WI 53202
(414) 297-3473

WYOMING
Served by Denver, CO, district office

Appendix B   Directory of Small Business Development Centers

ALABAMA
John Sandefur
State Director
Alabama SBDC Consortium
University of Alabama at Birmingham
Medical Towers Building
1717 11th Avenue, Suite 419
Birmingham, AL 35294

ALASKA
Jan Fredericks
State Director
Alaska Small Business Development Center
University of Alaska Anchorage
430 West Seventh Avenue, Suite 110
Anchorage, AK 99501
Tel: (907) 274-7232
Fax: (907) 274-9524

ARIZONA
Michael York
State Director
Arizona SBDC Network
2411 West 14th Street, Suite 132
Tempe, AZ 99501
Tel: (602) 731-8720
Fax: (602) 731-8729
E-mail: in%"york@maricopa.edu

ARKANSAS
Janet Nye
State Director
Arkansas Small Business Development Center
University of Arkansas at Little Rock
100 South Main, Suite 401
Little Rock, AR 72201
Tel: (501) 324-9043
Fax: (501) 324-9049
E-mail: jmney@ualr.edu

CALIFORNIA
Maria Morris
State Director
California SBDC Program
Department of Commerce
801 K Street, Suite 1700
Sacramento, CA 95814
Tel: (916) 324-5068
Fax: (916) 322-5084

COLORADO
Rick Garcia
State Director
Colorado Small Business Development Center
Colorado Office of Business Development
1625 Broadway, Suite 1710
Denver, CO 80202
Tel: (303) 892-3809
Fax: (303) 892-3848

CONNECTICUT
John P. O'Connor
State Director
Connecticut Small Business Development Center
University of Connecticut
Rte. 44, U-94
Storrs, CT 06269-5094
Tel: (203) 486-4135
Fax: (203) 486-1576

DELAWARE
Clinton Tymes
State Director
Delaware Small Business Development Center
University of Delaware

Purnell Hall, Suite 005
Newark, DE 19716-2711
Tel: (302) 831-2747
Fax: (302) 831-1423

DISTRICT OF COLUMBIA
Woodrow McCutchen
State Director
District of Columbia SBDC
Howard University
6th and Fairmont Streets, NW, Room 128
Washington, DC 20059
Tel: (202) 806-1550
Fax: (202) 806-1777

FLORIDA
Jerry G. Cartwright
State Director
Florida Small Business Development Center Network
University of West Florida
19 West Garden Street, Suite 300
Pensacola, FL 32501
Tel: (904) 444-2060
Fax: (904) 444-2070
E-mail: jcartwri@uwf.cc.upw.edu

GEORGIA
Henry Logan, Jr.
State Director
Georgia Small Business Development Center
University of Georgia
Chicopee Complex, 1180 East Broad Street
Athens, GA 30602-5412
Tel: (706) 542-5760
Fax: (706) 542-6776
E-mail: sbdcdir@uga.cc.uga.edu

HAWAII
Darryl Mleynek
Acting State Director
Hawaii Small Business Development Center Network
University of Hawaii at Hilo
200 West Kawili
Hilo, HI 96720
Tel: (808) 933-3515
Fax: (808) 933-3683

IDAHO
James Hogge
Acting State Director
Idaho Small Business Development Center
Boise State University
1910 University Drive
Boise, ID 83725
Tel: (208) 385-1640
Fax: (208) 385-3877
E-mail: aidhogge@cobfac.idbsu.edu

ILLINOIS
Jeff Mitchell
State Director
Illinois Small Business Development Center
Department of Commerce and Community Affairs
620 East Adams Street, 6th Floor
Springfield, IL 62701
Tel: (217) 524-5856
Fax: (217) 785-6328
E-mail: jeff.mitchell@accessil.com

INDIANA
Steven G. Thrash
Executive Director
Indiana Small Business Development Centers
Economic Development Council
One North Capitol, Suite 420
Indianapolis, IN 46204
Tel: (317) 264-6871
Fax: (317) 264-3102
E-mail: sthrash@inforum.indycom.com

IOWA
Ronald A. Manning
State Director
Iowa Small Business Development Center
Iowa State University
137 Lynn Avenue
Ames, IA 50014
Tel: (515) 292-6351
Fax: (515) 292-0020
E-mail: rmanning@iastate.edu

KENTUCKY
Janet S. Holloway
State Director

Kentucky Small Business Development Center
University of Kentucky, Center for Business Development
225 Business and Economics Building
Lexington, KY 40506-0034
Tel: (606) 257-7668
Fax: (606) 258-1907
E-mail: cbejh.@uk.cc.uky.edu

LOUISIANA
John P. Baker
State Director
Louisiana Small Business Development Center
Northeast Louisiana University, CBA
700 University Avenue
Monroe, LA 71209-6435
Tel: (318) 342-5506
Fax: (318) 342-5510
E-mail: brwall@merlin.nlu.edu

MAINE
Charles Davis
State Director
Maine Small Business Development Center
University of Southern Maine
96 Falmouth Street
Portland, ME 04103
Tel: (207) 780-4420
Fax: (207) 780-4810
E-mail: tisdale@maine.maine.edu

MARYLAND
Brenda Townsend-Milton
Acting State Director
Maryland Small Business Development Center
Department of Economic & Employment Development
217 East Redwood Street, 10th Floor
Baltimore, MD 21202
Tel: (410) 333-6995
Fax: (410) 333-4460

MASSACHUSETTS
John F. Ciccarelli
State Director
Massachusetts Small Business Development Center
University of Massachusetts-Amherst
Room 205, School of Management

Amherst, MA 01003
Tel: (413) 545-6301
Fax: (413) 545-1273
E-mail: j.ciccarelli@dpc.umass.edu

MICHIGAN
Ronald Hall
State Director
Michigan Small Business Development Center
2727 Second Avenue
Detroit, MI 48201
Tel: (313) 964-1768
Fax: (313) 964-3648

MISSISSIPPI
Raleigh H. Byars
Executive Director
Mississippi Small Business Development Center
University of Mississippi
Old Chemistry Building, Suite 216
University, MS 38677
Tel: (601) 232-5001
Fax: (601) 232-5650

MISSOURI
Max E. Summers
State Director
Missouri Small Business Development Center
University of Missouri
300 University Place
Columbia, MO 65211
Tel: (314) 882-0344
Fax: (314) 884-4297
E-mail: sbdc-mso@ext.missouri.edu

MONTANA
Gene Marcille
Montana Small Business Development Center
Montana Department of Commerce
1424 9th Avenue
Helena, MT 59620
Tel: (406) 444-4780
Fax: (406) 444-2808
E-mail: proberts@win.com

NEBRASKA
Robert E. Bernier
State Director

Nebraska Business Development Center
University of Nebraska at Omaha
60th and Dodge Streets, CBA Room 407
Omaha, NE 68182
Tel: (402) 554-2521
Fax: (402) 554-3747
E-mail: rbernier@cbafaculty.unomah.edu

NEVADA
Sam Males
State Director
Nevada Small Business Development Center
University of Nevada, Reno
College of Business Administration-032, Room 411
Reno, NV 89557-0100
Tel: (702) 784-1717
Fax: (702) 784-4337
E-mail: nvsbdc@scs.unr.edu

NEW HAMPSHIRE
Liz Lamoureux
State Director
New Hampshire Small Business Development Center
University of New Hampshire
108 McConnell Hall
Durham, NH 03824
Tel: (603) 862-2200
Fax: (603) 862-4468
E-mail: hg@christa.unh.edu

NEW JERSEY
Brenda Hopper
State Director
New Jersey Small Business Development Center
Rutgers University Graduate School of Management
180 University Avenue
Newark, NJ 07102
Tel: (201) 648-5950
Fax: (201) 648-1110
E-mail: bhopper@andromeda.rutgers.edu

NEW MEXICO
Frank Hatstat
State Director
New Mexico Small Business Development Center
Santa Fe Community College

P.O. Box 4187
Santa Fe, NM 87502-4187
Tel: (505) 438-1362
Fax: (505) 438-1237

NEW YORK
James L. King
State Director
New York State Small Business Development Center
State University of New York
SUNY Central Plaza, S-523
Albany, NY 12246
Tel: (518) 443-5398
Fax: (518) 465-4992
E-mail: kingjl@snycenvm.bitnet

NORTH CAROLINA
Scott R. Daugherty
Executive Director
North Carolina SBDC
University of North Carolina
4509 Creedmoor Road, Suite 201
Raleigh, NC 27612
Tel: (919) 571-4154
Fax: (919) 571-4161
E-mail: srdaughesbdc.@mhs.unc.edu

NORTH DAKOTA
Walter Kearns
State Director
North Dakota Small Business Development Center
University of North Dakota
118 Gamble Hall, UND, Box 7308
Grand Forks, ND 58202
Tel: (701) 777-3700
Fax: (701) 777-5099
E-mail: auwjk@undjes2.bitnet

OHIO
Holly Schick
Ohio Small Business Development Center
77 South High Street
P.O. Box 1001
Columbus, OH 43266-0101
Tel: (614) 466-2711

Fax: (614) 466-0829
E-mail: rising%sbd%edd@odod.ohio.gov

OKLAHOMA
Grady L. Pennington
State Director
Oklahoma Small Business Development Center
Southeastern Oklahoma State University
P.O. Box 2584, Station A
Durant, OK 74701
Tel: (405) 924-0277
Fax: (405) 920-7471

OREGON
Edward Cutler, Ph.D.
State Director
Oregon Small Business Development Center
Lane Community College
44 West Broadway, Suite 501
Eugene, OR 97401-3021
Tel: (503) 726-2250
Fax: (503) 345-6006
E-mail: ecutler@aol.org

PENNSYLVANIA
Gregory L. Higgins
State Director
Pennsylvania Small Business Development Center
The Wharton School, University of Pennsylvania
444 Vance Hall, 3733 Spruce Street
Philadelphia, PA 19104-6374
Tel: (215) 898-1219
Fax: (215) 573-2135
E-mail: ghiggins@secl.wharton.upenn.edu

PUERTO RICO
Mariluz Frontera
Acting State Director
Puerto Rico Small Business Development Center
University of Puerto Rico
P.O. Box 5253 College Station
Mayaguez, PR
Tel: (809) 834-3590
Fax: (809) 834-3790

RHODE ISLAND
Douglas H. Jobling
State Director

Rhode Island Small Business Development Center
Bryant College
1150 Douglas Pike
Smithfield, RI 02917
Tel: (401) 232-6111
Fax: (401) 232-6416

SOUTH CAROLINA
John M. Lenti
State Director
The Frank L. Roddey Small Business Development Center
University of South Carolina College of Business Administration
Columbia, SC 29201-9980
Tel: (803) 777-4907
Fax: (803) 777-4403
E-mail: lenti@darla.badm.scarolina.edu

SOUTH DAKOTA
Robert E. Ashley, Jr.
State Director
South Dakota Small Business Development Center
University of South Dakota
414 East Clark
Vermillion, SD 57069
Tel: (605) 677-5279
Fax: (605) 677-5272

TENNESSEE
Kenneth J. Burns
State Director
Tennessee Small Business Development Center
Memphis State University
Bldg. 1, South Campus
Memphis, TN 38152
Tel: (901) 678-2500
Fax: (901) 678-4072
E-mail: gmivkle@admin1.memphis.edu

TEXAS (Dallas)
Liz Klimback
State Director
North Texas-Dallas SBDC
Bill J. Priest Institute for Economic Development
1402 Corinth Street
Dallas, TX 75215
Tel: (214) 565-5833

Fax: (214) 565-5813
E-mail: emk9402@dcccd.edu

TEXAS (Houston)
Betsy Gatewood
Regional Director
University of Houston Small Business Development Center
University of Houston
1100 Louisiana, Suite 500
Houston, TX 77002
Tel: (713) 752-8444
Fax: (713) 752-8484
E-mail: uhsbdc@jetson.uh.edu

TEXAS (Lubbock)
Craig Bean
Regional Director
N.W. Texas Small Business Development Center
Texas Tech University
2579 S. Loop 289, Suite 114
Lubbock, TX 79423
Tel: (806) 745-3973
Fax: (806) 745-6207
E-mail: odaus@ttacs.ttu.edu

TEXAS (San Antonio)
Robert M. McKinley
Regional Director
UTSA South Texas Border SBDC
UTSA Downtown Center
1222 North Main Street, Suite 450
San Antonio, TX 78212
Tel: (210) 244-0791
Fax: (210) 222-9834
E-mail: mpenn@ clan.utsa.edu

UTAH
David A. Nimkin
Executive Director
Utah Small Business Development Center
102 West 500 South, Suite 315
Salt Lake City, UT 84101
Tel: (801) 581-7905
Fax: (801) 581-7814

VERMONT
Donald L. Kelpinski
State Director

Vermont Small Business Development Center
Vermont Technical College
P.O. Box 422
Randolph, VT 05060
Tel: (802) 728-9101
Fax: (802) 728-3026
E-mail: dkelpins@night.vtc.vsc.edu

VIRGIN ISLANDS
Chester Williams
State Director
UVI Small Business Development Center
Sunshine Mall, Suite 104
Frederiksted, St. Croix, VI 00840
Tel: (809) 776-3206
Fax: (809) 778-7629 (St. Croix); (809) 778-7629 (St. Thomas)

VIRGINIA
Dr. Robert D. Smith
State Director
Virginia Small Business Development Center
901 East Byrd Street, Suite 1800
Richmond, VA 23219
Tel: (804) 371-8253
Fax: (804) 225-3384

WASHINGTON
Lyle M. Anderson
State Director
Washington Small Business Development Center
Washington State University
Kruegel Hall, Suite 135
Pullman, WA 99164-4727
Tel:(509) 335-1576
Fax: (509) 335-0949
E-mail: andersol@wsuvm1.csc.wsu.edu

WEST VIRGINIA
Hazel Kroesser
State Director
West Virginia Small Business Development Center
GOCID
1115 Virginia Street East
Charleston, WV 25301
Tel: (304) 558-2960
Fax: (304) 558-0127

WISCONSIN
William Pinkovitz
State Director
Wisconsin Small Business Development Center
University of Wisconsin
432 North Lake Street, Room 423
Madison, WI 53706
Tel: (608) 263-7764
Fax: (608) 262-3878
E-mail: pinkovitz@admin.uwex.edu

WYOMING
Dave Mosley
State Director
WSBDX/State Network Office
P.O. Box 3275
Laramie, WY 82071-3275
Tel: (307) 766-3505
Fax: (307) 766-4028

ASSOCIATE MEMBERS
Anne Hope
Director
St. Mary's University Business Development Center
The Sterns Building, 81 Alderney Drive
Dartmouth, Nova Scotia
CANADA B2Y 2N7
Tel: (902) 469-2992
Fax: (902) 469-4244

Jay Krysler
Senior Advisor
Economic Development and Tourism
8th Floor, Sterling Place, 9940 106th Street
Edmonton, Alberta
CANADA T5K 2P6
Tel: (403) 427-3685
Fax: (403) 427-5926

Conrad Rosing
Management Advisory System
A Division of Moss Adams
1001 Fourth Street, Suite 2700
Seattle, WA 98154-1199
Tel: (206) 442-2616
Fax: (206) 442-9617

R. J. Sandoval
AmericanBank Corpus Christi
P.O. Box 6469
Corpus Christi, TX 78466-6469
Tel: (512) 992-9900

Izabella Firkowska
Director
Small Business Advisory Center—Lodz
UL Piltrkowska 109/191
90-447 Lodz, Poland

Andrzej Stasiek
Director
Small Business Advisory Center—Warsaw
4A Zurawia Street
Warsaw, Poland

Appendix C   Directory of State International Trade Contacts

ALABAMA
International Development
Alabama Development Center
Alabama Center for Commerce
401 Adams Avenue
Montgomery, AL 36130
(205) 242-0400

ALASKA
International Finance and Insurance
3601 C Street, Suite 798
Anchorage, AK 99503
(907) 561-5585

ARIZONA
International Trade and Investment Division
Department of Commerce
3800 North Central, Suite 1500
Phoenix, AZ 85012
(602) 280-1371

ARKANSAS
Arkansas Industrial Development Commission
One State Capitol Mall, Room 4C 300
Little Rock, AR 72201
(501) 682-7690

CALIFORNIA
California State World Trade Commission
1121 L Street, Suite 310
Sacramento, CA 95814
(916) 324-5511

COLORADO
Colorado International Trade Office
1625 Broadway, Suite 680
Denver, CO 80202
(303) 892-3856

CONNECTICUT
International Division
Department of Economic Development
865 Brook Street
Rocky Hill, CT 06067
(203) 258-4261

DELAWARE
Business Development
Division of Economic Development
99 Kings Highway, Box 1401
Dover, DE 19903
(302) 739-4271

DISTRICT OF COLUMBIA
Office of International Business
1250 I Street, NW, Suite 1003
Washington, DC 20005
(202) 727-1576

FLORIDA
Division of International Trade and Development
Florida Department of Commerce
107 West Gaines Street
366 Collins Building
Tallahassee, FL 32399-2000
(904) 488-9050

GEORGIA
Department of Industry, Trade & Tourism
P.O. Box 1776
Atlanta, GA 30301
(404) 656-3571

HAWAII
Trade & Industry Development
Department of Planning and Economic Development
P.O. Box 2359
Honolulu, HI 96804

IDAHO
Division of International Business
Idaho Department of Commerce
700 West State Street
Boise, ID 83720
(208) 334-2470

ILLINOIS
International Business Division
Illinois Department of Commerce & Community Affairs
100 West Randolph, Suite C-400
Chicago, IL 60601
(312) 814-7164

INDIANA
International Trade Division
Indiana Department of Commerce
One North Capitol, Suite 700
Indianapolis, IN 46204-2288
(317) 232-3527

IOWA
Division of International Trade
Iowa Department of Economic Development
200 East Grand Avenue
Des Moines, IA 50309

KANSAS
Trade Development Division
Kansas Department of Commerce
700 Harrison Street, 13th Floor
Topeka, KS 66603-3957
(913) 296-4027

KENTUCKY
Office of International Trade
Kentucky Commerce Cabinet
Capitol Plaza Tower, 24th Floor
Frankfort, KY 40601
(502) 564-2170

LOUISIANA
Louisiana Department of Economic Development
P.O. Box 94185
Baton Rouge, LA 70804-9185
(504) 342-4320

MAINE
International Commerce
Department of Economic and Community Development
State House Station 59
Augusta, ME 04333
(207) 289-5700

MARYLAND
International Trade
Maryland International Division
401 East Pratt Street, Suite 752
Baltimore, MD 21202
(410) 333-8180

MASSACHUSETTS
Office of International Trade
100 Cambridge Street, Room 902
Boston, MA 02202
(617) 367-1830

MICHIGAN
International Office
Michigan Department of Commerce
P.O. Box 30225
Lansing, MI 48909
(517) 373-6390

MINNESOTA
Minnesota Trade Office
1000 World Trade Center
30 East 7th Street
St. Paul, MN 55101-4902
(612) 297-4227

MISSISSIPPI
Export Office
Department of Economic Development
P.O. Box 849
Jackson, MI 39205
(601) 359-6672

MISSOURI
Economic Development Programs
P.O. Box 118
Jefferson City, MO 65102
(314) 751-4999

MONTANA
International Trade Office
Montana Department of Commerce
1424 9th Avenue
Helena, MT 59620
(406) 444-3923

NEBRASKA
Department of Economic Development
301 Centennial Mall South
P.O. Box 94666
Lincoln, NE 68509
(402) 471-3111

NEVADA
International Program
Nevada Commission on Economic Development
5151 South Carson
Carson City, NV 89710
(702) 687-4325

NEW HAMPSHIRE
Office of International Commerce
International Trade Resource Center
601 Spaulding Turnpike, Suite 29
Portsmouth, NH 03801-2833
(603) 334-6074

NEW JERSEY
Division of International Trade
Department of Commerce & Economic Development
P.O. Box 47024
Newark, NJ 07102
(201) 648-3518

NEW MEXICO
Economic Development Division
Economic Development and Tourism Department
1100 St. Francis Drive

Santa Fe, NM 87503
(505) 827-0272

NEW YORK
International Division
Department of Economic Development
1515 Broadway, 51st Floor
New York, NY 10036
(212) 827-6210

NORTH CAROLINA
International Division
North Carolina Department of Economic Development
430 North Salisbury Street
Raleigh, NC 27611
(919) 733-7193

NORTH DAKOTA
North Dakota World Trade
1833 East Bismarck Expressway
Bismarck, ND 58504
(701) 221-5300

OHIO
International Trade Division
Department of Development
77 South High Street, 29th Floor
P.O. Box 1001
Columbus, OH 43266-0101
(614) 466-2317

OKLAHOMA
International Trade and Investment
Oklahoma Department of Commerce
P.O. Box 26980
Oklahoma City, OK 73126-0980
(405) 841-5217

OREGON
International Trade Division
Oregon Economic Development Department
One World Trade Center
121 Southwest Salmon, Suite 300
Portland, OR 97204
(503) 229-5625

PENNSYLVANIA
Office of International Trade
Pennsylvania Department of Commerce
464 Forum Building
Harrisburg, PA 17120
(717) 787-7190

PUERTO RICO
Puerto Rico Department of Commerce
G.P.O. 4275
San Juan, PR 00905
(809) 725-7254

RHODE ISLAND
International Trade Division
Department of Economic Development
7 Jackson Walkway
Providence, RI 02903
(401) 277-2601

SOUTH CAROLINA
South Carolina State Development Board
P.O. Box 927
Columbia, SC 29202
(803) 737-0400

SOUTH DAKOTA
Export, Trade and Marketing Division
Governor's Office of Economic Development
711 Wells Avenue
Capitol Lake Plaza
Pierre, SD 57501
(605) 773-5735

TENNESSEE
Department of Economic and Community Development
320 6th Avenue North, 7th Floor
Nashville, TN 37243-0405
(615) 741-5870

TEXAS
International Trade Relations
Texas Department of Commerce
P.O. Box 12728
Austin, TX 78711
(512) 320-9672

UTAH
International Business Development
Economic & Industrial Development Division
324 South State Street, Suite 200
Salt Lake City, UT 84111
(801) 538-8737

VERMONT
Department of Economic Development
Pavilion Office Building
Montpelier, VT 05602
(802) 828-3221

VIRGINIA
Trade Development Group
Virginia Department of Economic Development
P.O. Box 798
Richmond, VA 23206-0798
(804) 371-8107

VIRGIN ISLANDS
Virgin Island Department of Economic Development and Agriculture
Bureau of Economic Research
P.O. Box 6400
St. Thomas, VI 00804
(809) 774-8784

WASHINGTON
Domestic and International Trade Division
Department of Trade and Development
2001 6th Avenue, Suite 2700
Seattle, WA 98121-2522
(206) 464-7143

WEST VIRGINIA
International Trade and Investment
Governor's Office of Community Industrial Development
State Capitol, Room M-146
Charleston, WV 25306
(304) 558-2234

WISCONSIN
Bureau of International Development
Department of Development
P.O. Box 7970

Madison, WI 53707
(608) 266-9487

WYOMING
International Trade Office
Wyoming Division of Economic and Community Development
4th Floor North, Barrett Building
Cheyenne, WY 82002

2

Export Distribution Channels

Key Questions Answered in This Chapter

Introduction

Establishing distribution networks overseas is one of the most important and complex hurdles for the exporter. Basic decisions such as which market segment to target can become major problems in markets such as China and Brazil, which may not have readily accessible demographic figures. In addition, foreign markets may force exporters to face markedly different issues relating to infrastructure (e.g., rail, truck, and air services) and relationships with agents and other intermediaries.

Since most exporters will not be selling directly to buyers, establishing relationships with agents and other intermediaries will be the most crucial step in setting up a distribution network. Agent intermediaries include sales agents, sales representatives, and distributors.

Although working with agent intermediaries may be the best way to break into a foreign market, once a company has established a presence, it may want more control over the sales, distribution, manufacturing, or assembly processes. This can be accomplished by working with joint-venture partners, logistics companies, or foreign retailers, or by using direct mail or piggyback marketing methods.

This chapter discusses the various types of distribution channels available to U.S. firms. It also discusses how an exporter can work with a freight forwarder to ease distribution and other aspects of international trade. Topics covered include overseas manufacturing, organizing a company for export, distribution methods and actors, establishing an overseas sales force, and negotiating agency and distribution agreements.

2.1 MANUFACTURING ABROAD

How a company will set up distribution networks depends largely on where it chooses to manufacture its goods. That decision will depend, in part, on:

- Company resources
- Availability of raw materials
- Labor costs
- Foreign market location

There is a wide difference in the efficiency and quality of work processes in different nations. Therefore, if overseas manufacturing is contemplated, it is best to visit a country and investigate all facilities, local regulations, and the labor pool before proceeding. These differences can quickly turn into significant hidden costs if they are not considered early on.

EXAMPLE

Manufacturing goods in China offers U.S. firms the advantages of avoiding some import restrictions and tariffs. However, many Chinese firms have mixed experience in operating a profit-making enterprise. The lack of basic experience in Western-style management and hiring practices can lead to a considerable investment in time and resources to bring the personnel up to a level in line with U.S. operations. In many instances, Chinese plants have to be completely retooled to bring them up to appropriate quality standards.

Numerous regulations need to be considered as well. China is divided into twenty-nine provinces, autonomous regions, and municipalities. In addition to different climates, tastes, dialects, and infrastructure, most of the regions have different regulations and laws. U.S. manufacturers in China will encounter municipal, regional, provincial, and national government regulations concerning:

- Foreign exchange
- Land use rights
- Import/export licenses
- Taxation
- Environmental regulations
- Operations in special economic zones
- Labor management
- Technology transfer
- Customs tariffs
- Local content or labor requirements

2.1.1 Pros and Cons of Overseas Manufacturing

Companies do not have to be large to manufacture goods overseas. The right joint-venture arrangement can mean on-site production for even the smallest firm. There are many economic advantages and disadvantages to overseas manufacturing. Advantages include:

- Lower labor costs
- Reduced shipping
- Elimination of foreign customs duties
- Easier access to end markets
- More direct connection to the customer

EXAMPLE

A New York City manufacturer of women's sleepwear produced most of its goods domestically until 1988, when a substantial part of the manufacturing was moved to the Caribbean region to take advantage of exemptions from customs duties. Garments were cut in the United States and sent offshore (to Costa Rica, the Dominican Republic, and Haiti) for labor-intensive operations. Because of special customs regulations for this region, the returning import duty on these garments was only on the added value—mostly labor. Ordinarily, the company would have been required to pay duty on the entire value of the goods. (For more information on customs duty management, see Chapter 11.)

Disincentives related to overseas manufacturing include:

- Transport and shipping costs
- Expense and delay of shipping extra raw materials

- Poorer quality of offshore work
- Difficulty in supervising overseas operations

In addition to concerns relating to finances, overseas manufacturing presents operational and cultural hurdles. Here are a few to consider:

- Management will have to learn the local culture and language to work effectively in that market.
- In the event of a language barrier, management is dependent on locals or interpreters to conduct business.
- There is a potential loss of control of the operation due to distance and reliance on foreign intermediaries.
- Knowledge of foreign tax structures, as well as trade customs surrounding financial transactions (e.g., payoffs, kickbacks), is necessary.
- Political problems can threaten the operation.

2.1.2   Offshore Quality-Control Issues

There is a difference in attitude between offshore and domestic management. In North America, the emphasis is on efficiency, speed, and quality. By contrast, in some foreign countries, management is not always able to exercise as much authority over employees.

Example

The New York manufacturer of the previous example hired a full-time quality-control employee who traveled from plant to plant in the Dominican Republic. Even with an executive overseeing manufacturing quality, however, the work in some of the Caribbean countries did not measure up to the quality standards of other overseas and domestic plants.

Note. Quality levels vary from country to country. In the Caribbean, Costa Rica had much better quality control than the other countries in question. Quality levels also appear to be high for garments imported from China, Taiwan, and Bangladesh. Even so, experienced manufacturers warn other Americans to allow for mishaps when manufacturing abroad.

2.1.3   Other Issues Related to Offshore Manufacture

The following are other issues that commonly arise when Americans produce their goods overseas for sale in the United States:

1. *Language barriers.* It is best to find managers who are fluent in English. Otherwise, serious communication problems are bound to arise.

2. *Shipment of materials.* In many cases of offshore manufacture, most or all materials have to be exported from the United States. The expense and delay of these shipments is a significant problem facing offshore manufacturers.

3. *U.S. Customs Service.* Although recent legislation is designed to streamline customs activities, there are always some problems associated with working with this sort of large bureaucracy. Those who manufacture overseas and then import goods back into the United States will have to deal with U.S. Customs on a regular basis.

EXAMPLE

During the course of one import, Caribbean packers placed one shipping label on top of another label, covering important customs information. Initially, U.S. Customs permitted the U.S. company to correct the problem in the customs warehouse at the goods' destination. When more goods were flown in, with the same labeling problem, U.S. Customs refused to release them for nearly eight months, even after the problem was corrected. By the time the goods were released, the value of the merchandise had decreased.

4. *Foreign regulations.* In many countries, there are labor, technical, and quality control regulations that even experienced international attorneys may have difficulty clarifying. Although the North American Free Trade Agreement (NAFTA) has done away with certain "local labor and local content" rules pertaining to American manufacturing in Mexico, those types of regulations still exist in many countries. In addition, it is often difficult to determine which foreign government agencies are charged with making sure that foreign companies are in compliance with local laws.

EXAMPLE

Manufacturers seeking to establish facilities in China must contend with a myriad of local government regulations, including:

⊛ *Foreign exchange laws.* The way an enterprise is structured (e.g., as a wholly owned foreign venture, joint venture, or other business format) determines the rules governing transfer and conversion of capital and profits.

⊛ *Local land use rights.* Each village or district may have different laws governing land use and may require special licenses and permits.

⊛ *Import/export licenses.* Whether the goods are intended for export or for sale in the Chinese market has a bearing on which licenses are required. Also, if the enterprise is a joint-venture company, the Chinese partner may be required to obtain import and other licenses.

⊛ *Taxation.* Attorneys experienced in Chinese tax law are needed to determine the tax rates at the local, regional, and national levels.

⊛ *Operations in special economic zones.* Just as the United States has designated free trade zones, China has special economic zones that restrict or permit business operations in a number of ways.

⊛ *Labor laws.* China, like most countries in the world, has strict laws and policies regarding labor, wages, trade unions, and related issues.

⊛ *Technology transfer and intellectual property rights.* U.S. manufacturers need to be aware of laws relating to technology and intellectual property. For instance, the U.S. restricts the transfer of certain technologies to other countries; these restrictions could affect manufacturing operations located abroad. Once technology and other intellectual properties are in China, manufacturers need to take steps to protect patents, copyrights, trademarks, and trade secrets from pirating and other forms of infringement.

⊛ *Customs tariffs*. China imposes high tariffs on certain items imported for use by foreigners; tariffs are imposed on refrigerators, automobiles, consumer electronics, and appliances. U.S. manufacturers establishing plants in China must be aware of these tariffs when importing items needed for the operation of the manufacturing facility.

2.2 ORGANIZING FOR EFFECTIVE EXPORT

How a company organizes and plans its exporting efforts determines, to a large part, the success of the venture. A comprehensive plan should be developed well in advance of any sales. The plan should cover all phases of the export process, from early market research to shipment of and payment for the goods.

Effective Communication

Good communication, both within a company and with a foreign buyer, is critical to effective exporting. Communicating clearly with the foreign buyer helps ensure that the goods arrive and the exporter is paid in a timely fashion. Effective internal communication is the key to ensuring that all of a company's bases are covered when it exports goods.

Exporting is a many-faceted enterprise and all of the details are important. Correctly completing documentation will be for naught if the exported goods are improperly packed or labeled and are damaged or impounded in transit. All or most of a firm's departments will be involved with the exporting effort. All employees involved with exporting need to understand the process if the work is to be completed in the most thorough and efficient fashion.

EXAMPLE

A novice export manager in a small company assigns one person to track logistics and shipping, and another to arrange letters of credit and act as a liaison with banks. However, these two components of the export process are, in practice, the same function: Issuance of a letter of credit payment depends on shipping documentation. Good up-front organization would have told the export manager that one reliable employee should handle both functions. Moreover, that employee must work with the person who is negotiating sales terms with the foreign buyer, since those terms dictate the terms of a letter of credit.

Export Compliance

The exporter needs to be aware of all U.S. and foreign laws relating to export. Exporters who do not scrupulously follow U.S. and foreign regulations and shipping requirements could face long delays in shipment, fines, and possible confiscation of goods.

In particular, exporters must be aware of the following issues:

- Export regulations (see Chapter 3)
- Foreign import licenses
- Valuation of goods and classification under the Harmonized Tariff Schedule (see Chapter 9)
- Foreign government regulations
- Export documentation (see Chapter 5)
- Terms of sale (see Chapter 4)
- Shipping and labeling requirements (see Chapter 6)
- Bonding and insurance compliance (see Chapter 11)
- Export costs (see Chapter 4)

Internal Organization

One of the best ways to organize for effective exporting is to look at a company that is doing it successfully. The Waters Corporation has been exporting products all over the world for twenty years. Good organization and a thorough understanding of the export process are the keys to their success.

EXAMPLE

The Waters Corporation is a Massachusetts-based manufacturer of liquid chromatography instruments. Its customers are hospitals, universities, and other medical institutions. The company has approximately 1,000 employees worldwide with subsidiaries in twenty-six countries. Its export department has seven staff members; export processes are segmented into the following functions:

- Preparation of export documentation
- International order entry
- Export compliance and regulatory functions
- Tracking of domestic and international freight budgets
- Tracking importation of materials used in the manufacture of instruments
- Computer systems management

Professional Assistance

Waters maintains a relationship with a freight forwarder who provides the company with information on trends and developments in export licensing regulations and a working knowledge of foreign laws and regulations.

Overseas Organization

Waters has twenty-six subsidiaries in twenty-six countries. The managers of each subsidiary report directly to the U.S. general manager. Foreign subsidiaries sell directly to the customer. As a result, shipments from the United States are not made to the customers directly; they are intracompany shipments for which the subsidiary has already been paid or has arranged payment terms. Waters has realized significant savings in shipping costs by opening a European distribution center in Holland. Instead of shipping to thirteen different

European countries, it makes daily shipments into Amsterdam, from whence goods are shipped to subsidiaries in other European countries. The Dutch distribution center is also able to maintain a larger inventory so that when customers are looking for a product, they can go directly to Holland instead of waiting for a shipment from the United States.

2.3   OVERVIEW OF DISTRIBUTION CHANNELS

Automation makes it possible for even the smallest company to market overseas. Even so, technology has not obliterated the need to make human contact with customers. How a company establishes distribution channels is a factor of company size and culture.

Although companies generally design a distribution channel to match their operating style and products, the methods available for promoting those products or services internationally fall into the following general categories:

* *Direct sale.* The company makes contacts with potential customers on its own through trade shows, overseas contact-making trips, or by establishing an overseas office, to name a few methods.

* *Marketing intermediaries.* Domestic U.S. firms are hired to market goods or services in foreign markets. These firms provide most, if not all, of the customer contact, using whatever methods they have designed.

* *Foreign marketing intermediaries.* Foreign companies and/or individuals are employed to market products or services.

* *Foreign trade organizations.* Foreign government agencies are used to market products and services. This arrangement is usually found in state-run or centrally controlled economies. Under these circumstances, direct contact with the potential end user of a product or service may not be possible.

These are broad categories. In practice, the arrangements that companies and individuals make for selling their goods and services overseas are quite variable and depend largely on financial resources, the foreign culture in question, the product, and foreign market demands.

2.4   DISTRIBUTION METHODS

Many arrangements are possible when it comes to manufacturing and selling overseas. When a company enters a foreign market and begins the selling process, it may pursue one of these common arrangements:

* Agents, distributors, and sales representatives
* Joint-venture partners and alliances
* Logistics companies
* Foreign retailers

- Direct mail
- Piggyback marketing

2.4.1 *Commissioned Sales Agents and Sales Representatives*

Commissioned sales agents represent a company in a defined overseas market. Unless working under an exclusive arrangement, they may work for more than one firm, but generally do not handle competing products.

Commissioned sales agents rarely stock products. Orders are usually relayed to the home office and the agent earns a commission or percentage of the order after the customer pays the U.S. supplier. Under this arrangement, the supplier both ships and bills the customer directly. Customers tend to be wholesale or retail chains. Agents are generally quite effective when selling high-volume, low-priced consumer goods; they may be able to undercut distributor prices because they do not charge markups for shipping and other costs.

In selecting an agent, exporters should ensure that agents are well connected in their target field and knowledgeable about the product in question.

Commissioned sales representatives may be individuals or firms. Whichever form they take, they operate in the same way as sales agents. The term *sales representative* is normally used when the U.S. supplier sells high-unit-value or industrial products. *Sales agent* is the term more commonly used when consumer goods or low-unit-value commodities are being supplied. Because of the nature of the products they sell, sales representatives may more commonly sell directly to individual buyers within the assigned territory.

Guidance

Exporters should be cautioned that the entire balance of power between the seller and agent intermediaries in a foreign country can be dramatically tilted in favor of the agent. This is especially true if the exporter is selling a product or service without wide brand-name recognition. Often, the agent is the only source of sales for the exporter. In addition, the agent has all of the contacts and relationships necessary for the growth of the business. In some cases, the agent may have connections with officials who issue licenses or permits.

This imbalance can be righted if the exporter has explored a variety of options and does not forward all its business to one agent. In addition, all terms and conditions in any contracts should be carefully spelled out under the guidance of an attorney or other professional who is familiar with the laws of that particular country.

2.4.2 *Distributors*

In foreign markets, distributors offer the advantage of stocking inventory so that orders from customers can be shipped immediately. Distributors often maintain their own sales force and will call on foreign accounts.

Distributors handle all costs pertaining to sales, credit risks, and collection of receivables. Their margin is usually 50–70 percent of the final sales price to cover a variety of costs and their profit margin. Usually, distributors depend on the manufacturer to set pricing. Businesses may work with several different types of distributors.

Importing Distributors

Importing distributors order goods from the U.S. supplier and pay for them directly at prearranged prices and terms. They then mark up the goods to cover their costs and profit and sell directly to customers, retailers, or lower-level distributors. Distributors can be nonexclusive or exclusive for a given market area. If they are exclusive, they agree not to sell competing products in the territory.

Exclusive Distributors

Exclusive distributors stock products, manage inventory, and assume all responsibility for sales promotion and servicing in their area.

Sometimes an exclusive distributor might act as a sales representative on specific transactions. This arrangement occurs most frequently when the competitive situation, the customs of the country involved, or the desires of a particularly large customer call for a more normal "commission" markup, rather than the distributor's typically higher markup. If a sales representative arrangement is desired, an agreement should be made in writing in advance and treated as a specific amendment to the basic agreement between the supplier and the foreign distributor.

Nonexclusive Distributors

Nonexclusive distributors assume less risk and reserve the option to sell competing products if the market seems to support that approach. They also may rely on the supplier for sales support and literature.

2.4.3 *Export Agents, Merchants, and Remarketers*

Export agents, merchants, and remarketers purchase products directly from the manufacturer, packing and marking the products according to their own specifications. They then sell overseas in their own name and assume all risks for accounts.

Guidance

When working with export agents, merchants, or remarketers, a U.S. firm should be aware of the following:

• The U.S.-based company often relinquishes control over the marketing and promotion of its product. Loss of control may have an adverse effect on future sales efforts abroad. The product could be underpriced or incorrectly positioned in the market. Service could be neglected.

⊛ Manufacturers can save marketing and research time, obtaining sales leads that would take a great deal of time and money to procure on their own.

2.4.4 Piggyback Marketing

Sometimes, especially when an exporter seeks to enter a new market, it is advantageous to enter into piggyback marketing relationships. For instance, a company may ask an overseas manufacturer to distribute goods in its (the manufacturer's) market. Other arrangements might call for one manufacturer to handle production for another.

EXAMPLE

A common piggyback scenario is as follows:

1. Company A (the U.S.-based firm) manufactures cowboy boots and wants to add belt buckles to its line for sale in Germany. However, Company A is not organized to produce belt buckles.
2. Company A commissions another U.S.-based firm—Company B—to manufacture the desired products.
3. Company B produces the belt buckles, making an arrangement with Company A to ship some of the belt buckles with the cowboy boots.
4. Company B's products therefore "piggyback" on Company A's products.
5. Company A generally bears all distribution costs.

Note. To be successful, the product lines must be complementary and appeal to the same customer.

2.4.5 Foreign Retailers

A company may also sell directly to a foreign retailer. This approach is usually limited to consumer product lines. Manufacturers generally rely on traveling sales representatives to contact foreign retailers directly. Catalogs, brochures, and other literature may be used.

2.4.6 Direct Mail

The direct mail approach has the benefits of eliminating commissions, reducing traveling expenses, and reaching a broader audience. But there are disadvantages to direct mail. It requires intense follow-up; it may be difficult to obtain foreign mailing lists; and creating copy that breaches language barriers and appeals to foreign cultures is a challenge.

2.4.7   In-Country Representatives

Some foreign governments require nonnationals to work through a native or in-country representative to do business, even if a foreign partner or other intermediary is involved. The intermediary sets up the in-country contact.

Two countries that required this sort of arrangement in the past were the former Soviet Union and China. However, with political barriers falling and former communist nations embracing some form of capitalism, such arrangements may no longer be required. It is best to check with foreign consulates in former communist countries and regions that still operate under some form of state control.

2.4.8   Government-Run Trading Organizations

The economies of some nations are still state-controlled or centrally planned. For example, this is the case in some African nations, to a certain extent in China, and in certain Eastern European countries. Under these situations, state-run trading organization purchase imports to the country. These organizations are usually divided among the various industry/product sectors.

Note. There are some approximations of government trading organizations in the United States. One example is the export trading company of the Port Authority of New York and New Jersey. This state-financed agency assists importers and exporters.

2.4.9   Quasi-Governmental Trading Companies

Unlike totally state-run trading organizations, quasi-government trading companies are usually substantial, private-sector corporations formed specifically for the purpose of buying and selling goods and services in international markets. What sets these companies apart from other distributors or agents is the sanction of local governments to extend their operations to cover not only the buying of imports, but also to handle distribution, transportation, and even the co-manufacture, final assembly, and testing of products in their country.

While Japan is best known for promoting trading companies, some developing countries have adopted this approach. Because trading companies usually operate under a set of broad capabilities (not to mention flexible charters), the U.S. supplier can structure agreements according to a wide spectrum of terms. The characteristics of deals struck with quasi-government trading companies tend to be more like exclusive distributorships rather than agent-representative agreements.

2.4.10   Logistics Companies

Logistics companies offer a variety of services for storage, packing, and sorting of goods for shipment. Some logistics companies—especially those associated with major trucking companies—are starting to offer warehouse/distribution services.

For example, Frans Maas in the Netherlands now handles some light assembly work for manufacturers. Finished goods are stored in the Frans Maas warehouse and shipped upon customer demand.

Small exporters should inquire about this approach because it means quicker access to a foreign market. Although major logistics companies prefer to work with large companies, they may make an exception for a steady client. In one case, Frans Maas made such an arrangement with its American partner, Yellow Freight, to assist a Yellow Freight customer producing diagnostic equipment for motorcycles. Frans Maas stores upwards of ten of the bulky units in its warehouse in Dordrecht, the Netherlands, at any given time.

2.4.11 *Joint-Venture Partners*

Sometimes it is more desirable to set up direct linkages with a sister company overseas for manufacturing, distributing, and marketing of a product—or any combination of the three. Under these circumstances, U.S. companies may seek out joint-venture partners. Small and midsize companies frequently find this arrangement allows them almost immediate penetration into a foreign market without having to set up their own operation. Even some large companies work in this fashion.

Example

A Dutch trade booth manufacturer was seeking a joint-venture partner in the United States. The Dutch company was not interested in manufacturing its product in the U.S., although it was considering having the partner do assembly work. Mainly, it wanted to create a reciprocal arrangement whereby an American company would shepherd the Dutch booths to U.S. shows and the Dutch company would do the same for an American company overseas. An American trade booth manufacturer was located and arrangements were made for a trial run.

There are also different types of joint-venture arrangements. The exporter interested in forging such an alliance should consider all of the options before deciding which type of arrangement best suits the needs and resources of the company.

Example

Two types of joint ventures are available for exporters interested in China:

● *Contractual joint ventures.* Contractual joint ventures represent the primary means for small business investment in China. No minimum contributions are required, and contributions can be made in nonmonetary resources such as services, labor, or materials. The Chinese government allows for great flexibility in structuring the management, assets, and organization of the contractual joint venture. In addition, registered capital may be withdrawn during the term of the contract.

● *Equity joint ventures.* Equity joint ventures allow for a fifty-year term and offer profit and risk sharing proportionate to the amount of investment. A U.S. manufacturer exporting in China under an equity joint-venture agreement has limited access to the Chinese market; most of the goods must be exported from China. The financial and corporate structure of the venture is closely regulated by the Chinese government. No registered capital can be withdrawn for the duration of the contract. The equity joint-venture partner must also contend with a myriad of municipal, regional, and government regulations and restrictions.

Note. As in any partnership, joint ventures have their pitfalls. Partners must get along to do business. This places an extra burden on both parties to cope with differences in style and especially in culture—both indigenous and corporate.

2.4.12   *Alliances*

Alliances are limited versions of joint ventures. Two companies agree to assist each other in specified, usually reciprocal fashions in their home markets. There is no formal partnership.

EXAMPLE

The American shipping company Yellow Freight formed an alliance with the Dutch shipping/freight forwarder Frans Maas to provide one-stop international shipping between the United States, Europe, and other world markets. This was just one of many such alliances between carriers burgeoning in the late 1990s.

2.5   CHOOSING A DISTRIBUTION METHOD

Selecting a distribution method depends to a great extent on a company's:

* *Resources.* Financial resources play a major role in how goods are marketed and distributed. For example, a small company may not have the resources for mass mailings, especially overseas.

* *Product.* Different products require different shipping and distribution methods. It is possible to air-freight computer chips but not steel plates. Overseas buyers of computer chips may be located in modern industrial parks not far from a major airport, whereas many steel warehouses are located close to ports.

* *Style.* Every company has a different style, which affects distribution choices. Some companies are geared to direct mailings, others to in-person sales. The product may sometimes dictate these choices, but not always.

* *Government or trade requirements.* The conditions may differ depending on the destination country.

Guidance

Here are some examples of how companies of various sizes might distribute goods overseas:

● *Less than 10 employees.* A company of this size usually enters the international marketplace because of knowledge of a demand for goods either in the United States or overseas. Often, a member of the company has personal contacts in a foreign country who are ready to assist on the other end. Or the company has made contacts through trade shows and other methods introduced by marketing. Usually, the only way a very small company with limited financial resources can function is through joint-venture arrangements or alliances. These sorts of arrangements can prove highly lucrative and may propel the company into a larger trade arena.

● *Less than 100 employees.* The circumstances for these "small" companies may not be that different from a company with under ten employees. Management may have more resources with which to enter a foreign market, but it must contend with the high costs of accurately marketing goods and services overseas over a long period of time. Joint ventures and alliances still may be the best way to enter a foreign market for a company of this size. However, any number of sales and distribution arrangements would also be feasible. The product, the market, corporate style, and resources should be considered before a decision is reached.

● *Midsize companies (less than 500 employees).* A business this size may have the option of opening up offices overseas or even company headquarters in different parts of the world. Most midsize companies choose sales agents or representatives. Once again, the product, market, company style, and resources must be considered before a decision is made to hire intermediaries, establish an overseas operation. or create joint ventures or alliances.

● *Large companies/multinationals.* Multinationals frequently establish headquarters and manufacturing facilities in foreign countries. The new trend is toward creating seamless global corporations. Under these circumstances, control returns to the U.S. operations and international headquarters are dismantled. Automation links suppliers worldwide. The corporate purchasing department, in the meantime, sources goods and services throughout the global "company" network.

EXAMPLE

The global approach is still in its infancy, but is emerging as the corporate trend of the 1990s. Ford Motors is a prime example of this approach. Components of its automobiles are produced all over the world for assembly in the United States, or sourced worldwide for assembly in regional plants in other countries.

2.6 ESTABLISHING AN OVERSEAS SALES FORCE

From the perspective of control, direct entry to an overseas market is almost always desirable. A direct presence yields more accurate sales and marketing information and helps the exporter increase name recognition. However, this approach is costly and fraught with risk.

In some circumstances—commercial aviation, industrial capital machinery, and space-related equipment, for example—direct sales may be the preferred method. In those instances, products tend to be unique and target marketing is both cost-effective and feasible as the customer or user population is relatively limited in number. Customers can be identified and contacted directly.

Note. In some countries, direct sale is not possible, no matter how feasible in a pure market sense. In China, for example, there are still many areas of the country closed to foreigners. Foreign intermediaries must be sought for trade to take place.

Guidance

Companies new to international sales most commonly employ direct sales when contacts for overseas marketing are long established. For example, someone may work for several years as an overseas buyer or agent for a major company and then choose to strike out on his or her own. The contacts and working relations exist, making for fairly easy market entry.

Direct sales are more challenging—and perhaps too costly—for international trade novices who have a good product and good marketing sense but lack an overseas network. Some sort of intermediary approach—a joint-venture partnership, an alliance, or a sales agents—may be necessary. Once customer relationships have been developed, it is more common to deal with overseas customers directly to discuss new products requirements for subsequent orders.

EXAMPLE

Because food has been traded for centuries, international food distribution networks are varied. Various professionals play different roles in international food distribution:

Importers

Importers receive a ''placing phone call'' (from a distributor, agent, or other party), bring in a particular product, handle the paperwork, and transfer food to distributors and other parties for direct sale. They may work in many industries simultaneously.

Exporters

After receiving a placing phone call from distributors or other parties, exporters often sell directly to importers. They may work in a variety of industries simultaneously.

Agents

Most commonly located in the importing country, agents act as overseas sales representatives for clients.

Brokers

Acting as intermediaries between a variety of parties, brokers place orders with importers, exporters, or distributors.

International Distributors

An international distributor often makes a personal investment in a product, then resells goods manufactured by others to a variety of parties on an international basis. Some distributors warehouse goods and sell wholesale. Others work directly with a customer.

Export and Import Distributors

Some distributors manufacture their own products and distribute them internationally. Others simply export or import other's goods.

Stocking Distributors

These are distributors who stock imported goods for sale to importers. (There is no correlation on the export side.)

Parallel Traders

Parallel traders are individuals who buy existing imported goods on the market for resale.

2.7 DISTRIBUTION AGREEMENTS

2.7.1 *Negotiating Distribution Agreements*

Every distributor provides customers with a distribution agreement. Most are "shell" agreements—boilerplate contracts that are then customized. Most distributor agreements cover the following areas:

- Territory
- Products
- Market segments
- Pricing agreements
- Confidentiality clauses
- Trademarks and trade names
- Contract duration
- Passage of title (i.e., which party will own the goods)

There are two types of contract arrangements: a single agreement between the manufacturer and the overseas party, or separate agreements—one between the manufacturer and distributor and another between the distributor and the overseas party.

Guidance

Agency and distributorship arrangements should be prepared with the assistance of legal counsel. All roles, details, and restrictions should be clearly established, including:

- Products to be distributed or sold
- Channels of distribution
- Specific outline of authorized territory
- Inventory requirements
- Minimum sales levels that agents/distributors must maintain to continue representing the company in question
- Pricing (i.e., how much the merchandise costs the agents/distributors)
- Sales price
- Duration of the agreement (**Note.** Appoint a distributor or agent for a short trial period of mutual accord. Six months should be sufficient time to determine if the relationship is satisfactory. The arrangement can then be extended.)
- Conditions for termination (**Note.** When terminating an agent or distributor, the exporter must have proper legal grounds. It is prudent to specify in the contract under what conditions the agreement can be terminated.)

2.7.2 *Dealing With Currency Fluctuations*

Currency fluctuations should be factored into an agreement with an agent/distributor. The value of the U.S. dollar against foreign currencies varies daily. This variation is a crucial factor in price negotiations. In terms of an agent/distributor agreement, the currency-fluctuation provision should establish the fluctuation level that is acceptable when prices are being negotiated with a foreign customer.

Some companies ignore currency fluctuations and choose to have firm prices in dollars, regardless of currency changes. Experienced importers and exporters know that this rigid approach is imprudent. Flexibility in the currency arena means an additional negotiating point and a means of controlling an agent or distributor.

Agents and distributors usually operate from a loosely supervised distance. It is not uncommon—or unacceptable in some circles—for these business representatives to pocket the difference when a currency fluctuation takes place during negotiations. Although practices such as this are not illegal, they will not be possible if company officials monitor the negotiations and insist on flexibility in the face of ever-changing currencies.

Note. A two percent fluctuation of currency values is usually acceptable to either party. Beyond that, some provision should be included in an agreement. Once again, flexible handling of currency fluctuations may mean additional profits.

A German distributor of auto parts is working out a shipment from the United States to German repair shops when the dollar drops in value against the deutsche mark. Instead of one deutsche mark equaling 50 cents, the ratio drops to 30 cents. On the American side, the fluctuations mean a loss. The 1,000 deutsche marks drop in value from $500 to $300. But for Germans, the dollar drop is a gain in value of their currency.

The result is an influx of immediate funds. The distributor has several options when deciding how to handle the additional cash the fluctuation has produced; they include:

- Pocketing the difference
- Reinvesting the cash into sales and advertising promotions
- Lowering the retail price in the hope of increasing sales

Take the same scenario with a significant rise in the dollar. The same German distributor will have to increase retail prices to cover its loss. Price increases may inhibit product sales.

2.8 EXPORT MANAGEMENT COMPANIES

Export management companies (EMCs) provide valuable services for companies of all sizes. They can:

- Act as the export department for one or several producers of goods or services
- Solicit and transact business in the name of the producers
- Work on a commission, salary, or retainer-plus basis.

Note. EMCs usually specialize either by product, by foreign market, or both. Because of their specialization, the best EMCs know their products and the markets they serve very well and usually have well-established networks of foreign distributors already in place.

Immediate access to foreign markets is one of the principal reasons for using an EMC. Establishing a productive relationship with a foreign representative may be a costly and lengthy process. Again, EMCs do pose threats to manufacturers in the sense that they act as go-betweens and can control rather than support foreign sales on behalf of their client.

Advantages to Working with an EMC

Here are the most commonly realized advantages of working with an EMC:

- The EMC helps realize foreign sales quickly through its network of contacts, distributors, and even industry customers. This arrangement allows U.S. companies to test market goods and services with little up-front investment.

• The EMC staff can educate novice exporters about international sales and assist them in developing their own expertise.

Disadvantages to Working With an EMC

Here are some common problems that arise when working with an EMC:
• The exporter loses some control over the overseas market and customers. The EMC usually handles pricing policy, selection of distributors, purchasing, and promotion.
• Some loss of profit margin can be expected. Because of the potential for lack of control over the EMC's sales efforts, one product line may be pushed to the detriment of others. The same goes for countries or regions.
• There is a risk that the EMC may go bankrupt, a possibility if the EMC is dealing in high-risk zones internationally.

Negotiating With an EMC

EMCs all operate differently. Exporters must determine what they want from such an arrangement and negotiate as they would any business partnership. Some factors to consider in the negotiating process are:

• Means of retaining control over the EMC
• Operating styles
• Market compatibility
• Knowledge of a given product line
• Advertising and service arrangements

Locating an EMC

Because EMCs are independent businesses, it may take some searching to find the right company to handle custom export needs. Sources that can assist in the search include:

• Other exporters
• Export assistance centers (see Chapter 1, Appendixes A and C, for a list of export assistance centers)
• International Trade Administration (ITA) district offices
• Publications that specialize in international trade

The Overseas Trading Network in Darien, IL (708-769-4338) is also a source. Other active regional or national EMC groups are:

Export Managers Association of California
110 East 9th Street
Suite A669
Los Angeles, CA 90079

Tel: (310) 606-0161
Fax: (310) 606-3150

National Association of Export Companies (NEXCO)
P.O. Box 1330
Murray Hill Station
New York, NY 10156
Tel: (212) 725-3311

2.9 FREIGHT FORWARDERS

Freight forwarders often call themselves transport architects. They act as agents for exporters in moving cargo to overseas destinations. As such, forwarders must be familiar with:

- Import rules and regulations of foreign countries
- Shipping methods
- U.S. government export regulations
- Documents connected with foreign trade

Freight forwarders can advise the exporter of the freight costs, port charges, consular fees, costs of special documentation and insurance, as well as handling fees—all of which help in selecting a distribution method and in preparing price quotations for a foreign business transaction.

Forwarders also work with exporters on meeting foreign documentation requirements. Some, but not all, maintain branch offices overseas. In these cases, their foreign offices may help with entry documentation when cargo reaches its destination.

2.9.1 Freight Forwarder Services

Standard Services

Typically, a freight forwarder performs the following services:

1. Arranges the pickup from the manufacturer-exporter for delivery to the airport or ocean terminal. (Some trucking companies also perform this service.)
2. Chooses the appropriate airline or ocean freight company servicing the destination.
3. Makes the arrangements for the cargo space required.
4. Recommends the type of packing required to protect merchandise during shipping.
5. May arrange for packing or containerization at the port.
6. Delivers the product to the designated carrier.

7. Arranges for the delivery of the consignment to the end party in the transaction.
8. Reviews the letter of credit, commercial invoices, and packing list when goods are ready to be shipped, ensuring that all is in order.
9. May make arrangements with customs brokers at the port of export to ensure that the goods comply with U.S. Customs export documentation, if applicable.
10. May prepare the bill of lading and any special documentation required.
11. After shipment, forwards all documents directly to the customer or bank, if so requested.

Specialty Services

In addition, freight forwarders may offer extra services, such as:

- Packing and crating facilities for those clients who do not have this function
- Specialty departments to improve the handling of letter of credit transactions and restricted articles (e.g., chemicals)
- Specially skilled staff to handle export licensing requirements
- International networks of freight forwarders to replicate services abroad
- Distribution and warehouse facilities in the United States and abroad
- Marketing departments to help their client base make overseas contacts
- Legal departments to keep track of the documentation requirements of each foreign country and ensure that consignments depart with documentation

2.9.2   *Working With a Freight Forwarder*

The average exporter usually requires the services of export professionals such as freight forwarders. Recent changes in export enforcement (outlined in detail in Chapter 3) impose the increased legal liability for violations of export laws and regulations; therefore, only the most seasoned exporters should consider handling their own shipments without professional help.

It is crucial to hire a conscientious and knowledgeable freight forwarder. Because freight forwarders are not licensed by any official body, exporters should diligently investigate any companies with which they plan to work. Trucking companies, airlines, and ocean shippers, as well as other exporters and national associations, can provide referrals. Exporters should make sure that the company selected is financially stable and is not undergoing any major reorganization. When selecting a freight forwarder, look for a freight forwarder who has:

- Experience handling the product in question
- An overseas network and market penetration that meets the requirements of the exporter and the product
- Competitive pricing for documentation services and reasonable shipping rates

- A fully computerized operation that offers computer hookup to major federal export licensing programs
- In-depth knowledge of Bureau of Export Administration requirements
- Packing and labeling expertise

Preparing to Work With a Freight Forwarder

To ensure reliable, speedy service from freight forwarders, exporters should make sure that they understand the basic components of an export transaction. These include general knowledge of:

- Terms of sale and how they affect business transactions (see Chapter 4)
- Export regulations (see Chapter 3)
- Letters of credit (see Chapter 5)
- Boycott regulations (see Chapter 3)
- Bills of lading (see Chapter 5, section 5.4)
- Export insurance (see Chapter 11, sections 11.1 to 11.5)

The following example illustrates how freight forwarders and exporters collaborate.

EXAMPLE

An exporter wants to ship ten cartons of computer disks to Holland. The freight forwarder would operate as follows:

1. The forwarder quickly determines that Holland is a free-world country and that no special export controls exist on this product. A general export license is sought.

2. The next issue is determining the appropriate shipping service. Main factors in deciding between air and ocean shipping are time, price, quantity, and weight. Given the small size of the shipment, air freight seems most reasonable. In general, small quantity shipments mean higher freight costs, while larger shipments yield lower costs; this is particularly true for ocean freight.

3. The forwarder determines that the exporter can save on freight costs if the computer disks are consolidated with goods from other exporters. This usually adds a day or two to delivery time.

4. Because time is not of the essence in the transaction, the exporter and freight forwarder decide to wait for a time slot that best suits the shipper, rather than calling for a more expensive rush order.

5. Packing, labeling, documentation, and shipping are the final concerns.

2.9.3 *Legal Issues*

In recent years, the laws and regulations affecting international transactions have changed markedly. As will be discussed more fully in Chapter 3, the ongoing reorganization of the Commerce Department's Bureau of Export Administration is having a major impact on how exporters and freight forwarders collaborate. New regulations place more responsibility on exporters, requiring them to ensure that the export of their products will not endanger U.S. national or economic security. For both exporters and freight forwarders, there is increased liability for inaccurate export declarations.

By making the freight forwarder a partner in liability, the export regulations force forwarders to become more scrupulous in scrutinizing their customers and in completing documentation. The impact of these changes is that freight forwarders are assuming an oversight role; they are no longer merely "paper merchants." Freight forwarders are on alert as never before when they see shipments bound for controlled regions of the world.

EXAMPLE

One freight forwarder recalls that a year ago, it was possible to send a large shipment of paper clips to India's Atomic Energy Commission without any need for special clearance. Now, however, clearance is required: The product itself is innocuous, but the end user presents possible national security dangers.

Most freight forwarders require exporters to sign a power of attorney before acting on their behalf. (See Forms 2.01 and 2.02 for sample freight forwarder powers of attorney.) These documents allow the freight forwarder to effect shipping and prepare required documentation. Exporters must note, however, that while the power of attorney legally permits freight forwarders to carry out their duties, it does not exempt exporters for ultimate liability for the shipment. Prudent exporters should therefore familiarize themselves with export controls and regulations (discussed in depth in Chapter 3).

Summary of Key Points Raised in This Chapter

1. When choosing where to locate a manufacturing facility abroad, a U.S. company should consider the social and political scene, as well as financial issues such as currency exchange laws, conversion of profit laws, and investment requirements.

2. Overseas manufacturing can result in significantly reduced labor costs, but it also has disadvantages, including increased shipping expenses and loss of control over the operation.

3. Methods for distributing products abroad include direct sales, marketing intermediaries, and foreign trade organizations.

4. Commissioned sales agents and representatives seek out product orders that are fulfilled by the U.S. firm itself.

5. Distributors maintain inventory in the foreign market so that orders can be shipped directly to customers. Distribution agreements can be exclusive or nonexclusive.

6. Export agents, merchants, and remarketers purchase products directly from U.S. firms, then sell them overseas.

7. Piggyback marketing is a distribution method whereby the products of two U.S. firms are shipped and marketed abroad together.

8. Some countries require foreign businesses to work through in-country representatives or government or quasi-government trading organizations.

9. When negotiating price with a foreign agent or distributor, a U.S. firm should monitor exchange rates and insist on an agreement that takes into account the fluctuation of currency values.

10. Export management companies can act as the export department for a U.S. firm, transacting business in exchange for a commission, a salary, or a retainer.

Form 2.01   Power of attorney.

Know all men by these presents, that   *[name of exporter]* , organized and doing

business under the laws of the State of _____ and having an office and place

of business at _____ hereby authorizes   *[name of freight forwarder]*

of _____ from this day forward to act as its forwarding agent for export

control and customs purposes.

    IN WITNESS WHEREOF, the said exporter has caused these presents to be

sealed and signed by its   *[owner, partner, or, if corporation, president or other duly*

authorized officer or employee] . City of _____, State of _____ this _____

day of _____, 19____

_____

Exporter

By: _____

Title: _____

[SEAL]

Form 2.02 Power of attorney to execute shipper's export declarations.

Know all men by these presents, that   *[name of exporter or forwarding agent]* ,

organized and doing business under the laws of the State of _____ and having

an office and place of business at _____ hereby designates the following

officers or employees of the exporter or forwarding agent named above _____

as true and lawful agents of the exporter or forwarding agent named above for and in

the name, place and stead of said exporter or forwarding agent from this day forward

and in no other name, to make, endorse, sign, declare or swear to any shipper's export

declaration required by law or regulation in connection with the exportation of any

commodity shipped, consigned or forwarded by said exporter or forwarding agent

and to perform any act or condition which may be required or authorized by any law

or regulation relating to export control and customs purposes.

   IN WITNESS WHEREOF, the said exporter or forwarding agent has caused

these presents to be sealed and signed by its   *[owner, partner or if corp., president, or*

other duly authorized officer or employee] . City of _____ , State

of _____ this _____ day of _____ , 19____

_____

[ ] Exporter or [ ]Forwarding agent

_____

By: _____

Title: _____

[SEAL]

3

Export Controls and Licenses

Key Questions Answered in This Chapter

Introduction

Once the decision to export has been made and target markets are identified, an exporter must consider export regulations and controls.

Sweeping geopolitical changes throughout the world, the opening of new markets such as China, and major advances in computer technology all significantly affect the regulatory atmosphere. As new economic alliances such as the North American Free Trade Agreement (NAFTA) and the European Union are formed, and power blocs such as the Soviet Union disappear, the need for export controls, which at once protect the national interest while allowing for free trade, becomes more compelling.

The Bureau of Export Administration (BXA) controls and regulates exports under a four-part policy:

* To control exports that would make a significant contribution to the military potential of any other country, or combination of countries, and thus would prove detrimental to the national security of the United States
* To further the foreign policy of the United States and to fulfill the United States' international obligations
* To protect the domestic economy from excessive drain of scarce materials and to reduce foreign trade's impact on inflation
* To promote nonproliferation of controlled items, including military and nuclear technologies and items that have dual military and civilian uses

Since 1994, the BXA—the arm of the Commerce Department that oversees export controls and licensing—has been reorganized to reflect international geopolitical change. New BXA licensing regulations went into effect in the spring of 1995. The aim of these changes has been to streamline and simplify BXA operations and open channels to increased trade and exports. Many products have been decontrolled in the process and the cold war era emphasis on controlling goods to "enemy" countries has been eliminated. Now in place is an enforcement system that relies on spot checks and increased surveillance to world trouble areas.

At the time the new regulations were issued, then Commerce Secretary Mickey Kantor said, "The bottom line is that BXA is determined to be more customer-friendly, more effective, and more practical without sacrificing the very real security concerns we have been entrusted with." Here are some highlights of the BXA regulation changes:

* Regulations adopt "plain English," to improve their readability and to standardize the use of terms and definitions.

* No license or other authorization will be required for any transaction unless the regulations affirmatively state it. Under the previous regulations, all exports were prohibited unless an applicable general license had been established or a validated license or other authorization was granted by BXA.

* The term *general license* is dropped. This change eliminates confusion because general license was often mistaken to mean prior BXA review, and authorization was required.

* The regulations consolidate information on when to obtain a license (information previously scattered in various sections). One part contains the license review policy for all license requirements contained in the Commerce Control

List (CCL). Another part provides requirements and review policies for licenses based on the end use or end user involved in a proposed export or re-export.

⦁ The CCL states more specifically the reasons for control of items within each Export Control Number and can be used with a new Country Chart, indicating whether a license is required to a particular country.

⦁ The special licenses are eliminated and replaced by the Special Comprehensive License (SCL). Under the SCL, all commodities, except those controlled for missile technology reasons, are eligible for export to all destinations except for embargoed countries and countries that support terrorism.

Note. Under the new regulations, more emphasis is placed on "dual use" goods—those products that can serve both military and civilian purposes. Exporters and export professionals must be aware of the end use of their shipments and must be able to prove that products and goods are not falling into the wrong hands for the wrong purposes. They bear more responsibility for accurate documentation and face stiff fines and penalties for noncompliance.

This chapter provides an analysis of the controls exporters typically confront. Topics covered include the export license application process, antiboycott regulations, antidiversion regulations, and export documentation. A final section on creating an in-house export management system helps exporters organize their compliance efforts.

3.1 UNDERSTANDING THE EXPORT CONTROL PROCESS

Because of the volume of regulations and issues that confront each export decision, this brief section generally outlines the export process so that details described in the remainder of the chapter can be read in context. The following are steps that all exporters, even those with experience, should complete when beginning the process:

1. Recognize, first, that there are export regulations and determine which agencies hold jurisdiction over the particular shipment of goods or products. In addition to the Commerce Department, the Defense and State Departments as well as the Treasury Department's Office of Foreign Assets (OFAC) most commonly hold jurisdiction over a particular export. The State Department offers foreign policy advice and the Defense Department offers military advice in the event that a license application is questioned. The OFAC may hold jurisdiction when an embargo is in place.

2. Most commercial commodities fall under the Commerce Department's jurisdiction—including so-called dual-use commodities that can be used for both civilian and military applications.

Note. Export professionals can help determine which agency will hold jurisdiction over an export. The Commerce Department maintains export counseling centers in many parts of the country; these centers can also provide help.

3. If the commodity falls under the Commerce Department's authority (as it will in most cases), it is the exporter's responsibility to determine the classification of the good or product under the CCL and cross-check with the new country list to see if a license is required. (See section 3.6 for more details.)

4. Under the current system, there are two basic categories—Licenses and No License Required (NLR)—which replace the former validated licenses and general license designations. (See section 3.6.)

5. Two major factors will always come under consideration when determining whether a license is required: the product type and the product's end destination. In general, exports of products are controlled when they have a dual use, meaning they can be applied to civilian and military purposes. Exports are also controlled to various "hot" parts of the world that fall under U.S. embargo because of terrorism or other political threats.

6. NLR applies to goods that fall under the Export Administration Regulations (EAR) 99 category, or goods that are included in the Commerce Control List but are not bound for any destination that poses a problem, as defined by the BXA country chart.

7. Rewrite of the Export Administration Regulations has been designed so that laypersons can easily determine whether or not an export license is required. BXA officials have provided more detail in these regulations for the purpose of answering exporter questions up-front. There is the general hope that exporters will not have to rely as much on BXA officials to answer preliminary questions.

8. If a licensing requirement is ascertained, exporters should set up internal procedures for completing export documentation. These procedures should include provisions for record retention, since all export documentation must be maintained for five years.

3.2 THE BUREAU OF EXPORT ADMINISTRATION

Before learning more about the requirements that affect an export, exporters should gain an understanding of the structure of the Bureau of Export Administration. This awareness will assist exporters in their work with professionals such as freight forwarders, potentially saving the exporter time and money in the long run.

As noted, the BXA, which is an arm of the U.S. Department of Commerce, is the federal agency charged with overseeing enforcement of export laws. Besides controlling U.S. exports (especially high-tech exports), the BXA is responsible for a wide range of policy and technical matters related to maintaining the vitality of the U.S. defense industrial base. BXA officials also work overseas with new exporting countries to coordinate export controls.

The BXA controls exports in order to accomplish the following goals:

* To promote national security
* To further U.S. foreign policy

- To rectify shortages in the supply of certain goods
- To promote nonproliferation of controlled items (e.g., weapons, chemicals, and missile technology)

In furtherance of these goals, the BXA:

- Enforces the principal regulatory scheme—the Export Administration Regulations
- Issues licenses on controlled exports
- Advises the U.S. Commerce Department and other agencies on export control requirements
- Works to streamline export regulations
- Provides counseling and outreach to U.S. businesses through its Exporter Counseling Division

The BXA's main purpose is the enforcement of U.S. export laws. The following subsections discuss the laws that the BXA is charged with regulating; the BXA's function and how individual BXA departments carry out enforcement functions in specific ways.

3.2.1 Export Administration Laws

The Export Administration Act of 1979 (EAA) expired on August 20, 1994. This act used to control dual-use commodities and technologies—those that are designed for civilian use but have potential military applications. In August 1994, President Clinton invoked the International Emergency Economic Powers Act and continued, in effect, the provisions of EAA and the Export Administration Regulations as part of a sweeping export control reform effort.

Export control reform aims to promote the following key provisions:

- Streamlining the export licensing process
- Allowing broader industry rights to petition against export controls that have "unfair impact" on U.S. competitiveness
- Eliminating the distinction between national security and foreign policy controls, thereby encouraging multilateral cooperation in building common standards for lists of controlled items and enforcement programs
- Requiring U.S. economic interests to be considered before the imposition or extension of unilateral controls
- Increasing penalties for export control violations

Controls are implemented on exports of these products for reasons of national security, foreign policy, and short supply. Controls are also maintained in cooperation with other governments, for purposes of nuclear nonproliferation as well as to limit the proliferation of chemical and biological weapons and missile technology.

3.2.2 *The Export Administration Regulations*

The Export Administration Regulations are administered by the BXA as a means of implementing the general policy guidelines of the BXA. The EAR also control the movement of specific categories of U.S.-made goods, notably:

* Materials and materials processing
* Electronics
* Computers
* Software
* Telecommunications equipment
* Transportation equipment
* Propulsion systems
* Sensors, avionics, and navigation equipment
* Marine technologies

Note. This is a broad listing of the goods regulated by the EAR. Exporters are urged to obtain copies of the regulations, which contain a highly specific and technical listing of controlled goods. U.S.-made goods are defined as those that are of U.S. origin, have entered the U.S. economy, or contain a specified percentage of U.S. parts and components.

A major portion of the EAR deals with export licensing. The EAR and the practical applications of these regulations are discussed in greater detail in the sections on export licensing (see sections 3.6–3.7).

3.2.3 *The BXA's Export Control and Licensing Offices*

As discussed previously, one of the BXA's functions is assessing the impact of exports on national and world security, U.S. foreign policy, and the U.S. economy. A number of offices have been established to screen particular types of U.S. exports. Each of the export control offices participates in interagency and international deliberations to determine the list of items that will be controlled. The licensing officers in these divisions have responsibility for:

* Making decisions on export license applications based on their technical analysis of the specific transaction. Licensing officers are actively involved with the interagency dispute resolution process when a consensus cannot be reached among the various reviewing agencies.

* Providing preapplication commodity classifications and advisory opinions, which help exporters determine the licensing requirements for their export transactions.

* Providing assistance to the Technical Advisory Committee and support to the BXA seminar program.

Note. As discussed earlier, in recent years the BXA has undergone a substantial reorganization. Experienced exporters should note that the Office of Export

Licensing (OEL) and the Office of Technology and Policy Analysis (OTPA) were eliminated outright. The Office of Industrial Resource Administration is now called the Office of Strategic Industry and Economic Security. Some BXA offices, notably the enforcement offices, were not affected.

The following sections discuss the functions and policies of each BXA office.

The Office of Export Administration

The Office of Export Administration implements and administers the export controls reflected in the EAR. Export Administration consists of five offices located in Washington, D.C. and two field offices in California. Mailing addresses and phone and fax numbers for BXA headquarters and its two field offices are listed here:

Exporter Counseling Division
U.S. Department of Commerce
14th and Pennsylvania Ave., NW, Room H1099D
Washington, DC 20230
Tel: (202) 482-4811
Fax: (202) 482-3617

Western Regional Office
U.S. Department of Commerce
3300 Irvine Ave., Suite 345
Newport Beach, CA 92660
Tel: (714) 660-0144
Fax: (714) 660-9347

The Office of Exporter Services

The Office of Exporter Services (OES) is usually an exporter's first contact with the BXA. As the coordinating and administrative arm of the BXA, it is responsible for the following functions:

- Maintaining the EAR and the Special Comprehensive License
- Initial screening of export license applications
- Responding to requests for advisory opinions and commodity classifications
- Computer processing of license applications
- Issuing export licenses
- Counseling to exporters and re-exporters
- Providing educational seminars
- Coordinating activities between various BXA offices

The OES is made up of the following divisions and field offices:

- *The Exporter Counseling Division.* Responsible for responding to inquiries from the exporting community. Personnel conduct outreach efforts to help exporters understand and comply with the EAR. They also analyze requests for expedited licensing.

* *The Western Regional Office.* This office undertakes similar responsibilities for twelve Western states.

* *The Regulatory Policy Division.* Drafts new regulations and coordinates all changes to the Export Administration Regulations.

* *The Special Licensing and Compliance Division.* Responsible for analyzing applications for special licenses and for consulting with the export community on license procedures and export management.

* *The Operations Division.* Maintains all export licensing forms and screens all incoming license applications, checking them for completeness before they are routed to appropriate licensing offices for review and analysis. This office also issues import certificates.

Chemical/Biological Controls and Treaty Compliance Office

This office conducts day-to-day export licensing, commodity classification, and advisory opinions in the chemical and biological weapons area. It also assists in the implementation of multilateral weapons controls.

Strategic Industries and Economic Security Office

This office has three important functions:

* Scrutinizing U.S. export controls to ensure that they enforce national security while also protecting the market compatibility of U.S. exports
* Providing technical expertise to other BXA divisions
* Assessing foreign industry and research and development efforts to ensure that American capabilities remain equal with foreign trading partners

This office has two main divisions:

1. *The Defense Programs Division.* Responsible mainly for identifying foreign market opportunities for U.S. defense manufacturers, facilitating the conversion of military enterprises in Eastern Europe's newly independent states, and administering the Defense Priorities and Allocations System
2. *The Strategic Analysis Division.* Responsible for analyzing the effect of offsets in defense trade on the U.S. defense industrial base and developing initiatives in this arena, assessing the impact of foreign imports on the U.S. defense industrial base, and related functions

Nuclear and Missile Technology Controls Office

This office is responsible for all policy issues, export licenses, and other issues relating to nuclear and missile technology. The office consists of two divisions:

the Nuclear Technology Controls Division and the Missile Technology Controls Division.

The Office of Strategic Trade and Foreign Policy Controls

This office is responsible for implementing multilateral export controls dealing with conventional arms and related dual-use items. This office also manages computer export control policies, and implements U.S. foreign policy controls (e.g., crime control, antiterrorism, and regional stability). It also has licensing responsibility for items controlled for national security and foreign policy reasons.

3.2.4 *Export Enforcement Offices*

In addition to its licensing duties, the BXA directly enforces export laws and regulations. Several offices are responsible for these tasks.

The Office of Export Enforcement

The Office of Export Enforcement (OEE) investigates export control violations. OEE and its criminal investigators gather information on their own and from intelligence sources in order to detect export control diversion schemes and to close down networks that divert controlled goods to proscribed destinations or end uses. The OEE also manages the Safeguards Verification Program, which carries out checks of export license applications and verifies the post-shipment disposition of exported goods. Appendix A lists OEE regional offices.

The types of violations investigated by the OEE include:

- Violations of the terms set forth in an export license (e.g., where goods or technical data end up in a controlled country or are used for military purposes)
- Violations of an export control order
- False statements on license applications, boycott reports, shipping documents, investigations, compliance proceedings, or appeals
- Transactions with parties subject to denial of export privileges
- Violation of record-keeping or reporting requirements

If the OEE detects a potential violation, it launches several enforcement procedures:

1. *Investigations.*
2. *Warning letters.* The OEE sends warning letters when it detects minor violations of export administration regulations; the letters are used to inform exporters about specific circumstances requiring greater compliance efforts.
3. *Administrative sanctions.* For more serious violations, OEE can impose ad-

ministrative sanctions—either monetary penalties, denials of export privileges, or both.

4. *Criminal indictments.* The most serious export violations are punishable by criminal sanctions, which may be imposed on companies or individuals.

5. *Interdictions.* OEE officials can suspend goods that are suspected of being the subject of illegal export or diversion.

The Office of Enforcement Support

Serving as an informational link between OEE special agents and the Office of Export Licensing, the Office of Enforcement Support (OES) performs the following functions:

- Screens automated license applications to identify cases for enforcement review
- Requests prelicense checks and postshipment verifications
- Coordinates input from Foreign Commercial Service staff overseas
- Analyzes the end-user reliability and diversion risk potential of pending license applications
- Tracks license applications receiving enforcement review

The Office of Strategic Industry and Economic Security

Focusing primarily on foreign security matters as they relate to industry, the Office of Strategic Industry and Economic Security (OIRA) investigates the impact of exports on U.S. security, an area that increasingly affects the high-tech industry.

Office of Antiboycott Compliance

The Export Administration Regulations contain rules prohibiting U.S. companies from adhering to foreign boycotts against countries friendly to the United States. The Office of Antiboycott Compliance enforces these rules by:

- Monitoring international boycott developments
- Conducting investigations of alleged violations
- Providing support in administrative actions and criminal prosecutions

For more information on antiboycott laws, see section 3.5.

Technical Advisory Committees

The Technical Advisory Committees (TACs) provide advice and assistance to BXA from U.S. industry regarding the creation and implementation of export controls. Among existing TACs are those covering the following industries: computers, electronics, materials/materials processing, materials processing equipment, regulations and procedures, sensors, telecommunications equipment, and transportation and related equipment.

Note. For more information on the establishment of TACs, see Supplement No. 2 to part 730 of the Federal Register.

3.2.5   *Other Government Agencies Involved With Export Controls*

The U.S. Customs Service is charged with enforcing the laws and regulations of more than sixty government agencies. Exporters need to know whether their products fall under the purview of any of those agencies and what they need to do to ensure that their shipments are in compliance with those laws and regulations.

The following are some examples of major government agencies whose regulations exporters may encounter.

Food and Drug Administration (FDA)

The FDA enforces U.S. laws designed to ensure that foods, drugs, medical devices, and cosmetics are safe. The FDA also cooperates with the regulatory arms of friendly nations. If an item regulated by the FDA is intended for export only, it must meet foreign purchaser specification, foreign government regulations, as well as foreign labeling requirements.

Exporters should check with their nearest FDA field office to determine if FDA regulations pertain to the goods being exported. Freight forwarders, too, are often good sources of information on foreign regulation.

Environmental Protection Agency (EPA)

Although the EPA has no authority to control the export of hazardous wastes, it has established an export notification system in recognition of the potential environmental, health, and foreign policy problems that may arise from these exports.

The Resource Conservation and Recovery Act (RCRA) requires exporters of hazardous waste to notify the EPA prior to shipment; shipments may not be made until the exporter has received written approval from the government of the consignee to whom the exporter is shipping.

Note. The following is a partial list of government departments that may hold jurisdiction over narrower classes of exports and re-exports. For more information on government agencies, consult Supplement No. 3 to part 730 of the Export Administration Regulations (EAR).

Defense Services and Defense Articles

Department of State
Office of Defense Trade Controls
Fax: (703) 875-6647

(703) 875-5663
(703) 875-6681
22 CFR parts 120 through 130

Drugs, Chemicals, and Precursors

Drug Enforcement Administration
International Chemical Control Unit
Tel: (202) 307-7202
Fax: (202) 307-8570
21 CFR parts 1311 through 1313

(Controlled Substances)
Drug Enforcement Administration
International Drug Unit
Tel: (202) 307-2414
Fax: (202) 307-8570
21 CFR 1311 through 1313

(Drugs and Biologics)
Food and Drug Administration
Import/Export
Tel: (301) 594-3150
Fax: (301) 594-0165
21 U.S.C. 301 *et seq.*

(Investigational Drugs Permitted)
Food and Drug Administration
International Affairs
Tel:(301) 827-4480
Fax: (301) 443-0235
21 CFR 312.1106

Fish and Wildlife Controls; Endangered Species

Department of the Interior
Chief Office of Management Authority
Tel: (703) 358-2093
Fax: (703) 358-2280
50 CFR 17.21, 17.22, 17.31, 17.32

Foreign Assets and Transactions Controls

Department of the Treasury
Office of Foreign Assets Control, Licensing
Tel: (202) 622-2480
Fax: (202) 622-1657
31 CFR parts 500 through 590

Medical Devices

Food and Drug Administration
Office of Compliance
Tel: (301) 594-4699
Fax: (301) 594-4715
21 U.S.C. 301 *et seq.*

Natural Gas and Electric Power

Department of Energy
Office of Fuels Programs
Tel: (202) 586-9482
Fax: (202) 586-6050
10 CFR 205.300 through 205.379 and 590

Nuclear Materials and Equipment

Nuclear Regulatory Commission
Office of International Programs
Tel: (301) 415-2344
Fax: (301) 415-2395
10 CFR part 110

Nuclear Technology; Technical Data for Nuclear Weapons/Special Nuclear Materials

Department of Energy
Office of Arms Control and Non-Proliferation
Export Control Division
Tel: (202) 586-2112
Fax: (202) 586-6977
10 CFR part 810

Ocean Freight Forwarders

Federal Maritime Commission
Office of Freight Forwarders
Tel: (202) 523-5843
Fax: (202) 523-5830
46 CFR part 510

Patent Filing Data Sent Abroad

Department of Commerce
Patent and Trademark Office
Licensing and Review
Tel: (703) 308-1722

Fax: (703) 305-7765
37 CFR part 5

Prohibition of Movement of American Carriers and Prohibition on Transportation of Goods Destined for North Korea

Department of Transportation
Office of International Law, General Counsel
Tel: (202) 366-2972
Fax: (202) 366-9188
44 CFR part 403

U.S. Flagged or U.S. Manufactured Vessels Over 1,000 Gross Tons

U.S. Maritime Administration
Division of Vessel Transfer and Disposal
Tel: (202) 366-5821
Fax: (202) 493-2180
46 CFR part 221

3.2.6 BXA Reorganization and Regulatory Reform

Recognizing the need to control exports without stifling trade, the U.S. Department of Commerce implemented a major reorganization of the BXA on October 1, 1994, consolidating its many divisions into the major offices discussed previously.

The purpose of the reorganization is to streamline operations and strengthen the BXA's efforts to control proliferation of chemical, biological, conventional, and nuclear weapons. With respect to individual exports, reorganized BXA offices focus on two main areas:

- The uses of the goods being exported
- The "end use" as stated by the exporter

This new emphasis places increased responsibility on exporters and their professional counselors. Under the reorganization, exporters are liable for false declarations or misrepresentations regarding shipments; they must therefore become familiar with export controls and must make sure that their professional advisers (e.g., customs brokers, freight forwarders, and attorneys) are well acquainted with the new structure and focus of the BXA. To minimize problems, exporters should:

- Make sure all BXA requirements are met; strict compliance with BXA requirements will help ensure that the shipping process goes more smoothly
- Alert overseas customers of changes that have taken place in the BXA
- Monitor the application review process to safeguard against delays caused by the reorganization

Regulatory Reform

The BXA has been working on streamlining the Export Administration Regulations and further reducing regulatory burdens on international trade. As a result of changes made by the now-defunct Coordinating Committee for Multilateral Export Controls (COCOM), the number of license applications required from U.S. exporters has been declining.

Note. In 1996, the Wassenaar Agreement effectively replaced COCOM. Under this agreement, participating states worldwide promote transparency and greater responsibility in transfers of conventional arms and dual-use goods and technologies. Participating states agree through their national policies to ensure that transfers of these items do not contribute to the development or enhancement of military capabilities that undermine these nonproliferation goals. These same states control all items as outlined in the List of Dual-Use Goods and Technologies and the Munitions List.

BXA's Trade Promotion Coordinating Committee (TPCC) is working on further streamlining the U.S. export licensing system and liberalizing export control. The TPCC—which is chaired by the Secretary of Commerce and includes, among others, the secretaries of Defense, Energy, and State—directs immediate actions to reduce unnecessary regulatory burdens on exporters.

EXAMPLE

Regulatory reform is expected to increase exports of high-tech products while reducing costly export safeguard burdens. Examples include:

- Allowing increased export of computer equipment
- Allowing export of additional types of supercomputers
- Removing prior licensing requirements for telecommunications equipment

3.3 EXPORT CONTROLS

Exports are controlled when they pose economic, security, or foreign policy risks to the United States. There are two primary targets of export controls:

- "Short supply" goods that must be regulated to protect the country from the excessive drain of scarce materials and to reduce the inflationary impact of excessive foreign demand
- Goods or technical data that will contribute to the proliferation of nuclear or military technologies, or that have potential dual-use applications

The Export Administration Regulations list comprehensive procedures and controls to address the concerns associated with export of these items.

Responding to short supply concerns, and the concerns of exporters affected by short supply restrictions, in 1993, the BXA increased the existing ban on export of unprocessed timber from Washington State. That same year, in contrast, the BXA removed export licensing requirements on unprocessed red cedar from federal and state lands in Alaska.

If the item in question is under a short supply quota, a U.S. firm may petition the BXA to gain a share of the quota. Two of the criteria the BXA uses to determine if the firm is eligible to export the commodity in question are past participation in the export of the commodity and/or a statement showing that being prohibited from exporting the commodity would cause the firm undue hardship.

For a sample of short supply restrictions and licensing controls, see Appendix B.

Proliferation Controls

Categories of goods that are affected by proliferation controls include:

* Nuclear technology
* Chemical and biological weapons
* Missile technology
* Crime control and detection equipment
* Computers with a CTP (composite theoretical performance) above 2,000 MTOPS

Note. As of December 1996, special regulations became operative that widely revise the computer revisions of the EAR. The aim is to make these regulations "more friendly" and to provide that No License Required is available for the export and re-export of digital computers whose performance is measured at 2,000 MTOPS or less. Exceptions are computers sold for possible military use or computers being exported to embargoed or terrorist-supporting destinations.

For more detailed information on new computer regulations, consult parts 740, 770, and 774 of the EAR.

There are a number of documents that the exporter must file with the BXA when submitting a license application to export any goods in these categories. Whether or not the goods in question fall under any proliferation controls is determined by the BXA during the course of the export licensing application process.

In addition, there are countries with special controls regarding nuclear nonproliferation and dual-use chemical and biological equipment. See Appendixes C and D for lists of these countries. See section 3.7 for a discussion of special licensing procedures relating to goods subject to proliferation controls.

Technology Data

Regulations affect technology data contained in many forms, including:

* Software (**Note.** Most commercial software, meaning software that is generally available and designed for installation by the user without substantial

support by the supplier, can be shipped to all destinations, except Iran and
Syria.)

- Publications and journals
- Conferences and educational forum
- Research, correspondence, and informal scientific exchange
- Contracts and commercial consulting

Note. The computer industry is battling to lift controls on export of encoded
software. Legislation is pending before Congress on the encryption issue.

Technical data is divided into three control categories:

10 Data available to all destinations
20 Data under restriction
30 Data requiring a special export license

Chemicals

The Commerce Department also heavily monitors chemical by-products,
called precursors, useful in chemical warfare. Working with other nations under
the auspices of the Australia Group, the United States has helped create a list of
fifty-four chemicals it considers essential to curbing the development of chemical
weapons. The group also shares information on the possible proliferation of such
weapons. Parties seeking chemical precursors from member nations are noted
and watched.

To export controlled chemical precursors requires an export license to all destinations except members of the Australia Group. The State Department generally
reviews all such applications and makes an approval when confident that the
export will not make a material contribution to the design, development, production, stockpiling, or use of chemical weapons. Exports of chemical precursors are
generally denied to Iran, Iraq, Libya, and Syria. For more information on individual validated licenses, see section 3.7.

Note. Members of the Australia Group are Australia, Austria, Ireland, NATO
member countries (except Iceland and Turkey), New Zealand, and Switzerland.

Biological Agents

Several microorganisms (e.g., viruses, rickettsias, bacteria, and fungi) have
been identified for export control because of concerns over their potential use as
biological warfare agents. Exports of these microorganisms are unilaterally controlled. Licenses are required for all destinations except Canada.

Record-keeping Requirements

One of the most common mistakes that exporters make in violation of EAA
and EAR regulations is failure to keep the appropriate records for the prescribed
period of time. Depending on the nature of the transaction, many types of records
need to be kept on file, including:

- Export control documents, including purchase orders, invoices, bills of lading, and Shipper's Export Declarations
- Memoranda, notes, and correspondence
- Contracts
- Invitations to bid
- Books of account and financial records
- Restrictive trade practice and boycott documents and reports

Records should be kept in active files for two years and in dead storage for three years, for a total of five years.

The OEE, U.S. Customs Service, or any government agency may ask an exporter to produce records for a variety of reasons. These include the investigation of export control violations or financial audits. Record-keeping requirements are complex and exporters are advised to seek the assistance of a customs broker, freight forwarder, or attorney to ensure compliance.

Penalties and Sanctions

If the OEE suspects a violation of export controls, it generally issues a charging letter to an exporter. This letter states the specific regulation involved and the essential facts concerning the allegation. The exporter has thirty days to respond to the letter, either admitting or denying the charges and requesting a hearing or a decision by an administrative law judge. Failure to respond to the letter means an exporter is in default.

Default or an unfavorable initial decision can result in administrative sanctions, including:

- Suspension or revocation of validated export licenses
- Temporary denial of export privileges
- General denial of export privileges

Note. A temporary or general denial of export privileges may include all parties and entities with whom the defaulting exporter deals.

More serious violations of the EAA can result in criminal sanctions, including substantial fines or prison sentences. Violations of this nature include exporting goods to controlled countries for military or intelligence-gathering purposes or making false statements.

3.4 ANTIDIVERSION REQUIREMENTS

Under U.S. law, goods can be shipped to legally authorized destinations only. The procedures that take place to ensure compliance with the law are called antidiversion requirements. The main tool of the antidiversion requirements is the destination control statement. This statement is attached to shipping documents to ensure that U.S. exports are directed only to legally authorized destinations.

Destination control statements should read as follows:

These [*commodities*] [*technical data*] licensed by the United States for ultimate destination [*name of country*]. Diversion contrary to U.S. law prohibited.

3.5 ANTIBOYCOTT REGULATIONS

U.S. antiboycott laws are intended to encourage or require U.S. firms to refrain from participating in foreign boycotts that do not have U.S. government sanction. These laws also prohibit U.S. firms from taking any actions that support such boycotts.

Many countries that sponsor international boycotts use companies and individuals as fronts, in order to evade the U.S. antiboycott laws. U.S. firms must be aware that it is unlawful to do business with these fronts.

3.5.1 Antiboycott Laws

The two main antiboycott laws in the United States are:

  * *The 1977 Amendments to the Export Administration Act.* The EAA prohibits companies from participating in unsanctioned foreign boycotts.

  * *The Ribicoff Amendment to the 1976 Tax Reform Act.* The Tax Reform Act does not explicitly prohibit boycott-related conduct, but denies certain tax advantages for such actions. Tax benefits that are jeopardized by participation in an unsanctioned boycott include domestic international sales corporation (DISC) status, foreign sales corporation (FSC) status, foreign subsidiary tax deferrals, and foreign tax credits.

Actions that are penalized and/or prohibited under Tax Reform Act and EAA include:

  * Agreeing to refuse or actual refusing to do business with Israel or with companies blacklisted because they do business with Israel
  * Agreeing to discriminate or actual discriminating against individuals based on race, religion, sex, or national origin
  * Furnishing information about business relationships with Israel or with blacklisted companies
  * Furnishing information about the race, religion, sex, or national origin of another person
  * Implementing letters of credit that include prohibited boycott terms or conditions

3.5.2 Enforcement of Antiboycott Laws

The Compliance Policy Division is responsible for developing and coordinating policies and initiatives to promote compliance with the antiboycott policies and requirements of the Export Administration Act. The division retains investigative teams, which are involved in the following activities:

- Conducting compliance reviews
- Investigating potential violations
- Issuing precharging letters for alleged violations
- Negotiating settlements where violations are alleged
- Preparing settlement documentation or charging letters initiating administrative proceedings
- Preparing cases for referral to the Office of the Chief Counsel for Export Administration for litigation
- Assisting the Office of the Chief Counsel for Export Administration in litigation of charges brought under the antiboycott provisions of the Act
- Preparing cases for referral to the Department of Justice for criminal prosecution

3.6 EXPORT LICENSES

With the abolition of the general license category, fewer goods require export licenses today. That does not mean the BXA has stopped requiring licenses. If anything, exporters should be more vigilant than ever in complying with BXA regulations. As noted previously, the BXA administers export controls, including licenses, for three primary reasons:

- To protect the U.S. economy from being drained of scarce materials and to reduce the inflationary impact of foreign demand
- To further U.S. foreign policy
- To enhance U.S. national security

3.6.1. Export Administration Regulations and Export Licensing

In recent years BXA officials have spent a great deal of time traveling the country and meeting with exporters to determine the best way to improve the export system. The aim has been to decontrol as many products as possible and require as few licenses as possible in an effort to increase U.S. exports while still protecting U.S. economic and military interests.

Much of the BXA focus has been on rewriting the Export Administration Regulations to make them accessible. On the other hand, the trick has also been to make the EAR detailed enough to give exporters the information they require to make as many licensing decisions as possible on their own.

Note. The EAR can be found in the government documents sections of many public and university libraries. Likewise, the BXA regional offices and help lines are notable for their prompt and efficient service.

Some people find the great length of the EAR and their extensive use of technical terms to be intimidating. BXA officials contend, however, that such detail and precision can and does serve public interests. The detailed listing of technical parameters in the CCL, for example, establishes precise, objective criteria that should help exporters and re-exporters ascertain the appropriate control status. They believe that broader and more subjective criteria would only leave exporters and re-exporters more dependent upon interpretations and rulings of the BXA.

The BXA further points out that much of the detail in the CCL is derived from multilaterally adopted lists. The specificity serves to enhance the uniformity and effectiveness of international control practices and to promote a "level playing field." Furthermore, the detailed presentation of such elements as licensing and export clearance procedures allows exporters and re-exporters to find in one place what is needed to comply with pertinent requirements.

Note. Of special importance in the EAR is the detailed listing of License Exception criteria, which allow exporters and re-exporters to determine quickly and confidently whether it is possible to proceed with a transaction without delay.

Additional Categories Covered by EAR Cover Outside of Exports

The core of the export control provisions of the EAR concerns exports from the United States. However, some provisions give broad meaning to the term *export* and apply to transactions outside the United States or to activities other than exports. For example:

* *Re-exports.* Commodities, software, and technology that have been exported from the United States are generally subject to the EAR with respect to re-export. Many such re-exports, however, may go to many destinations without a license or qualify for an exception from licensing requirements.

  Note. Re-exports can pose major legal issues. For example, in 1997 the Supreme Court agreed to review the issue of whether the U.S. copyright laws protect goods that are sold abroad by a manufacturer at discount prices and then re-exported for sale here without permission from the manufacturer.

* *Foreign products.* In some cases, authorization to export technology from the United States is subject to assurances that items produced abroad that are the direct product of that technology will not be exported to certain destinations without authorization from BXA.

* *Scope of exports.* Certain actions that might not be regarded as an export in other contexts do, in fact, constitute an export subject to the EAR. The release of technology to a foreign national in the United States through such means as demonstration or oral briefing is deemed an export. Other examples of exports under the EAR include the return of foreign equipment to its country of origin after repair in the United States, shipments from a U.S. foreign trade zone, and the electronic transmission of nonpublic data that is received abroad.

* *U.S. person activities.* To counter the proliferation of weapons of mass destruction, the Export Administration Regulations restrict the involvement of "United States persons" anywhere in the world in either exporting foreign-origin items or providing services or support that may contribute to such proliferation.

EAR Self-Help Section

The Export Administration Regulations provide self-help information for exporters and re-exporters attempting to determine whether a license is required. Here are some frequently asked questions and their answers:

How the Export Administration Regulations Are Organized

The Export Administration Regulations are structured in a logical manner. In dealing with the EAR, it is helpful to be aware of the overall organization of these regulations. To determine what the rules are and what exporters need to do, review the titles and the introductory sections of the parts of the EAR.

 • *How do exporters determine their obligations under the EAR?* Part 732 of the EAR provides steps exporters may follow to determine their obligations under the EAR. This guidance tells exporters whether or not a transaction is subject to the EAR and, if it is, whether it qualifies for a License Exception or must be authorized through issuance of a license.

 • *Are the items or activities subject to the EAR at all?* Part 734 of the EAR defines the items and activities that are subject to the EAR. Note that the definition of "items subject to the EAR" includes, but is not limited to, items listed on the Commerce Control List in part 774 of the EAR.

 • *If subject to the EAR, what do the regulations require?* Part 736 of the EAR lists all the prohibitions that are contained in the EAR. Certain prohibitions (e.g., General Prohibitions one through three) apply to items as indicated on the CCL, and other (e.g., General Prohibitions four through ten) prohibit certain activities and apply to all items subject to the EAR unless otherwise indicated.

 • *Is a license needed for the item or activity? What policies will BXA apply if a license application must be submitted?* The Export Administration Regulations have several ways of describing license requirements:

1. The EAR may require a license to a country if the item is listed on the CCL and the Country Chart in part 738 of the EAR states that a license is required to that country. Virtually all Export Control Classification Numbers (ECCN) on the CCL are covered by the Country Chart in part 738 of the EAR. That part identifies the limited number of entries that are not included on the Chart. These ECCNs state the specific countries that require a license or refer the exporter to a self-contained section (i.e., short supply in part 754 of the EAR, or embargoes in part 746 of the EAR). If a license is required, consult part 740 of the EAR, which describes the License Exception that may be available for items on the CCL. Part 742 of the EAR describes the licensing policies that BXA applies in reviewing an application that is filed. Note that part 754 of the EAR on short supply controls and part 746 on embargoes are self-contained parts that include the available exceptions and licensing policy.
2. A license requirement may be based on the end use or end user in a trans-

action, primarily for proliferation reasons. Part 744 of the EAR describes such requirements and relevant licensing policies and includes both restrictions on items and restrictions on the activities of U.S. persons.

3. A license is required for virtually all exports to embargoed destinations, such as Cuba. Part 746 of the EAR describes all the licensing requirements, license review policies, and License Exceptions that apply to such destinations. If the transaction involves one of these countries the exporter should first look at this part. This part also describes controls that may be maintained under the EAR to implement UN sanctions.

* *How do exporters file a license application and what happens to the application once it is filed? What if authorization is needed for multiple transactions?* Parts 748 and 750 of the EAR provide information on license submission and processing. Part 752 of the EAR provides for a Special Comprehensive License that authorizes multiple transactions. If an application is denied, part 756 of the EAR provides rules for filing appeals.

* *How does the exporter clear shipments with the U.S. Customs Service?* Part 758 of the EAR describes the requirements for clearance of exports.

* *Where are the rules on restrictive trade practices and boycotts?* Part 760 of the EAR deals with restrictive trade practices and boycotts.

* *Where are the rules on record keeping and enforcement?* Part 762 of the EAR sets out your record-keeping requirements and parts 764 and 766 of the EAR deal with violations and enforcement proceedings.

* *What is the effect of foreign availability?* Part 768 of the EAR provides rules for determining foreign availability of items subject to controls.

* *Do the Export Administration Regulations provide definitions and interpretations?* Part 770 of the EAR contains interpretations and part 772 of the EAR lists definitions used.

Where to Get Help

Throughout the EAR, exporters can find information on offices to contact for various purposes and types of information. General information, (including assistance in understanding the EAR); information on how to obtain forms, electronic services, and publications; and information on training programs offered by BXA, is available from the Office of Exporter Services.

Note. The BXA provides EAR Online subscription services for $252 a year. A paper-based service costs $89 a year. For more information on the scope of services, call 703-605-6060.

3.6.2   Types of Licenses

The vast majority of exports and re-exports do not require a license today. Before moving on to further describe the process for determining whether a license is required, here is a short summary of the former license system, in contrast to how the BXA handles export licenses today.

The Old System

In the past, exporters had to contend with two major types of licenses: validated licenses and general licenses.

A validated license was a specific grant of authority from the BXA to an exporter allowing the export of a particular product. Validated licenses were granted on a case-by-case basis for either a single transaction or for a specified period of time. All validated licenses were secured through an application process.

Under the former system there were two major types of validated licenses—individual validated licenses and special validated licenses. The individual category covered a wide range of products and destinations and was the most commonly issued license. Special validated licenses generally authorized the export of technical data or commodities for specified time frames to specified countries. These were called project licenses, distribution licenses, and service supply licenses.

In the past, general licenses covered certain categories of products where the government granted authority to export without gaining written authorization first. No document was issued from the Commerce Department as a precondition to export.

The vast majority of U.S.-manufactured exports did not require prior Commerce Department approval before being shipped and therefore fit into this category. Under the former general license umbrella, there were twenty-three different types of licenses covering everything from any product listed on the CCL that did not require a validated license, to low-value orders and returns, repairs, and replacements of unwanted foreign goods.

The New Simplified System and End Use

The BXA is responding to changing world events with a refocus on commodities, technology, software, and services that could be used to develop or deliver weapons of mass destruction. The Enhanced Proliferation Control Initiative (EPCI) regulations were issued in 1991 and place greater emphasis on the end use or end user of exported items.

The aim of the simplified license system is to allow more exports with fewer controls while still providing protection for national security reasons. Under this system there are three major license categories: License, No License Required (NLR), and Special Comprehensive License.

Note. As a result of EPCI regulations, exporters need to be more vigilant in screening their customers and transactions. As will be described in the next few sections, the end use of a shipment plays a major role in determining whether an export license, or further government agency review, is required. Under the nonproliferation regulations, items that might otherwise be exported using a general license may require the designation of an end user.

3.6.3   *Determining Whether a License Is Required*

An Overview

Several changes have taken place in terms of determining when a license is required. BXA officials advise thinking of the new system in baseball terms. Exporters and re-exporters move from scope (first base) to prohibitions (second base) to license categories (third base) and then home when they determine they do not need a license or are granted a license to export.

The decision about whether a product requires an export license is based on the commodity being exported and the export destination. To make this determination, exporters will need to know:

- The classification of the product or goods
- The destination
- The end user
- The end use
- Conduct (**Note.** Conduct refers to contracting, financing, and freight forwarding in support of a proliferation project as defined in part 744 of the EAR.)

To classify products and goods for export license purposes, exporters and re-exporters must determine the following:

- *The Export Control Classification Number (ECCN).* This number consists of a code followed by a code letter. The code letter indicates the country group level of control for all goods on the Commerce Control List (CCL). This number also determines documentation requirements.

- *The country group of the country to which the goods are being shipped.* Each country group is assigned a different level of control. It is the exporter's responsibility to ensure that the country of ultimate destination is properly identified on all export documentation.

If an exporter determines that no license is required, then application does not have to be made to the BXA and no written authorization is required for that particular export. Licenses require both an application and the issuance of an actual license by the BXA. In some cases, especially if the goods in question are dual-use items, a substantial amount of supporting documentation is required before the issuance of a license; the process can become quite complex.

Procedural Steps

The following are the new procedural steps exporters and re-exporters must follow when determining their license status:

• *Scope.* Scope essentially means "subject to the EAR." When exporters or re-exporters enter this step they are answering whether or not their export activities are subject to the EAR. The following are some categories subject to the EAR:

1. Certain activities of U.S. persons related to proliferation of chemical or biological weapons or of missile technology
2. Activities of U.S. or foreign persons prohibited by any denial order
3. Re-export controls, including: U.S. origin items wherever located; foreign-made items, only if subject to general prohibition two (parts and components rule) or general prohibition three (foreign-produced product rule)
4. Exports of technology released to foreign nationals

Note. Most exporters and re-exporters are subject to the EAR. That does not mean a license is required. There are some situations in which exporters or re-exporters will not be subject to the EAR. For example, products are outside the scope of the EAR (1) if they are subject to the exclusive jurisdiction of another agency, such as items on the munitions list or regulated by the Nuclear Regulatory Commission; (2) when the technology being exported or re-exported is "publicly available"; (3) if the item is not on the CCL and is listed in EAR 99, which is a catchall category for noncontrolled goods such as pencils.

Note. Exports and re-exports that are not subject to the EAR do not require a license application. And they do not fall into the No License Required category.

• *General prohibitions.* Exports that fall under the scope category next must be examined to determine whether they are subject to any export prohibitions. There are ten prohibitions that exporters and re-exporters must examine. The first three prohibitions are based on the Commerce Control List when examined in conjunction with the country chart. Whether a license is required depends on the product classification and the end destination. Prohibitions two and three focus on the percentage of foreign-made parts or components a product is carrying compared to U.S. parts and technology.

Note. Encryption items are now transferred from the U.S. Munitions List to the Commerce Control List. Exporters and re-exporters of commercial communications satellites and "hot-section" technology for the development, production, or overhaul of commercial aircraft engines are also subject to new regulations. Products that are used for biological warfare may also be subject to new controls.

In early 1998, the industry's battle with government over export controls for encrypted software was heading to the U.S. House of Representatives where House Speaker Newt Gingrich was expected to provide a final decision. The issue was still to appear before the U.S. Senate, and there was discussion that the Supreme Court might hear a case relating to this subject. President Clinton imposed additional controls that curbed sales of high-performance computers to China, Russia, and other nations that posed a nuclear threat in the fall of 1997. Protesting this move, the computer industry was conducting talks with the Commerce Department in an attempt to soften the implementation rules governing exports of these products.

It should be noted that the U.S. software industry is not satisfied with controls on encrypted software and is currently battling in Congress to have them overhauled. In September 1997 the House Commerce Committee voted to lift government restrictions on common software with encoding features. But it is not certain that this vote will be sustained beyond this committee.

The following are the ten general prohibitions:

1. Exports and re-exports of controlled items to listed countries
2. Re-exports of foreign-made items incorporating more than a *de minimis* amount of controlled U.S. content
3. Re-exports of foreign-produced direct product

(Prohibitions four through seven are transaction based.)

4. Export or re-export (and certain transfers) to denied parties as defined in the EAR, mainly criminal elements or dictators (Denied Persons List)
5. Export or re-export to prohibited end uses or end users (includes nuclear, missile technology, and chemical or biological weapons end use; refer to EAR part 744)
6. Export or re-export to embargoed or special destinations (e.g., Cuba, Libya, North Korea, Iran, and Iraq; refer to EAR part 746)
7. Support proliferation activities (refer to EAR part 744)
8. In transit shipments and items to be unladed from vessels or aircraft
9. Violate and order, term and condition
10. Proceed with transaction with the knowledge that a violation has occurred or is about to occur

Exporters and re-exporters subject to prohibitions one, two, and three must now determine if a license is required. They will either find a special license is required or that they may fit under the No License Required category.

License Exceptions

At this stage exporters and re-exporters must also check to see if they are subject to one of five list-based license exceptions that are spelled out in part 740 of the EAR.

If the product or good does not qualify for a license exception, then it is time to apply for a license. If the BXA grants the license, then the export to re-export can be shipped. If a license is denied, then there may be a question of redesign, a decision to ship to noncontrolled parts of the world, or appeals can be filed.

The five main license exception categories can be divided roughly into two major groups:

1. *Situational exceptions.* These are not commodity-based exceptions but rest on the context of the export. Gift parcels under $2,500 (GFT) may fit this category,

or materials being exported to governments and international organizations (GOV).

2. *Commodity-based license exceptions.* These exceptions cover shipments to countries in Group B ("friendly" nations); low-value shipments (LVS); civilian end-user (CIV) shipments; and others. Restricted technology and software may be allowed under this category, depending on the ECCN number.

Note. Beware that the EAR only lists restrictions. There will be no instructions in the affirmative that tell exporters and re-exporters that it is acceptable to go ahead and ship without a license. When in doubt, contact either export counselors in regional BXA offices, consultants, or attorneys.

How to Use the Commerce Country Chart

The Commerce Country Chart—generally known as Country Chart—allows exporters and re-exporters to determine if they need a license to export or re-export their item to a particular destination.

The first column of the Country Chart lists all countries in alphabetical order (see Figure 1). There are a number of destinations not listed on the actual chart that are contained in Supplement No. 1 to part 738 of the EAR. Contact BXA counseling centers for help working through the chart on the first attempt.

Note. For colonies that are dependents of major countries, refer to the major country in question. For example, if exporting to the Cayman Islands, which is a dependent of the United Kingdom, look under the United Kingdom on the Country Chart.

Stretching out to the right on the Country Chart are horizontal headers identifying the various reasons for control. These include categories such as nuclear proliferation, antiterrorism, national security controls, regional stability, short supply controls, and chemical and biological weapons. Each column identifier consists of a letter—Reason for Control—and a column number (e.g., CB Column 1). The column identifiers correspond to those listed in the Country Chart header within the License Requirement section of the ECCN.

Note. The symbol X is used to denote licensing requirements on the Country Chart. If an X appears in a particular cell, transactions subject to that particular Reason for Control/Destination combination require a license. There is a direct correlation between the number of X's applicable to a transaction and the number of licensing reviews an application must undergo.

Guidance

The BXA has prepared the following sample entry and related analysis to illustrate the type of process exporters and re-exporters should follow to determine whether a license is required:

1. An item valued at $10,000 is classified under ECCN 2A000.a. The entire entry is controlled for national security and anti-terrorism reasons.
2. Because this item is classified under paragraph 2A000.a, and not 2A000.b,

Figure 1. Commerce country chart.

Reason for Control

Countries	Chemical & Biological Weapons			Nuclear Nonproliferation		National Security		Missile Tech	Regional Stability		Crime Control			Anti-Terrorism	
	CB Column 1	CB Column 2	CB Column 3	NP Column 1	NP Column 2	NS Column 1	NS Column 2	MT Column 1	RS Column 1	RS Column 2	CC Column 1	CC Column 2	CC Column 3	AT Column 1	AT Column 2
Afghanistan	X	X	X	X		X	X	X	X	X	X		X		
Albania	X	X		X		X		X	X	X	X	X			
Algeria	X	X		X	X	X	X	X	X	X	X		X		
Andorra	X	X		X	X	X	X	X	X	X	X		X		
Angola	X	X		X	X	X	X	X	X	X	X		X		
Antigua & Barbuda	X	X		X		X	X	X	X	X	X		X		
Argentina	X			X		X	X	X	X	X	X		X		
Armenia	X	X	X	X		X	X	X	X	X	X	X	X		
Australia	X					X		X	X	X					
Austria	X					X		X	X	X	X		X		
Azerbaijan	X	X	X	X		X	X	X	X	X	X	X	X		
Bahamas, The	X	X		X		X	X	X	X	X	X		X		
Bahrain	X	X	X	X		X	X	X	X	X	X		X		
Bangladesh	X	X		X		X	X	X	X	X	X		X		
Barbados	X	X		X		X	X	X	X	X	X		X		
Belarus	X	X	X	X		X	X	X	X	X	X	X	X		
Belgium	X					X		X	X		X	X			
Belize	X	X		X		X	X	X	X	X	X		X		

it means that nuclear proliferation controls apply to a portion of the entry, but not to this particular item.

3. The appropriate Country Chart column identifiers are NS column 2 and AT column 1.
4. Turning to the Country Chart, locate the specific destination—India—and see that an X appears in the NS column 2 cell for India, but not in the AT column 1 cell.
5. The appearance of these X's means that a license is required unless the transaction qualifies for a License Exception or Special Comprehensive License.
6. From the License Exception (LVS) value listed in the entry, it is immediately evident that the proposed transaction exceeds the value limitation associated with LVS.
7. Noting that the License Exception is "yes" for this entry, the last step is to seek out part 740 of the EAR to review provisions for this category.

Note. Experienced exporters and re-exporters find this process far simpler in practice than it may seem from the examples listed. It's easier to dig into a process than read about it.

When a License Is Required

There is very little correspondence between the old export license system and today's system. This fact may prove confusing to those who worked under the old system and are returning for the first time. It is possible to think about the new license category in terms of the former validated license, but that is where the similarities end. Here are the areas they cover:

- *License.* Covers products on the CCL list that are bound for countries that exist on the BXA Country Chart.

- *No License Required.* Covers either those commodities listed in EAR 99, or commodities listed on the CCL with no country restrictions.

- *Special Comprehensive License.* Covers all commodities (except missile technology) that are eligible for export, except to embargoed countries or countries that support terrorism. Field experts report that the Special Comprehensive License is rarely used because it imposes so many conditions on companies, and opens them up to audits, that exporters and re-exporters would rather make other provisions than seek this license.

Note. More controls exist today in the area of imparting information to foreign nationals. The question of whether imparting information to foreign nationals equals an "export" is a matter of debate and controversy that is beyond the scope of this book. Exporters and re-exporters should know that this debate exists and seek professional advice before inviting foreign business delegations to tour a plant in the United States, offering training courses to foreign nationals either in the United States or on foreign soil, or releasing technology or software to foreign nationals.

3.7 THE LICENSE APPLICATION PROCESS

When entering the application process, it is important to know the parties to the transaction. Applicants for export licenses must disclose information on all of the parties to the transaction. The licensee is responsible for the accuracy of all information. Exporters need to become familiar with the following terms, because the application and supporting documents will require that these parties be identified:

1. *Ultimate consignee.* The ultimate consignee is the person located abroad who is actually receiving the export for the designated end use. A bank, freight forwarder, forwarding agent, or other party, when acting as an intermediary, is not acceptable as the ultimate consignee.

2. *Intermediate consignee.* The intermediate consignee is the bank, forwarding agent, or other intermediary (if any) who acts in a foreign country as an agent for the exporter, the purchaser, or the ultimate consignee for the purpose of effecting delivery of the export to the ultimate consignee. More specifically:

* If the intermediate consignee is unknown at the time of application or none is to be used, this must be stated on the application. If, at the time of filing an application, an exporter is unable to determine at which port the commodities will be unloaded from the exporting carrier, optional intermediate consignees may be shown.

* Before any shipment is made, the name and address of any intermediate consignee must be determined and produced on a shipper's export declaration (SED), whether or not named on the license application or validated license. However, the intermediate consignee need not be named on the commercial invoice. See section 3.8 for more information on the shipper's export declaration.

1. *Purchaser.* The purchaser is the person abroad who enters into the export transaction with the applicant to purchase the commodities or technical data for delivery to the ultimate consignee. An intermediary such as a bank, freight forwarder, or forwarding agent may not be identified as the purchaser.

2. *Order party.* The order party is the person in the United States who conducts the direct negotiations or correspondence with the foreign purchaser or ultimate consignee and who, as a result of these negotiations, receives the order from the foreign purchaser or ultimate consignee.

Completed applications should be mailed, along with all supporting documentation, reports and forms to:

The Office of Export Licensing
P.O. Box 273
Washington, DC 20044

Applications can also be filed electronically (as will be discussed in section 3.7.3).

Within ten days after receiving the application, the BXA either accepts it for further processing or, if the application is not completed properly or more information is needed, returns it to the applicant. If the application is returned without action, the BXA informs the applicant what needs to be corrected or added. If the corrected application does not need be referred to another government agency or does not need corrective action, the BXA issues or denies a license within sixty days.

Note. The average processing time for applications that do not require referral to another agency is about nine days; for applications requiring referral, the average is about forty-eight days.

3.7.1 The License Referral Process

The Commerce Department refers certain applications to other agencies for further review and recommendations. Decisions for referral are based on:

* The level of technology
* The appropriateness of the items for the stated end use
* The destination country

The principal referral agencies that handle license issues are:

* The Defense Department's National Security-Controlled Items
* The Energy Department's Nuclear Non-Proliferation Controlled Items
* The State Department's Foreign Policy and Certain Non-Proliferation Controlled Items

Under certain agreed procedures, applications are also referred to what are known as working-level interagency groups. Agencies represented at the working level include the Departments of Commerce, Defense, Energy, and State and the Arms Control and Disarmament Agency (ACDA).

If the Operating Committee (OC) of any involved agency cannot reach a consensus on an application, this is the process an exporter may follow with the backing of one of the OC's government agency members:

1. The application is sent next to the Advisory Committee on Export Policy (ACEP). A Commerce Department unit, this group is made up of officials at the assistant secretary level who make a recommendation regarding the disposition of the application.

2. If a member agency disagrees with the ACEP's recommendations, it can bring the claim to the Export Administration Review Board (EARB). The EARB is a Cabinet-level group that Commerce chairs, and also includes State and Defense. Energy and ACDA participate in matters dealing with their respective statutory and policy-making authorities and non-proliferation matters.

3. If an agency disagrees with the recommendations of the EARB, it can refer the decision to the president.

The following is an example of the course of a license application for a controlled commodity—in this case, commodities relating to missile technology:

1. The application is considered to determine whether the export would make a material contribution to the proliferation of missiles.
2. Following a thorough BXA review, the application is referred to other related government agencies.
3. Before final approval is granted, missile technology assurances may be requested from the government of the country receiving the controlled items. The State Department is responsible for acquiring all government-to-government assurances.
4. If the foreign government confirms the stated end user and end use, and assures the U.S. government that the equipment will not be used, modified, or retransferred for other than civilian purposes, the license may be granted.

Exporters should take the following actions to ensure compliance with all laws and regulations:

- Establish good communication with the foreign buyer and obtain thorough knowledge of their operations and reputation
- Check the Table of Denial Orders in the EAR for possible restrictions on any parties to the transaction (see Appendix E)
- Employ an experienced and reputable customs broker or freight forwarder
- Document all shipments completely and accurately

3.7.2   Documentation Requirements

License applications forms must be obtained through the BXA; each form has a preprinted control number consisting of a letter followed by six digits. This number is used by applicants when communicating with the BXA about the status of their applications.

When applying for an export license, the parties to the transaction may be asked to supply supporting documentation.

3.7.3   Electronic Licensing

Pursuant to ongoing export control reform, the Department of Commerce has introduced the Automated Export System (AES), which has been up and running in pilot phase since the summer of 1995.

A joint venture between the U.S. Customs Service, the Bureau of Census, Bureau of Export Administration, and other state and federal agencies, AES provides an information gateway designed to improve trade statistics, manage

Harbor Maintenance Fee collection, improve customer service, and ensure compliance.

Data collection is one of the main purposes behind AES. As it now stands, most information the U.S. Commerce Department provides on import/export activity is, by necessity, seven years old. That is because the information is based on U.S. Census figures. AES, through creation of a central repository for source information and as an electronic gateway for the routing of export data, is expected to allow for the quick dissemination of pertinent import/export marketing statistics.

Since July 3, 1995 five vessel ports—Baltimore, Norfolk, Houston, Charleston, and Los Angeles/Long Beach—have been successfully operating "live" as phase I of the AES pilot project. During this phase, participating companies are required to dual report to U.S. Customs, meaning they submit both paper and electronic shipper's export declarations (SEDs), allowing the Bureau of Census to audit the integrity of the electronic system.

AES requires exporters and carriers to file some specific export information in advance of exportation the same way today's regulations require paper filing. AES is supposed to be extended to all vessel ports in the United States by the late 1990s. Commodity data will be accepted into the system from all transport modes—air, ocean, and truck—starting in the winter of 1997. By the end of 1997, transportation data of all sorts was expected to start entering the system.

However, this has not taken place. By the end of 1997, only two exporters, two ocean carriers, and twelve freight forwarders were participating. Although the transportation community has supported AES in concept, there is a major dispute over the requirements the U.S. Customs Service has outlined for the shippers export declaration. Customs has insisted the SED be filed before the vessel or aircraft leave the country. Exporters say that it's impossible to supply all the information required for an SED predeparture, but they can complete all documentation within several days of departure. For example, exporters of agricultural products often sell their goods while the shipment is in transit. That means they can't give Customs the destination or consignee in a predeparture fashion.

In late 1997 the U.S. General Accounting Office (GAO) recommended that the U.S. Customs Service create one form that fits all for the thirteen government agencies supposed to file reports under AES. The GAO considered the AES system as then designed to be too unwieldy and troublesome for both government officials and exporters alike.

Because AES is strictly voluntary, most exporters and transport professionals have refused to participate.

Automated Export System—Postdeparture Authorized Special Status (AES-PASS)

While agreeing to formal talks with the international trade community on the AES issue, Customs has come up with a related program called the Customs "gold card," which is designed to simplify the paper needed to export goods and conduct documentation electronically. Officially the new program is called AES-PASS for Automated Export System—Postdeparture Authorized Status.

Exporters have to be preapproved to participate in AES-PASS and earn their gold card. Customs is making it relatively easy to qualify. The only major restrictions will be on exports that are generally considered controlled such as weapons or on exports to locations that are controlled, such as Iraq.

Those exporters that earn their gold card will need to submit only two pieces of information predeparture: the exporter's identification number—known as the Data Universal Numbering System (DUNS) number, and a unique number identifying each shipment. The remaining data can be filed after departure.

Currently, there are a number of other online programs exporters can access during the licensing process.

The Export License Application and Information Network (ELAIN)

This BXA system is designed to streamline the export licensing process. It can receive applications and issue licenses electronically. About 30–40 percent of exporters currently use ELAIN, saving about three to four days of processing time.

The ELAIN system is not completely paperless. Supplementary documentation materials must be faxed or sent to the BXA by overnight mail. Exporters must take care to submit these materials within the deadlines prescribed by the BXA. Currently, forty-eight hours are allowed for a fax transmission and seventy-two hours for an express mail package.

System for Tracking Export License Applications (STELA)

STELA issues a computer-generated, up-to-the-minute status report on the progress of an export license application and can issue authorizations to ship goods for those applications approved without conditions.

Licensing Officer Access (LOA)

The LOA system allows BXA licensing officers instant access to past licensing history. The system also permits electronic application review and approval (or denial). Once an application is approved, the license is transmitted electronically to the exporter.

3.8 MAKING SHIPMENTS UNDER LICENSE

Once licensing documentation is received, the exporter proceeds to the shipping of goods. The following sections discuss shipping under different license categories.

Shipping Under No License Required

Exporters whose goods fall under the NLR category should follow these procedures:

* *Include a destination control statement on all documentation.* For more information on destination control statements, see section 3.4.

* *Complete a shipper's export declaration.* A shipper's export declaration is a form filed with the U.S. Customs Service. An SED is required if the value of the shipment is more than $2,500 or if shipped under an individual validated license, regardless of value. (Shipments valued at $2,500 or less, or mail shipments valued at $500 or less, are exempt.) On the declaration, the exporter indicates the NLR category. (See Form 3.10 for a sample SED.)

Shipping Under a License

A destination control statement and shipper's export declaration are required for all licensed shipments. The SED must include an export authorization number.

3.9 DEVELOPING AN EXPORT MANAGEMENT SYSTEM (EMS)

Given the growing complexity of compliance with export controls, the Commerce Department recommends that exporters develop an export management system (EMS). This is an optional program each company can establish to ensure that its exports and export decisions are consistent with the EAR.

As noted, the Enhanced Proliferation Control Initiative (EPCI) regulations require the exporter to assume greater responsibility in screening export transactions. Items usually eligible for general licenses may require specific Commerce Department authorization in the form of a validated license when a particular transaction raises proliferation concerns. Firms that participate in the export of items that would normally be eligible for general license treatment, but that require a Commerce Department validated license because of the nature of the end use or end user, may be held liable under EPCI.

Note. Firms could lose their export privileges, be fined a fee, or even be criminally prosecuted if they fail to obtain the required validated license.

The main purpose of the EMS is establishing in-house mechanisms to provide checks and safeguards at key steps in the order processing system. Continued checks should lead to better management of the overall export process. The aim is to help complies comply with U.S. export controls, saving valuable time and money.

The establishment of an EMS will not protect an exporter from being liable for criminal or administrative prosecution if a violation occurs. However, export specialists report that the implementation of an EMS—coupled with good judgment—can greatly reduce the risk of inadvertently exporting to an unauthorized party or for an unauthorized end use.

An EMS system asks an exporter a series of questions as a form of self-auditing throughout the export process. Issues include:

- Knowing the customer
- Understanding the EAR
- Identifying those sections of the export regulations that apply to the exporter's international activities
- Determining the types of business that form the exporting company's focus
- Identifying the types of foreign firms that make up the bulk of the company's customers
- Learning who the ultimate foreign end user will be

To assist companies in identifying firms with which trade is prohibited, the Commerce Department maintains a "Table of Denial Orders" that lists companies and individuals whose export privileges have been suspended. An exporter should check these lists before doing business with any company or individual suspected of operating in an embargoed area. See Appendix E for an excerpt from the Table of Denial Orders.

Note. Exporters can contact their regional BXA office for a copy of *EMS Guidelines*. These are merely recommendations and are not mandated approaches to exporting. Businesses are advised to adopt those BXA recommendations that fit their particular concerns.

Summary of Key Points Raised in This Chapter

1. The U.S. government controls exports to protect national security, promote foreign policy, and safeguard U.S. economic interests.

2. The Department of Commerce, through its Bureau of Export Administration (BXA), enforces export controls.

3. Other U.S. government agencies, such as the Defense Department, the State Department, Food and Drug Administration, and the Environmental Protection Agency, are also involved in controlling U.S. exports.

4. Export licenses are the primary means of controlling U.S. exports.

5. Antiboycott laws prohibit U.S. companies from doing business with countries that boycott U.S. allies; these laws also prohibit dealing with countries that encourage discrimination on the basis of sex, race, religion, or national origin.

6. U.S. companies are required to state on their shipping documents that shipments are permitted for authorized destinations only.

7. Dual-use commodities are those that have both civilian and military applications.

8. Only specialized exports require an export license.

9. Licenses are required for controlled products and destinations; No License Required fits commodities that appear under EAR 99, or the Commerce Control List.

10. To obtain a license, exporters must complete an application and go through a Commerce Department approval process.

11. Exporters are responsible for the truth and accuracy of all export documentation, including documentation prepared by professionals such as customs brokers, freight forwarders, and customs attorneys.

12. No License Required requires no application.

13. Exporters must ascertain the end use of the commodities they export.

Appendix A   Bureau of Export Administration Offices

Export Counseling Division
Tel: (202) 482-4811
Fax: (202) 482-3617

Western Regional Office
3300 Irvine Avenue
Suite 348
Newport Beach, CA 92660-3198
Tel: (714) 660-0144
Fax: (714) 660-9347

Eastern Regional Office
547 Amherst Street
4th Floor
Nashua, NH 03063
Tel: (603) 598-4300
Fax: (603) 598-4323

Portland Office
121 SW Salmon Street
Suite 241
Portland, OR 97204
Tel: (503) 326-5159
Fax: (503) 326-5972

Office of Export Enforcement (OEE)
Tel: (202) 482-1208
Fax: (202) 482-0964
Enforcement Hotline: (800) 424-2980

OEE/Boston Field Office
O'Neill Federal Building
10 Causeway Street
Room 350
Boston, MA 02222
Tel: (617) 565-6030
Fax: (617) 565-6039

OEE/Chicago Field Office
2400 E. Devon Avenue

Suite 300
Des Plaines, IL 60018
Tel: (312) 353-6640
Fax: (312) 353-8008

OEE/Dallas Field Office
525 Griffin St.
Room 622, Box 122
Dallas, TX 75202
Tel: (214) 767-9294
Fax: (214) 767-9299

OEE/Los Angeles Field Office
2601 Main St.
Suite 310
Irvine, CA 92714-6299
Tel: (714) 251-9001
Fax: (714) 251-9103

OEE/LAX Satellite Office
222 N. Sepulveda Blvd.
Suite 720
El Segundo, CA 90245
Tel: (310) 297-0360
Fax: (310) 297-0507

OEE/Miami Field Office
200 E. Las Olas Blvd.
Suite 1260
Ft. Lauderdale, FL 33301
Tel: (954) 356-7540
Fax: (954) 356-7549

OEE/JFK Office
Cargo Building #75
JFK International Airport
Jamaica, NY 11430
Tel: (718) 553-1702
Fax: (718) 553-1704

OEE/San Jose Field Office
96 N. 3rd St.
Suite 250
San Jose, CA 95112-5519
Tel: (408) 291-4204
Fax: (408) 291-4320

Appendix B Short Supply License Controls (Excerpt)

PETROLEUM AND PETROLEUM PRODUCTS SUBJECT TO SHORT SUPPLY LICENSING CONTROLS

Schedule B Number[1]	Commodity Description[2]	Unit of Quantity[3]
	Petroleum Licensed Only in Accordance With § 777.6(d)(1)	
	Group A	
475.0710	Crude petroleum, including reconstituted crude petroleum, tar sands and crude shale oil.	Bbl. Bbl.
	Petroleum Products Subject to Validated Licensing in Accordance with § 777.6(d)(2) and (3)	
	Group B	
475.2520	Aviation gasoline	Bbl.
	Group C	
475.2520	Gasoline, except aviation type	Bbl.
475.6781	Gasoline blending agents, hydrocarbon compounds only, n.s.p.f.	Bbl.
	Group D	
475.3000	Kerosene derived from petroleum, shale oil, or both (except motor fuel)	Bbl.
	Group E	
475.2530	Jet fuel, naphtha-type	Bbl.
475.2550	Jet fuel, kerosene-type	Bbl.
	Group F	
475.0720	Distillate fuel oils (light)	Bbl.
475.0740	Distillate fuel oils (No. 4 type)	Bbl.
475.2560	Other motor fuel (including tractor and stationary turbine fuel)	Bbl.
	Group G	
475.0760	Residual fuel oils (heavy fuel oils)	Bbl.
	Group K	
475.1545	Butane	Bbl.
	Group L	
475.1525	Propane	Bbl.
	Group M	
475.6720	Natural gas liquids, including LPG, n.s.p.f.	Bbl.
	Group N	
475.3500	Naphthas, derived from petroleum, shale oil, or both but excluding specialty naphthas which are packaged and exported in containers not exceeding 55 U.S. gallons per container.	Bbl.
	Petroleum Products Subject to Provisions of Either § 771.16 or § 777.6(d)(3)	
	Group Q	
415.2400	Helium	M Cu. Ft.
415.2900	Hydrogen	X
417.2000	Ammonia, aqueous	Cnt. ton
423.1010	Carbon dioxide and carbon monoxide	X
475.1505	Synthetic natural gas[4]	M Cu. Ft.
475.1515	Ethane with a minimum purity of 95 liquid volume percent	Bbl.

[1]Schedule B Nos. are provided only as a guide to proper completion of the Shipper's Export Declaration, Form No. 7625 V.
[2]Commodity description determines the product under control.
[3]Report commodities in units of quantity indicated.
[4]Natural gas and liquefied natural gas (L.N.G.), and synthetic natural gas commingles with natural gas, require export authorization from the U.S. Department of Energy. See § 770.10(g).

Appendix C   Nuclear Non-Proliferation: Special Country List

Afghanistan
Albania
Algeria
Andorra
Burma
Comoro Islands
Djibouti
Guyana
India
Iran
Iraq
Israel
Libya
Mauritania
Mozambique
Niger
Oman
Pakistan
St. Kitts
Tanzania
United Arab Emirates
Vanuatu
Zambia
Zimbabwe

Appendix D   Dual-Use Chemical and Biological Equipment: Regions, Countries, and Other Restrictions

Bulgaria
China (People's Republic of)
Cuba
Middle East
Myanmar (Burma)
North Korea
Romania
South Africa
Southwest Asia
The geographic area formerly known as the Union of Soviet Socialist
    Republics
Taiwan
Vietnam

Appendix E   Table of Denial Orders

Denial Orders Sorted by Name
Feb. 28, 1995

Name ....: Diago, Michel V.
Address ....: 1183 Calle del Arroyo, Sonoma, California 95476, United States
Effective Date ....: 19940907
Expiration Date .....: 20030225
Fed. Register Date .: 19940915
F.R. Citation ....: 59 F.R. 47299
Privileges Affected: General and validated licenses, all commodities, any destination, also exports to Canada

Name ....: Felber, Manfred R.
Address ....: FCI Milan, P.O. Box 9999, Milan, Michigan 48160, United States
Effective Date ....: 19941117
Expiration Date .....: 20040606
Fed. Register Date .: 19941201
F.R. Citation ....: 59 F.R. 61583
Privileges Affected: General and validated licenses, all commodities, any destination, also exports to Canada

Name ....: Felber, Manfred R.
Address ....: 1150 John Street, 13-15 Vienna, Austria
Effective Date ....: 19941117
Expiration Date .....: 20040606
Fed. Register Date .: 19941201
F.R. Citation ....: 59 F.R. 61583
Privileges Affected: General and validated licenses, all commodities, any destination, also exports to Canada

Name ....: Giangrandi, Augusto
Address ....: Via Roja 4863, Santiago, Chile
Effective Date ....: 19940915
Expiration Date .....: 19990915
Fed. Register Date .: 19940922
F.R. Citation ....: 59 F.R. 48595
Privileges Affected: General and validated licenses, all commodities, any destination, also exports to Canada
See Also ....: Valenzuela, Augusto Giacomo Giangrandi

Name ....: Govaerts, Franciscus B. individually and d/b/a Printlas Europa
Address ....: Van Lokvenstraat 117, 5731, Mierlo, Netherlands
Effective Date ....: 19910306
Expiration Date .....: 19960306
Fed. Register Date .: 19941110
F.R. Citation ....: 56 F.R. 10532; 59 F.R. 56033
Privileges Affected: General and validated licenses, all commodities, any destination, also exports to Canada
See Also ....: Printlas Europa

Name ....: Li, Jing Ping
Address ....: Federal Correctional Institution, Registry No. 25208—P.O. Box 1000, Petersburg, Virginia 23804-1000, United States
Effective Date ....: 19940907
Expiration Date .....: 20030917

Fed. Register Date .: 19940915
F.R. Citation ....: 59 F.R. 47300
Privileges Affected: General and validated licenses, all commodities, any destination, also exports to
    Canada

Name ....: Li, Jing Ping
Address ....: 125 Castillan Drive, Virginia Beach, Virginia 23462, United States
Effective Date ....: 19940907
Expiration Date .....: 20030917
Fed. Register Date .: 19940915
F.R. Citation ....: 59 F.R. 47300
Privileges Affected: General and validated licenses, all commodities, any destination, also exports to
    Canada

Name ....: Libra Electronics, Inc.
Address ....: 5255 Via Cartagena, Yorba Linda, California 92687, United States
Effective Date ....: 19941209
Expiration Date .....: 19961209
Fed. Register Date .: 19941219
F.R. Citation ....: 59 F.R. 65317
Privileges Affected: General and validated licenses, all commodities, any destination, also exports to
    Canada
See Also ....: Sharma, Rajeev individually and formerly doing business as Libra Electronics, Inc.

Name ....: Mega Computer Corporation
Address ....: 10840 Thornmint Road, San Diego, California 92127, United States
Effective Date ....: 19940810
Expiration Date .....: 20020323
Fed. Register Date .: 19940819
F.R. Citation ....: 59 F.R. 42804
Privileges Affected: General and validated licenses, all commodities, any destination, also exports to
    Canada

Name ....: Printlas Europa
Address ....: Van Lokvenstraat 117, 5731, Mierlo, Netherlands
Effective Date ....: 19910306
Expiration Date .....: 19960306
Fed. Register Date .: 19941110
F.R. Citation ....: 56 F.R. 10532; 59 F.R. 56033
Privileges Affected: General and validated licenses, all commodities, any destination, also exports to
    Canada
See Also ....: Govaerts, Franciscus B.

Name ....: Rosen, David R.
Address ....: 15 Sheffield Road, Natick, Massachusetts 01760, United States
Effective Date ....: 19940907
Expiration Date .....: 20000626
Fed. Register Date .: 19940915
F.R. Citation ....: 59 F.R. 47301
Privileges Affected: General and validated licenses, all commodities, any destination, also exports to
    Canada

Name ....: Shahamat, Vida
Address ....: 6318 Green Spring Avenue, Apartment 208, Baltimore, Maryland 21209, United
    States
Effective Date ....: 19940921
Expiration Date .....: 19970921

Fed. Register Date .: 19940929
F.R. Citation ....: 59 F.R. 49642
Privileges Affected: General and validated licenses, all commodities, any destination, also exports to
  Canada

Name ....: Sharma, Rajeev individually and formerly doing business as Libra Electronics, Inc.
Address ....: 5255 Via Cartagena, Yorba Linda, California 92687, United States
Effective Date ....: 19941209
Expiration Date .....: 19961209
Fed. Register Date .: 19941219
F.R. Citation ....: 59 F.R. 65317
Privileges Affected: General and validated licenses, all commodities, any destination, also exports to
  Canada
See Also ....: Libra Electronics, Inc.

Name ....: Teledyne Wah Chang, a Division of Teledyne Industries, Inc.
Address ....: 1600 N.E. Old Salem Road, P.O. Box 460, Albany, Oregon 97321-6990, United
  States
Effective Date ....: 19950301
Expiration Date .....: 19950531
Fed. Register Date .: 19950203
F.R. Citation ....: 60 F.R. 6696
Privileges Affected: General and validated licenses, all commodities, any destination, also exports to
  Canada

Name ....: Valenzuela, Augusto Giacomo Giangrandi
Address ....: Via Roja 4863, Santiago, Chile
Effective Date ....: 19940915
Expiration Date .....: 19990915
Fed. Register Date .: 19940922
F.R. Citation ....: 59 F.R. 48595
Privileges Affected: General and validated licenses, all commodities, any destination, also exports to
  Canada
See Also ....: Augusto Giangrandi

Name ....: Wu, Bin
Address ....: 201 North Palm Avenue, Virginia Beach, Virginia 23462, United States
Effective Date ....: 19940907
Expiration Date .....: 20030917
Fed. Register Date .: 19940915
F.R. Citation ....: 59 F.R. 47302
Privileges Affected: General and validated licenses, all commodities, any destination, also exports to
  Canada

Name ....: Wu, Bin
Address ....: Federal Correctional Institution, Schuylkil, Registry No. 25213-083, P.O. Box 759,
  Minersville, Pennsylvania 17954, United States
Effective Date ....: 19940907
Expiration Date .....: 20030917
Fed. Register Date .: 19940915
F.R. Citation ....: 59 F.R. 47302
Privileges Affected: General and validated licenses, all commodities, any destination, also exports to
  Canada

Name ....: Zhang, Peter
Address ....: Federal Correctional Institution, Registry No. 25241-083, P.O. Box 1000, Petersburg, Virginia 23804-1000, United States

Effective Date ....: 19940907
Expiration Date .....: 20030917
Fed. Register Date .: 19940915
F.R. Citation ....: 59 F.R. 47303
Privileges Affected: General and validated licenses, all commodities, any destination, also exports to
   Canada
See Also ....: Pinzhe Zhang

Name ....: Zhang, Peter
Address ....: 82 W. 49th Street, Apartment Á, Norfolk, Virginia 23518, United States
Effective Date ....: 19940907
Expiration Date .....: 20030917
Fed. Register Date .: 19940915
F.R. Citation ....: 59 F.R. 47303
Privileges Affected: General and validated licenses, all commodities, any destination, also exports to
   Canada
See Also ....: Pinzhe Zhang

Name ....: Zhang, Peter
Address ....: 82 W. 49th Street, Apartment A, Norfolk, Virginia 23518, United States
Effective Date ....: 19940907
Expiration Date .....: 20030917
Fed. Register Date .: 19940915
F.R. Citation ....: 59 F.R. 47303
Privileges Affected: General and validated licenses, all commodities, any destination, also exports to
   Canada
See Also ....: Peter Zhang

Name ....: Zhang, Pinzhe
Address ....: Federal Correctional Institution, Registry No. 25241-083, P.O. Box 1000, Petersburg, Virginia 23804-1000, United States
Effective Date ....: 19940907
Expiration Date .....: 20030917
Fed. Register Date .: 19940915
F.R. Citation ....: 59 F.R. 47303
Privileges Affected: General and validated licenses, all commodities, any destination, also exports to
   Canada
See Also ....: Peter Zhang

Appendix F   Export License Country Groups

Country Groups

Terms and Symbols:	
Freeworld:	T, V
Proscribed	Q, W, Y
Embargoed:	S, Z
^	GCT, GFW eligible
#	GFW eligible
+	GLX eligible
*	Other embargoed countries

Country Group Q

Romania

Country Group S

Libya

Country Group T

North America

Greenland #
Grenada #
Mexico (including Cozumel and
    Revilla Gigedo) #
Miquelon and St. Pierre Islands #

Central America and Caribbean

Anguilla #
Bahamas #
Barbados #
Belize #
Bermuda #
Cayman Islands #
Costa Rica #
Dominica #
Dominican Republic #
El Salvador #
French West Indies #
Guadaloupe #
Guatemala #
Haiti (including Gonave and Tortuga Islands) #
Honduras (including Bahia and Swan Islands) #
Jamaica #
Leeward and Windward Islands #
Martinique #
Montserrat #
Netherlands Antilles #
Nicaragua #
Panama #
Saint Kitts-Nevis #
Saint Lucia #

San Vincent and the Grenadines #
Turks & Caicos Islands #
Trinidad and Tobago #

South America

Argentina #
Bolivia #
Brazil #
Chile #
Colombia #
Ecuador (including the Galapagos Islands) #
Falkland Islands (Islas Malvinas) #
French Guiana (including Inini) #
Guyana #
Paraguay #
Peru #
Suriname #
Uruguay #
Venezuela #

Country Group V

Afghanistan #
Algeria #
Andorra #
Angola #
Anguilla #
Ashmore and Cartier Islands #
Australia ^
Austria ^
Bahrain #
Bangladesh #
Belgium ^
Benin #
Bhutan #
Bouvet Island #
Bosnia-Herzegovina #
Botswana #
British Indian Ocean Territory #
Brunel #
Burkina Faso (Upper Volta) #
Burundl #
Cameroon #
Cape Verde #

Central African Republic #
Chad #
China, People's Republic of +
Christmas Island #
Cocos Island #
Cook Islands #
Coral Sea Islands Territory #
Comoros #
Congo, Democratic Republic of the #
Congo, Republic of the #
Croatia #
Czech Republic
Cyprus #
Denmark ^
Djiboutl, Republic of #
Egypt #
Equatorial Guinea #
Ethiopia #
Faroe Islands #
Federal Republic of Germany ^
Fiji #
Finland ^
France ^
French Polynesia #
French Southern and Antarctic Lands #
Gabon #
Gambia, The #
Ghana #
Gibraltar #
Greece ^
Guernsey #
Guinea #
Guinea-Bissau #
Heard Island and McDonald Islands #
Hong Kong ^
Hungary #
Iceland #
India #
Indonesia #
Iran #
Iraq #
Ireland ^
Israel #
Italy ^
Ivory Coast #
Jan Mayen #
Japan ^
Jersey #
Jordan #
Kenya #
Kiribatl #
Korea, Republic of #
Kuwait #
Lebanon #
Lesotho #
Liberia #
Liechtenstein #
Luxembourg ^
Macau #
Macedonia #

Madagascar #
Malawi #
Malaysia #
Maldives #
Mali #
Malta #
Man, Isle of #
Mauritania #
Mauritius #
Martinique #
Monaco #
Montenegro *
Montserrat #
Morocco #
Mozambique #
Myanmar (Burma) #
Namibia #
Nauru #
Nepal #
Netherlands ^
New Caledonia #
New Zealand ^
Niue #
Nigeria #
Norfolk Island #
Norway ^
Oman #
Pakistan #
Papua New Guinea #
Philippines #
Pitcairn Islands #
Poland
Portugal ^
Qatar #
Reunion #
Rwanda #
Saint Helena #
San Marino #
Sao Tome and Principe,
    Democratic Republic of #
Saudi Arabia #
Senegal #
Serbia *
Seychelles #
Sierra Leone #
Singapore #
Slovak Republic
Slovenia #
Solomon Islands #
Somalia #
South Africa, Republic of #
Spain ^
Sri Lanka #
Sudan #
Svalbard #
Swaziland #
Sweden ^
Switzerland ^
Syria
Taiwan #

Tanzania #
Thailand #
Togo #
Tokelau #
Tonga #
Tunisia #
Turkey ^
Tuvalu #
Uganda #
United Arab Emirates #
United Kingdom ^
Vanuatu #
Vatican City #
Wallis and Futuna #
Western Sahara #
Western Samoa #
Yemen #
Yugoslavia (Serbia & Montenegro) *
Zambia #
Zimbabwe #

Azerbaijan +
Belarus +
Bulgaria +
Cambodia +
Estonia +
Georgia +
Kazakhstan +
Kyrgystan +
Laos +
Latvia +
Lithuania +
Moldova +
Mongolia +
Russia +
Tajikistan +
Turkmenistan +
Ukraine +
Uzbekistan +
Vietnam +

Country Group W

Reserved +

Country Group Y

Albania +
Armenia +

Country Group Z

Cuba
North Korea

Appendix G   Commerce Control List (Excerpt)

CATEGORY 4—COMPUTERS

Note 1: Computers, related equipment or "software" performing telecommunications or "local area network" functions must also be evaluated against the performance characteristics of the telecommunications entries in Category 5.

N.B. 1: Control units that directly interconnect the buses or channels of central processing units, "main storage" or disk controllers, are not regarded as telecommunications equipment described in the telecommunications entries in Category 5.

N.B. 2: For the control status of "software" that provides routing or switching of "datagram" or "fast select" packets (i.e., packet by packet route selection) or for "software" specially designed for packet switching, see the telecommunications entries in Category 5.

Note 2: Computers, related equipment or "software" performing cryptographic, cryptanalytic, certifiable multi-level security or certifiable user isolation functions, or that limit electromagnetic compatibility (EMC), must also be evaluated against the performance characteristics of the "information security" entries in Category 5.

A. EQUIPMENT, ASSEMBLIES & COMPONENTS

4A01A Electronic computers and related equipment, as follows, and "assemblies" and specially designed components therefor.

Requirements

Validated License Required: QSTVWYZ

Unit: Computers and peripherals in number; parts and accessories in $ value

Reason For Control: NS, MT, NP, FP (see *Notes*)

GLV: $5000 for 4A01.a *only;* $0 for 4A01.b

GCT: Yes, except MT (See *Notes*) and except supercomputers as defined in 776.11(a) (no supercomputer restriction for Japan)

GFW: No

Notes: 1. MT controls apply to 4A01.a.

2. NP controls apply to computers with a CTP exceeding 500 Mtops to countries listed in Supplement No. 4 to part 778.

3. FP controls apply to all destinations except Japan, for supercomputers (See § 776.11).

List of Items Controlled

Electornic computers and related equipment, as follows, and "assemblies" and specially designed components therefor:

a. Specially designed to have either of the following characteristics:

1. Rated for operation at an ambient temperature below 228 K (− 45° C) or above 358 K (85° C);

Note: The temperature limits in 4A01.a.1. do not apply to computers specially designed for civil automobile and train engine applications.

4. Radiation-hardened to exceed any of the following specifications:

a.	Total Dose	5×10^6 Rads (Si)
b.	Dose Rate Upset	5×10^4 Rads (Si)/sec
c.	Single Event Upset	1×10^{-7} Error/bit/day; *or*

Note: Equipment designed or rated for transient ionizing radiation is controlled by the ITAR.

b. Having characteristics or performing functions exceeding the limits in the "information security" entries in Category 5.

Related ECCNs: See 4A21B for MT controls on electronic computers and related equipment, not controlled by 4A01A, that are designed or modified for airborne applications.

4A02A "Hybrid computers," as follows, and "assemblies" and specially designed components therefor.

Requirements

Validated License Required: QSTVWYZ

Unit: Computers and peripherals in number; parts and accessories in $ value

Reason For Control: NS, MT, NP, FP (see *Notes*)

GLV: $5000

GCT: Yes, *except* MT (see *Notes*) and except supercomputers as defined in § 776.11(a) (no supercomputer restrictions for Japan)

GFW: No

Notes: 1. MT controls apply to hybrid computers combined with specially designed "software," for modeling, simulation, or design integration of complete rocket systems and unmanned air vehicle systems described in § 787.7.

2. NP controls apply to computers with a CTP exceeding 500 Mtops to countries listed in Supplement No. 4 to part 778.

3. FP controls apply to all destinations, except Japan, for supercomputers (see § 776.11).

List of Items Controlled

"Hybrid computers," as follows, and "assemblies" and specially designed components therefor:

a. Containing "digital computers" controlled by 4A03;

b. Containing analog-to-digital or digital-to-analog converters having both of the following characteristics:

1. 32 channels or more; *and*

2. A resolution of 14 bits (plus sign bit) or more with a conversion rate of 200,000 conversions/s or more.

4A03A "Digital computers," "assemblies," and related equipment therefor, as described in this entry, and specially designed components therefor.

Requirements

Validated License Required: QSTVWYZ

Unit: Computers and peripherals in number; parts and accessories in $ value

Reason For Control: NS, MT, NP, FP (see *Notes*)

GLV: $5000

GCT: Yes, *except* MT and FP, and except supercomputers as defined in § 776.11(a) (no supercomputer restriction for Japan); (see *Notes*)

GFW: Yes, *except* MT and FP (see *Notes*), for computers with a CTP not exceeding 1,000 Mtops (500 Mtops for eligible countries listed in Supp. 4 to part 778) and specially designed components therefor, exported separately or as part of a system, and related equipment therefor when exported with these computers as part of a system.

N.B. 1: General License *GFW* is *not* available for the export of commodities that the exporter knows will be used to:

    a. Enhance the performance capability (i.e., CTP) of a computer to the "supercomputer" level; or

    b. Enhance the performance capability of a "supercomputer" (see § 776.11 for definition of "supercomputer").

N.B. 2: To determine whether General License *GFW* may be used to export related equipment controlled under another entry in the CCL, consult the *GFW* paragraph under the Requirements heading of the appropriate entry.

Notes: 1. MT controls apply to digital computers used as ancillary equipment for test facilities and equipment that are controlled by 9B05 or 9B06.

    2. NP controls apply to computers with a CTP exceeding 500 Mtops to countries listed in Supplement No. 4 to part 778.

    3. FP controls apply to computers for computerized fingerprint equipment to all destinations except Australia, Japan, New Zealand and members of NATO.

    4. FP controls apply to all destinations, except Japan, for supercomputers (see § 776.11).

    5. FP controls apply to Iran and Syria for computers controlled by 4A03A or 4A94F (i.e., computers with a CTP of 6 Mtops or greater). See § 785.4(d)(1).

List of Items Controlled

Note 1: 4A03 includes vector processors, array processors, digital signal processors, logic processors, and equipment for "image enhancement" or "signal processing."

Note 2: The control status of the "digital computers" or related equipment described in A403 is governed by the control status of other equipment or systems provided:

    a. The "digital computers" or related equipment are essential for the operation of the other equipment or systems;

    b. The "digital computers" or related equipment are not a "principal element" of the other equipment or systems; *and*

N.B. 1: The control status of "signal processing" or "image enhancement" equipment and specially designed for other equipment with functions limited to those required for the other equipment is determined by the control status of the other equipment even it it exceeds the "principal element" criterion.

N.B. 2: For the control status of "digital computers" or related equipment for telecommunications equipment, see the telecommunications entries in Category 5.

    c. The technology for the "digital computers" and related equipment is governed by 4E.

"Digital computers," "assemblies," and related equipment therefor, as follows, and specially designed components therefor.

    a. Designed or modified for "fault tolerance";

Note: For the purposes of 4A03.b, "digital computers" and related equipment are not considered to be designed or modified for "fault tolerance," if they use:

    1. Error detection or correction algorithms in "main storage";

    2. The interconnection of two "digital computers" so that, if the active central processing unit fails, an idling but mirroring central processing unit can continue the system's functioning;

    3. The interconnection of two central processing units by data channels or by use of shared storage to permit one central processing unit to perform other work until the second central processing unit fails, at which time the first central processing unit takes over in order to continue the system's functioning; *or*

    4. The synchronization of two central processing units by "software" so that one central processing unit recognizes when the other central processing unit fails and recovers tasks from the falling unit.

    b. "Digital computers" having a "composite theoretical performance" ("CTP") exceeding 260 million composite theoretical operations per second (Mtops);

    c. "Assemblies" specially designed or modified to be capable of enhancing performance by aggregation of "computing elements" ("CEs"), so that the "CTP" of the aggregation exceeds the limit in 4A03.b.

Note 1: 4A03.d applies only to "assemblies" and programmable interconnections not exceeding the limits in 4A03.b, when shipped as unintegrated "assemblies." It does not apply to "assemblies" inherently limited by nature of their design for use as related equipment controlled by 4A03.d to 4A03.f.

Note 2: 4A03.d does not control "assemblies" specially designed for a product or family of products whose maximum configuration does not exceed the limits of 4A03.b.

    d. Graphics accelerators or graphics coprocessors exceeding a "3-D Vector Rate" of 1,600,000;

    e. Equipment performing analog-to-digital or digital-to-analog conversions exceeding the limits in 3A01.a.5;

    f. Equipment containing "terminal interface equipment" exceeding the limits in 5A02.c;

Note: For the purposes of 4A03.f, "terminal interface equipment" includes "local area network" interfaces, modems and other communications interfaces. "Local area network" interfaces are evaluated as "network access controllers."

    g. Equipment, specially designed to provide for the external interconnection of "digital computers" or associated equipment, that allows communications at data rates exceeding 80 Mbytes/s.

> Note: 4A03.g does not control internal interconnection equipment (e.g., backplanes, buses) or passive interconnections equipment.

4A04A Computers, as follows, and specially designed related equipment, "assemblies" and components therefor.

Requirements

Validated License Required: QSTVWYZ

Unit: Computers and peripherals in number; parts and accessories in $ value

Reason For Control: NS

GLV: $5000

GCT: Yes

GFW: No

List of Items Controlled

   a. "Systolic array computers";
   b. "Neural computers";
   c. "Optical computers."

4A21B Analog computers, digital computers, or digital differential analyzers designed or modified for use in "missiles" not controlled by 4A01 and having either of the following characteristics: rated for continuous operation at temperatures from below −45° C to above +55° C; or designed as ruggedized or "radiation hardened."

Requirements

Validated License Required: QSTVWYZ

- *Unit:* Number

Reason For Control: MT

GLV: $0

GCT: No

GFW: No

4A80C Computers for fingerprint equipment, n.e.s.

Requirements

Validated License Required: QSTVWYZ, except Australia, Japan; New Zealand, and NATO

Unit: Number

Reason for Control: FP (See *Note*)

GLV: No

GCT: No

GFW: No

> Note: FP controls apply to the items described in this entry because they can be used for crime control and detection purposes. Applications will generally receive favorable consideration on a case-by-case basis unless there is evidence that the government of the importing country may have violated internationally recognized human rights.

4A94F Computers, "assemblies" and related equipment not controlled by 4A01, 4A02, or 4A03, and specially designed components therefor.

Requirements

Validated License Required: SZ, Iran, Syria

Unit: Computers and peripherals in number; parts and accessories in $ value

Reason for Control: FP

GLV: $0

GCT: No

GFW: No

List of Items Controlled

    a. Electronic computers and related equipment, and "assemblies" and specially designed components therefor, rated for operation at an ambient temperature above 343 K (70° C), but not above 358 K (85° C);

    b. "Digital computers" not controlled by 4A03 having a "composite theoretical performance" ("CTP") equal to or greater than 6 million theoretical operations per second (Mtops);

    c. "Assemblies" not controlled by 4A03 that are specially designed or modified to enhance performance by aggregation of "computing elements" ("CEs"), as follows:

        1. Designed to be capable of aggregation in configurations of 16 or more "computing elements" ("CEs"); *or*

        2. Having a sum of maximum data rates on all channels available for connection to associated processors exceeding 40 million Bytes/s;

> Note 1: 4A94.c applies only to "assemblies" and programmable interconnections with a "composite theoretical performance" ("CTP") not exceeding 12.5 million theoretical operations per second (Mtops), when shipped as unintegrated "assemblies." It does not apply to "assemblies" inherently limited by nature of their design for use as related equipment controlled by 4A03 or 4A94.

> Note 2: 4A94.c does not control any "assembly" specially designed for a product or family of products with a maximum configuration that does not exceed a "CTP" of 12.5 Mtops.

    d. Disk drives and solid state storage equipment:

        1. Magnetic, erasable optical or magneto-optical disk drives with a "maximum bit transfer rate" exceeding 25 million bit/s;

        2. Solid state storage equipment, other than "main storage" (also known as solid state disks or RAM disks), with a "maximum bit transfer rate" exceeding 36 million bit/s;

    e. Input/output control units designed for use with equipment controlled by 4A94.d;

    f. Equipment for "signal processing" or "image enhancement", not controlled by 4A03, having a "composite theoretical performance" ("CTP") exceeding 8.5 million theoretical operations per second (Mtops);

    g. Graphics accelerators or graphics coprocessors, not controlled by 4A03, that exceeds a "3-D vector rate" of 400,000 or, if supported by 2-D vectors only, a "2-D vector rate" of 600,000;

> Note 1: The provisions of 4A94.g do not apply to work stations designed for and limited to:
>
>   a. Graphic arts (e.g., printing, publishing); *and*
>
>   b. The display of two-dimensional vectors.

    h. Color displays or monitors having more than 120 resolvable elements per cm in the direction of the maximum pixel density;

> Note 1: 4A94.h does not control displays or monitors not specially designed for electronic computers.
>
> Note 2: Displays specially designed for air traffic control (ATC) systems are treated as specially designed components for ATC systems under Category 6.

    i. Equipment containing "terminal interface equipment" exceeding the limits of 5A91F.

> Note: For the purposes of 4A94.h, "terminal interface equipment" includes "local area network" interfaces, modems and other communications interfaces. "Local area network" interfaces are evaluated as "network access controllers."

4A96G Other computer equipment, "assemblies" and components, n.e.s.

Requirements

• *Validated License Required:* SZ

Unit: Computers and peripherals in number; parts and accessories in $ value

Reason For Control: FP

GLV: $0

GCT: No

GFW: No

B. TEST, INSPECTION & PRODUCTION EQUIPMENT

4B94F Equipment for the "development" and "production" of magnetic and optical storage equipment, as described in this entry.

Requirements

Validated License Required: SZ, Iran, Syria

Unit: $ value

Reason for Control: FP

GLV: $0

GCT: No

GFW: No

List of Items Controlled

a. Equipment specially designed for the application of magnetic coating to controlled non-flexible (rigid) magnetic or magneto-optical media;

> Note: 4B94F does not control general-purpose "sputtering" equipment.

b. "Stored program controlled" equipment specially designed for monitoring, grading, exercising, or testing controlled rigid magnetic media;

c. Equipment specially designed for the "production" or alignment of heads or head/disk assemblies for controlled rigid magnetic and magneto-optical storage, and electro-mechanical or optical components therefor.

4B96G Computer test, production and inspection equipment, n.e.s.

Requirements

Validated License Required: SZ

Unite: $ value

Reason For Control: FP

GLV: $0

GCT: No

GFW: No

Appendix H   Authorities Administering IC/DV Systems

AUTHORITIES ADMINISTERING IMPORT CERTIFICATE/DELIVERY VERIFICATION SYSTEM IN FOREIGN COUNTRIES[1]

Country	IC/DV Authorities	System Administered[2]
Australia	Director, Technology Transfer and Analysis, Industry Policy and Operations Division, Department of Defense, Russell Office, Canberra, A.C.T. 2600	IC/DV
Austria	Bundesministerium fur Handel Gewerbe und Industrie Landstr. Haupstr. 55-57, Vienna 1031	IC/DV
Belgium	Ministere Des Affaires Economiques Office Central des Contingenta et Licences 24-26 Rue De Mot, Bruxelles-1040	IC/DV
China, People's Republic of	Technology Import and Export Department MOFERT No. 2 Dong Chang An Street Bejing, PRC Telephone: 553031 Telex: 22478 MFERTCN	PRC End-User Certificate
Czech Republic	Federal Ministry of Foreign Trade Head of Licensing Politickych Veznu 20 112 49 Praha 1	IC/DV
Denmark	Handelsministeriets Licenskontor Kampmannsgade 1, DK 1604, Copenhagen V IC's also issued by Danmarks Nationalbank Holmens Kanal 17, Copenhagen K Custom-houses	IC/DV DV
Finland	Hensingin Pilritullikamari, Kanavakatu 6 (or P.O. Box 168) 00161 Helsinki	ID/DV
France	Ministere de l'Economie et des Finances Direction Generale des Douanes et Drolta Indirects Division des Affaires Juridiques et Contentleuses 8, Rue de la Tour des Dames, Bureau D/3, 75436 Paris Codex 09	IC/DV
Germany	Bundesamt fur gewerbliche Wirtschaft Frankfurter Strasse 29-81 6236 Eschborn /Ts	IC/DV
Greece	Banque de Greece, Direction des Transactions Commerciales avec l'Etranger Athens	IC/DV
Hong Kong	Trade Department, Ocean Centre, Canton Road, Tsimshatsul, Kowloon, Hong Kong	IC/DV
Hungary	Ministry of International Economic Relations Export Control Office 1054 Budapest P.O. Box 728 H-1365, Hold Str. 17	IC/DV
India	Deputy Chief Controller of Imports and Exports Udyog Bhawan, Maulana Azad Road New Delhi—11011—: For small scale industries and entities, and those not elsewhere specified	Indian Import Certificate
	Directorate General of Technical Development, Udyog Bhawan, Maulana Azad Road, New Delhi—11011—: For the "organized" sector, except for computers and related equipment	Indian Import Certificate
	Defense Research and Development Organization Room No. 224, "B" Wing Sena Bhawan, New Delhi—110011—: For Defense organizations	Indian Import Certificate
	Department of Electronics, Lok Nayak Bhawan, New Delhi—110003—: For computers and related electronic items	Indian Import Certificate
	Assistant Director, Embassy of India, Commerce Wing, 2536 Massachusetts Ave. NW, Washington, D.C. 20008—: On behalf of any of the above	Indian Import Certificate
Ireland, Republic of	Department of Industry, Trade, Commerce and Tourism, Frederick House, South Frederick Street, Dublin 2	IC/DV
Italy	Ministero del Commercio con l'Estero Direzione Generale delle Importazioni e delle Esportazioni, Div. III, Rome Dogana Italiana (of the town where takes place)	IC DV
Japan	Ministered of International Trade and Industry in Fukuoka, Hiroshima, Kanmon (Kitakyushu-shi), Kobe, Nagoya, Osaka, Sapporo, Sendai, Shikoku (Takamatsu-shi), Shimizu, Tokyo, and Yokohama	IC
	Japanese Customs Offices	DV

Country	IC/DV Authorities	System Administered[2]
Korea, Republic of	Trade Administration Division Trade Bureau Ministry of Trade and Industry Jungang-Dong, Kyonggi-Do, Building 3 Kwachon, Republic of Korea	IC
	Republic of Korea Customs House	DV
Liechtenstein	Swiss Federal Office for Foreign Economic Affairs, Import and Export Division Zieglerstrasse 30, CH-3003 Bern	IC/DV
Luxembourg	Office des Licences Avenue de la Liberte, 10	IC/DV
Netherlands	Centrale Dienst voor In-en Ultvoer Engelse Kamp 2, Groningen	IC/DV
New Zealand	Comptroller for Customs P.O. Box 2218 Wellington, New Zealand	IC/DV
Norway	Handelsdepartmentet Direktoratet for Eksport-og-Importregulering Fr. Nansens plass 5, Oslo	IC/DV
Pakistan	Chief Controller of Imports and Exports—5, Civic Center Islamabad, Pakistan	IC
	Joint Science Advisor, Ministry of Science and Technology, Secretariat Block '8', Islamabad, Pakistan	DV
Poland	Ministry of Foreign Economic Relations Department of Commodities and Services Plac Trzech Krzyzy 5, Room 358 00-507 Warsaw	IC/DV
Portugal	Reparticao do Comercio Externo Direccao-Geral do Comercio Secretaria de Estado do Comercio Ministerio da Economia, Lisbon	IC/DV
Singapore	Controller of Imports and Exports, Trade Development Board, World Trade Centre, 1 Maritime Square, Telok Blangah Road, Singapore	IC/DV
Slovak Republic	Ministry of Foreign Affairs Licensing-Registration Department Spitalska 8, 813 15 Bratislava Slovak Republic	IC
Spain	Secretary of State for Commerce Paseo la Cistellana 162, Madrid 28046	IC/DV
Sweden	The Association of Swedish Chambers of Commerce and Industry P.O. Box 16050, S-103 22 Stockholm Office: Vastra Tradegardsgatan 9	IC/DV
Switzerland	Swiss Federal Office for Foreign Economic Affairs, Import and Export Division, Zieglerstrasse 30 CH-3003 Bern.	IC/DV
Taiwan (Hsinchu Science-based Industrial Park)	Science-based Industrial Park Administration No. 2 Hsin Ann Road Hsinchu, Taiwan, R.O.C.	IC/DV
Turkey	Ministry of Commerce, Department of Foreign Commerce, Ankara	IC
	Head Customs Office at the point of entry	DV
United Kingdom	Department of Trade and Industry Export Licensing Branch Millbank Tower Millbank London, SW1P 4QU	IC
	H.M. Customs and Excise, § 22 King's Beam House, Mark Lane London, E.C. 3	DV
Yugoslavia	Yugoslav Chamber of Economy, Knez Mihailova 10, Belgrade.	Yugoslav End-Use Certificate

[1]Facsimilies of Import Certificates and Delivery Verifications issued by each of these countries may be inspected at the Bureau of Export Administration Western Regional Office, 3300 Irvine Avenue, Suite 345, Newport Beach, California 92660-3198 of at any U.S. Department of Commerce District Office (see listing in Commerce Office Addresses section of these regulations) or at the Office of Export Licensing, Room 1099D, U.S. Department of Commerce, 14th Street and Pennsylvania Avenue, N.W., Washington, D.C. 20230.

[2]IC—Import Certificates and/or DV—Delivery Verification.

Form 3.01   Individual validated license.

EXPORT LICENSE NO.: A030043	UNITED STATES DEPARTMENT OF COMMERCE
VALIDATED: 7/19/88	BUREAU OF EXPORT ADMINISTRATION P.O. BOX 273 BEN FRANKLIN STATION
EXPIRATION DATE: 7/31/90	WASHINGTON, D.C. 20044

CONSIGNEE IN COUNTRY OF ULTIMATE DESTINATION:

ABU DHABI TRADING ESTABLISHMENT
2345 LIAM DUK WAY
ABU DHABI, UNITED ARAB EMIRATES

LICENSEE:

A P CIRCUIT CORPORATION
513 EAST 86 STREET
NEW YORK, NY 10028

APPLICANT'S REFERENCE NO.: A030043

PURCHASER:

AEG TELEFUNKEN
STEINHOEFT 9
HAMBURG, WEST GERMANY

INTERMEDIATE CONSIGNEE:

ZINCOR INFOSYSTEMS, INC.
4456 PASQUATCH LET
BOMBAY, INDIA

PROCESSING CODE: CS

COMMODITIES:

QUANTITY	DESCRIPTION	ECCN	UNIT PRICE	TOTAL PRICE
50 EACH	MODEL 2345 6.50 MATH COPROCESSORS	1565	14000.00	700000.00
2 EACH	MCS68 3.40 HUMPHREY ANALYZERS	1565	30000.00	60000.00

VOID

                                          TOTAL: 760000

THE EXPORT ADMINISTRATION REGULATIONS REQUIRE YOU TO TAKE THE FOLLOWING ACTIONS WHEN EXPORTING UNDER THE AUTHORITY OF THIS LICENSE.

A.   RECORD THE EXPORT CONTROL COMMODITY NUMBER IN PARENTHESES DIRECTLY BELOW THE CORRESPONDING SCHEDULE B NUMBER ON EACH SHIPPERS EXPORT DECLARATION (SED).

B.   RECORD YOUR LICENSE NUMBER IN THE COMMODITY DESCRIPTION COLUMN ON EACH SED.

C.   PLACE A DESTINATION CONTROL STATEMENT ON ALL BILLS OF LADING, AIRWAY BILLS, AND COMMERCIAL INVOICES.

THIS LICENSE AUTHORIZES THE LICENSEE TO CARRY OUT THE EXPORT TRANSACTION DESCRIBED ON THE LICENSE (INCLUDING ALL ATTACHMENTS). IT MAY NOT BE TRANSFERRED WITHOUT PRIOR WRITTEN APPROVAL OF THE BUREAU OF EXPORT ADMINISTRATION. THIS LICENSE HAS BEEN GRANTED IN RELIANCE ON REPRESENTATIONS MADE BY THE LICENSEE AND OTHERS IN CONNECTION WITH THE APPLICATION FOR EXPORT AND IS EXPRESSLY SUBJECT TO ANY CONDITIONS STATED ON THE LICENSE, AS WELL AS ALL APPLICABLE EXPORT CONTROL LAWS, REGULATIONS, RULES, AND ORDERS. THIS LICENSE IS SUBJECT TO REVISION, SUSPENSION, OR REVOCATION WITHOUT PRIOR NOTICE.

Form 3.02   Application for export license.

FORM BXA-622P APPLICATION FOR EXPORT LICENSE

A full-page reproduction of the U.S. Department of Commerce, Bureau of Export Administration, Application for Export License form (FORM BXA-622P). Key visible fields include:

- **BB** FORM BXA-622P (REV. 9-89) FORM APPROVED: OMB No. 0694-0005
- **U.S. DEPARTMENT OF COMMERCE — Bureau of Export Administration — APPLICATION FOR EXPORT LICENSE**
- **DATE RECEIVED (Leave Blank)**
- 1. CONTACT PERSON — Name — Telephone Number
- 2a. FORM(S) ATTACHED: BXA-622P-A, BXA-622P-B, BXA-622P, TECH. SPECS.
- 2b. DOCUMENT(S) ON FILE WITH APPLICANT: ITA-629P, LETTER OF ASSURANCE, OTHER
- **APPLICATION CONTROL NUMBER** — This is NOT an export license number. **C**
- I.C. and/or END-USE CERTIFICATE(S) COUNTRY / COUNTRY
- 3. RESUBMISSION OF CASE NUMBER
- 4. SPECIAL PURPOSE
- 5. APPLICANT — ADDRESS — CITY — STATE — ZIP CODE
- 7. PURCHASER — Same as Item #5 — ADDRESS — CITY — POSTAL CODE — COUNTRY — TELEPHONE NO.
- 6. ULTIMATE CONSIGNEE — ADDRESS — CITY — POSTAL CODE — COUNTRY — TELEPHONE NO.
- 8. INTERMEDIATE CONSIGNEE — Same as Item #7 — ADDRESS — CITY — POSTAL CODE — COUNTRY — TELEPHONE NO.
- 9 (a) QUANTITY — (b) COMMODITY PDR — MANUFACTURER'S DESCRIPTION OF COMMODITY (Place model # before description, followed by a colon. End description with ECCN Paragraph Reference) — PROCESSING CODE — (c) ECCN — (d) NET VALUE U.S. DOLLARS: UNIT PRICE / TOTAL PRICE
- TOTAL OF ENTIRE TRANSACTION $
- 10. PARTY OTHER THAN APPLICANT AUTHORIZED TO RECEIVE LICENSE — ADDRESS — CITY — STATE — ZIP CODE
- 11. MANUFACTURER(S)
- 12. SPECIFIC END-USE OF COMMODITIES OR TECHNICAL DATA BY CONSIGNEE IN ITEM #6 ABOVE
- 13. END-USER if different from Item #6 — NAME — ADDRESS — CITY — POSTAL CODE — COUNTRY — TELEPHONE NO.
- 15. ADDITIONAL INFORMATION
- 14. FOREIGN AVAILABILITY SUBMISSION ATTACHED — YES / NO
- 16. APPLICANT'S CERTIFICATION: I hereby make application for a license to export...
- SIGN HERE IN INK — (SIGNATURE of person authorized to execute this application) — Type or Print (NAME and TITLE of person whose signature appears on line to the left) — DATE OF APPLICATION
- 17. ORDER PARTY'S CERTIFICATION (See §372.8 (b) of the Export Administration Regulations)...
- Type or Print (Order Party) — SIGN HERE IN INK (Signature of Person authorized to sign for the order party) — Type or Print (NAME and TITLE of person whose signature appears on line to the left) — **BB**
- This license application and any license issued pursuant thereto are expressly subject to all rules and regulations of the Department of Commerce...
- **ORIGINAL**
- USCOMM-DC 86-84002

General Instructions Regarding
Form BXA-622P

FORM BXA-622P
(REV. 6-88)
FORM APPROVED: OMB No. 0694-0005

U.S. DEPARTMENT OF COMMERCE
Bureau of Export Administration

Application for Export License

GENERAL INSTRUCTIONS

A.   **WHEN TO USE THIS FORM.** Use this form to apply to the U.S. Department of Commerce for a validated license, when required, as authorization to export commodities or technical data.

B.   **WHO MAY APPLY.** A license application may be made only by a person subject to the jurisdiction of the United States who is in fact the exporter, or by his duly authorized agent. An application may be made on behalf of a person not subject to the jurisdiction of the United States by an authorized agent in the United States, who then becomes the applicant.

C.   **WHAT TO SUBMIT.** Submit everything in this packet except this cover sheet and the last page. Do *not* separate the remaining parts of the packet.

D.   **DUPLICATE APPLICATIONS.** Do not submit an application for export license if a pending application covers the same transaction.

E.   **COMPLIANCE WITH REGULATIONS.** Instructions for filling out and filing an application for export license, and information on other export control matters may be found in the Export Administration Regulations. An applicant must comply with the provisions relating to individual or other validated licenses and special provisions of the Export Administration Regulations relating to the desired export. These regulations are codified at 15 C.F.R. 368 et seq. Changes to the regulations are published in the Federal Register. The Department of Commerce also publishes a looseleaf version to the Regulations. Supplements to the Regulations are issued as Export Administration Bulletins. Subscription to the Export Administration Regulations, including the Bulletins may be placed with the Superintendent of Documents, U.S. Government Printing Office, Washington, D.C. 20402.

F.   **LICENSEE:** The applicant to whom the license is issued becomes the licensee and will be held strictly accountable for the use of the license. Exports under a validated license may be made only for the account of the licensee.

G.   **ASSISTANCE AND COPIES OF APPLICATION.** For assistance regarding export matters, consult with the Exporter Assistance Staff on (202) 377-4811 or any District Office of the International Trade Administration. You can obtain small quantities of this form from a District Office. To order large quantities write to the following address and include a completed address label. Operational Support Staff, P.O. Box 273, Washington, D.C. 20044.

MAIL APPLICATION TO:	COURIER DELIVERIES TO:
OFFICE OF EXPORT LICENSING P.O. BOX 273 WASHINGTON, D.C. 20044	OFFICE OF EXPORT LICENSING ROOM 2705 14TH ST. & PENNSYLVANIA AVE., N.W. WASHINGTON, D.C. 20230

INCOMPLETE APPLICATIONS WILL BE RETURNED FOR THE NECESSARY INFORMATION AND/OR DOCUMENTATION.
DETACH THIS SHEET AT PERFORATION. SEE SPECIFIC INSTRUCTIONS ON REVERSE SIDE.

Export Administration

INSTRUCTIONS FOR COMPLETING AND FILING FORM BXA-622P

Application for Export License

This application will be processed using an Optical Character Recognition (OCR) system. Type using 10 or 12 pitch. Do not use script type faces. Information must be placed within the space provided. *Do not go through or outside lines.* Failure to complete the form as requested will significantly delay processing of the application.

PROVIDE COMPLETE NAMES, ADDRESSES AND TELEPHONE NUMBERS FOR ITEMS 5, 6, 7, 8, 10 & 13.

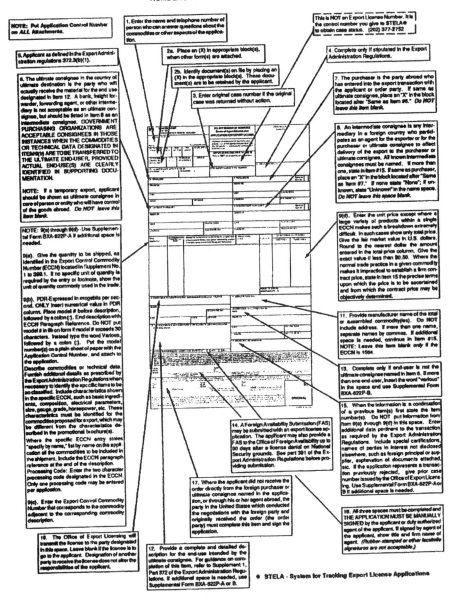

NOTE: Put Application Control Number on *ALL* Attachments.

1. Enter the name and telephone number of person who can answer questions about the commodities or other aspects of the application.

This is NOT an Export License Number. It is the control number you give to STELA® to obtain case status. (202) 377-2752

5. Applicant as defined in the Export Administration regulations 372.3(b)(1).

2a. Place an (X) in appropriate block(s), when other form(s) are attached.

4. Complete only if stipulated in the Export Administration Regulations.

6. The ultimate consignee in the country of ultimate destination is the party who will actually receive the material for the end use designated in Item 12. A bank, freight forwarder, forwarding agent, or other intermediary is not acceptable as an ultimate consignee, but should be listed in Item 8 as an intermediate consignee. GOVERNMENT PURCHASING ORGANIZATIONS ARE ACCEPTABLE CONSIGNEES IN THOSE INSTANCES WHEN THE COMMODITIES OR TECHNICAL DATA DESIGNATED IN ITEM 9(h) ARE TO BE TRANSFERRED TO THE ULTIMATE END-USER, PROVIDED ACTUAL END-USE(S) ARE CLEARLY IDENTIFIED IN SUPPORTING DOCUMENTATION.

NOTE: If a temporary export, applicant should be shown as ultimate consignee in care of person or entity who will have control of the goods abroad. *Do NOT leave this item blank.*

NOTE: 9(a) through 9(d)—Use Supplemental Form BXA-622P-A if additional space is needed.

9(a). Give the quantity to be shipped, as identified in the Export Control Commodity Number (ECCN) located in Supplement No. 1 to 399.1. If no specific unit of quantity is required by the entry or footnote, show the unit of quantity commonly used in the trade.

9(b). PDR-Expressed in megabits per second. ONLY insert numerical value in PDR column. Place model # before description, followed by a colon (:). End description with ECCN Paragraph Reference. Do NOT put model # in 9b on form if model # exceeds 30 characters. Instead type the word Various, followed by a colon (:). Put the model number(s) on a plain sheet of paper with the Application Control Number, and attach to the application.

Describe commodities or technical data. Furnish additional details as prescribed by the Export Administration Regulations when necessary to identify the specific items to be so classified. Include characteristics shown in the specific ECCN, such as basic ingredients, composition, electrical parameters, size, gauge, grade, horsepower, etc. These characteristics must be identified for the commodities proposed for export, which may be different from the characteristics described in the promotional brochure(s).

Where the specific ECCN entry states "specify by name," list by name on the application all the commodities to be included in the shipment. Include the ECCN paragraph reference at the end of the description.
Processing Code: Enter the two character processing code designated in the ECCN. Only one processing code may be entered per application.

9(c). Enter the Export Control Commodity Number that corresponds to the commodity adjacent to the corresponding commodity description.

2b. Identify document(s) on file by placing an (X) in the appropriate block(s). These document(s) are to be retained by the applicant.

3. Enter original case number if the original case was returned without action.

7. The purchaser is the party abroad who has entered into the export transaction with the applicant or order party. If same as ultimate consignee, place an "X" in the block located after "Same as Item #6." *Do NOT leave this item blank.*

8. An intermediate consignee is any intermediary in a foreign country who participates as an agent for the exporter or for the purchaser or ultimate consignee to effect delivery of the export to the purchaser or ultimate consignee. All known intermediate consignees must be named. If more than one, state in Item #15. If same as purchaser, place an "X" in the block located after "Same as Item #7." If none state "None"; if unknown, state "Unknown" in the name space. *Do NOT leave this space blank.*

9(d). Enter the unit price except where a large variety of products within a single ECCN makes such a breakdown extremely difficult. In such cases show only total price. Give the fair market value in U.S. dollars. Round to the nearest dollar the amount entered in the total price column. Give the exact value if less than $0.50. Where the normal trade practice in a given commodity makes it impractical to establish a firm contract price, state in Item 15 the precise terms upon which the price is to be ascertained and from which the contract price may be objectively determined.

11. Provide manufacturer name of the total or assembled commodity(ies). Do NOT include address. If more than one name, separate names by commas. If additional space is needed, continue in Item #15. NOTE: Leave this Item blank only if the ECCN is 1564.

13. Complete only if end-user is not the ultimate consignee named in Item 6. If more than one end-user, insert the word "various" in the space and use Supplemental Form BXA-622P-B.

15. When the information is a continuation of a previous item(s) first state the Item number(s). Do NOT put information from Item 9(a) through 9(d) in this space. Enter additional data pertinent to the transaction as required by the Export Administration Regulations. Include special certifications, names of parties in interest not disclosed elsewhere, such as foreign principal or supplier, explanation of documents attached, etc. If the application represents a transaction previously rejected, give prior case number issued by the Office of Export Licensing. Use Supplemental Form BXA-622P-A or B if additional space is needed.

14. A Foreign Availability Submission (FAS) may be submitted with an export license application. The applicant may also provide a FAS to the Office of Foreign Availability up to 90 days after a license denial on National Security grounds. See part 391 of the Export Administration Regulations before providing submission.

17. Where the applicant did not receive the order directly from the foreign purchaser or ultimate consignee or through his or her agent abroad, the party in the United States which conducted the negotiations with the foreign party and originally received the order (the order party) must complete this item and sign the application.

18. All three spaces must be completed and THE APPLICATION MUST BE MANUALLY SIGNED by the applicant or duly authorized agent of the applicant. If signed by agent of the applicant, show title and firm name of agent. (Rubber-stamped or other facsimile signatures are not acceptable.)

10. The Office of Export Licensing will transmit the license to the party designated in this space. Leave blank if the license is to go to the applicant. Designation of another party to receive the license does not alter the responsibilities of the applicant.

12. Provide a complete and detailed description for the end-use intended by the ultimate consignee. For guidance on completion of this item, refer to Supplement 1, Part 372 of the Export Administration Regulations. If additional space is needed, use Supplemental Form BXA-622P-A or B.

● STELA - System for Tracking Export License Applications

DETACH THIS INFORMATION SHEET BEFORE SUBMITTING APPLICATION

Form 3.03 Service supply license statement.

**FORM BXA-6026P, SERVICE SUPPLY (SL) LICENSE
STATEMENT BY U.S. EXPORTER**

FORM APPROVED: OMB NO. 0694-0002

FORM BXA-6026P
(REV. 1-92)-LF

U.S. DEPARTMENT OF COMMERCE
BUREAU OF EXPORT ADMINISTRATION

SERVICE SUPPLY (SL) LICENSE STATEMENT BY U.S. EXPORTER

INSTRUCTIONS--All items on this form must be completed. The signature required in item 7 must be that of an official of the exporter's firm. If more space is needed, attach an additional copy of this form or add a page signed as in item 7.

REFERENCE NO.
(if desired) ➤

Public reporting burden for this collection of information is estimated to average five minutes per response, including the time for reviewing instructions, searching existing data sources, gathering and maintaining the data needed, and completing and reviewing the collection of information. Send comments regarding this burden estimate or any other aspect of this collection of information, including suggestions for reducing this burden, to the Office of Security and Management Support, Bureau of Export Administration, U.S. Department of Commerce, Washington, D.C. 20230; and to the Office of Management and Budget, Paperwork Reduction Project (0694-0002), Washington, D.C. 20503.

No export from the United States of spare or replacement parts under a Service Supply (SL) License may be made unless the U.S. exporter completes this Form BXA-6026P and submits it, together with other documentation, to the Office of Export Licensing. Information furnished herewith is subject to the provisions of Section 12(c) of the Export Administration Act of 1979, 50 U.S.C. App. 2411 (c), and its unauthorized disclosure is prohibited by law.

1. Name and address of firm *(Street, City, State and ZIP Code)*

2. Request

I (We) request that this statement be considered a part of my (our) application (Reference No. as above) for export license submitted to the Office of Export Licensing covering exports of commodities described in item 4 below to the destinations listed in item 3d below for use solely in servicing U.S. equipment, as defined in Section 773.7 of the Export Administration Regulations.

3. Nature of Business

  a. Nature of my (our) usual business: _____
        (Specify as aircraft manufacturer, machine manufacturer, merchant exporter, etc.)

  b. Number of years in business: _____

  c. Types of equipment to be serviced: _____
        (Specify as computers, aircraft, radar, scientific instruments, etc.)

  d. Destinations to be served: _____
        (Specify by country)

4. Commodity Description

I (We) expect to export the following commodities as spare or replacement parts: *(Description in general terms: e.g., electronic parts, communications parts and equipment, parts for scientific instruments and apparatus, etc.)*

5. Comments *(Add any additional pertinent facts relating to the servicing activities or nature of business).*

REVERSE OF FORM BXA-6026P, SERVICE SUPPLY (SL)
LICENSE STATEMENT BY U.S. EXPORTER

6. Assistance in preparing statement
(Specify names and addresses of persons other than employees of the firm who assisted in the preparation of this statement.) If assistance has not been obtained, enter the word "None".

7. Certification
I (We) certify that:

a. I (We) will export the spare or replacement parts described in Item 4 for the sole purpose of servicing the equipment described in Item 3c to the destination(s) listed in Item 3d. Servicing this equipment is a normal function of my (our) firm and these commodities will not be resold or used for any other purpose.

b. The commodities described in Item 4 will not be exported to any person or firm listed on the Office of Export Licensing's Table of Denial Orders, or to Syria, Iran, Libya, North Korea, Vietnam, Cambodia, or Cuba. Further, these commodities will not be exported to any destination under the SL procedure without the specific prior authorization of the Office of Export Licensing if such commodities will improve or change the basic design characteristics of the commodities to be serviced.

c. The equipment to be serviced was manufactured and/or exported by my (our) firm or by its subsidiary.

d. I (We) will export from the United States the commodities described in Item 4 to any country in Eastern Europe, excluding Yugoslavia, or the People's Republic of China, or Afghanistan only if the commodities are for use as replacement parts. Such commodities will not be shipped in a quantity in excess of immediate current requirements to service the equipment; and any commodities identified by the symbol "A" on the Commodity Control List published by the Office of Export Licensing will not be used on any equipment also identified by the symbol "A", if the value of such commodities exceeds $25,000.00 or $75,000.00 for the People's Republic of China.

e. No commodity excluded from the SL Procedure under the Export Administration Regulations will be exported to any consignee in any destination under this procedure.

f. I (We) will maintain records of all exports of the commodities referred to in Paragraph "a" of this certification in the detail set forth in the Export Administration Regulations, for a period of two years from the date the commodities are exported. These records will be available for inspection, upon demand, by the Office of Export Licensing or by any other U.S. Government agency. Further, I (we) agree to submit a quarterly report on all exports to the former U.S.S.R., Eastern European countries, the People's Republic of China and Afghanistan of commodities as required by Section 773.7(k) of the Export Administration Regulations.

g. I (We) certify that all of the facts contained in this statement are true and correct to the best of my (our) knowledge and belief and I (we) do not know of any additional facts that are inconsistent with the above statement. A supplemental statement will be sent to the Office of Export Licensing disclosing any change of facts or intentions set forth in this statement that occurs after the statement has been prepared and forwarded.

_____   _____
(Signature of Official or firm named in Item 1)   (Date of signing)

Type or print _____
                      (Name and title of person signing this document)

DO NOT WRITE BELOW THIS LINE--FOR DEPARTMENT OF COMMERCE USE ONLY

NOT APPROVED UNLESS THE OFFICIAL VALIDATION STAMP APPEARS HEREON	ACTION TAKEN BY U.S. DEPARTMENT OF COMMERCE	
	☐ APPROVED	Expiration Date
	☐ NOT APPROVED	SL License No.
	U.S. DEPARTMENT OF COMMERCE Bureau of Export Administration Office of Export Licensing P.O. Box 273 Washington, D.C. 20044	
	_____ (Date)	

BXA-6026P (REV.1-92)

Form 3.04   International import certificate.

FORM BXA-645P/ATF-4522/DSP-53, INTERNATIONAL IMPORT CERTIFICATE

FORM BXA-645P/ATF-4522/DPS-53 (REV. 8-89)   Form Approved: OMB No. 0625-0064 · Modèle approuvé: OMB No. 0625-0064

U.S. DEPARTMENT OF COMMERCE Bureau of Export Administration U.S. DEPARTMENT OF THE TREASURY Bureau of Alcohol, Tobacco and Firearms U.S. DEPARTMENT OF STATE Office of Munitions Control	INTERNATIONAL IMPORT CERTIFICATE (CERTIFICAT INTERNATIONAL D'IMPORTATION)
NOTE: Read instructions on the reverse side before completing and submitting this form. (Lire les instructions au verso avant de remplir et de présenter la présente formule.)	Certificate Number
1. U.S. Importer/Importateur (Name and address – Nom et adresse)	FOR U.S. GOVERNMENT USE (Réservé pour le Gouvernement des Etats-Unis)
2. Exporter/Exportateur (Name and address – Nom et adresse)	If this form has been approved by the Department of Commerce or the Department of State, it is not valid unless the official seal of the Department of Commerce, or the Department of State, appears in this space. If this form is approved by the Treasury Department, a seal is not required. (Si ce formulaire a été approuvé par le Ministère du Commerce, ou le Ministère des Affaires Etrangères, il n'est pas valide à moins qu'un sceau officiel du Ministère du Commerce ou du Ministère des Affaires Etrangères soit apposé sur le document. Si ce formulaire est approuvé par le Ministère des Finances, un sceau officiel n'est pas nécessaire.

3. Description of goods (Désignation de la Marchandise)	TSUS Anno. No. (Numéro de la liste)	Quantity (Quantité)	Value (Valeur) (FOB, CIF, etc.)

4. Representation and undertaking of U.S. importer or principal

The undersigned hereby represents that he has undertaken to import into the United States of America under a U.S. Consumption Entry or U.S. Warehouse Entry the commodities in quantities described above, or, if the commodities are not so imported into the United States of America, that he will not divert, transship, or reexport them to another destination except with explicit approval of the Department of Commerce, the Department of State, or the Department of the Treasury, as appropriate. The undersigned also undertakes to notify the appropriate immediately of any changes of fact or intention set forth herein. If a delivery verification is required, the undersigned also undertakes to obtain such verification and make disposition of it in accordance with such requirement. Any false statement wilfully made in this declaration is punishable by fine and imprisonment. (See experts from U.S. Code on reverse side.)

Déclaration et engagement de l'importateur ou du commettant des Etats-Unis

Le soussigné déclare par la présente qu'il a pris l'engagement d'importer aux Etats-Unis d'Amérique, en vertu d'une Déclaration américaine de Mise en Consommation, ou d'une Déclaration américaine d'Entrée en entrepôt, la quantité de produits ci-dessus, et que, dans le cas où ces produits ne seraient pas ainsi importés aux Etats-Unis d'Amérique, il ne les détournera, ne les transbordera, ni les réexportera à destination d'un autre lieu, si ce n'est avec l'approbation explicite du Ministère du Commerce, du Ministère des Affaires Etrangères ou du Ministère des Finances, comme il est requis. Le soussigné prend également l'engagement d'aviser le Ministère intéressé des Etats-Unis de tous changements survenus dans les actes ou les intentions énoncés dans la présente déclaration. Si demande est faite d'une confirmation de la livraison, le soussigné prend également l'engagement d'obtenir cette confirmation et d'en disposer de la manière prescrite par cette demande. Toute fausse déclaration faite intentionnellement expose l'auteur aux pénalités prévues par la loi. (Voir Extrait du Code des Etats-Unis au verso.)

Type or Print (Prière d'écrire à la machine ou en caractères d'imprimerie) Name of Firm or Corporation (Nom de la Firme ou de la Société)	Type or Print (Prière d'écrire à la machine ou en caractères d'imprimerie) Name and Title of Authorized Official (Nom et titre de l'agent ou employé autorisé)
Signature of Authorized Official (Signature de l'agent ou employé autorisé)	Date of Signature (Date de la signature)

This document ceases to be valid unless presented to the competent foreign authorities within six months from its date of issue. (Le présent document perd sa validité s'il n'est pas remis aux autorités étrangères compétentes dans un délai de six mois à compter de sa délivrance.)

No import certification may be obtained unless this International Import Certificate has been completed and filed with the appropriate U.S. Government agency (Department of Commerce: 50 U.S.C. app. §2411, E.O. 12214, 15 C.F.R. §368; Department of the Treasury: 22 U.S.C. §2778, E.O. 11959, 27 C.F.R. §47; Department of State: 22 U.S.C. 2778, 2779, E.O. 11958, 22 C.F.R. §123). Information furnished herewith is subject to the provisions of Section 12(c) of the Export Administration Act of 1979, 50 U.S.C. app. 2411(c), and its unauthorized disclosure is prohibited by law.

FOR U.S. GOVERNMENT USE (Réservé au Gouvernement des Etats-Unis)

Certification: This is to certify that the above declaration was made to the U.S. Department of Commerce, State, or Treasury through the undersigned designated official thereof and a copy of this certification is placed in the official files.	**Certification:** Il est certifié par la présente que la déclaration ci-dessus a été faite au Ministère du Commerce, des Affaires Etrangères, ou des Finances des Etats-Unis par l'intermédiaire du fonctionnaire soussigné de ce Ministère et qu'une copie de ce certificat a été conservée dans les archives officielles.

Designated Commerce, State, or Treasury Official (Fonctionnaire compétent du Ministère du Commerce, d'Etat, ou du Trésor)   Date

USCOMM-DC 89-24414

Form 3.05   Delivery verification certificate.

Form Approved: OMB No. 0694-0016

FORM BXA 647P
(REV.1-90)

U.S. DEPARTMENT OF COMMERCE
BUREAU OF EXPORT ADMINISTRATION

DELIVERY VERIFICATION
CERTIFICATE

Public reporting burden for this collection of information is estimated to average 15 minutes per response, including the time for reviewing instruments, searching existing data sources, gathering and maintaining the data needed, and completing and reviewing the collection of information. Send comments regarding this burden estimate or any other aspect of this collection of information, including suggestions for reducing this burden, to Office of Security and Management Support, Bureau of Export Administration, U.S. Department of Commerce, Washington, D.C. 20230; and to the Office of Management and Budget Paperwork Reduction Project (0694-0016) Washington, D.C. 20503

Instructions - When required to obtain a delivery verification, the U.S. Importer shall submit this form in duplicate, to the Customs Office. U.S importer is required to complete all items on this form except the portion to be completed by the U.S. Customs Service. The Customs Office will certify a Delivery Verification Certificate only after the import has been delivered to the U.S. importer. The duly certified form shall then be dispatched by the U.S. importer to the foreign exporter or otherwise disposed of in accordance with instructions of the exporting country.

No delivery verification may be obtained unless a completed application form has been received. (50 U.S.C. App. § 2401 et seq.; 15 C.F.R. § 768).

EXPORTER *(Name and address)*	This certification applies to the goods described below, shown on U.S. Department of Commerce International Import Certificate No. _____
	ARRIVED *(Name of port)*	DATE OF ARRIVAL
IMPORTER *(Name and address)*	NAME OF SHIP, AIRCRAFT, OR CARRIER *(Include numbers on bills of lading, airway bills, etc.)*

DESCRIPTION OF GOODS	QUANTITY	VALUE (FOB, CIF, etc.)

TO BE COMPLETED BY U.S. CUSTOMS SERVICE	REGION NO:

(Custom's Seal)	CERTIFICATION - It is hereby certified that the importer has produced evidence that the goods specified above have been delivered and brought under the Export Administration Regulations of the United States.

Signature   Date

ENTRY	☐ WAREHOUSE	☐ CONSUMPTION	NUMBER	DATE

USCOMM-DC 90-24078

Form 3.06   Notification of delivery verification requirement.

FORM BXA-648P, NOTIFICATION OF DELIVERY VERIFICATION REQUIREMENT

Form Approved: OMB No. 0625-0005

FORM BXA-648P (REV. 2-88)	U.S. DEPARTMENT OF COMMERCE BUREAU OF EXPORT ADMINISTRATION	Date
NOTIFICATION OF DELIVERY VERIFICATION REQUIREMENT		Export License No.
		Applicant's Reference No.
Information furnished herewith is subject to the provisions of Section 12 (c) of the Export Administration Act of 1979, 50 U.S.C. app. 2411 (c), and its unauthorized disclosure is prohibited by law. Your failure to complete and return this form along with required delivery verification(s) may subject you to administrative action under the Export Administration Act.		International Import Certificate No.

IMPORTANT NOTICE

LICENSEE: You are required to provide the Office of Export Licensing with a document verifying the delivery of each shipment made against the attached license. For your information, instructions on what you must do about obtaining and submitting delivery verification documents will be found on the reverse side of the Duplicate Copy of this Form.

AGENT OR FREIGHT FORWARDER: When this Form BXA-648P is attached to a license which has been forwarded by the Office of Export Licensing to an agent or freight forwarder of the licensee, it is the responsibility of the agent or freight forwarder to notify the licensee that verification of delivery is required for exports made against the license.

Check Item 1, 2, or 3, as applicable, and complete Item. The ORIGINAL of this form must be return to the Office of Export Licensing, P.O. Box 273, Washington, D.C. 20044, as soon as you have received all delivery verification documents for shipments made against the attached License. (See paragraph A3 on the back of the Duplicate Copy.)

1. ☐ The total quantity authorized for export by this license has been exported and all delivery verification documents are attached hereto.

2. ☐ A part of the quantity authorized for export by this license will not be exported. Delivery verification documents covering all commodities exported are attached hereto.

3. ☐ No shipment has been made against this license and none is contemplated.

4. The License:

 a. ☐ is returned herewith for cancellation.

 b. ☐ Was returned to the Office of Export Licensing as required by 386.2(d) (4) of the Export Administration Regulations.

Remarks:

Print or type name of licensee	Print or type name and title of authorized representative
Date signed	Signature of authorized representative

USCOMM-DC 88-24089

(See Instructions on reverse side of Duplicate Copy)

FORM BXA-648P, INSTRUCTIONS FOR FULFILLING DV REQUIREMENT

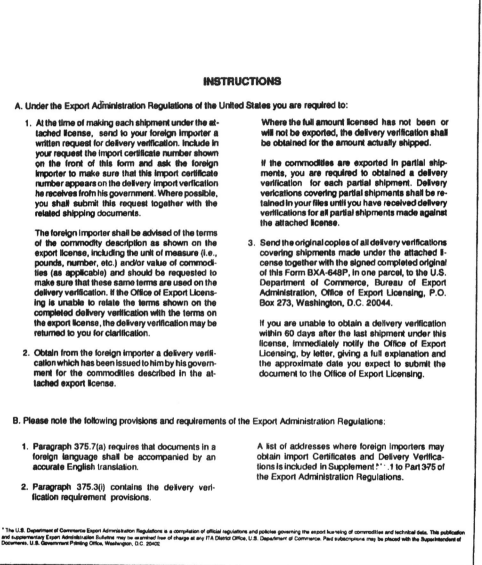

INSTRUCTIONS

A. Under the Export Administration Regulations of the United States you are required to:

1. At the time of making each shipment under the attached license, send to your foreign importer a written request for delivery verification. Include in your request the import certificate number shown on the front of this form and ask the foreign importer to make sure that this import certificate number appears on the delivery import verification he receives from his government. Where possible, you shall submit this request together with the related shipping documents.

   The foreign importer shall be advised of the terms of the commodity description as shown on the export license, including the unit of measure (i.e., pounds, number, etc.) and/or value of commodities (as applicable) and should be requested to make sure that these same terms are used on the delivery verification. If the Office of Export Licensing is unable to relate the terms shown on the completed delivery verification with the terms on the export license, the delivery verification may be returned to you for clarification.

2. Obtain from the foreign importer a delivery verification which has been issued to him by his government for the commodities described in the attached export license.

Where the full amount licensed has not been or will not be exported, the delivery verification shall be obtained for the amount actually shipped.

If the commodities are exported in partial shipments, you are required to obtained a delivery verification for each partial shipment. Delivery verications covering partial shipments shall be retained in your files until you have received delivery verifications for all partial shipments made against the attached license.

3. Send the original copies of all delivery verifications covering shipments made under the attached license together with the signed completed original of this Form BXA-648P, in one parcel, to the U.S. Department of Commerce, Bureau of Export Administration, Office of Export Licensing, P.O. Box 273, Washington, D.C. 20044.

   If you are unable to obtain a delivery verification within 60 days after the last shipment under this license, immediately notify the Office of Export Licensing, by letter, giving a full explanation and the approximate date you expect to submit the document to the Office of Export Licensing.

B. Please note the following provisions and requirements of the Export Administration Regulations:

1. Paragraph 375.7(a) requires that documents in a foreign language shall be accompanied by an accurate English translation.

2. Paragraph 375.3(i) contains the delivery verification requirement provisions.

A list of addresses where foreign importers may obtain import Certificates and Delivery Verifications is included in Supplement *.1 to Part 375 of the Export Administration Regulations.

* The U.S. Department of Commerce Export Administration Regulations is a compilation of official regulations and policies governing the export licensing of commodities and technical data. This publication and supplementary Export Administration Bulletins may be examined free of charge at any ITA District Office, U.S. Department of Commerce. Paid subscriptions may be placed with the Superintendent of Documents, U.S. Government Printing Office, Washington, D.C. 20402

FORM BXA-648P (REV. 2-86)

Form 3.07 Statement by ultimate consignee and purchaser.

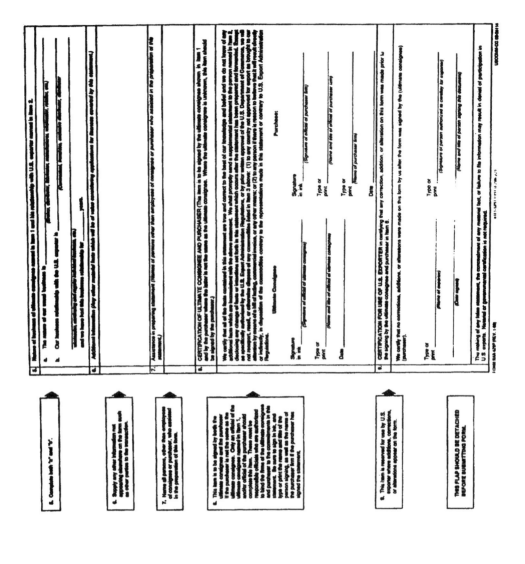

Form 3.08 End-user supplement.

Form BXA-622P-B

SUPPLEMENTAL FORM BXA-622P-B (REV. 3-88) FORM APPROVED: OMB No. 0625-0001	U.S. DEPARTMENT OF COMMERCE Bureau of Export Administration	DATE RECEIVED (Leave Blank)
1. APPLICATION CONTROL NUMBER (Insert from the original, BXA-622P, or BXA-699P)	**END-USER SUPPLEMENT** *If End-User(s) are different from Items #6 on form BXA-622P and/or BXA-699P*	
2. CONTACT PERSON Name _____ Telephone No. _____	Information furnished herewith is subject to the provisions of Section 12(c) of the Export Administration Act of of 1979, 50 U.S.C. app. 2411(c), and its unauthorized disclosure is prohibited by law.	

13. END-USER		13. END-USER	
ADDRESS		ADDRESS	
CITY	POSTAL CODE	CITY	POSTAL CODE
COUNTRY	TELEPHONE NO.	COUNTRY	TELEPHONE NO.
13. END-USER		13. END-USER	
ADDRESS		ADDRESS	
CITY	POSTAL CODE	CITY	POSTAL CODE
COUNTRY	TELEPHONE NO.	COUNTRY	TELEPHONE NO.
13. END-USER		13. END-USER	
ADDRESS		ADDRESS	
CITY	POSTAL CODE	CITY	POSTAL CODE
COUNTRY	TELEPHONE NO.	COUNTRY	TELEPHONE NO.
13. END-USER		13. END-USER	
ADDRESS		ADDRESS	
CITY	POSTAL CODE	CITY	POSTAL CODE
COUNTRY	TELEPHONE NO.	COUNTRY	TELEPHONE NO.
13. END-USER		13. END-USER	
ADDRESS		ADDRESS	
CITY	POSTAL CODE	CITY	POSTAL CODE
COUNTRY	TELEPHONE NO.	COUNTRY	TELEPHONE NO.
13. END-USER		13. END-USER	
ADDRESS		ADDRESS	
CITY	POSTAL CODE	CITY	POSTAL CODE
COUNTRY	TELEPHONE NO.	COUNTRY	TELEPHONE NO.

12. CONTINUATION OF INFORMATION REGARDING SPECIFIC END-USE OF COMMODITIES OR TECHNICAL DATA BY CONSIGNEE.

ORIGINAL

USCOMM-DC 88-04003

Form 3.09   Statement by foreign consignee in support of special license.

**FORM BXA-6052P, STATEMENT BY FOREIGN CONSIGNEE
IN SUPPORT OF SPECIAL LICENSE APPLICATION**

OMB No. 0694-0050

Form BXA-6052P (Rev. 5-88)	STATEMENT BY FOREIGN CONSIGNEE IN SUPPORT OF SPECIAL LICENSE APPLICATION	U.S. DEPARTMENT OF COMMERCE BUREAU OF EXPORT ADMINISTRATION

No shipment may be made under the Special Licenses procedure unless a completed Form BXA-6052P has been received. (50 U.S.C. 2401 et seq.; 15 C.F.R. Part 773.	**1. NAME AND ADDRESS OF CONSIGNEE**
	Name
	Street and Number
	City Country

INSTRUCTIONS: This form must be submitted by the consignee, in three copies, to the exporter named in item 2, below . Only items 1 through 9, inclusive, are to be completed by the consignee. Item 10 is to be completed by the U.S. exporter. In all cases, the signatures required must be those of responsible officials who are authorized to bind the firms for which they sign. If more space is needed, attach an additional copy of this form or sheet of paper signed as required in items 9 and 10. The information furnished herewith is to be used in connection with an application for a license from the U.S. Government for the export of U.S. commodities. In the case of a Project License, technical data may also be included. Information furnished herewith should not be published or disclosed except in accordance with the provisions of Section 12(c) of the Export Administration Act of 1979, 50 U.S.C. app. 2411(c), and its unauthorized disclosure is prohibited by law. Public reporting for this collection of information is estimated to average 10 minutes per response, including the time for reviewing instructions, searching existing data sources, gathering and maintaining the data needed, and completing and reviewing the collection of information. Send comments regarding this burden estimate or any other aspect of this collection of information, including suggestions for reducing this burden, to Office of Security and Management Support, Bureau of Export Administration, U.S. Department of Commerce, Washington, D.C. 20230; and to the Office of Management and Budget, Paperwork Reduction Project (0694-0050), Washington, D.C. 20503.

2. Request
I (We) request that this statement be considered a part of the ☐ . Distribution)
☐ Service Supply) License Application
☐ Project)

filed by _____
(Name and address of exporter with whom we have placed or may place an order.)

for export to us of the commodities/technical data shown in item 3 below during the validity period of the relevant export license issued to the exporter.

3. Description of commodities/technical data
I (We) expect to use, sell, install, or reexport the following commodities/technical data: *(Describe briefly)*

4. Consignee's business and relationship with exporter named in Item 2
a. Nature of business is: Distributor, broker, sales agent, manufacturer. etc. *(Specify)*

b. Our business relationship with the exporter is: Franchise, exclusive sales agency, authorized sales agency, customer, etc. *(Specify)*

c. We have had this business relationship for _____ years.

5. Disposition or use of commodities by ultimate consignee named in Item 1 *(check and complete the appropriate box(es))*
I (We) certify that the commodities listed in Item 3 will be:
Used by us (as capital equipment) in the form in which received in a manufacturing process in the country named in Item 1 and will not be reexported or incorporated into an end product.

b. ☐ Processed or incorporated by us into the following products(s) _____
(Specify)
to be manufactured in the country named in Item 1 for distribution in _____
(Name of country or countries)

c. ☐ Used to service the following commodities _____
(Specify computers, aircraft, etc.)
in the following destinations _____

d. ☐ Resold by us in the form in which received in the country named in Item 1. The specific end-use by our customer will be
_____
(Specify, if known)

e. ☐ Reexported by us in the form in which received to _____
(Name of country or countries)

f. ☐ Other *(Describe fully)* _____

6. Disposition or use of commodities/ data by Project License ultimate consignee name in Item 1
I (We) certify that the ☐ commodities ☐ technical data listed in Item 3 will be used soley for the purposes described in the project description included as an attachment to this form.

USCOMM-DC 89-24446

REVERSE OF FORM BXA-6052P, STATEMENT BY FOREIGN CONSIGNEE IN SUPPORT OF SPECIAL LICENSE APPLICATION

7. Additional Information *(Any material facts which will be of value in considering this statement.)*

8. Assistance in preparing statement *(Name of persons other than employees of firm named in Item 1, who assisted in preparing this statement.)*

9. CERTIFICATION OF CONSIGNEE

I (We) certify that all of the facts contained in this statement are true and correct to the best of my (our) knowledge and belief and I (we) do not know of any additional facts which are inconsistent with the above statement. I (We) shall promptly send a supplemental statement to the exporter named in Item 2, disclosing any change of facts or intentions set forth in this statement which occurs after the statement has been prepared and forwarded, except as specifically authorized by the U.S. Export Administration Regulations. I (We) (a) will not use, reexport, sell, distribute, install or otherwise dispose of any commodities/technical data covered by this statement contrary to U.S. Export Administration Regulations; and (b) will not sell or otherwise dispose of any of these commodities to any person or firm listed on the U.S. Department of Commerce Table of Denial Orders or where there is reason to believe that the commodities will be reexported to a destination not authorized by the Office of Export Licensing.

Signature of official of firm named in Item 1 *(See instructions on front of form) (Sign here in ink)*	Date signed
Name of person signing this document *(Print or type)*	Title

10. Request and Certification of U.S. Exporter

We request that the firm named in Item 1 be approved as a consignee to whom we may export commodities/technical data, under the special license specified in Item 2. We understand that all undertakings, commitments, obligations, and responsibilities under the applicable special licensing procedure, and the Export Administration Regulations related thereto, are fully applicable to any export to the above mentioned consignee if this form is validated by the Office of Export Licensing. No corrections, additions, or alterations were made on this form by us after the form was signed by the official named in Item 9 above. We certify that we will not export or otherwise dispose of any commodities/technical data covered by the special license issued to use for the consignee names in Item 1, until this form has been validated or after it has expired or been revoked.

Signature of person authorized to certify for exporter *(Sign here in ink)*	Date signed
Name of exporter firm *(Print or type)*	Name of and title of person signing this document

The making of any false statement or the concealment of any material fact or failure to file required information may result in denial of participation in U.S. exports. Notarial or Government certification is not required.

DO NOT WRITE BELOW THIS LINE—FOR DEPARTMENT OF COMMERCE USE ONLY

| NOT APPROVED UNLESS THE OFFICIAL VALIDATION STAMP APPEARS HEREON

Validation | Approval of this form by the U.S. Government does not remove the need to obtain authorization from any other government for the proposed use or disposition of the commodities/technical data covered. If authorization for the use or disposition of these commodities is required under the laws of any other government, such authorization should be obtained in additional to that of the U.S. Government.

☐ Approved ☐ Not Approved

Expiration Date: _____

U.S. Department of Commerce
Bureau of Export Administration
Office of Export Licensing
P.O. Box 273
Washington, D.C. 20044

_____
(Date) |

FORM BXA-6052P (5-89)

USCOMM-DC 89-24448

Form 3.10 Shipper's export declaration.

FORM 7525-V-ALT., SHIPPER'S EXPORT DECLARATION

U.S. DEPARTMENT OF COMMERCE — BUREAU OF THE CENSUS — INTERNATIONAL TRADE ADMINISTRATION		CONFIDENTIAL — For use solely for official purposes authorized by the Secretary of Commerce (13 U.S.C. 301(g)).	
FORM 7525-V-ALT. (Intermodal)(1-1-88) SHIPPER'S EXPORT DECLARATION			DO NOT USE THIS AREA

2. EXPORTER (Principal or seller-licensee and address including ZIP Code)
Jones Manufacturing Company
190 Patricia Drive
Washington, D.C.
ZIP CODE 20233

4. DOCUMENT NUMBER
5. EXPORT REFERENCES

1b. B/L OR AWB NUMBER
B-22246

AUTHENTICATION (When required)

28. THE UNDERSIGNED HEREBY AUTHORIZES
Alan Joel
TO ACT AS FORWARDING AGENT FOR EXPORT CONTROL AND CUSTOMS PURPOSES.

EXPORTER Jones Manufacturing
(BY DULY AUTHORIZED OFFICER OR EMPLOYEE)

3. CONSIGNED TO
Gary-Donna LTD
2015 Dorothy Street
Zurich, Switzerland

7. FORWARDING AGENT (Name and address — reference)
Alan Joel Forwarders
322 Phyllis Avenue
Baltimore, MD 21202

6. POINT (STATE) OF ORIGIN OR FTZ NUMBER
VA

30. METHOD OF TRANSPORTATION (Mark one)
☒ Vessel ☐ Other — Specify
☐ Air

4. NOTIFY PARTY/INTERMEDIATE CONSIGNEE (Name and address)
Harold Delivery
17 George Road
Rotterdam, Netherlands

8. DOMESTIC ROUTING/EXPORT INSTRUCTIONS

31. ULTIMATE CONSIGNEE (City name and address if this party is not shown in item 3.)

32. DATE OF EXPORTATION (Not required for vessel shipment)

33. COUNTRY OF ULTIMATE DESTINATION
Switzerland

34. EXPORTER'S EIN (IRS) NUMBER
12-012345678

12. PRE-CARRIAGE BY

13. PLACE OF RECEIPT BY PRE-CARRIER

5B. PARTIES TO TRANSACTION
☒ Related ☐ Non-related

14. EXPORTING CARRIER
Michael (US)

16. PORT OF LOADING/EXPORT
Baltimore

11. TYPE MOVE

Export shipments are subject to inspection by U.S. Customs Service and/or the Office of Export Enforcement.

15. FOREIGN PORT OF UNLOADING (Vessel and air only)
Rotterdam

17. PLACE OF DELIVERY BY ON-CARRIER
Zurich

11b. CONTAINERIZED (Vessel only)
☒ Yes ☐ No

MARKS AND NUMBERS (18)	NUMBER OF PACKAGES (19)	DESCRIPTION OF COMMODITIES in Schedule B detail (20)	GROSS WEIGHT (Kilos) (21)	MEASUREMENT (22)	D OR F (23)		
						CD — Check digit	
						Value — Selling price or cost if not sold (U.S. dollars, omit cents)	
						Quantity — Schedule B unit(s) (Nearest whole unit)	
XYZ/07	1 Crate	Maps and Charts	7,841		D	24. SCHEDULE B NO. 4905.99.0000	CD 0
						25a. QUANTITY 1 X	25b. QUANTITY 2
						26. VALUE 86,265	
MNO-46370	6 Boxes	Men's Swimwear	400		D	24. SCHEDULE B NO. 6211.11.0000	CD 9
						25a. QUANTITY 1 334 Doz.	25b. QUANTITY 2 300 Kg
						26. VALUE 25,000	
RST U-123456	1	Passenger Automobile tires, New radial	12,151		D	24. SCHEDULE B NO. 4011.10.0010	CD 5
						25a. QUANTITY 1 1,000	25b. QUANTITY 2
						26. VALUE 31,616	

27. VALIDATED LICENSE NO./GENERAL LICENSE SYMBOL
G-DEST

28. ECCN (When required)

34. I certify that all statements made and all information contained herein are true and correct and that I have read and understand the instructions for preparation of this document, set forth in the "Correct Way to Fill Out the Shipper's Export Declaration." I understand that civil and criminal penalties, including forfeiture and sale, may be imposed for making false or fraudulent statements herein, failing to provide the requested information, or for violation of U.S. laws on exportation (13 U.S.C. Sec. 305; 22 U.S.C. Sec. 401; 18 U.S.C. Sec. 1001; and 50 U.S.C. App. 2410).

(Signature) Alan Joel
(Title) Manager
(Date) 7-8-88

This form may be privately printed. Sample copies may be obtained from the Bureau of the Census, Washington, D.C. 20233, and local Customs District Directors. The "Correct Way to Fill Out the Shipper's Export Declaration," is available from the Bureau of the Census, Washington, D.C. 20233.

OMB No. 0607-0152

FORM 7525-V, SHIPPER'S EXPORT DECLARATION

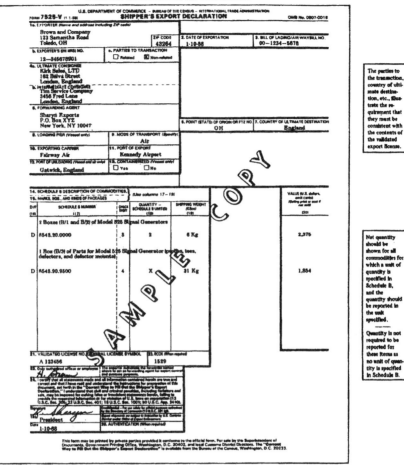

4

Export Costs and Pricing

Key Questions Answered in This Chapter

Introduction

Once the first steps in the export process have been completed—researching the market, understanding the regulatory environment, and obtaining the appropriate license—the exporter must next consider the costs associated with exporting. Those costs are a major factor in setting a price at which the goods or services are sold. A successful pricing strategy also hinges upon having clear foreign market objectives, understanding market demand, and grasping the political and competitive environments.

Before undertaking any sales negotiations with a foreign buyer, the exporter must fully understand export costs. These differ in important ways from the costs in a domestic sales transaction. For example, the international sales terms that are a part of any export sales transaction describe not only which party pays the freight but also the point in the transaction at which one party assumes responsibility for the goods. The exporter may have negotiated favorable shipping terms but may unknowingly bear full responsibility for the safekeeping of the goods, even though they are stored in a warehouse in a foreign port over which the exporter has no control.

Similarly, there may be a number of costs the exporter failed to take into account when setting a price for the goods. These include landed costs and other fees. When all costs are totaled, the exporter may find that he or she has not made a profit or has even lost money on the sale.

Careful attention to pricing and costs allows exporters to negotiate successful sales transactions and helps ensure long-term exporting success. This chapter examines all of the pricing and cost issues associated with an export transaction. Topics covered include foreign market objectives, market demand, shipping terms, landed costs, and foreign costs.

4.1 PRICING

One of the most important decisions an exporter makes is the price at which the goods will be sold. The four most important components in setting a price are:

- Foreign market objectives
- Market demand
- Competition
- Costs

Adopting a pricing strategy is something all firms have experienced. Whatever strategy a firm employs, these four components must be considered from an exporting perspective.

There are a number of elements that are unique to exporting when it comes to setting a price. In some instances, a strong brand name will command a higher price in a foreign market. In other instances, a generic or private-label brand will surpass a market leader. The extent of product modification or packaging required to bring an export up to foreign standards sometimes drives the price to a higher point than the market will bear. In some cases, the foreign target market will just not pay for goods or services that in the United States command a premium.

As a general rule, exporters need to know that in today's global marketplace, the pressure to keep prices low is relentless and intense. Competition is everywhere, as are low-cost imitations and copies. In many of the world's biggest markets, such as China and Brazil, goods are pirated, sometimes displaying the manufacturer's brand name. According to the National Trade Data Bank, 80 percent of the software in use in Brazil today is counterfeit.

An effective pricing strategy is predicated on the fact that a firm has fully analyzed its target market in terms of the benefits of that particular market, the risks involved, and the firm's own competitive advantages.

4.1.1 Foreign Market Objectives

Firms seek out export markets for many different reasons. In all cases, however, it is important to clearly identify all of the objectives for entering a foreign market and to ensure that the commitment in time and resources is there to see those goals through.

Some of the reasons firms export include:

- Slow growth in the U.S. market
- Change in domestic demographics
- Achieving a certain percentage of sales through export
- Supplementing sales in the United States or unloading surplus goods
- Developing a product that suits a particular export market
- Establishing a foothold in an emerging market

EXAMPLE

A U.S. manufacturer of soup-base products for the food service industry undertook a passive market research campaign to try to generate sales to international cruise ship lines. International sales were not a priority and were conducted in spare time. U.S. sales were strong, and the firm felt that if export sales could be gained through a minimal commitment of time and resources, it was worth the effort.

McDonald's, by contrast, extended its global reach to more than fifty countries because globalization was where the growth was. Changing demographics caused a decline in sales in the late 1980s; serving more than 18 million Americans per day, McDonald's had reached the pinnacle of its domestic growth. More fast food was being consumed off premises (62 percent in 1990 versus 23 percent in 1982). Families with children were increasingly likely to order a take-home pizza or other fast-food alternative. To McDonald's, export growth meant survival in an increasingly competitive and changing business.

The emergence of new global trading blocs has greatly expanded export opportunities. For example, in South and Central America, MERCOSUR (Argentina, Paraguay, Brazil), ANCOM (Peru, Bolivia, Ecuador, Bolivia, Colombia, and Venezuela), and CARICOM (the Caribbean nations) all aim to ease the flow of goods between countries. Firms that never considered exporting to these regions are now establishing linkages should the new markets pan out as expected.

EXAMPLE

Twenty of the world's auto companies were asked to submit concepts and financing plans at the China Family Car Forum in Beijing in November 1994. The Chinese government was seeking a joint-venture partner to produce a family car for the Chinese market. Although an eventual deal may be ten years and many millions of dollars away, the risks and associated costs are worth it to the auto companies: 80 million Chinese families may buy their first car by 2010.

In some cases, export opportunities present themselves because a product is especially suited to a foreign market or the price of a product is sufficiently low to allow the exporter to gain an advantage over the competition overseas.

EXAMPLE

An American entrepreneur found that he could purchase used ski equipment for a fraction of the cost of new gear. The equipment was virtually worthless in the U.S. market but commanded a premium in Europe where the market was growing and equipment was scarce.

EXAMPLE

A U.S. specialty-food manufacturer never considered exporting until it discovered at a trade show that its product—single-serving desserts with an extended shelf life—did not exist overseas. Moreover, there was a huge market for the desserts.

Foreign Market Objectives and Pricing Strategies

How a firm prices its export goods is clearly influenced by its foreign market objectives. For example, the used-ski equipment entrepreneur mentioned previously will look to price the goods as high as possible as long as he can sell them quickly. He has no current competition. However, there are no guarantees that he can obtain the same equipment again, if ever.

Similarly, the dessert manufacturer has a novel product but likely is looking to a longer-term presence overseas. Moreover, the firm expects low-cost competition from foreign baking giants in a short period of time. The price must reflect the unique nature of the goods but be low enough to continue to attract consumers when the competition arrives.

A firm seeking a certain percentage of sales from exports in a given time frame will have a different pricing strategy than a firm looking only to supplement sales in its main home market. The dessert company, hoping to establish a long-term presence, will face different pricing considerations than the used-ski equipment firm that can afford to charge whatever the market will bear at the moment.

Many exporters do not have much leeway in terms of pricing. As with domestic markets, most export markets are highly competitive with narrow margins. Also, pricing strategies depend on which products a firm chooses to sell in export markets.

EXAMPLE

The two market leaders in the power-tool industry, Black & Decker and Makita Electric Works Ltd. of Japan, have completely different export product lines and pricing strategies. Black & Decker makes different tools for each of its markets: The U.S. division makes light hand tools for American consumers, who like tools portable, and the German subsidiary makes the more expensive, high-powered, heavy tools that Germans prefer. In contrast, Makita makes one good, low-priced drill that it sells to all of its markets, reasoning that a high-quality, low-cost item will sell in any market.

EXAMPLE

One year after its 1995 venture into the Brazilian market, retailing giant Wal-Mart Stores Inc. posted heavy losses at its Supercenters and Sam's Club outlets. Some analysts felt that by trying to establish a final price to the consumer of 15 percent below that of its competitors, Wal-Mart failed to consider that those same competitors—many of whom have developed a history of consumer loyalty and goodwill—would then cut their own prices.

4.1.2   Market Demand

When assessing market demand, a company can take years to study the marketplace or can simply ask suppliers and salespersons a few questions, then quickly begin to test the waters. How a company proceeds depends on its objectives, resources, and commitment.

Exporters operate in an environment that consists of a number of factors and trends. These include demographic, economic, political, and technological factors.

Demographic Factors

The demographic environment is extremely important to exporters trying to establish a long-term presence in a given market. It consists of:

- Geographical and aging trends in the population
- Ethnic, racial, and educational factors
- Cultural, social, and personal preferences

EXAMPLE

Companies such as Benetton, The Coca-Cola Co., Pepsico Inc., Levi Strauss Associates Inc., and Swatch are among the first to identify a global generation; they market products as if there were one type of teenager in all the world's markets. These companies believe that market demand for soft drinks, fashion, music, watches, and other consumer goods will be the same in Japan as Italy, Germany, Mexico, or Russia. Swatch, in particular, has developed a series of global television ads and syndicated shows that play the same all over the world.

However, in most cases companies ignore cultural and social differences at their own peril. Consider these examples:

- Procter & Gamble Company absorbed $200 million in losses in Japan from 1971 to 1987 before it modified its diapers into the thin, fitted disposable kind preferred by Japanese consumers

- Mattel Toys successfully marketed its Barbie dolls throughout the world except in Japan, until its subsidiary polled Japanese schoolgirls and discovered the doll's anatomy did not appeal to conservative Japanese tastes
- Crest failed to penetrate the Mexican market because its scientifically oriented advertising did not attract Mexican consumers
- Hallmark cards were a failure in France because the French disdained the overtly sentimental messages
- Two-liter bottles of Coca-Cola did not sell in Spain because most Spaniards did not have refrigerators that were large enough to accommodate them

Information technology also allows firms to take advantage of niche marketing, or micromarketing, which breaks down demographic groups into smaller segments. For example, the Claritas Company in Alexandria, Virginia has segmented over 240,000 U.S. neighborhoods into 40 prototypes. Based on these profiles a firm can niche market, through direct mail or advertising, to those segments where the demand for a given product is strongest. A number of firms develop specific product lines based on demographic profiles, allowing them to price their goods accordingly.

Cultural Environment

Sometimes changing cultural norms can open up export markets in the most unlikely places. Between June and November of 1995, Japanese retail chain Kojima Co. sold 53,000 General Electric American-style refrigerators, a number that astounded GE's own top executives. Part of the reason was Kojima's ability to bypass traditional distribution systems and keep costs low. But a major factor was that more Japanese women remain in the workplace after marriage and cannot shop for food daily, as was the custom in their parent's generation. Suddenly, huge two-door refrigerators filled a pressing consumer need and there were none being made in Japan. (*The Wall Street Journal*, 10/31/95)

It is important to remember that market demand can change on a dime; foreign consumers are just as fickle as their American counterparts and are as subject to the whims of fashion. Moreover, it doesn't take long for foreign producers to jump on any profitable bandwagon and bring their local connections and expertise to bear on the marketplace.

In 1996 the market share growth of consumer imports in Russia came to a halt. For a number of reasons—savvier competition, a newfound pride in their own traditions—domestic producers began to retake their turf. Russian juice producer Wimm-Bill-Dann discarded its American-style advertising in favor of a Russian image. The Russian subsidiary of Nestle SA introduced Shok to compete directly with the Snickers bar; the domestic product features the bitter dark chocolate that Russians prefer. Russkoye Radio's Russian-only music format has made it the second-most popular FM station in Moscow, and Russian pop star Filipp Kirkorov now sells out his concerts as fast as does Michael Jackson. (*The Wall Street Journal*, 12/9/96)

Economic Environment

Major factors in determining the economic environment of a target market include:

- Per-capita income
- The availability of credit
- Average savings and the allocation of income
- How people spend (e.g., percentages of total household income spent on food, clothing, rent, medical care, education)
- Human development index (a measure of health, education and purchasing power)
- Stock market and currency fluctuations

These economic indicators are a useful gauge for determining market demand but are not the only yardstick. For example, in Mexico and Poland the average household spends 45 percent and 38 percent of its income, respectively, on food and housing, compared to 16 percent in the United States. However, these are two of the best markets for relatively expensive, brand-name consumer goods.

Economic factors are changing in many parts of the world. Consider these growth markets of the future:

- Consumers in the Pacific Rim countries are expected to purchase 58 million cars over the next six years and like numbers of television sets, kitchens, bathrooms, living rooms, and bedrooms. Consumption of industrial exports such as steel, plastic, petrochemicals, and energy is also greatly increasing, as is the demand for housing.

- The growth of the middle class in India, now numbered between 100 and 300 million people, coupled with the fast-growing reach of television, has created a huge demand for branded goods and telecommunications equipment.

- Poland is considered the hottest market in Eastern Europe. Economic growth was 6.5 percent in 1995, the highest mark in Europe. Privatization of state-owned companies is increasing and unemployment and inflation are declining. Foreign investment in infrastructure projects such as electric power grids and roads is increasing. U.S. exports to Poland totaled $400 million in 1990 and $900 million in 1993; they are expected to grow to $7 billion by the year 2000. (*Business-Week*, 12/4/95; *Nation's Business*, 6/95)

- South America and Latin America have increasingly affluent and youthful markets that are causing companies such as RJR Nabisco and Proctor & Gamble to increase acquisitions and investments there. Brand-name consumer goods are extremely popular in countries such as Chile, Argentina, and Mexico. Argentina's total imports increased 400 percent between 1990 and 1993 as the government privatized state-owned industries such as natural gas, oil, airlines, and electric power.

⦿ In China, the demand for telecommunications, chemicals, and pharmaceuticals will be huge. Moreover, as the population's source of protein shifts from grain to animal products—common in growing economies—the demand for imported feed and grain to support livestock could increase seven-fold. For example, a 15 percent increase in the caloric intake of the average Chinese would mean an additional 150 million tons of grain would be needed annually.

Guidance

The National Trade Data Bank offers a great deal of helpful information concerning economic, political, and demographic factors that affect pricing. For example, it points out that pricing is a very inexact science in a country such as Brazil, where inflation has in the recent past run at 30 percent per month. According to the NTDB, many firms that want to increase the price of goods but still maintain market share use very high markups followed immediately by deep discounts. For information on accessing the National Trade Data Bank, see section 1.3.3.

Economic indicators are only part of the picture in terms of market demand for a given product. Consumers will find a way to purchase goods that really matter to them. Once seen as dumping grounds for low-cost and low-quality merchandise, many developing nations boast a healthy demand for high-quality goods. When goods are perceived as being high-quality or have a certain status, the exporter has a great deal of leeway in terms of setting a price.

EXAMPLE

In Mexico, the number of homes with color television sets is greater than the number of homes with running water. There are approximately 70,000 VCRs in the poorest neighborhoods of Calcutta. In Guangdong province in China, according to experts, 29-inch television sets with flat-screen technology are the top sellers. In addition:

⦿ In Warsaw, Poland, where the annual per-capita income is $2,500, boutiques selling Christian Dior perfume and Valentino shoes are doing exceedingly well.
⦿ In China, where per capita income is $600, Procter & Gamble charges ten times the U.S. price for its Whisper brand sanitary napkins. Johnson & Johnson charges 500 percent more for its Band-Aids and Baby Shampoo. These products are perceived as being of the highest quality.
⦿ Bausch & Lomb sells its Ray-Ban sunglasses to Indonesia's middle-class consumers for between $50 and $100 more than Americans pay for similar styles. The company has seen its Asian sales increase by 23 percent per year between 1988 and 1992.

Note. The demand for industrial exports such as steel, plastics, petrochemicals, and energy is increasing in the Pacific Rim, the Middle East, and Asian countries, except Japan. The demand for housing is also expected to explode worldwide as middle-class spending power increases in countries such as India. Changing economies also portend changes in food consumption. A Taiwanese food company, President Foods, segments China into five regional markets, each capable of generating up to $5 billion per year in sales.

The prices of industrial goods and food products are generally not subject to the whims and trends of consumer goods pricing. Currency fluctuations and political environments, notably tariff and nontariff trade barriers, have a far greater impact on industrial goods and food and agricultural products.

EXAMPLE

The devaluation of the Mexican peso in December 1994 had a huge impact on the trade balance between that country and the United States. The ensuing political fallout could jeopardize not only the North American Free Trade Agreement (NAFTA) but U.S. involvement in multilateral trade agreements worldwide.

The devalued peso made Mexican exports more competitive in world markets while weakening the ability of Mexico's consumers and industries to purchase imports. In 1994 the United States had a trade surplus with Mexico; by December 1996 the United States was running a trade deficit with Mexico of nearly $18 billion. Combined with the $22 billion United States trade deficit with Canada, the total NAFTA deficit is the third largest in the world for the United States, right behind those of China and Japan.

In the auto industry alone Mexico had an $11.9 billion trade surplus with the United States in 1996. But more troubling to many American trade specialists is the perception that there has been permanent shift away from U.S. goods; more industrial equipment, chemicals, and electronics goods are being imported from Asia and Europe.

The trade deficit and other factors will likely hurt the chances of extending the trade pact to Chile and other Latin American nations and may even put pressure on Congress and the president to reexamine the pact when it comes up for a mandatory review in July 1997. (*BusinessWeek*, 12/9/96, *The Wall Street Journal*, 1/4/95 and 10/26/95)

EXAMPLE

The U.S. stock market and many of the factors that drive it, such as currency fluctuations, can have an enormous impact on importing and exporting costs and policies. World markets are intertwined with one another as never before. The stock market and currency crises that sent many Asian economies reeling in the latter half of 1997 also had a significant impact on the U.S. stock market and on many U.S. businesses that depend on global customers for their livelihood.

Though the link between investment in new and existing businesses and the stock market is a subject of debate between economists, when stock markets are rising, banks are much more willing to fund start-up companies and business expansion. The bull market that has been running since 1990 has fueled a boom in business investment, which has increased at a rate of 9 percent between 1993 and 1997.

Many of the companies that have benefited from the positive investment climate are exporters. Computer manufacturers are one example, but there has also been a boom in investment in new machinery and factories. In spite of the stock market correction that hit U.S. markets in October 1997, a plastic mold company in Middletown, Connecticut, with sales of less than $10 million per year went ahead with an investment of $200,000 in new machinery to fill an order from a Canadian customer.

Certain types of businesses may benefit from the turmoil in Asia. Pier 1 Imports Inc. expects to realize a savings of up to $5 million in 1997 due to falling prices in China, India, and Southeast Asia, from which it buys almost 75 percent of its goods. And retail giants Kmart Corporation and J.C. Penney Co. plan to pass savings on imported goods to consumers; the price of imported apparel fell by 1.2 percent in the twelve months beginning in September 1996. Import prices for specialized machinery and computers fell by 6.2 percent in the same twelve-month period, according to the Bureau of Labor Statistics.

The relative strength of the dollar may also benefit other types of businesses as well. Between July 1 and October 27, 1997, the dollar gained 6.1 percent and 10.1 percent, respectively, against the Japanese and Taiwanese currencies. That could lower prices on numerous categories of goods, including autos, electronic components, consumer electronics, telecommunications equipment, toys, and sporting goods.

If the turmoil in Asia continues, burgeoning inventories may also deflate prices on a wide range of goods. In China, the price of chicken fell by 25 percent as of November 1997, as tens of thousands of tons piled up in refrigerated warehouses. Inventory at China's Harbin Power Equipment Company equaled 80.6 percent of a revenue in 1996 compared with 64.2 percent a year earlier; at Shangling, a manufacturer of appliances, inventory as a percentage of revenue was 52.1 percent for 1996 compared to 18 percent a year earlier.

By November 1997, Thailand's Sahaviriya Steel Industries had almost 200,000 tons of unsold steel sitting in fields near the company's main mill. At Hyundai Motor Corp. in South Korea workers hours were cut back due to a bulging inventory of 65,000 cars. Throughout Asia, vast inventories of glass, copper, wood pulp, and petrochemicals are expected to put considerable downward pressure on prices.

U.S. shipping ports may also benefit from the Asian currency crisis. The port in Long Beach, California, saw an 18 percent jump in import traffic during the first nine months of 1997 as compared with a 3.5 percent increase in export traffic. The numbers were largely attributed to the increasing strength of the dollar against Southeast Asian currencies. (*The Wall Street Journal*, 10/27/97, 10/28/97, 10/29/97, and 11/26/97, UBS Global Research, International Trade Administration, J.P. Morgan)

Political Environment

The political environment of a given market has a significant impact on whether U.S. exporters have access to that market. As recently as a few years ago, both China and the republics of the former Soviet Union were seen as the growth markets of the future. Many U.S. exporters and investors have now reassessed their export strategies in light of political chaos in many of the republics and unpredictable relations between the United States and China.

Political environments and decisions can also have an impact on the price an exporter can charge for a product. For example:

⚬ After intensive lobbying by Chrysler, the government of Thailand changed its import classification for cars to include a new category for recreational vehicles.

The new classification lowered the cost of the imported Chrysler Cherokee while at the same time increasing the costs of Japanese rival products.

⊕ Antitrust officials in the European Union granted Sony Corporation a rare exclusive-distribution agreement, meaning electronics dealers can only buy Sony products from Sony or authorized dealers. The arrangement allows Sony to keep its prices down by providing protection from wholesalers and dealers who can undercut the company on its own products and from counterfeit goods carrying the Sony name.

EXAMPLE

As the U.S. stock market fell in response to the decline in foreign markets in October 1997, there was significant political fallout that could impact U.S. trade policy in the future. Republican presidential contender Steve Forbes called the Clinton administration the "chief culprit for the stock market debacle." Some analysts think the political heat was a factor in the defeat of "fast track" legislation that would have given the president authority to negotiate international trade agreements.

The political fallout from the stock and currency crises could also impact the debate on global warming, which has enormous cost implications for many U.S. exporters.

Some economists feel that stock market volatility in Europe and Asia could also affect the European Union's plans to create a common currency. As European currencies appreciate against depressed Asian currencies, growth could be slowed throughout the continent. Others speculate that the Asian turmoil could keep interest rates from rising in Europe and could actually speed up plans for European companies with their sites on acquisition targets in the U.S. whose market valuations may have plummeted. (*The Wall Street Journal*, 10/27/97, 10/28/97, and 10/29/97)

Other important political factors affecting the price of exported goods include:

⊕ Deregulation of industries
⊕ Privatization of industries

EXAMPLE

In 1992 Ben & Jerry's Homemade Inc. started a joint venture to sell its gourmet ice cream in the northern province of Karelian in the former U.S.S.R. The fledgling business had 100 employees in five franchises and distributed ice cream to outlets in Moscow and St. Petersburg.

In addition to quality control problems, the venture ran into trouble when tax liabilities for joint ventures were greatly increased. Then a local bank successfully sued the South Burlington, Vermont, ice cream maker for a 20 percent stake in the business.

In February 1997, Ben & Jerry's announced that it was pulling out of the venture. (*The Wall Street Journal*, 2/7/97)

Note. Exporters are advised to closely monitor the political and trade policies of the countries to which they export goods or services. Sources of information include:

* Trade publications and associations
* Major newspapers
* U.S. government publications and trade offices

Legal Environment

Because trade laws differ from country to country, it is imperative for exporters to be fully aware of the legal implications of all sales contracts, distribution agreements, or joint-venture arrangements they may enter into. Researching the trade laws of another country can be expensive, but so can the costs of being caught unaware.

EXAMPLE

In 1987 specialty software manufacturer Acme Corporation signed an exclusive distribution agreement with SofTouch, a Japanese company, to distribute Acme products in Japan. To solidify their Japanese presence, Acme and SofTouch then formed a corporate joint venture, Acme Corp. Kabushiki Kaishun (ACKK), with two large corporations as minority partners. By 1991 the venture generated over $5 million in revenues.

Acme directors were therefore startled when another Japanese high-tech reseller called and said it was considering acquiring SofTouch but the company was saddled with debt. It was true; by 1992 SofTouch announced it could not meet its obligations.

Acme Corporation never collected the $900,000 in receivables it was owed by SofTouch. Moreover, since SofTouch never actually declared bankruptcy, Acme had to pay Japanese taxes on the receivables plus $200,000 in legal fees. (*INC.*, 1/94)

Small export transactions are often conducted without the input of international trade attorneys. However, when significant amounts of money are involved, exporters should at least consult with an attorney or other trade expert.

Note. A good online resource is the International Trade Law Project (http://ananse.irv.uit.no/trade_law/). Although much of the information is general, it provides links to the West Legal Directory and Martindale-Hubbell Legal Locator, both good resources for finding attorneys with a specific area of expertise.

Technological Environment

The advent of high-technology consumer goods such as personal computers has greatly changed the notion of a product life cycle. A new video game or laptop computer may be the most popular item on the market and then become obsolete in six months. As a result, many firms with products incorporating the latest technology introduce the goods into the marketplace at a very high cost with a great deal of promotion. The goal is to make profits as quickly as possible before the product becomes obsolete or low-cost competition arrives.

One of the results of speeding high-tech goods to market is a much faster product development time. It is a high-stakes game that requires a great deal of capitalization and promotional expenses. Many smaller software firms may have the technology but cannot compete with the giants because they are undercapitalized. Another risk is that many firms introduce products before all of the glitches have been worked out.

4.1.3 Competition

It cannot be overemphasized that the pressure to keep prices low in the global marketplace is relentless; competition is everywhere. The Levi's and the Ray-Bans are the exceptions, as are the new pharmaceutical or technological breakthroughs. Most exporters face consumers with a number of choices at all levels of quality and price ranges.

Exporters should ensure that their products are differentiated from the foreign competition by:

- A lack of substitute products
- A unique niche product
- Significantly lower costs
- Higher quality or technological improvement

Exporters may face a myriad of competitive disadvantages in the form of significant barriers to entry, including:

- Pressure from low-cost competitors
- Higher costs for setting up a foreign operation, including licensing fees, new advertising and promotional materials, duties and tariffs, currency conversions, and shipping costs
- Lack of access to effective distribution
- Need to establish a reputation if the product or service is not an internationally recognized brand

EXAMPLE

In Indonesia, most wholesale and retail distribution channels are reserved for Indonesian companies (i.e., companies that are at least 51 percent Indonesian owned). Foreign companies can open up a trade office but are limited to only one. Moreover, the company's foreign trade representatives cannot engage in direct selling; they may work in sales promotion and provide technical and marketing assistance only. Exporters of certain goods, such as heavy equipment, cars, trucks, and motorcycles, are required to work with a national franchise holder or sole agent.

As in the United States, the emergence of discount superstores and private-label brands in much of the world has put more pressure on prices in a number of industries.

Private-label yogurts hold second place in the large French yogurt market, behind market leader Danone but ahead of popular brand names such as Yoplait and Nestle's Chambourcy.

Germany's Aldi food-store chain may offer only about 1,000 basic products on a daily basis as opposed to between 5,000–7,000 offered by European superstores. But by selling almost nothing but its own private-label brands and taking in gross margins of 12.5 percent (as opposed to the 16 percent and 25 percent taken in by French and British grocery stores, respectively), Aldi has become the market leader in Germany and Belgium and is making inroads in the French market as well.

The demands of emerging markets will sometimes spur the growth of a domestic industry to the extent that repercussions are felt on prices worldwide. Exporters need to constantly assess long-term trends and shifting competitive balances.

EXAMPLE

Escalating demand and economic growth rates have triggered a massive growth in Asian chemical production. Exports from South Korea and China have flooded the world market and driven down prices on some plastics and petrochemicals to decade-low levels, driving down earnings at such large corporations as Dow Chemical Company and BASF. Western exports of polyethylene could be cut in half within two years. The region is expected to double its production to $604 billion annually by the year 2002 and to account for 35 percent of the global market.

Opportunities for Small Firms

Small firms can compete internationally if they understand their markets and have clear-cut objectives. With innovative products and savvy marketing, an exporter can target niches that want something different from what the market leaders are offering. Also, exporters content to increase their sales reach without seeking a major market share can do very well in the global marketplace. For instance:

* A small machine shop in western Massachusetts was able to sell specialized photo-processing equipment to a large West German firm, despite strong competition from German machine shops. The U.S. firm emphasized its successful track record as a supplier to Polaroid and was able to import at low costs the components it needed to manufacture the machinery.

* A Dutch specialty-food and catering business almost single-handedly created a market in Western Europe for Mexican food by introducing a cone-shaped taco shell that made it fun and easy to eat. The firm supplies most of the Mexican food restaurants in Europe.

* A small U.S. market research company landed a contract with one of Europe's largest temporary employment agencies seeking to enter the U.S. market.

The U.S. company learned of the European firm's plans by monitoring international newspapers and made direct contact with the manager in charge of U.S. operations; the American company impressed the manager with its access to information on U.S. temporary employment markets and statistics.

* A small U.S. software concern developed software to run digital LED equipment and became a supplier to a number of South American stadiums and sports equipment manufacturers.

* A U.S. wallpaper manufacturer became a supplier to an international hotel chain by creating innovative designs tailored to the specific regions and styles of each hotel.

4.2 INTERNATIONAL SALES TERMS

International sales terms (incoterms), or terms of sale, are a standard set of shipping terms used in import/export transactions to define the roles and responsibilities of the buyer and the seller. The terms spell out the costs and risks that each party must bear during the shipping process and can have a significant impact on the total cost of an import transaction.

It is extremely important that exporters understand incoterms and how they are used. They have an impact on Customs clearance and, in the event goods are lost, damaged, or stolen, can dictate which party is responsible for the shipment.

Note. The incoterms were developed by the International Chamber of Commerce (ICC) to assist importers and exporters. They were last revised in 1990. Exporters might obtain two ICC guides to incoterms to keep as references. They are *Incoterms 1990* ($29.95), which defines the incoterms themselves, and the *Guide to Incoterms* ($49.95), which uses examples and discussion to explain how buyers and sellers divide risks and obligations in international transactions. Both are available from ICC Publishing Corporation, 156 Fifth Avenue, Suite 308, New York, N.Y. 10010; telephone (212-206-1150); fax (212-633-6025).

4.2.1 Incoterms and Export Pricing

Incoterms can be applied to any mode of transport—ship, rail, or air. They can also be applied to intermodal or multimodal arrangements.

Whatever arrangements importers make for their goods—called "carriage" during the shipping process—will bear directly on overall costs at some point in the importation. For instance, if an importer insists that the seller bear total responsibility for the shipment, the seller will most likely reflect that added burden in the price of the goods. Similarly, importers who agree to bear total responsibility for the shipment will most likely request price concessions. And, as will be shown, there are other variables offered under the incoterms as well. Shipping costs can be significant, typically 5 to 10 percent of the cost of goods.

As in any business transaction, costs play a major role in deciding what shipping arrangement to negotiate. Facilities, trucking resources, and staffing also influence the decision. But exporters should bear in mind that costs can be deceptive. What appears to be a less expensive way to operate on paper may prove more costly in the long run.

EXAMPLE

> It is always less costly in the abstract to have goods or carriage shipped to a destination and left in a warehouse, container stripping facility, or even on the dock. The exporter then has the prerogative of negotiating separate trucking rates with the foreign buyer. If the foreign buyer is a large company, it may prefer to handle pickup and delivery, but smaller companies may not have the wherewithal to do so.

Note. The sections that follow discuss incoterms in descending order of buyer responsibility.

4.2.2 The Ex Works Term: Buyer Bears Maximum Responsibility

When the ex works or ex factory term is used, the buyer bears maximum responsibility for transport; the seller's obligations are the most minimal offered under the incoterms. The seller fulfills the obligation to deliver after making the goods available at his or her premises (i.e., works, factory, warehouse) to the buyer. In particular, the seller is not responsible for loading the goods on a vehicle provided by the buyer or for clearing the goods for export, unless otherwise agreed. The buyer bears all costs and risks involved in taking the goods from the seller's premises to the desired destination.

Guidance

The ex works term should not be used unless the buyer is able to carry out directly or indirectly the export formalities. If the buyer is unable to perform these duties, the free carrier (FCA) term should be used (as described in the next section).

4.2.3 The "F" Series: Buyer Pays Main Carriage Costs

In general, under "F" series incoterms, the buyer bears the cost of carriage of the goods. With the exception of inland freight costs, such as sending the goods by truck to the dock or airport, the seller does not pay main carriage costs.

Free Carrier (FCA)

Under the free carrier term, the seller fulfills the obligation to deliver when he or she has handed over the goods, cleared for export, into the charge of a carrier named by the buyer at the named place or point. If no precise point is indicated by the buyer, the seller may choose the place within a stipulated range where the carrier will take the goods into its charge. The FCA term may be used for any mode of transport, including multimodal transport.

Guidance

FCA terms allow the seller a great deal of leeway to deliver the goods to the carrier and discharge his or her responsibility. The buyer should indicate the precise point at which the carrier takes charge of the goods to minimize the risks of lost or stolen goods.

When, according to commercial practice, the seller's assistance is required in making the contract with the carrier (such as in rail or in air transport) the seller may act at the buyer's risk and expense.

Free Alongside Ship (FAS)

Under this term, the seller fulfills the obligation to deliver when the goods have been placed alongside the vessel on the quay or in lighters (i.e., barges used to load and unload ships) at the named port of shipment. This means that the buyer has to bear all costs and risks of loss or damage to the goods from that moment. The FAS term requires the buyer to clear the goods for export.

Guidance

The FAS term should not be used when the buyer cannot carry out directly or indirectly the export formalities. This term can only be used for sea or inland waterway transport.

Free on Board (FOB)

When this term is used, the seller fulfills the obligation to deliver when the goods have passed over the ship's rail at the named port of shipment. This means that the buyer has to bear all costs and risks of loss or of damage to the goods from that point. The FOB term requires the seller to clear the goods for export.

Guidance

FOB terms can only be used for sea or inland waterway transport. When the ship's rail serves no practical purpose as a measuring point, such as in the case of roll-on/roll-off or container traffic, the FCA term is more appropriate.

4.2.4   The "C" Series: Seller Pays Main Carriage

The "C" series incoterms generally oblige the seller to pay the main carriage of the goods—subject, in some cases, to some additional requirements.

Cost and Freight (CFR)

Under the cost and freight term, the seller must pay the costs and freight necessary to bring the goods to the named port of destination. But the risk of loss or damage to the goods—as well as any additional costs owing to events occurring after the time the goods have been delivered on board the vessel—is transferred from the seller to the buyer when the goods pass the ship's rail in the port of shipment. The CFR term requires the seller to clear the goods for export.

Guidance

This term can only be used for sea or inland waterway transport. When the ship's rail serves no practical purpose, such as in the case of roll-on/roll-off or container traffic, the CPT (carriage paid to) term, discussed below, is more appropriate.

Cost, Insurance, and Freight (CIF)

Under the cost, insurance, and freight term (used only for sea and inland waterway transport), the seller has the same obligations under CFR, but with the additional requirement that the seller must procure insurance against the buyer's risk of loss or damage to the goods during the carriage. The seller contracts for insurance and pays the insurance premium.

The buyer should note that under CIF terms, the seller is only required to obtain insurance on minimum coverage. The CIF term requires the seller to clear the goods for export. When the ship's rail serves no practical purpose, such as in the case of roll-on/roll-off or container traffic, the CIP (carriage and insurance paid to) term is more appropriate.

Guidance

For the importer, there are several disadvantages to buying on a CIF basis:

The insurance coverage may not be adequate.
Costs may not be competitive or acceptable for general average purposes. (See section 12.1.3 for a discussion of general average.)
U.S. excise tax may be payable on foreign insurance.
The foreign judicial process may affect claim settlements if the terms of sale dictate that disputes be resolved in a foreign jurisdiction.

Carriage Paid To (CPT)

Under this term, the seller pays the freight for the carriage of the goods to the named destination. The risk of loss or damage to the goods, as well as any additional costs due to events occurring after the time the goods have been delivered to the carrier, is transferred from the seller to the buyer when the goods have been delivered into the custody of the carrier. The CPT term requires the seller to clear the goods for export.

Guidance

The CPT term may be used for any mode of transport, including multimodal transport.

Carriage and Insurance Paid To (CIP)

This term involves additional obligations of the seller regarding the procurement of cargo insurance against the buyer's risk of loss or damage to the goods during the carriage. The seller contracts for insurance and pays the insurance premium. The buyer should note that under the CIP term, the seller is only required to obtain insurance to cover the minimum coverage. The buyer may want to stipulate that the seller contract for an insurance policy to cover the entire replacement value of the shipment in the event of theft, loss or damage. The minimum coverage generally is insufficient to cover those costs.

The CIP term requires the seller to clear the goods for export.

Guidance

This term may be used for any mode of transport, including multimodal transport.

4.2.5   The "D" Series: Seller Makes Goods Available at Destination

Under the "D" series of incoterms, the seller makes goods available at the destination and in certain cases may have additional responsibilities.

Delivered at Frontier (DAF)

Under this term, the seller fulfills the obligation to deliver when the goods have been made available and cleared for export at the named point and place at the frontier, but before the customs border of the adjoining country. The term *frontier* may be used for any frontier, including that of the country of export. It is of vital importance that the frontier in question be defined precisely by naming the point and place in the term. The frontier can be a port, airport, or Customs checkpoint.

Guidance

The DAF term is primarily intended to be used when the goods are to be carried by rail or road, but it may be used for any mode of transport.

Delivered Ex Ship (DES)

Under this term, used only for sea and inland waterway transport, the seller fulfills the obligation to deliver when the goods have been made available to the buyer on board the ship (uncleared for import) at the named port of destination. The seller has to bear all the costs and risks involved in bringing the goods to the named port of destination.

Delivered Ex Quay Duty Paid (DEQ)

Under this term, used only for sea and inland waterway transport, the seller fulfills his or her obligation to deliver when the goods have been made available to the buyer on the quay (wharf) at the named port of destination, cleared for importation. The seller has to bear all risks and costs including duties, taxes and other charges for delivering the goods thereto.

Guidance

This term should not be used if the seller is unable, directly or indirectly, to obtain the import license. If the parties wish the buyer to clear the goods for importation and pay the duty the words "duty unpaid" should be used instead of "duty paid." If the parties wish to exclude from seller's obligation some of the costs payable upon importation of the goods, such as a value-added tax (VAT), this should be made clear by adding words to this effect: "Delivered ex quay, VAT unpaid (. . . named port of destination)."

This term may be used for sea or inland waterway transport only.

Delivered Duty Unpaid (DDU)

Under this term, the seller fulfills the obligation to deliver when the goods have been made available at the named place in the country of importation. The seller has to bear the costs and risks involved in bringing the goods thereto (excluding duties, taxes, and other official charges payable upon importation), as well as the costs and risks of carrying out customs formalities. The buyer has to pay any additional costs and bear any risks caused by his or her failure to clear the goods for import in time.

Guidance

If the parties wish the seller to carry out customs formalities and bear the costs and risks resulting therefrom, the DDU term must be specified. For example, if the parties wish to include in the seller's obligations some of the costs payable upon importation of the goods, such as the value-added tax, this should be made clear by adding words to this effect: "Delivered duty unpaid, VAT paid (. . . named place of destination)."

This term may be used irrespective of the mode of transport.

Delivered Duty Paid (DDP)

Under this term, the seller fulfills the obligation to deliver when the goods have been made available at the named place in the country of importation. The seller has to bear the risks and costs, including duties, taxes, and other charges, of delivering the goods thereto, cleared for importation. While the ex works term represents the minimum obligation for the seller, DDP represents the maximum obligation. This term should not be used if the seller is unable directly or indirectly to obtain an import license.

Guidance

If the parties wish the buyer to clear the goods for importation and to pay the duty, the term DDU (delivered duty unpaid) should be used. If the parties wish to exclude from the seller's obligations some of the costs payable upon importation of the goods (such as the value-added tax), this should be made clear by adding words to this effect: "Delivered duty paid, VAT unpaid (. . . named place of destination)."

This term may be used irrespective of the mode of transport.

4.3 LANDED COSTS

In addition to the costs of transportation itself, exporters face a variety of expenses related to shipping goods for export. As a group, these assorted fees, charges, and premiums are known as landed costs. The parties to whom the exporter must pay landed costs include:

- Customs
- Insurance companies
- The port authority or airport
- Freight forwarders
- Courier services
- Banks
- Trucking companies
- Steamship lines or airlines

Note. Many exporters are unaware that U.S. ports are for-profit enterprises. As such, they are in heated competition with one another. There is a great deal at stake; in Los Angeles port-related commerce is responsible for 270,000 jobs and almost $9 billion in wages, while in New York the combined ports account for 165,000 jobs and $6.3 billion in wages. (*The Wall Street Journal*, 10/18/96)

As a result, ports spend heavily to upgrade their facilities and to attract customers. That is good news for exporters, as some ports are offering incentives to users. For example, on August 9, 1996, a Massachusetts law went into effect that offers a dollar-for-dollar tax credit to firms that pay the Harbor Maintenance Tax on goods shipped through the Port of Boston. (There is also litigation in some states challenging the collection of harbor maintenance fees.) Importers and exporters should contact state maritime agencies or ports directly to find out about similar incentive programs.

The contested Harbor Maintenance Tax is slated for Supreme Court review sometime in 1998. At least two lower courts, including the Federal Circuit Court, found the tax unconstitutional. At stake are refunds of at least $1 billion to companies that have paid the tax regularly in recent years. The government has appealed to the high court, arguing that the tax is not only constitutional, but necessary as a revenue source of the maintenance of ports and harbors.

Guidance

The size and configuration of the overall load determines the ocean freight charges. Shipping a container of goods is generally cheaper than shipping goods that require special handling, such as a yacht resting in a shipping cradle. The cost of shipping a forty-foot container of goods from major East Coast ports such as Port Elizabeth in New Jersey or the Port of Baltimore to the Port of Rotterdam or Bremerhaven in Germany is between $2,000 and $4,000 on most steamship lines. Special restrictions or handling increase costs. (See Chapter 6 for more information on shipping.)

Form 4.01 is a worksheet for keeping track of landed costs. Exporters can expect to encounter the following landed costs:

1. *Export packing fees.* Export packing fees pay for the crating and packing of shipments and may cover the use of wood products, plastics, cardboard, liquid fillers, and other materials required to protect goods from humidity, shock, and vibration. Costs range widely, according to the nature of each shipment.

2. *Banking fees.* Banking fees include the processing of bank documents such as letters of credit and similar instruments. Fees vary within the industry, but one can expect to pay from $15 to $40 per transaction, or an hourly rate, which may be higher. (For more information on banking issues generally, see Chapter 5.)

3. *Forwarder fees.* Freight forwarders customarily charge a basic handling fee per transaction, ranging between $10 and $25. Hazardous items may be subject to surcharges.

4. *Documentation charges.* Invoices, packing lists, certificates of origin, export licenses, export declarations, faxes, and telexes cost $10 to $20 per document. The exporter may choose to pay a freight forwarder for the acquisition and preparation of these documents.

5. *Messenger fees.* When an outside document delivery company (such as DHL, Federal Express, or the U.S. Postal Service) helps with a shipment, a messenger fee is charged.

6. *Transfer fees.* Transporting a product from the freight forwarder's facility to an airline or ocean carrier costs about $0.06 to $0.10 per kilo. The fee applies whether the exporter's vehicle or that of an outside vendor is used.

7. *Insurance premiums and placement fees.* All forwarders maintain open insurance policies that allow for maximum amounts of coverage per shipment. (For a shipment of unusually high value, an exporter may have to make special insurance arrangements in advance.) When an exporter requests insurance coverage for a shipment through a forwarder, the premium depends not only on the product being shipped but also on the destination country's stability and economic conditions. The normal range is $0.50 to $0.95 per $100 in value. In addition to

insurance premiums, exporters are expected to pay a placement fee, the forwarding industry charge for physically producing an insurance certificate. (See Chapter 12 for more information on insurance.)

8. *Ocean pier loading, wharfage, and handling charges.* These charges, also called pier handling, are levied by the receiving pier or terminal to remove cargo from the inland drayage vehicle and deposit it onto the pier.

9. *Heavy lift charges.* These are fees assessed for lifting outsized containers that require a crane or other specialized equipment. These fees are generally assessed by the port or subcontractor working for the port authority.

10. *Ocean currency adjustment factor (CAF).* This charge, levied by the ocean lines, covers the cost of adjusting for fluctuating currency values between the time of departure and the time of arrival when an export transaction requires converting one currency into another.

11. *Bunker fuel, bunker adjustment fee (BAF).* The ocean lines charge for the expense of bringing a bunker fuel barge alongside a vessel to refuel it at foreign ports. (Note that this is not a fee for fuel.)

12. *Harbor maintenance fees (HMF).* U.S. Customs collects a fee to support the overall maintenance of U.S. harbors and ports. Both exporters and importers pay based on a percentage of the transactional value of the import or export. Currently, fees of 0.125 percent are charged.

13. *Ocean freight/full container load (FCL).* These charges, also known as base ocean freight (BOF), are levied by the steamship lines to cover the cost of transporting a full container from origin to destination port.

14. *Ocean freight/less than container load (LCL), weight/volume.* Ocean lines and carriers like freight forwarders assess charges to cover the cost of transporting less than full container loads from origin to destination port. These charges are usually calculated on a weight or volume basis. Most lines calculate the ocean freight rate based on one metric ton (1,000 kilograms equals 2,204 pounds) or one cubic meter (one CM equals 35.312 cubic feet) of space. The exporter pays this fee.

15. *Ocean destination delivery charge/full container load or container service charge (CSC).* A destination charge is one that the steamship line levies for the inward handling of full containers from the vessel to the ocean line's designated terminal. This fee is collected from the consignee named on the bill of lading.

16. *Ocean container usage fee.* The port authority or the responsible local agency at the port charges for the outward or inward movement of FCL cargo through the port terminal or facility. The fee is charged to the exporter or importer named on the ocean bill of lading.

17. *Terminal handling charges (THC).* This charge, also known as a port surcharge or origin charge, is levied by the steamship line for the movement of cargo from the line's terminal to the ocean vessel. It is based on weight or measure and is calculated in the same way as base ocean freight. Both the ports of shipment and destination may assess this fee to each party to the transaction.

18. *Preshipment inspection cost.* A preshipment inspection is undertaken at the request of the buyer or seller to confirm the condition, quantity, or any other factors regarding the goods. The buyer generally bears this cost depending on the terms of sale. The inspection may be conducted by an agent of the insurance or bonding company or an independent agency.

19. *Document transfer fee.* Whenever a forwarder receives documents from overseas and must transfer them to a customs broker or another forwarder, a document transfer fee is charged to the exporter.

20. *Certification fee.* This is a charge for special authentication of visas and other documents. The exporter pays this fee.

21. *Brokerage/entry fee.* A customs broker charges a fee for filing the documents necessary to release a shipment for entry into another country. The exporter pays this fee.

22. *Customs duties.* When goods are shipped for export, the country of final destination assesses import taxes, called duties. The importer generally pays the duties. Duties may be based on the value of the goods (*ad valorem* duties), specific factors such as weight or quantity (specific duties), or a combination of value and other factors (compound duties). Duties vary from country to country. For example, Hong Kong imposes no duty on textiles or computers, whereas Mexico charges 30.68 percent for each of these products. (For more information on duties, see section 4.4 and Chapter 10.)

23. *Sales and value-added tax (VAT).* In most cases, a value-added tax is imposed on the stated value of the goods as described on the commercial invoice, including the transportation cost and the customs duty. As with foreign duties, these taxes vary widely among countries. In Europe, they range from 15 percent in Spain to 25 percent in Denmark. The buyer generally pays the value-added tax and has taken that expense into account in the sales negotiation.

24. *Customs examination fee.* A fee is assessed by Customs if opening and reclosing parcels is required for customs inspection.

25. *Congestion surcharge.* At high-traffic times of the year, ports may impose an additional fee on vessels trying to land cargo.

26. *Delivery charge.* This is a fee for delivering goods after they have been released from Customs.

27. *Various fines and penalties.* Improperly marking goods, attempting to enter goods whose importation is forbidden, falsifying declarations or values, or violating any of a number of other regulations can result in unnecessary charges.

4.4 FOREIGN COSTS

The costs assessed by officials in the country of ultimate destination vary according to the country in question. The following example is intended to give exporters a sense of the types of costs they can expect to pay when shipping goods abroad.

EXAMPLE

When shipping goods to Brazil, exporters can expect the following costs:

- *Duties.* The average duty rate for goods shipped into Brazil is 14 percent of the CIF value of the shipment.
- *Syndicate fee.* This fee is 2.2 percent of the CIF value.
- *Brokerage fee.* This fee is 1 percent of the CIF value.
- *Administrative commission.* Approximately $50.
- *Port tax.* Taxed at 3 percent of the CIF value.
- *Industrial products tax.* This tax is assessed at the point of sale and varies from 0 to 15 percent of the CIF value, depending on the nature of the product. Raw materials imported for manufacturing purposes are exempt from this and other taxes.
- *Merchandise circulation tax.* This tax is imposed by state governments within Brazil. It is a value-added tax based on the CIF value of the goods and is generally 17 percent. Construction, mining, and energy equipment; most fuels; and other industrial products are exempt from this tax.

Exporters need to remember that if the documentation required by Brazilian authorities is incorrect or if an import license has not been secured, substantial fines may be levied and the goods impounded. Valuable information on import regulations of individual countries may be found in the National Trade Data Bank. Exporters are also encouraged to work with a freight forwarder familiar with the requirements of the country in question.

Summary of Key Points Raised in This Chapter

Exporters must take into consideration a wide range of export transaction costs when establishing an export price.

In pricing for export, exporters must consider their foreign market objectives, foreign market demand, competition, and costs.

To determine a pricing strategy, exporters must clearly define their foreign market objectives—whether that objective is to enter the market to test the waters or to sell a product developed especially for that market.

Market demand depends on demographic, economic, political, and technological factors.

Currency fluctuations play an important part in defining a foreign market objective.

Costs associated with international transactions include shipping costs, landed costs, and foreign customs costs.

Incoterms are standardized shipping terms used in international transactions to define the roles and responsibilities of the buyer and seller.

Some incoterms impose additional responsibilities (including payment of insurance premiums and tariffs) on parties to the transaction.

When the ''ex works'' shipping term is used, the buyer bears maximum responsibility for shipping.

Under the ''F'' series of incoterms, the buyer pays the main carriage costs.

Under the "C" series of incoterms, the seller pays the main carriage costs and may have additional responsibilities such as payment of insurance premiums.

Under the "D" series of incoterms, the seller is responsible for main goods available at the destination and may be required to pay duties and taxes on the shipment.

Landed costs are the fees, charges, and premiums associated with shipping goods for export, separate from the cost of transportation itself.

Form 4.01   Landed cost worksheet.

Export packing charges   ———
Banking charges   ———
Foreign inland freight to port of export   ———
Transfer charges*   ———
Forwarder fees   ———
Pier loading and wharfage**   ———
Ocean freight per container** (FCL)†   ———
Destination delivery charge**   ———
Ocean freight (cubic meters x rate/m^3) (LCL)††   ———
Airfreight charges* (kilos x rate/kilo)   ———
Currency adjustment fee (CAF)   ———
Insurance   ———
Pier handling charges   ———
Container usage**   ———
Document transfer fee*   ———
Terminal handling fee*   ———
Entry fee   ———
Customs duty and user fees   ———
Harbor maintenance fee   ———
Customs examination fee   ———
Inland freight charges   ———
Total estimated cost to land goods from ex factory   ———

  *Applicable to air shipments only
 **Applicable to ocean shipments only
  †Full container load (i.e., 20- or 40-foot ocean container)
 ††Less than container load (i.e., consolidated)

5

International Sales Transactions

Key Questions Answered in This Chapter

193

Why are shipping documents essential to a letter of credit
    transaction?   **5.5.6**
What payment methods serve as alternatives if the buyer can-
    not obtain a letter of credit?   **5.4, 5.**

Introduction

For small and midsize companies, receiving payment for goods and services can
be one of the most complex aspects of international trade. The legal protection
available to exporters is greatly enhanced when payment from a foreign customer
is guaranteed by means of well-negotiated sales documents and use of appropriate methods of payment.

    The key to a smooth transaction is accurate documentation. Whether working
with contract or through a lending institution to obtain payment, exporters must
keep channels of communication with the foreign customer clear. Both parties
must take into account:

- The terms and conditions of the transaction
- The types of documents involved
- The order in which documents are prepared and exchanged
- The method of payment

5.1 QUOTATIONS

5.1.1 The Request for Quotation

Many export transactions, particularly first-time transactions, begin with an inquiry from a foreign buyer. Generally, the prospective buyer requests a price quotation for a quantity of goods; he or she may also specify a particular delivery
date, method of delivery, shipping term, or other sales terms.

    For example, in Form 5.01, Request for Quotation, the prospective buyer re-
quests goods to be shipped on a CIF (cost, insurance, and freight) basis. Whenever
a seller receives a quotation request, he or she should note all terms and clarify
conditions of sale that are vague or unspecified.

5.1.2 Preparing a Cost Sheet

Before responding to a request for quotation, the seller should carefully consider
all expenses associated with the sale and should contact a freight forwarder regarding costs about which the seller may be unaware. These costs are itemized on
a cost sheet, a worksheet prepared for the exporter's internal use only. When
preparing a cost sheet, exporters should consider:

- The price of the goods
- Landed costs (discussed in section 4.3)

   ● Shipping costs
   ● Shipping terms (see section 4.3)
   ● Insurance costs (see Chapter 12)
   ● Foreign duties, if any

See Form 5.02 for a sample export cost sheet.

5.1.3 Issuing a Quotation to a Foreign Buyer

A quotation is the seller's formal estimate of the price of the goods, taking into account all expenses. Quotations are contractual documents and consequently must be prepared with care. The seller must ensure that all of its terms and conditions are clear. With the quotation, the buyer and seller should also resolve any differences in the terms and conditions of sale.

The quotation should contain the following information:

1. The buyer's name and address.
2. The buyer's reference number and date of inquiry.
3. A list of products.
4. A brief description of the products. (Because the buyer may be unfamiliar with the product, a brief description will clarify exactly what is being sold.)
5. The unit price of each item, in U.S. dollars.
6. Gross and net shipping weight, in metric units where appropriate.
7. Total cubic volume and dimensions of goods when packed for shipping, in metric units where appropriate.
8. Trade discounts offered, if applicable.
9. The delivery point.
10. The terms of sale under which the transaction will be carried out.
11. Insurance and shipping costs.
12. The estimated shipping date to the buyer's factory or from a U.S. port. (**Note.** It is preferable to specify the shipping date from the U.S. port.)
13. The estimated date of shipment arrival.
14. A validity period for the quotation. Price quotations should state explicitly that they are subject to change without notice. If a specific price has been determined, the exporter should state a precise period during which the offer remains valid.

See Form 5.03 for a sample quotation.

5.1.4 Pro Forma Invoices

A pro forma invoice is essentially a quotation in invoice format. Depending on the laws of the buyer's country, the buyer may need a pro forma invoice from the seller in order to apply for an import license or arrange for financing.

In addition to the items included in the quotation, the pro forma invoice may need to include the following:

- A statement certifying that the invoice is true and correct.
- A statement noting the country of origin of the goods.

See Form 5.04 for a sample pro forma invoice.

Note. Exporters should consider submitting a pro forma invoice with all quotations.

5.2   PURCHASE ORDERS AND ACCEPTANCES

5.2.1   The Buyer's Purchase Order

In response to the seller's quotation, the buyer forwards an order to purchase goods. At this stage, the seller should make certain that the terms and conditions of the purchase order do not conflict with those contained in the quotation. Buyers can and do include additional or conflicting terms, which can become binding on the seller if no precautions are taken.

Guidance

To safeguard against problems caused by conflicting sales terms, sellers should object immediately to all different terms and state expressly in all documents that the seller agrees to make sales only on its own terms.

See Form 5.05 for a sample buyer's purchase order.

5.2.2   Seller's Response to Buyer's Purchase Order

On receipt of a purchase order, the seller has several response options, depending on whether he or she wishes to commit immediately to the sales agreement.

Purchase Order Acknowledgement

The purchase order acknowledgement confirms receipt of the buyer's purchase order, but, if worded properly, does not commit the seller to the sale. This form allows the seller to take time to object to conflicting terms, check the buyer's credit, and generally prepare for or decide against accepting the order. For maximum protection, the acknowledgement should state clearly that the seller has not yet accepted the purchase order.

For a sample purchase order acknowledgement, see Form 5.06.

Purchase Order Acceptance

By contrast, the purchase order acceptance is a confirmation of the sale and its terms. In the acceptance, the seller should provide a detailed list of all terms and conditions, to ensure that these control the transaction.

Note. If the purchase order contains different terms, the seller should include in the purchase order acceptance a statement that the order is accepted only on the seller's terms and only if the buyer confirms its acceptance of the seller's terms.

See Form 5.07 for a sample purchase order acceptance.

5.3 COMMERCIAL INVOICES

The commercial invoice documents the entire transaction between the buyer and seller; it is the seller's request for payment. The commercial invoice must be as complete and accurate as possible because it serves as a record of the price of the goods and as such is scrutinized by the customs service of the importing country for purposes of assessing duties and tariffs. If a letter of credit is used as the method of payment (see section 5.5), the commercial invoice is sent to the banks involved in the transaction and is used to clear payment to the seller.

See Form 5.08 for a sample commercial invoice.

Invoice Requirements

Most foreign countries have their own invoicing requirements for customs purposes. Before preparing a commercial invoice, sellers should consult a buyer or a freight forwarder for information on the requirements of the receiving country. The Department of Commerce and its regional export assistance centers are also sources of reliable information on commercial invoice requirements. (See Chapter 3, Appendix A, for a directory of assistance centers.)

5.4 METHODS OF PAYMENT

In an export transaction, the exporter has a number of methods of international payment, each offering varying degrees of risk to both parties. In choosing a payment method, the seller must assess the risks of the transaction and select the method that best protects the parties' interests.

The different methods of payment are described in the following sections. For a chart comparing the relative risks of each method of payment, see Appendix A at the end of this chapter.

Cash in Advance

A transaction in which payment is made in cash in advance poses the least risk to the seller, since payment is made prior to shipment of the exported goods. However, this method poses great risks to the buyer: Because goods are made available only after payment has been made, the buyer is compelled to rely on the exporter to ship the goods as ordered and has little recourse if the goods do not conform to the order.

Letter of Credit

From the perspective of both the importer and exporter, a letter of credit is one of the safest ways to ensure that the seller is paid and that the buyer receives the goods as ordered. A letter of credit is a contract between the exporter's and importer's banks containing the terms and conditions of the sale. The exporter's risks are minimal and the buyer is assured of adequate quality and quantity. Goods are available after payment, and payment is made after the appropriate documents are made available at shipment.

The letter of credit process is detailed in section 5.5. In addition, Form 5.09 is a sample of a letter of credit.

Sight Draft

A sight draft is similar to a letter of credit, in that banks are used to effect payment. Unlike a letter of credit, however, payment is not guaranteed by the buyer's bank. Goods are available after payment, and payment is made when appropriate documents are presented to the importer's bank.

For the buyer, a sight draft is advantageous because it assures him or her that the received goods are adequate in quality and quantity. But the sight draft is somewhat riskier for the seller because if the draft is unpaid, goods must be returned or disposed of, often at a loss. The sight draft payment process is detailed in section 5.6.

Time Draft

A time draft is similar to a sight draft, except that it permits the buyer to make payment within a specified time after receipt of the goods. For the buyer, this method is advantageous because it allows him or her to check the shipment before payment. There are risks for the seller, though: If the buyer fails to pay, the goods must be returned or disposed of, usually at a loss. The time draft payment process is detailed in section 5.6.

Consignment

In a consignment sale, goods are forwarded to the buyer, but the exporter retains legal title to them. This presents no risk for the buyer, but substantial risk to the exporter, who is not paid until the consigned goods are sold or used.

Open Account

When the buyer maintains an open account, goods are shipped before payment and the buyer agrees to pay within a certain period of time. The seller bears complete risk in the event that the buyer defaults.

5.5   LETTERS OF CREDIT

The method of payment that offers the best assurances to both parties is the letter of credit. The exporter is guaranteed payment and the buyer is guaranteed a shipment that conforms to the sales agreement.

A letter of credit is a contract between the exporter's and importer's banks, under which the banks verify the sale before issuing payment. The banks never see or examine the goods, but they examine all documents related to the transaction and make sure that they are issued in exact accordance with the terms of sale as described in the letter of credit. When all terms and conditions have been met, the seller is paid and the goods are released.

The key to a smooth letter of credit transaction is proper documentation and an understanding of the payment process. This section details each element in the process:

- The parties involved in the transaction
- The different types of letters of credit
- The letter of credit cycle
- The elements of a letter of credit
- The documents that are required along with the letter of credit

5.5.1   *Parties to a Letter of Credit*

A letter of credit transaction involves the following parties:

1. *The account party.* Also known as the accountee, this is the buyer-importer who arranges to have the letter of credit established (e.g., "opened").

2. *The beneficiary.* The beneficiary is the seller, exporter, or shipper for whom the letter of credit is opened.

3. *The opening bank.* Also known as the issuing bank, this is the account party's bank, which issues the letter of credit. The opening bank usually requires the buyer to submit an application form for the letter of credit and may require collateral or sufficient funds to cover the letter of credit. See Form 5.10 for a sample letter of credit application.

4. *The advising bank.* The advising bank notifies the seller-beneficiary that another bank has opened a letter of credit in its (the seller's) favor. The seller works with the advising bank throughout the course of the transaction. The advising bank reviews the shipping and sales documents to ensure that they meet the terms described in the letter of credit.

5. *The confirming bank.* The advising bank becomes the confirming bank when, by adding its confirmation, it assumes the obligation to pay the seller. The letter of credit then becomes a confirmed letter of credit.

Note. The seller-exporter should insist that the advising or confirming bank be a bank in the seller's home country, as it is the role of the bank or banks to verify all signatures on the letter of credit and ensure that the opening bank has a valid obligation to pay the seller.

6. *The negotiating bank.* This is the bank that advances funds upon presentation of the documents described in the letter of credit.

Note. Generally, the same bank performs the advising, confirming, and negotiating functions. Separate negotiating banks are not commonly used in the United States. However, a U.S. exporter may wish to choose as a negotiating bank one with which it has a long-standing relationship in order to take advantage of lower fees and quicker payment of credit. To do so, the letter of credit must state that it is "freely negotiable with any bank," and all documents must be forwarded to the negotiating bank.

7. *Freight forwarders and customs brokers.* For all but the most experienced exporters, or those with in-house documentation specialists, a freight forwarder or customs broker will help ensure that all documents conform exactly to the terms outlined in the letter of credit.

5.5.2 *Types of Letters of Credit*

There are several types of letters of credit, presenting varying degrees of risk to the buyer and seller.

Commercial Letter of Credit

This is the general term describing all the various types of letters of credit. See Form 5.09 for a sample letter of credit.

Confirmed Letter of Credit

In a confirmed letter of credit, a second bank, in addition to the issuing bank, assumes the responsibility of payment to the seller. Because the second bank is usually in the seller's own country and adds its own guarantee to the seller, the confirmed letter of credit, when it is irrevocable, gives the seller an extra measure of protection. See Form 5.11 for a sample confirmation.

Irrevocable Letter of Credit

An irrevocable letter of credit is one for which the issuing bank waives all rights to cancel or amend any terms of the credit without the consent of the seller or beneficiary. An irrevocable letter of credit gives the seller greater assurance of payment, but payment remains dependent on a foreign issuing bank. The buyer has less flexibility with an irrevocable credit, as terms can only be amended or canceled if all parties to the transaction are in agreement.

Note. U.S. exporters should insist that letters of credit be irrevocable. This locks parties into the terms agreed upon in the sales transaction and outlined in the letter of credit.

Revolving Credit

A revolving credit is used in ongoing sales transactions, pursuant to which there are regularly scheduled shipments of goods. It saves both parties the expense of opening a new letter of credit with each shipment. For a sample revolving letter of credit, see Form 5.12.

Transferable Letter of Credit

A transferable letter of credit is one that can be transferred by the original seller-beneficiary, in whole or in part, to other beneficiaries. This method is often used when third parties such as brokers or agents are involved. See Form 5.13 for a sample transfer of credit.

5.5.3 *The Letter of Credit Cycle*

The following is a list of steps in the process of obtaining payment via letter of credit:

1. The buyer and seller conclude a sales agreement in which both parties agree to use a letter of credit as the method of payment. It is important to remember that the terms described in the letter of credit are negotiable between the buyer and seller. The chosen terms (e.g., incoterms and type of insurance, among others) can mean greatly increased costs and risks to either party. Careful negotiating is required, since all later sales documents must conform to the letter of credit.

2. The buyer applies to the issuing bank for a letter of credit. The buyer is usually required to sign a letter of credit agreement form issued by the bank. Banks use different criteria for issuing letters of credit. In some cases, the buyer must post 100 percent collateral on the value of the credit. Most banks require that the applicant have an established account relationship with the bank. Buyers may be asked to sign a letter of commitment to guarantee payment. See Form 5.10 for a sample letter of credit application.

3. The letter of credit is issued by the opening bank as either an irrevocable or revocable letter of credit and is sent to the advising bank. The advising bank notifies the seller that another bank has opened the credit. The advising bank may confirm the credit.

4. The advising bank receives the letter of credit and delivers it to the seller. All signatures on the letter of credit are verified by the advising bank.

5. The seller reviews the letter of credit to make sure that the terms and conditions conform to those in the sales agreement.

6. The seller-beneficiary contacts a freight forwarder or customs broker, who assists in the preparation of shipping documents in accordance with the terms specified in the letter of credit.

7. The freight forwarder or customs broker issues the transport documents in accordance with the terms of the credit.

8. The goods are shipped and the original transport document is sent to the seller. The seller, with the assistance of the forwarder or broker, prepares the rest of the shipping documents according to the exact terms of the letter of credit, then submits the documents to the advising bank.

9. If the advising bank determines that the shipping documents are in accordance with the terms of the letter of credit, payment is made to the seller-beneficiary.

10. The advising bank sends the documents to the opening/issuing bank.

11. If the opening bank determines that the documents are in order, the bank debits the buyer's account and sends the documents to the buyer with a notice of debit to the account.

12. The buyer receives the documents and picks up the merchandise at the port of discharge.

Bank Fees

Numerous bank charges are associated with a letter of credit transaction, including:

- Advising fees
- Negotiating fees
- Charges for cables, telexes, and other forms of communications
- Reimbursement fees
- Amendment fees

5.5.4 Letter of Credit Elements

All U.S. exporters should ensure that the following elements are present when using a letter of credit:

1. The letter of credit and all related documentation and transactions should be in English.
2. The customer's purchase order number should be indicated on the letter of credit.
3. The name of the buyer's opening bank and the bank reference number should be clearly indicated.
4. Payment should be specified in U.S. dollars.
5. Payment terms should be "at sight."
6. The letter of credit should be irrevocable and confirmed by the advising U.S. bank. The advising bank's reference number should be clearly identified. If possible, the letter of credit should also be confirmed through the seller's bank.
7. The description of merchandise should be in clear and general terms.

8. The letter of credit must be subject to the terms described in the most recent revision of the International Chamber of Commerce, Publication 500, "Uniform Customs and Practice for Documentary Credit."

9. The seller should be described using a legal corporate name. Many banks will not issue letters of credit to individuals.

10. Shipping terms (i.e., incoterms) should be stated as clearly as possible and should match the terms that were agreed upon by the buyer and seller in the sales agreement.

11. The latest shipping date and the letter of credit expiration date should be clearly indicated. The expiration date should be at least twenty-one days after the date of shipment of the goods.

12. The seller-beneficiary should be allowed at least twenty-one days to present the shipping documents to the bank.

13. Transshipment and partial shipments should not be permitted under the letter of credit.

14. No freight forwarder should be specified by name. This will permit the seller to select a forwarder and to use consolidated shipping, which reduces costs.

15. No airline or shipping line should be specified by name. This gives the freight forwarder flexibility in obtaining routing with the lowest rates.

16. Airway bills of lading should be consigned to the issuing bank.

5.5.5 Reviewing the Letter of Credit

When the exporter/seller receives the letter of credit from his or her advising bank, certain points should always be checked. If there are discrepancies, the exporter should ask the buyer to formally amend the letter of credit. (See Form 5.14 for a sample letter of credit amendment form.) A thorough checklist includes:

- Whether the credit is revocable or irrevocable
- Whether the credit is confirmed or unconfirmed
- When the credit expires
- Where the credit expires
- The accuracy of the buyer's and seller's titles and addresses
- The amount of the credit
- The tenor of the draft (i.e., whether the payment is due at sight, a given number of days after sight, or a given number of days after presentation of a draft)
- The location of the paying bank
- Documents required to be presented by the beneficiary
- Description and unit price of the merchandise
- The point of shipment and destination
- Stipulations on partial shipments and transshipments
- Shipping terms (i.e., incoterms)
- Whether the letter of credit is subject to UCP (Uniform Customs and Practice) terms
- Special instructions

5.5.6 *Letter of Credit Documentation*

To ensure speed and accuracy in a letter of credit transaction, all documents must conform exactly to the terms and conditions specified in the letter of credit. Documents common to most letter of credit transactions include:

- Commercial invoice
- Ocean bill of lading or airway bill
- Insurance certificate
- Packing list (if necessary)
- Country of origin certificate (if necessary)
- Inspection certificate (if required by buyer)
- Dock receipt

Commercial Invoice

As noted in section 5.3, the commercial invoice is a document that memorializes all final terms and conditions of the export transaction. As such, it plays a critical role in the letter of credit, because the banks involved will base their decision to authorize payment on the terms and conditions in the invoice. Therefore, sellers must be sure that the commercial invoice is complete, accurate, and specific by verifying the following:

1. The invoice should be issued by the seller, unless otherwise stated in the letter of credit.
2. It should be made out to the buyer-account party unless otherwise stated in the letter of credit.
3. The amount should not be in excess of the credit amount or the available balance of the credit.
4. The full shipment should be covered if partial shipments are not permitted.
5. The weights, quantities, and measures should agree with those stated in the bill of lading or other documents.
6. The description of goods should be identical to that in the credit.
7. Unit prices should agree with the credit.
8. Marks, numbers, and other information should be consistent on all documents.
9. Shipping terms should be those specified in the letter of credit.
10. Calculations, extensions, and additions should be checked for accuracy.
11. The invoice should not describe any charges or merchandise not specified in the credit.
12. The invoice should not include terms such as "used," "rebuilt," or "secondhand" unless authorized in the credit.
13. The commercial invoice should be signed and certified, and should meet all foreign customs requirements.

Ocean and Airway Bills of Lading

The bill of lading is a document that establishes the terms of a contract between a shipper and a transportation company under which freight is to be moved between specified points for a specified charge. The bill of lading is usually prepared by the shipper on forms issued by the carrier; it serves as a document of title, a contract of carriage, and a receipt for the goods shipped.

Bills of lading are commonly used as documentation for letters of credit and as such must be carefully checked for errors and inconsistencies. Exporters should verify the following:

1. The ocean bill of lading should be the full, original set as indicated at the bottom of the document.
2. The ports of loading and discharge must be correct.
3. The document must be properly signed.
4. The "notify" party should be correct.
5. Marks and numbers must agree with other documents.
6. The number of packages and stated weights must be correct.
7. If so required, the document should indicate whether the goods are to be shipped "on board." The term "on deck" should not appear unless indicated in the credit.
8. The bill of lading should be clean, meaning that there are no clauses indicating damaged or defective goods or packages.
9. The document should be properly signed and dated, within the time frame indicated on the credit.
10. The bill of lading should be properly endorsed.
11. According to the terms of the credit, the bill of lading should be marked "freight collect" or "freight prepaid." Terms such as "freight payable" or "freight to be paid" are not acceptable.
12. The entire scope of the shipment of the goods should be covered in one bill of lading.
13. There should be no provisions for transshipments or partial shipments if not provided for in the credit.
14. Bills of lading should not be presented more than twenty-one days after their date of issuance or "on board" date.

See Form 5.15 for a sample bill of lading.

Insurance Documents

Commonly, proof of insurance (either an insurance policy or a certificate of insurance) is required under the terms of the sales agreement and letter of credit. Exporters should verify the following elements of the insurance documents:

1. The insurance document presented should be the exact one specified in the credit. For example, an insurance certificate is not acceptable when an

insurance policy is required; likewise, cover notes issued by customs brokers are not acceptable unless so specified in the credit.

2. The amount of insurance should be sufficient. A rule of thumb is that the amount should be at least equal to the CIF/CIP value (cost, insurance, and freight/carriage and insurance to be paid) or the greater of the draft amount or invoice values.

3. The insurance document should be properly signed and countersigned, if required.

4. The document should be endorsed by the party to whom any loss is payable.

5. All dates should agree with the bills of lading and other documents.

6. The policy should be in the same currency as the credit, unless otherwise specified.

7. The scope of the entire transit of the goods should agree with that shown on the credit.

8. All packaging and shipping marks should agree with the information on all the other documents. (For more information on packaging and shipping marks, see section 6.1.)

9. Specific risks should be covered as required by the credit.

See Form 5.16 for sample insurance certificate.

Packing List

A packing list shows the number and kinds of items being shipped, as well as other information needed for transport purposes. This form is sometimes required under the customs laws of the importing country. It should specify:

- The number of pieces contained in the shipment
- The gross and net weights of each piece
- The weight of each piece
- The dimensions of each piece
- The ship date
- The order number
- The carrier
- The quantity shipped
- Markings used on the packaging

See Form 5.17 for a sample packing list.

Certificate of Origin

Under the customs laws of some countries, exporters are required to provide a certificate showing the origin of the goods exported. This certificate is prepared and signed by the exporter and further certified by a local chamber of commerce. (See Form 5.18 for a sample certificate of origin.)

Inspection Certificate

The buyer may make an inspection certificate a condition of the sale and thus part of the letter of credit. This certificate, prepared by an inspection company, notifies the buyer that the goods conform to the sales agreement.

Note. Buyers may also require inspection certificates in other forms of payment, such as sight drafts and time drafts.

See Form 5.19 for a sample inspection certificate.

5.5.7 *Common Documentation Discrepancies*

The exporter should be alert to discrepancies in the documentation, which, if left uncorrected, could delay payment. Among the discrepancies to watch out for:

1. Drafts are presented after the letter of credit has expired or after the time allotted for shipment has expired.
2. The invoice value or the amount of the draft exceeds the amount specified under terms of the letter of credit.
3. Charges included in the invoice are not specified in the letter of credit.
4. The amount of insurance coverage is inadequate or the coverage does not include risks required by the letter of credit.
5. The insurance document is not endorsed or countersigned.
6. The date of the insurance policy or certificate is later than the dates specified on the bills of lading.
7. Bills of lading contain notations that qualify the condition of the goods or packing.
8. "On board" endorsements or changes on bills of lading are not signed by the carrier or its agent or initialed by the party that signed the bill of lading.
9. "On board" endorsements are not dated.
10. Bills of lading are not endorsed.
11. Bills of lading are made out "to order" when the letter of credit specifies a "straight" bill of lading direct to the consignee. In some countries, "to order" bills of lading are prohibited.
12. Bills of lading do not indicate "freight prepaid" or "freight collect" as stipulated on the letter of credit.
13. Bills of lading are marked "freight prepaid" and freight charges are not included in the invoice.
14. Descriptions, marks, numbers, weights, quantities, and measures are not consistent on all documents or are not as required by the terms of the letter of credit.
15. Documents required by the letter of credit are missing.
16. Documents are not presented within a reasonable time after issuance.
17. The invoice does not specify shipping terms (e.g., incoterms) as stated in the letter of credit.
18. The invoice is not signed as the letter of credit requires.

5.6   SIGHT DRAFTS AND TIME DRAFTS

If the foreign buyer is unable to open a letter of credit (e.g., when the buyer's bank will not guarantee payment), the exporter may have to consider another method of payment. Sight drafts and time drafts are the next best methods.

Sight Drafts

A sight draft is similar to a letter of credit except that payment to the seller is not guaranteed. However, since the buyer's bank takes possession of the shipping documents and will not release them to the buyer until payment has been made, the exporter can be reasonably assured that the goods are protected.

Steps in a sight draft collection are as follows:

1. In the sales agreement between the seller and buyer, the seller requests that the buyer secure the transaction by means of a direct collection, payable at sight.

2. The forwarder ships the goods according to the seller's instructions.

3. The transport document is issued in the name of the buyer's bank. This acts as a guarantee that the buyer will not take possession of the goods until payment is made to the seller.

4. The freight is shipped at the same time that all relevant shipping documents are sent from the seller's bank to the buyer's bank via direct collection, which has a collection number and instructions for the overseas bank.

5. When the documents are received by the overseas bank, the buyer is contacted. If the documents are in full compliance with the seller's instructions, the funds are transferred from the buyer's account to the seller's bank and the documents are released to the buyer. The buyer can then collect the goods at the port of entry.

6. The seller's bank releases the funds to the seller, less any charges.

Time Drafts

A time draft is similar to a sight draft except that the time draft generally allows the buyer to make payment within a specified time frame. This payment method presents a far greater risk to the exporter, especially if the buyer takes possession of the goods before payment has been made.

Summary of Key Points Raised in This Chapter

A quotation is the exporter's formal estimate of the price of the goods and is a contractual document.

Price quotations should state explicitly that they are subject to change without notice.

A pro forma invoice may be required under the customs laws of the buyer's country.

Exporters must take care to object to purchase order terms that conflict with the sales quotation.

A purchase order acknowledgement allows the exporter to take time to object to conflicting terms and prepare for or decide against accepting an order.

A commercial invoice documents the final terms and conditions of an export sale.

A letter of credit is a contract between banks which guarantees an export transaction.

There are several types of letters of credit—confirmed, irrevocable, revolving, and transferable.

Required documentation in a letter of credit usually includes a commercial invoice, a bill of lading, an insurance document, a packing list, a country of origin certificate, and an inspection certificate.

Sight drafts and time drafts are methods of payment that are available when a letter of credit cannot be obtained.

Appendix A   Comparison of Methods of Payment

Method	When Goods Are Available to Buyer	Time of Payment	Risks to Exporter	Risks to Importer
Cash in Advance	After payment	Before shipment	None	Maximum risk. Importer relies on exporter to ship goods as ordered.
Letter of Credit	After payment	When documents are made available at time of shipment.	Virtually none	Assured of quality and quantity of shipment, if inspection report is required.
Sight Draft	After payment	On presentation of draft to importer	If draft unpaid, goods must be returned or disposed of, usually at a loss.	Same as above
Time Draft	Before payment	On maturity of draft	Relies on the importer to pay draft. If unpaid, goods must be returned or disposed of.	Minimal. Importer can check quality of goods before payment.
Consignment	Before payment. Exporter retains title until goods are used or sold.	Varies in length	Substantial risk	None
Open Account	Before payment	As agreed.	Relies on importer to pay account as agreed— complete risk.	None

Form 5.01   Request for quotation.

Johnson Marina Ltd.
28 Hawthorne Road
Maitland 2000 NSW Australia

February 1, 1997

International Pleasure Boats, Inc.
West Industrial Park
Marblehead, MA
Attn: Ms. Valerie A. Smith

Dear Ms. Smith:

Pursuant to our meeting at the International Boating Exposition in Frankfurt last month, I would like to place an order for your IPB "Duro" sailcloth material, Model No. 1400-84.

Thus far, we have secured several clients, most whose interest lies on a sample basis. For this purpose, we will need approximately 1,000 yards.

Please supply us with a pro forma invoice on a CIF [cost, insurance, and freight] basis, so that we can prepare necessary import documents as soon as possible and initiate a letter of credit, if you so require.

Very truly yours,

JOHNSON MARINA
John S. Kennery
Vice President, Sales

Form 5.02   Export cost sheet.

General Information

Customer: _____   Reference No.: _____
Address: _____
Tel: _____
Fax: _____
Inquiry No./Date: _____
Payment Terms: _____
Product Description: _____

Shipment Information

Estimated Date of Shipment: _____
Origin: _____   Destination: _____
Weight (lbs.): _____ (kgs.): _____   Volume Weight (kgs.): _____

Dimensions	No. of Pieces	Length	Width	Height
_____	_____	_____	_____	_____
_____	_____	_____	_____	_____
_____	_____	_____	_____	_____
_____	_____	_____	_____	_____

Cost Worksheet

Item	Cost
Sale Price of Goods	$_____
Trade Discount	$_____
Packing	$_____
Air Freight	$_____
Ocean Freight	$_____
Handling	$_____
Inland Freight	$_____
Airport Transfer	$_____
Certificate of Origin	$_____
Letter of Credit and Banking Fees	$_____
Messenger Fees	$_____
Insurance	$_____
Dangerous Goods Surcharge	$_____
Other:	$_____
_____	$_____
_____	$_____
TOTAL	$_____

Prepared by: _____   Authorized by: _____
Date: _____   Date: _____

Form 5.03   Quotation.

From: _____

To: _____

Buyer's Reference/Inquiry No.: _____

PRODUCT

Quantity	Description	Price	Amount
_____	_____	_____	_____
_____	_____	_____	_____
_____	_____	_____	_____
_____	_____	_____	_____

SHIPMENT INFORMATION

Estimated Date of Shipment: _____
Estimated Date of Arrival: _____
Terms of Shipment: _____
Origin: _____   Destination: _____
Weight (lbs.): _____   Weight (kgs.): _____
Volume Weight (kgs.): _____

Dimensions	No. of Pieces	Length	Width	Height
_____	_____	_____	_____	_____
_____	_____	_____	_____	_____
_____	_____	_____	_____	_____

CHARGES

Sale Price of Goods	$_____
Trade Discount	$_____
Packing	$_____
Air Freight	$_____
Ocean Freight	$_____
Handling	$_____
Inland Freight	$_____
Airport Transfer	$_____
Certificate of Origin	$_____

Letter of Credit and Banking Fees $_____
Messenger Fees $_____
Insurance $_____
Inspection Fees $_____
Dangerous Goods Surcharge $_____
Other: $_____
_____ $_____
_____ $_____
_____ $_____
TOTAL $_____

Note: Rates are subject to change without notice. This offer remains valid until
  [date] .

Prepared By: _____   Authorized By: _____
Date: _____   Date: _____

Form 5.04   Sample pro forma invoice.

PRO FORMA INVOICE

International Pleasure Boats, Inc.
West Industrial Park
Marblehead, MA

February 7, 1997

Johnson Marina Ltd.
28 Hawthorne Road
Maitland 2000 NSW Australia
Attn: John Kennery

Dear Mr. Kennery:

Quantity:	1,000
Model:	1400-84
Description:	IPB Duro Sailcloth made in USA of 100 percent cotton weave canvas, unit of measure yards.
Unit Price:	$28.75
Extension:	$28,750.00
Handling Packaging:	$10.00
Forwarder's Airport Handling and Inland Freight	$26.00
Estimated Air Freight and Insurance	$344.50
Estimated CIF Sydney, Australia	$29,130.50
Estimated Gross Weight:	255 kilos
Estimated Net Weight:	250 lilos

Note: All prices quoted herein are U.S. dollars. Prices quoted for merchandise herein valid 60 days. Any changes in shipping costs or insurance are for the account of the buyer. Estimated shipment is 20 days from receipt of purchase order.

Form 5.05   Buyer's purchase order.

Johnson Marina Ltd.
28 Hawthorne Road
Maitland 2000 NSW Australia
Date: _____
Order No.: _____
(Order number must appear on all documents and correspondence re: this order.)

Vendor: _____
Vendor No.: _____
Terms: _____
Purchasing Contact and Telephone No.: _____
Ship to Arrive (Date): _____
Freight: _____
In-Plant Destination: _____
Requisition No.: _____
Accounting Code: _____
Ship to: _____

Quantity	Description /Part No.	Price	Total Cost
_____	_____	_____	_____
_____	_____	_____	_____
_____	_____	_____	_____

Form 5.06   Purchase order acknowledgment.

International Pleasure Boats, Inc.
West Industrial Park
Marblehead, MA

February 15, 1997

Johnson Marina Ltd.
28 Hawthorne Road
Maitland 2000 NSW
Australia
Attn: John Kennery

Dear Mr. Kennery:

This is to acknowledge your order of February 7, 1997. Please note that this is not an acceptance of your order; acceptance is conditioned on internal approval of all terms and conditions of sale. We are currently evaluating your order and will notify you of our decision as soon as possible.

Yours very truly,

INTERNATIONAL PLEASURE BOATS
Valerie A. Smith

Form 5.07   Purchase order acceptance.

International Pleasure Boats, Inc.
West Industrial Park
Marblehead, MA

February 15, 1997

Johnson Marina Ltd.
28 Hamilton Road
Maitland 2000 NSW Australia
Attn: John Kennery

Dear Mr. Kennery:

We are pleased to accept your order of February 7, subject only to the terms and conditions set forth as follows:

Quantity:	1,000
Model:	1400-84
Description:	IPB Duro Sailcloth made in U.S.A. of 100 percent cotton weave canvas, unit of measure yards.
Unit Price:	$28.75
Extension:	$28,750.00
Handling Packaging:	$10.00
Forwarder's Airport Handling and Inland Freight:	$26.00
Estimated Air Freight and Insurance:	$344.50
Estimated CIF Sydney, Australia	$29,130.50
Estimated Gross Weight:	255 kilos
Estimated Net Weight:	250 kilos

Yours very truly,
INTERNATIONAL PLEASURE BOATS
Valerie A. Smith

Form 5.08   Commercial invoice.

INVOICE

International Pleasure Boats, Inc.
West Industrial Park
Marblehead, MA USA

Bill to: Johnson Marina Ltd.   Ship to: Johnson Marina Ltd.
        28 Hawthorne Road   28 Hawthorne Road
        Maitland 2000 NSW   Maitland 2000 NSW
        Australia   Australia

Ship Date: _____   Order No.: _____   Salesperson: _____
Carrier: _____   Terms: _____
Quantity Ordered: _____   Quantity Shipped: _____
Part No. _____   Description: _____
Price: _____   Total: _____
These commodities are licensed by the United States for ultimate destination Australia.
Diversion contrary to U.S. law is prohibited.
Packed by: _____   No. of Pieces: _____
Gross Weight: _____ Net Weight: _____
Dimension: _____
TOTAL DUE: _____

Form 5.09   Sample letter of credit.

FIRST BANK, N.A.
Maitland, New South Wales Branch
P.O. Box 1000
Maitland 2000 NSW
Australia
Cable Address: FIRSTBANK

Irrevocable Commercial Letter of Credit
Drafts Drawn Hereunder Must Be Marked: "Drawn Under the First Bank, N.A.,
New South Wales, Credit No. 95-1000" and indicate the date hereof.

International Pleasure Boats, Inc.
West Industrial Park
Marblehead, MA USA

Gentlemen:

We hereby authorize you to draw on First Bank, N.A., New York, U.S.A. by order
of: _____
And for account of: _____
Up to an aggregate amount of: _____
Available by your drafts at sight for 100 percent of the invoice value.
Accompanied by:
 A signed commercial invoice stating the import license number.
 An insurance policy or certificate, endorsed in blank covering Institute Marine
  Cargo clauses (W.A.), Institute War, S.R.C.C. clauses including all risks for
  110 percent of the invoice value up to Buyer's Warehouse.
 Certificate of origin.
 Full set of clean "on board" ocean bills of lading made out to order and endorsed
  to First Bank, N.A., mentioning "freight prepaid" and dated not later
  than _____, covering shipment of _____ from _____ to CIP Port _____. Part
  shipments prohibited. Transshipments prohibited.

Drafts must be drawn and negotiated not later than _____.

The amounts thereof must be endorsed on this letter of credit.

The negotiating bank is to forward the draft(s) negotiated in compliance with the
terms above-mentioned to the drawee bank for reimbursement and the remaining
documents by airmail direct to us.

We hereby agree with the drawers, endorsers and bona fide holders of all drafts drawn
under and in compliance with the terms of this credit, that such drafts will be duly
honored upon presentation to the drawee.

This credit is subject to the Uniform Customs and Practice for Documentary Credits, International Chamber of Commerce Pub. No. 500.

Very truly yours,

FIRST BANK, N.A.
Authorized Signature: _____

Form 5.10   Sample letter of credit application.

COMMERCIAL LETTER OF CREDIT APPLICATION

NO. _____
DO NOT FILL IN

Gentlemen: Date: _____
Please issue an Irrevocable Letter of Credit and either
a) Notify through correspondent by ☐ Mail/Airmail: ☐ Airmail with brief advice by cable; or
b) ☐ Return to us for mailing to beneficiary; or
c) ☐ Mail directly to beneficiary; as follows:

| You are hereby authorized to instruct the negotiation bank to forward to you all documents relating to this letter of credit in one mailing only, *unless the box shown below has been checked by us.*

 ☐ Please instruct the negotiation bank to forward the relative documents to you in two mailings. | For Account of (Applicant)

 (Name)

 (Complete Address) |
| In Favor of (Beneficiary)

 (Name)

 (Complete Address) | Amount

 Drafts must be presented for negotiation or presented to drawee on or before (Expiry Date) |

Available by drafts at _____ drawn, at your option,
_____ Indicate Tenor
on you or your correspondent for _____ % of the invoice value.

DRAFTS MUST BE ACCOMPANIED BY THE FOLLOWING DOCUMENTS AS CHECKED:

(Invoices must include substantially the below commodity description, but only general description of the commodity on the remaining documents is required.)

1 ☐   Commercial Invoices in original and _____ copies
2 ☐   Special Customs Invoice in original and _____ copies
3 ☐   Weight list in _____ copies
4 ☐   Packing list in _____ copies
5 ☐   Other documents _____

6 ☐   Marine/War Insurance Policy or Certificate _____

(If Other insurance is Required, Please State Risks)
Full set Clean "On Board" Ocean Bills of Lading consigned
7 ☐   to order, endorsed in blank, or consigned to order of _____

Marked Notify: _____
COVERING: Merchandise described in the invoice as: (Mention commodity only in generic terms omitting details as to grade, quality, etc.)
_____
_____
_____

CHECK ONE: ☐ FAS   ☐ FOB   ☐ C & F   ☐ CIF   ☐ C & I   _____
                                                                (Indicate Place or Port)

| SHIPMENT FROM
 TO | Partial shipments are permitted/prohibited
 Transshipment is permitted/prohibited. |

☐ Draft(s) and documents must be presented to negotiating or paying bank within _____ days after the date of issuance of the Bill(s) of Lading or other shipping documents but within expiry date.
☐ Insurance effected by ourselves. We agree to keep insurance coverage in force until this transaction is completed.
The credit will be subject to the Uniform Customs and Practice for Documentary Credits of the International Chamber of Commerce recently in effect.
SPECIAL INSTRUCTIONS _____
_____
_____

| This Application is made subject to the Continuing Letter of Credit Agreement (Security Agreement) heretofore most recently executed by us and delivered to you, the provisions of which are hereby made applicable to this Application and the Credit.

 We warrant that no shipment involved in this Application is in violation of U.S. Treasury Foreign Assets Control or Cuban Assets Control Regulations. | _____
 (Applicant)
 _____
 (Address)
 _____
 (Authorized Signature)   (Title)
 _____
 (Authorized Signature)   (Title) |

Form 5.11   Confirmation of letter of credit.

FIRST BANK, N.A.
123 Main Street
New York, New York

Confirmed Irrevocable Credit
[*Date*]

Gentlemen:

We are pleased to advise that _____ has opened its irrevocable credit no. _____ in your favor in the amount of _____ against your drafts drawn at _____ on us to be accompanied by the following documents: [list]

The said issuer engages that each draft drawn under and in compliance with the terms of this advice will be duly honored if presented at our counters on or before _____. Each draft must recite that it is "drawn under confirmed irrevocable credit no. _____." This advice is subject to the Uniform Customs and Practice for Documentary Credits, ICC Publication No. 500.

We hereby confirm the said credit and engage to honor all drafts drawn under and in compliance with the terms hereof.

Yours truly,
FIRST BANK, N.A.
By: _____

Form 5.12   Revolving letter of credit.

FIRST BANK, N.A.
IRREVOCABLE LETTER OF CREDIT NO. 95-1000
March 5, 1997
To: International Pleasure Boats, Inc.
           West Industrial Park
           Marblehead, MA

We hereby establish this irrevocable letter of credit in favor of the aforesaid addressee ("Beneficiary") for drawings up to United States $_____ effective immediately. This letter of credit is issued, presentable and payable at our office at [*issuing bank's address*] and expires with our close of business on May 1, 1997.

We hereby undertake to promptly honor your sight draft(s) drawn on us indicating our Credit No. 8762, for all or any part of this Credit if presented at our office, specified in paragraph one, on or before the expiration date or any extended expiration date.

Except as expressly stated herein, this undertaking is not subject to any agreement, condition or qualification. The obligation of [*issuing bank*] under this letter of credit is the individual obligation of [*issuing bank*] and is in no way contingent on reimbursement with respect thereto.

It is a condition of this letter of credit that it is deemed to be automatically extended without amendment for one year from the expiration date hereof, or any future expiration date, unless thirty days prior to any expiration date we notify you by registered mail that we elect not to consider this letter of credit renewed for any such additional period.

This letter of credit is subject to and governed by the laws of the State of New York and the 1983 revision of the Uniform Customs and Practice for Documentary Credits of the International Chamber of Commerce (Publication 400) and, in the event of any conflict, the laws of the State of New York will control. If this credit expires during an interruption of business as described in Article 19 of said Publication 400, the bank hereby specifically agrees to effect payment if this Credit is drawn against within 30 days after the resumption of business.

Very truly yours,
FIRST BANK, N.A.

Form 5.13 Transfer of credit.

Transfer of Credit in Its Entirety
To: FIRST BANK, N.A.
From: [*Beneficiary's name and address*]
123 Main Street
New York, New York 10000

Re: Credit No._____   Issued By: _____
      Advice No. _____

We the undersigned beneficiary, hereby request you to transfer the referenced letter of credit in its entirety to _____ whose address is _____ (herein called the "Transferee"), with no changes in the terms and conditions of the letter of credit.

We are returning the original instrument to you in order that you may deliver it to the transferee, together with your customary letter of transfer.

Any amendments to the letter of credit that you may issue or receive are to be advised by you directly to the transferee, and the documents (including drafts if required under the credit) of the transfer are to be processed by you (or any intermediary) without our intervention and without any further responsibility on your part to us.

We also [ ] enclose our certified check or cashier's check [ ] authorize you to debit our account no. _____ with you for $_____ to cover your fee.

In addition, we agree to pay to you, on demand, any expenses that may be incurred by you in connection with the transfer.

Name of Beneficiary
By: _____
Authorized Signature

_____
Title

_____
Name of Bank
By: _____
Authorized Signature

_____
Title

_____

Form 5.14   Amendment to letter of credit.

FIRST BANK, N.A.
123 Main Street
New York, New York 10000

Amendment to Documentary Credit No.: _____

Dated _____, 19 _____
Advising Bank: _____   Amendment No.: _____
Beneficiary: _____

_____

_____

Applicant: _____

_____

_____

THIS AMENDMENT IS TO BE CONSIDERED PART OF THE LETTER OF
CREDIT DESCRIBED ABOVE AND MUST BE ATTACHED THERETO.

Dear Sirs:

The above-described credit is amended as follows:
[describe]

All other terms and conditions remain unchanged.

The advising bank is requested to inform the beneficiary of this amendment.

Sincerely,

_____
Issuing Bank's Authorized Signature

Advising Bank's Notification
Place: _____
Date: _____

Form 5.15 Bill of lading.

UNIFORM THROUGH BILL OF LADING **B. R. BAILEY & CO., INC.** (N.V.O.C.C. BILL OF LADING)

SHIPPER (Principal or Seller-licensee and address)	BOOKING NUMBER — B/L No.
	EXPORT REFERENCES
CONSIGNEE (Non-Negotiable unless consigned to order)	FORWARDING AGENT (References)
	POINT AND COUNTRY OF ORIGIN
NOTIFY PARTY/INTERMEDIATE CONSIGNEE (Name and address)	ROUTING INSTRUCTIONS
PIER	
EXPORT CARRIER (Vessel, voyage & flag) / PORT OF LOADING	TO OBTAIN DELIVERY, CONTACT:
PORT OF DISCHARGE / FOR TRANS-SHIPMENT TO	

MARKS AND NUMBERS	NO. OF PKGS.	DESCRIPTION OF PACKAGES AND GOODS PARTICULARS FURNISHED BY SHIPPER	GROSS WEIGHT	MEASUREMENT

Container No. Intended Vessel Sailing Date

These Commodities Licensed by U.S. for Ultimate Destination

* If weight shown by shipper is incorrect the figure should be circled, correct weight entered and the words "Carrier's Weight" written opposite the figures.

MARINE INSURANCE
Shipper Requests Insurance ☐ YES | Amount Requested | ☐ NO

(If neither of these is checked, shipment is not insured)

If shipper has requested insurance as provided for at the left hereof, shipment is insured in the amount specified (recovery is limited to actual loss) insurance is payable to shipper unless another payee is designated in writing by the shipper.

FREIGHT RATES, CHARGES, WEIGHTS AND/OR MEASUREMENTS SUBJECT TO CORRECTION	PREPAID	COLLECT
TOTAL PREPAID		
TOTAL COLLECT		

IN WITNESS WHEREOF, the undersigned, signing on behalf of B. R. Bailey & Co., Inc., has on the date indicated above affirmed to this bill of lading. IN WITNESS WHEREOF three (3) original bills of lading all of this tenor and date have been signed one of which being accomplished, the others to stand void.
B. R. BAILEY & CO., INC.

For the Company

ATTENTION OF SHIPPER. The terms and conditions of the Order Bill of Lading under which this shipment is accepted are printed on the back hereof. **NOTE:** Unless otherwise specified, the charges listed above DO NOT INCLUDE customs duties, taxes, customs clearance charges and similar non-transportation charges which are for the account of the consignee.

B/L No.

[*Reverse side*]

UNIFORM THROUGH BILL OF LADING

RECEIVED by **B. R. Bailey & Co., Inc.,** hereinafter (BAILEY), from the shipper named on the reverse side hereof, the goods, or packages, said to contain goods herein mentioned in apparent good order and condition unless otherwise indicated in this bill of lading, to be transported to the BAILEY distributing depot at the point of destination in accordance with the terms and conditions set forth herein.

1. In this bill of lading the word "carrier" shall include BAILEY and any person, individual, corporation, partnership or other entity, providing or assuming responsibility for any part of the transportation of the goods shipped pursuant to this bill of lading; the word "underlying carrier" shall include any water, air, rail, or motor carrier used by BAILEY for any part of the transportation of the goods or for any part of the transportation of the container into which the goods are loaded; the word "water carrier" shall include the ship, her owner, master, operator or demise or time charterer; the word "container" shall include any van, trailer or enclosed cargo box utilized by BAILEY in connection with the transportation of the goods; the word "shipper" shall include the person named as such in this bill of lading and the person for whose account the goods are shipped; the word "consignee" shall include the holder of this bill of lading, properly endorsed, or the person who owns or is entitled to receive delivery of the goods; the word "charges" shall include freight and all other expenses, losses, special charges, amounts and money obligations whatsoever, payable by or chargeable to or for the account of the goods, shipper or consignee, or any of them.

2. To the extent that the goods covered herein are carried by water, this shipment shall have effect subject to the provisions of the Carriage of Goods by Sea Act of the United States, approved April 16, 1936, which shall be deemed to be incorporated herein and nothing herein contained shall be deemed a surrender by BAILEY, or any underlying carrier, of any of their rights or immunities or an increase of any of their responsibilities er liabilities under said Act.

3. The rights and obligations, whatsover they may be, of each and every person having any interest or duty whatsoever in respect of the receipt, care, custody, carriage, delivery or trans-shipment of the goods whether as shipper, consignee, holder or endorsee of the bill of lading, receiver or owner of the goods, carrier, master of the ship, shipowner, demise charterer, operator, agent, bailee, warehouseman, forwarder or otherwise howsoever, shall be subject to and governed by the terms of the bill of lading, receipt, freight note, contract or other shipping document issued by the underlying water, air, rail or motor carrier participating in the transportation hereunder and accepted by BAILEY for the shipment of the goods or for the shipment of the container in which the goods are loaded, and which bill of lading, receipt, freight note, contract or other shipping document shall be deemed to be incorporated herein, including any amendment thereto or special provisions thereof which may be in effect at the time the goods are received for shipment and applicable to the intended transportation. The liability of BAILEY herein shall in no event be greater than that of the underlying carrier under its bill of lading, receipt, freight, note, contract or other shipping document, and BAILEY shall be entitled to all of the exemptions from liability therein contained. Copies of such underlying carriers' bill of lading(s), receipt(s), freight note(s), contract(s) or other shipping document(s) may be obtained on application to the office of BAILEY, or its agent, at the point of shipment or at the point of destination.

4. BAILEY shall not be obligated to transport the goods by any particular water, air, rail, or motor carrier, on any particular vessel, train or other means of conveyance, in any particular container, or in time for any particular market or otherwise than with reasonable dispatch. Selection of the underlying carriers shall be within the sole discretion of BAILEY.

5. In any situation whatsover which in the judgment of BAILEY is likely to give rise to risk of capture, seizure, detention, damage, delay or disadvantage to or loss of the goods of a container in which the goods are loaded, to make it unsafe, imprudent or unlawful for any reason to commence or proceed on or continue the transportation or to enter or discharge the goods at the port of discharge or agreed destination, BAILEY may, before the commencement of the transportation hereunder, require the shipper or other person entitled thereto to take delivery of the goods at the point of shipment and upon failure to do so, may warehouse the goods at the risk and expense of the goods; or the goods may be discharged at any port or place as BAILEY may consider safe or advisable under the circumstances, or the goods may be discharged and forwarded by any means at the risk and expense of the goods. BAILEY is not required to give notice of discharge of the goods or the forwarding thereof as herein provided. BAILEY shall have the right to withhold delivery of, reship to, dispose or discharge the goods at any place whatsoever, surrender or dispose of the goods in accordance with any direction, condition or agreement imposed upon or exacted from BAILEY by any government or department thereof, or any person purporting to act with the authority of either of them. In any of the above circumstances the goods shall be solely at their risk and expenses and charges so incurred shall be payable by the shipper or consignee thereof and shall be a lien on the goods.

6. The shipper and consignee shall be liable for, and BAILEY shall have a lien on the goods, for all expenses of mending cooperage, baling or reconditioning of the goods or packages, or for the expenses of gathering of loose contents of packages; also for any payment, expense, fine, dues, duty, tax, impost, loss, damage or detention sustained or incurred by or levied upon BAILEY in connection with the goods, howsoever caused, including any action or requirement of any government or governmental authority or person purporting to act under the authority thereof, seizure under legal process or attempted seizure, incorrect or insufficient markings, numbering or addressing of packages or description of the contents, failure of the shipper to procure Consular, Board of Health or other certificates to accompany the goods, or to comply with laws or regulations of any kind imposed with respect to the goods by the authorities at any port or place, or for any other act or omission of the shipper or consignee. The shipper or the consignee shall be obligated to pay all customs duties and clearance charges upon arrival of the goods. Goods not cleared through customs for any reason may be cleared by BAILEY at the expense of

the goods, and may be warehoused at the risk and expense of the goods, or may be turned over to the port authorities without any further responsibility on the part of BAILEY.

7. Unless otherwise stated in the bill of lading, the description of the goods and the particulars of the packages are those furnished by the shipper and BAILEY shall not be responsible for the correctness of marks, number, quantity, weight, gauge, measurement, contents nature, quality or value. All measurements must be based upon dimensions taken at the points of greatest length, width and breadth of the package regardless of shape. In case shipper's particulars are found to be erroneous and additional freight is payable, the shipper shall be liable for any expense incurred for examining, weighing, measuring and valuing the goods.

8. *In the event of loss and/or damage, BAILEY's liability shall not exceed $500.00 per package or other customary freight unit, unless such valuation is shown on the bills of lading and extra freight paid thereon in accordance with the tariff of BAILEY. In no event shall BAILEY's liability exceed actual value. BAILEY shall not be liable for any consequential or special damage and shall have the option of replacing any lost or replacing or repairing any damaged goods. The shipper expressly authorizes the lowest valuation of the goods or limitation of liability contained in the bills of lading or shipping document of any underlying carrier, which valuation or limitation shall apply even though lower than the valuation or limitation herein.*

9. Unless notice of loss or damage and the general nature of such loss or damage be given in writing to BAILEY, or its agent at the point of destination before or at the time of the removal of the goods into the custody of the person entitled to delivery thereof under this bill of lading, such removal shall be prima facie evidence of the delivery of the goods as described in the bill of lading. If the loss or damage is not apparent, notice must be given within three (3) days of delivery. Any claim against BAILEY for any adjustment, refund of, or with respect to charges or for delay or any claim other than for loss or damages to goods, must be given to BAILEY or its agent, in writing within twenty (20) days from the date when the goods are or should have been delivered. In any event BAILEY shall be discharged from all liability in respect of loss or damage unless suit is brought within one (1) year of the delivery of the goods or the date when the goods should have been delivered. Suit should not be deemed brought until jurisdiction shall have been obtained over BAILEY by service of process or by an agreement to appear.

10. BAILEY charges will be calculated in accordance with its tariff rate in effect at the time of shipment. All charges shall be due and payable in full on the date the goods are delivered to BAILEY and without any offset, counterclaim or deduction in United States currency. All BAILEY charges shall be deemed completely earned on receipt of the goods and are to be absolutely payable, ship or other conveyance and/or cargo lost or not lost. The shipper and the consignee shall remain jointly and severally liable to BAILEY for all charges due. BAILEY shall have a lien on the goods which shall survive delivery, for all charges due hereunder and may enforce this lien by public or private sale and without notice.

11. All agreements or freight engagements for the shipment of the goods are superseded by this bill of lading. If required by BAILEY, a signed original bill of lading, duly endorsed, must be surrendered to BAILEY upon delivery of the goods. The terms of this bill of lading shall be separable, and if any part or term thereof is invalid or unenforceable, such circumstances should not affect the validity of enforceability of any other part or term thereof.

12. Nothing herein contained, whether by express statement, reference, implication or otherwise, shall be deemed a surrender of any rights or immunities or an increase of responsibilities or liabilities which BAILEY, any carrier, the ship, her owner, charterer, operator, agent or master or bailee, warehouseman, or forwarder of the goods or the agent of any of them, would have in the absence of this bill of lading. None of the terms of this bill of lading shall be deemed to have been waived except by express waiver signed by a duly authorized agent of BAILEY.

Form 5.16   Certificate of marine insurance.

CERTIFICATE OF MARINE INSURANCE

National Marine Insurance Company
Boston, MA 00001

This is to certify that on _____ day of _____, 19_____, this company insured under
Policy No. _____ made for _____ for the sum of _____ Dollars, on _____.

Valued at sum insured. Shipped on board the S/S of M/S _____ and or following
steamers _____ at and from [*initial point of shipment*]
via [*port of shipment*] to [*port of places of destination*] and it is understood and agreed,
that in case of loss, the same is payable to the order of _____ on surrender of the
Certificate which conveys this right of collecting any such loss as fully as if the
property were covered by a special policy directed to the holder hereof, and free
from any liability for unpaid premiums. This certificate is subject to all terms of the
open policy, provided, however, that the rights of the bona fide holder of this
certificate for value shall not be prejudiced by any terms of the open policy that are
in conflict with the terms of this certificate.

SPECIAL CONDITIONS: _____
On Deck Shipments (subject to an on deck bill of lading) insured—Warranted free
of particular average unless caused by the vessel being stranded, sunk, burnt, on fire
or in collision, but including risk of jettison and/or washing overboard, irrespective of
percentage.

MARKS AND NUMBERS
_____
_____
Schedule B Code (commodity): _____
Schedule C-E Code (country): _____
Amount Insured
Marine Rate   Marine Premium
War Rate   War Premium
Disc.
Marine Comm.   War Comm.
By: _____
Authorized Agent

Form 5.17 Packing list.

PACKING LIST

International Pleasure Boats, Inc.
West Industrial Park
Marblehead, MA USA

Bill to: Johnson Marina Ltd.   Ship to: Johnson Marina
             28 Hawthorne Road   28 Hawthorne Road
             Maitland 2000 NSW   Maitland 2000 NSW
             Australia   Australia

Ship Date: _____   Order No.: _____   Salesperson: _____
Carrier: _____
Quantity Ordered: _____   Quantity Shipped: _____
Part No.: _____
Description: _____
Packed By: _____
No. of Pieces: _____
Gross Weight: _____
Net Weight: _____
Dimension: _____

Form 5.18   Certificate of origin.

CERTIFICATE OF ORIGIN

The undersigned [*owner or agent*] for [*name and address of shipper*] declares that the following mentioned goods shipped on S.S. _____ on the date of _____ consigned to _____ are the product of the United States of America.

Marks & Numbers	No. of Pkgs.	Gross. Wt.	Net Wt.	Dimensions
_____	_____	_____	_____	_____
_____	_____	_____	_____	_____
_____	_____	_____	_____	_____
_____	_____	_____	_____	_____

Dated at _____ on the _____ day of _____, 19_____.
Sworn to before me this _____ date of _____, 19_____.

_____
Signature of Owner or Agent

_____
The _____, a recognized Chamber of Commerce under the laws of the state of _____ has examined the manufacturer's invoice or shipper's affidavit concerning the origin of the merchandise, and, according to the best of its knowledge and belief, finds that the products named originated in the United States of North America.

Secretary: _____

Form 5.19 Inspection certificate.

Emerson & Associates
123 Main Street
Boston, MA 00001

March 1, 1997

Johnson Marina Ltd.
28 Hawthorne Road
Maitland 2000 NSW
Australia
Attn: John Kennery

Re: Order No. M1790-A

Dear Mr. Kennery:

We certify that we have examined "Duro" Sailcloth material comprising the above order and find it to be manufactured in the dimensions, quantity and quality as specified in said order.

Yours truly,

EMERSON & ASSOCIATES

6

Export Shipping and Distribution

Key Questions Answered in This Chapter

Introduction

As the world opens to global trade, the mechanisms for shipping, distribution, and fulfillment are rapidly changing. Automation means that a shipment of goods from Fargo, North Dakota to Pisa, Italy can be tracked electronically within seconds, with duties and shipping costs assessed in minutes.

But while the efficiency of international transport is increasing, there are many potential pitfalls in the shipping process. Exporters must deal with the safety and security of their shipments, international packaging requirements and inefficiencies in foreign distribution networks. To minimize costs, risks, and delays, it is imperative that exporters understand how shipping and distribution work. This requires paying attention to all facets of the export process, from sophisticated computer tracking to basic steps such as proper packaging and labeling of goods.

This chapter examines each step in the shipping process. First, the material examines how to pack and mark shipments for export in order to protect the goods and comply with U.S. and foreign shipping regulations. Consolidated shipments and requirements for shipping hazardous materials are also discussed.

Exporters are then introduced to the range of international shipping options; these sections focus on the processes by which freight forwarders, agents, and international shipping alliances transport goods. Called the shipping cycle, this process integrates all facets of exporting, from regulatory issues to costs.

A brief overview of international distribution provides exporters with information on how goods reach consumers in some of the world's major export markets. Understanding the various obstacles and advantages of distribution regionally can help exporters make informed decisions when targeting foreign markets. An introduction to foreign customs clearance gives exporters a sense of what to expect when goods arrive overseas.

The chapter concludes with a detailed look at future trends in international distribution and logistics. Anticipating changes and trends allows exporters to prepare and plan for the future.

6.1 PACKAGING AND MARKING

6.1.1 *Basic Packaging* Considerations

The four factors to consider when packing goods for export are:

* Breakage
* Moisture
* Theft
* Weights and dimensions

Packages in transit are subject to rough handling and wear and tear each time they are loaded or offloaded. Goods are often moved by conveyor, chute, crane, forklift, or sling. Cargo may be dragged, pushed, rolled, or dropped during un-loading. Because international shipments may be loaded onto four or five differ-ent trucks, ocean vessels, or planes, it is extremely important that goods be packaged for maximum protection. Buyers often specify packaging requirements when negotiating an international sales transaction.

Guidance

Some important guidelines for export packaging are as follows:

- Containers should be made of strong materials and must be adequately sealed and filled.
- Contents should be evenly distributed.
- Goods should be in oceangoing containers or on pallets whenever possible.
- Packing filler should be made of recycled or recyclable moisture-resistant material and should fill the box or crate.
- To avoid theft, external export packaging should not bear labels that iden-tify the contents of the shipment or the brand names of the goods inside.
- Because transportation costs are assessed by weight and volume, exporters should use specially designed and reinforced lightweight packaging.

Most customs brokers, freight forwarders and shipping companies can ad-vise exporters on proper packaging and marking. Many pack goods for a fee.

6.1.2   Oceangoing Packaging

Moisture and condensation are constant problems with ocean shipments, even if the ship's storage hold is equipped with air conditioning and dehumidifiers. Cargo may also be unloaded in rain or damp conditions, and some foreign ports do not have covered storage facilities.

Shipping goods in containers is the best protection against moisture. Ocean-going containers can be leased from private carriers and trucking companies. Containers are mostly semitruck trailers that have been detached from their wheels. These containers vary in size and can accommodate most cargo. Refriger-ated and liquid bulk containers are available for perishable and liquid cargo.

6.1.3   Air Shipment Packaging

Air shipments are not subject to the same rigors as ocean cargo but must still be protected against theft and rough handling. Standard domestic packaging is acceptable for most durable products if any display packaging is adequately con-cealed. For more fragile goods, high-test cardboard (250 lbs./psi) or specialized construction boxes should be used.

The size of the plane is a factor in air shipment packaging. Smaller planes used in connecting flights overseas often have a height limit of sixty-three inches for packages. Exporters should check with their freight forwarders or shipping companies to determine whether their goods are subject to that limit and pack accordingly.

Guidance

Many companies that ship goods internationally use custom-designed packing materials, such as Styrofoam supports that mold exactly to the end configurations of the goods. Companies also use specially designed reinforced cardboard boxes to provide proper bracing and to ensure that weight is evenly distributed. Shipping labels are often printed onto the boxes with adequate space for all important shipping information.

6.1.4 Packing for an Automated Warehouse Environment

More and more warehouses are using a variety of advanced technologies—from optical scanning of bar codes for sorting to mechanized conveyors—to speed up the sorting, packing, and shipping of goods. These are the so-called automated warehouses. In an automated warehouse environment a package may be stored on pallets that sit forty-feet high; the package must be able to travel unassisted on conveyors and go through repeated bar code scanning before moving out to its destination.

The number of times humans actually handle shipments in an automated warehouse is dwindling. That means that goods now have to be packaged to hold up in a new sort of environment. General issues manufacturers/shippers face when preparing packaging for an automated warehouse involve placement of labeling for bar codes, durability, and sizing.

Manufacturers/shippers are starting to design packaging to withstand an automated warehouse. Here are some tips from packaging and logistics experts on overall design and then, specifically, on bar code labeling and pallets.

Guidance

⦿ Design packaging for products so they fit on a pallet and stack well. Try to get an interlinked pallet pattern rather than a column pattern, which is not structurally sound.

⦿ Once carton dimensions that will occupy the pallet are worked out, and it is proven that the product fits onto the pallet, the next step is to design the packaging so that the weight of the product sits low in the carton. The idea is to keep the center of gravity low and make sure the carton offers sufficient protection for the product.

⦿ High-speed warehouses are not gentle on products. It is important to be able to cushion goods.

⦿ Packing materials do not make up for bad packaging, but they may prove useful as long as disposal on the user's end is arranged. Plastic mold-injected packaging is commonly used in the auto industry, for example, but is expensive to produce. That means that small parts may be packed in larger-than-size containers that will then require special packing materials.

⦾ Preprinting bar codes right on packing boxes is most efficient. When this step is not possible, the next best thing is to preprint small boxes on the packaging where the label is to be attached. Make sure the positioning is in line with industry standards.

Bar Code Labeling. Manufacturers and shippers should talk to distributors of their products to determine what distribution or logistics requirements they have to meet in the field. It is important to ask how the customer's shipper wants the label placed on the product and how it wants the product to be shipped. Every shipper's bar code needs and requirements are different.

Shock Testing. During the preshipment phase, consider having packages shock tested to avoid possible damage in shipping. Many firms do various kinds of recordings of shock levels so that a company can get a sense of how to package its goods before subjecting them to various distribution environments.

Pallets. Guidelines for utilizing pallets may be even more important for automated warehouses than for the nonmechanized facilities. This is especially true for vertically designed warehouses where goods are stacked stories high. A defective or poorly designed pallet can gum up the entire works. Guidelines are as follows:

⦾ *Ensure that the company is using quality pallets that are strong and durable.* The unitizing material that holds the pallet together should be strong enough for the use intended. There should be no shifting, especially in a vertical arrangement.

⦾ *Make sure pallets can fit within the bin location that various warehouse operators maintain.* This may mean fitting within the perimeter of the platforms on which they will be handled.

⦾ *Make sure the pallet is structured correctly for the warehouse environment being selected.* For example, it is doubtful that a pallet made of either light foam plastic (e.g., standard polystyrene or EPS-Styrofoam) or even one made out of fiberboard would work well in most automated environments. Such materials deform more easily than wood or plastic.

6.1.5   *Shipping Information Resources*

In addition to the National Trade Data Bank (see section 1.3), there are several resources available to exporters that offer valuable information on international shipping and related topics. For example:

⦾ *The Air Cargo Tariff Guidebook* lists country-by-country regulations affecting air shipments. Other information includes tariff rules and rates, transportation charges, air waybill information, and special carrier regulations. Contact the Air Cargo Tariff, P.O. Box 7627, 1117 ZJ Schiphol Airport, the Netherlands.

⦿ The Bureau of National Affairs' *Export Shipping Manual* contains complete country-by-country shipping facts as well as information on tariff systems, import and exchange controls, and mail regulations. Contact the Bureau of National Affairs, 1231 25th Street, N.W., Washington, D.C. 20037.

⦿ The National Council on International Trade Documentation (NCITD) offers several low-cost publications that contain information on specific documentation commonly used in international shipping. For a free listing of publications, contact the NCITD, 350 Broadway, Suite 1200, New York, N.Y. 10013 (212-925-1400).

6.1.5 Export Marking

It is extremely important that export shipments be properly marked. Marking helps prevent the goods from being lost or stolen. Additionally, many countries have marking requirements that must be met to ensure swift customs clearance.

Proper marking is necessary for:

⦿ Complying with shipping and customs regulations
⦿ Ensuring proper handling
⦿ Concealing the identity of the contents
⦿ Helping the consignee identify the shipment

Marking on packages must correspond with the declarations on all export documentation, because marking regulations are strictly enforced by customs agents throughout the world. The marking should be simple but contain sufficient detail to identify the shipment for delivery to its final destination. One recommended method for marking goods is to include the required information in the following order:

Line 1: Consignee
Line 2: Customer's order number
Line 3: Shipper's order number
Line 4: Destination city-via (e.g., "Paris via Havre")
Line 5: Port of discharge
Line 6: Number of cases (e.g., "case 1 of 20")
Line 7: Country of origin (e.g., "Made in U.S.A.")

All markings should be made using waterproof ink.

In addition to the export markings, all cases should contain the weights and dimensions of the box or carton. This information is mandatory in most countries, and many countries require that the weights and dimensions be shown in metric. Special handling instructions should be written in English and in the language of the country of destination.

Parts numbers and serial numbers may also be required. If spare parts are being shipped, these may be sent in an overpack as part of the shipment.

Size of Marks

Markings should be large enough to be read from a distance of ten to fifteen feet. For most standard-size cartons, the letters and numbers should be at least one-half inch in height. For larger cases, the size of the letters and numbers should be in proportion to the size of the case.

Location of Marks

Marks should be stenciled on at least four sides of every case. This is especially important when shipping containers are to be loaded by the steamship line or airline and are not being sent directly to the customer's warehouse. Even if a full container is being shipped from warehouse to warehouse, mark all cases. If shipping in bundles or on skids, mark all cases in the shipment; bundles and skids can sometimes break open and packages can be lost if not properly marked.

Markings on Shipping Documents

In addition to being placed on packaging, all markings should appear on the following shipping documents:

1. Inland bills of lading
2. Ocean or air bills of lading
3. Dock receipts
4. Packing lists
5. Commercial invoices
6. U.S. shipper's export declarations

6.2 CONSOLIDATED SHIPMENTS

Consolidation is the practice of grouping international shipments for cost or convenience. Many single or smaller international shipments are consolidated at some juncture in the shipping process, either by the manufacturer, trucking company, the logistics (warehousing) outfit, airline, or steamship line.

Consolidation takes place in a number of ways, including:

- The packing of a number of items from one manufacturer in one packing box or crate.
- The packing of a number of manufacturer-consolidated items in a specially designed shipping container for protection on board a ship or air carrier. Consolidations can involve goods from the same customer or any number of customers. The decision is based on pricing, arrangements made between the buyer and seller, and practical concerns.
- The grouping of goods bound for the same destination on air or ocean shipments.

Consolidations are also based on shipper's schedules. Unless otherwise stipulated, forwarders and shippers may hold or ship goods depending on predesigned schedules.

Guidance

Consolidating goods for shipment may mean that goods that would normally go by air freight become part of a containerized ocean shipment. This may be a concern to exporters of fragile goods, who do not want those goods exposed to the potential rigors of ocean shipment and handling.

If an exporter does not want goods to be part of a consolidated shipment, he or she must notify the forwarder prior to shipment so that alternative shipping arrangements can be made.

6.3 Hazardous Materials

Hazardous materials are subject to a number of special shipping regulations.

The United Nations Performance-Oriented Packaging Standards specify regulations for packing and labeling hazardous materials. Special labeling is required for hazardous materials; product labels must be printed in the language of the destination country.

Exporters must also pay attention to International Air Transportation Association (IATA) regulations, which stipulate that an airline pilot has the final say on whether goods categorized as hazardous can be shipped by air freight on a given day (e.g., because of severe weather conditions or other factors).

Guidance

When shipping hazardous materials, manufacturers must document the following information:

- The proper shipping name
- The United Nations number used to identify the proper shipping name
- The volume specified in metrics
- The class of hazards (e.g., poison, flammables)
- The packing instructions, including types of boxes, packing materials, and labeling

A freight forwarder or other export professional should always be consulted regarding U.S. and foreign regulation of hazardous materials shipments.

6.4 Export Labeling

An extremely important consideration for exporters is how to label goods that are intended for sale in foreign countries. The two main areas of concern are:

- Government regulations
- Commercial factors

6.4.1 *Government Regulations*

Most governments have health and safety regulations and requirements for labeling goods. They vary from country to country, but in most cases, at the very minimum all of the ingredients of a product must be identified in the language of the country in question. To avoid shipping delays, exporters should thoroughly research all of the labeling requirements of their target country early in the export process.

EXAMPLE

A major European manufacturer of high-quality soaps and body lotions did not understand U.S. Food and Drug Administration (FDA) requirements when designing product labeling for the U.S. market. The requirements were far more specific and complex than simply listing all of the ingredients in English. For example:

- Whether or not soap can be described on the label as antibacterial, antifungal, moisturizing, cleansing, natural, pure, organic, hypoallergenic, or a myriad of other classifications depends on the quality and quantity of the ingredients.
- Different criteria are used to determine whether the product qualifies as soap, liquid soap, cleansing agent, lotion, baby lotion, body lotion, or facial cream.
- The ingredients are required to be listed in a specified order, depending on the total percentage of each.
- Directions, warnings, contraindications, and manufacturer's claims regarding health, safety, and other benefits are closely regulated by the FDA and the Federal Trade Commission (FTC).

Some of the chemicals and dyes used in soap products may vary slightly from country to country and are sometimes not easily translated into the language of the target country. A few calls to the FDA and FTC would have clarified most of the regulatory labeling considerations for the European exporter. Trade associations are also good sources of information on product labeling requirements.

6.4.2 *Labeling Products for Specific Countries*

The National Trade Data Bank is a good source of information for general labeling requirements for specific countries. For example, the Brazilian Customer Protection Code requires that product labeling on imports provide consumers with clear, correct, and easily readable information concerning:

- Quality and quantity
- Ingredients
- Price
- Guarantees
- Shelf life (if applicable)
- The country of origin
- Risks

In addition, the labels must include a Portuguese translation of all pertinent information, and all quantities must be listed in metric weights and volume.

Note. For specific information on labeling requirements for products such as food, soap, pharmaceuticals, and chemicals, U.S. exporters must contact the specific government agency that regulates the import in question. That information can be found by contacting the foreign trade or commercial office, through a Commerce Department country desk, or through a related trade association in the United States.

Exporting to Europe poses a number of labeling problems for U.S. exporters. In some cases, different labels must be designed for each European country. However, the European Union is working on creating a pan-European labeling system to ease the burden for exporters.

Country-of-Origin Labeling

Many countries have "country of origin" requirements for product labeling. These generally require that labels must clearly identify the country of origin of the finished product, components, or ingredients; the country of origin determines the duties and tariffs payable on the export.

Note. The Mexican government's product labeling requirements under the North American Free Trade Agreement (NAFTA) have proved the source of many industry complaints to the Office of the United States Trade Representative (USTR) since the Mexicans published a proposal mandating standard labeling in 1994. Although the requirements did not present a strict trade barrier, they caused an uproar as industry considered them costly and burdensome. USTR helped bring the issue before the World Trade Organization (WTO) and NAFTA signatories. There was a long period of proposals when the Mexican party took proposals from interested parties. Eventually, new labeling requirements were developed that have proved more palatable to American business, in particular.

Note. The Mexican government's product labeling requirements under the North Atlantic Free Trade Agreement (NAFTA) have proved the source of many industry complaints to the Office of the United States Trade Representative (USTR) since the Mexicans published a proposal mandating standard labeling in 1994. Although the requirements did not present a strict trade barrier, they caused an uproar as industry considered them costly and burdensome. USTR helped bring the issue before the World Trade Organization (WTO) and NAFTA signatories. There was a long period of proposals when the Mexican party took proposals from interested parties. Eventually, new labeling requirements were developed that have proved more palatable to American business, in particular.

Labeling and Product Packaging

Many countries now have laws that regulate product packaging. These laws generally require that packaging be made of a certain percentage of recyclable material.

The European Union, in particular, has stringent requirements for the use of recyclable material in product packaging. In some cases, the product label must state that the packaging contains recyclable material or is in compliance with applicable packaging requirements. The laws also strictly regulate the number of potentially toxic or other controlled packaging materials.

To avoid claims of unfair competition, companies also need to ensure that their labels and packaging do not infringe the trademarks or designs of other products.

6.4.3   *Commercial Considerations*

Product labels should be geared to the tastes and preferences of the consumers in the target market. These vary considerably from country to country. For example:

⦿ Consumers in the Benelux countries and Denmark prefer to buy pastries packaged in cellophane so they can see the product. However, British consumers appreciate decorative boxes and wrapping.

⦿ The European soap manufacturer mentioned previously packaged its finest liquid soap product in a plastic bottle with a label that pictured an animated, smiling cow standing in a field of grass. While the image may suggest purity and wholesomeness to Europeans, Americans associate the picture with dairy products or children's soap.

Understanding the cultural tastes and preferences of a target market as they relate to packaging should be a basic component of any marketing research efforts.

6.5   THE SHIPPING CYCLE: OPTIONS FOR EXPORTERS

A technology-based revolution is vastly changing the way the transportation, logistics, and shipping industries conduct business. Electronic commerce, especially electronic data interchange (EDI), is taking over a myriad of paper functions, from bills of lading to messaging. Radio frequency technology coupled with optical scanning and computerization is automating warehouses. And satellite technology is moving from the realm of NASA to trucker's cabs, providing more accurate tracking and tracing capabilities.

Major transport and logistics companies have moved into the software business, establishing their own information services divisions to create proprietary products. Many transport companies consider themselves carriers of information as much as carriers of goods.

Technology provides the ability to transmit and process information on a shipment's whereabouts or its condition. This information arrives in almost real time, thanks to electronic transmissions, so decisions can be made quickly to meet customer demands. Manufacturers can purchase raw materials when needed and produce goods as close to just-in-time as possible.

Take an imaginary just-in-time shipment of computer components from Fuji, Japan to Minneapolis, Minnesota. Shipping information may flow via EDI the minute the components leave the Japanese manufacturer, with updates possible throughout the process. While en route the parts can be tracked via satellite or automatic equipment identification (AEI) if the containers are being transported via rail.

Radio frequency and optical scanning technology come into play when the containers arrive in the United States and are resorted for distribution in this country. Constant monitoring of the shipment's progress using a combination of EDI or Internet transmissions and satellite tracking, for example, can shave hours or even days off the shipping schedule if the goods meet a highway delay or equipment breaks down and rerouting is necessary.

What is underlying this technology revolution is changing business practices and the changing nature of global trade. Specifically:

- The global economy is creating heightened competitiveness.
- Manufacturers aim to reduce inventory and ship just-in-time.
- Just-in-time shipping requires greater speed and accuracy.
- The need for speed and accuracy means being able to track goods globally on an almost real-time basis.

Technology is not the only change taking place in shipping, transport, and logistics. In many cases, the lines are blurring between shippers, manufacturers, and logistics operators as companies attempt to reduce inventory and warehouse as little as possible. Both carriers—whether truckers, rail, or the combined forces of intermodal—and third-party logistics companies are providing a wide range of services besides the basic shipping of goods. These include tracking, assembly, light manufacturing, recycling of products and containers, and seamless door-to-door service.

The roles of freight forwarders, customs brokers, trucking firms, and other transport and logistics companies have changed in the process. As a result, U.S. exporters now have a number of options when choosing a firm to handle their international shipping needs.

This section explores the process by which goods are shipped—the shipping cycle—according to the various types of shipping service providers. The three types of providers commonly used by exporters are:

* Freight forwarders
* Agents
* International shipping alliances

By understanding how international shippers operate, exporters can make informed decisions regarding the shipment of goods abroad.

6.5.1 *Freight Forwarders*

Some freight forwarders maintain warehouses where goods are stored pending shipment. Companies generally have their goods driven by truck to the forwarder's warehouse for processing before shipment. Some larger companies maintain in-house forwarders and warehousing and truck goods directly to docks or airfields.

At this stage of the shipping cycle, the importance of the shipping terms, or incoterms, under which the exporter has contracted with the buyer to ship the goods becomes apparent. Incoterms determine where in the export process the exporter's responsibility for the goods ends. Freight forwarders often recommend working on "ex works" or "free carrier" terms rather than on a carriage-paid-to basis, under which exporters are responsible for delivering goods to their final destination. (For more information on shipping terms, see Chapter 4, section 4.2.)

Guidance

Freight forwarders and shippers use a number of terms with which exporters should become familiar, as the terms have a bearing on methods of shipment and freight charges. The terms are:

* Less than container loads (LCL)
* Less than truckload (LTL)
* Full truckload (FTL)
* Part loads (PL)

Once the goods are prepared for shipping, the freight forwarder considers:

1. The quantity of goods involved
2. The mode of transportation
3. The customer's requested time frame for shipping and preferences regarding consolidation
4. Whether or not the goods or products fit under a controlled export category

Freight Forwarder's Shipping Cycle

If the goods in question can be shipped immediately under the No License Required category, the next steps in the shipping cycle for a medium-size shipment of goods—up to a container load—are as follows:

1. The freight forwarder recommends a consolidated shipment. The aim is to tag the goods onto a regularly scheduled consolidation as an alternative to booking a separate shipment.
2. A consolidation is scheduled.
3. The first available flight or sailing is booked, depending on the customer's stipulations.
4. The forwarder reviews documents for accuracy, taking special care with export licensing.
5. The shipping documents are prepared next. These include:
   —The house airway bill
   —The cargo manifest
   —The master airway bill
6. Lot labels or cargo identification labels are attached. These carry the following information:
   —The house and master airway bill number
   —The origin and destination airports or ports
   —The total piece count
7. Goods are trucked from the warehouse and delivered to the dock or airfield.

Shipping and Banking Issues

If the exporter is working with a letter of credit or sight draft, the forwarder may assist in the banking process to secure financing for the shipment. The following are the five most common items exporters must provide their forwarder and the bank when seeking financing:

1. A letter of credit
2. An airway or ocean bill of lading
3. An invoice
4. A packing list
5. A certificate of origin

EXAMPLE

At Waters Corporation, a Massachusetts-based manufacturer of medical equipment, the in-house traffic department prepares the financial documents. All documents and the original letter of credit are then sent to financial experts at the freight forwarder, which then issues the airway bill. Shipping charges are assessed based on the incoterm arrangement the manufacturer has selected. The freight forwarder then "banks" the original documents, sending copies to the bank that is handling the letter of credit.

The freight forwarder can also advise the exporter as to all of the costs associated with the shipment. (See Chapter 4 for more information on export costs.)

Overseas Arrival of the Goods

The goods arrive at a foreign port either in ship or airline containers. They are offloaded and removed to stripping facilities where the freight is then categorized for distribution. In Europe, freight coming into major ports such as Rotterdam, Antwerp, or Hamburg would be categorized by country for long-distance hauling to the major city closest to the final destination.

Freight forwarders generally maintain agents in particular countries. They may also turn goods over to a broker for the consignee who then handles shipping to the final destination.

EXAMPLE

A couple with an infant plans to spend two weeks in Holland on a business trip. They decide to ship a two-week supply of the infant's formula and baby food. The shipment, along with some toys and clothes, weighs seventy-five pounds. Air freighted from Boston, Massachusetts, it arrives at Schiphol Airport near Amsterdam where the freight forwarder's agent arranges delivery to the guest house where the couple is staying. In this case, the couple pays the freight forwarder for both legs of the shipment.

How Freight Forwarders Operate With Other Transport Professionals

Freight forwarders operate differently in different parts of the world. In the U.S., forwarders may represent a shipper, buying cargo space in the marketplace according to the needs of their customers. Some receive brokerage payments from international transport companies such as:

- Airlines
- Steamship lines
- Non-vessel-owning common carriers (A NVOCC is a steamship line that does not own its own ships but piggybacks shipments on major steamship lines.)

6.5.2 Agents

Forwarders are not the only shipping professionals that maintain offices overseas to arrange foreign distribution. Air express companies also deliver internationally. And it is becoming more common for major U.S. trucking companies to extend their outreach beyond American shores to offer seamless, one-stop service.

In many parts of the world, agents tend to be international freight forwarders that handle all modes of shipping, as well as export licensing and customs clearance. Because of borders and other regional issues, forwarders in other countries usually handle a far wider array of tasks than their U.S. counterparts. In Europe, for instance, freight forwarders are also involved in consolidation and warehousing and may even handle deconsolidation of a shipment.

EXAMPLE

CaroTrans International is a subsidiary of the North Carolina–based Carolina Freight Corporation. In recent years, Carolina Freight, a general commodities carrier, has created offices in Canada, Mexico, the Netherlands, and Puerto Rico. Most recently, the company opened a foreign office in London.

Its European headquarters are in Rotterdam. Twelve agents operate on CaroTrans's behalf throughout Western Europe, handling sales and marketing as well as coordinating shipping efforts. The Rotterdam office also functions as a response center to the U.S. operations, handling problems that arise on a round-the-clock basis.

Most of CaroTrans's European agents act as full partners or full agents in their own country. They run their own operations under their own names and are independent from CaroTrans. For example, CaroTrans's French agents are L'Association Pour la Transporte et le Transit (A.T.T.), a subsidiary of the French group SDV. A.T.T. represents CaroTrans in the French market while maintaining its own operation.

Sample Agent's Shipping Cycle

An electronics company plans to ship twenty-five pallets of databoards to a French company. They may contact one of CaroTrans's U.S. offices to schedule the shipment or have their freight forwarder do so. The shipping cycle would proceed as follows:

1. If a freight forwarder is involved, he or she checks the shipping digest to determine which steamship line or airline is shipping to France. Caro-Trans offers Le Havre to Paris as a destination, which is considered highly desirable in terms of distribution.
2. The CaroTrans office in the U.S. produces a weekly sailing schedule from New York or Port Elizabeth, New Jersey. The vessels' names and voyage times are listed.
3. CaroTrans and the forwarder research the appropriate incoterm designation.
4. The forwarder also negotiates with CaroTrans the price of moving the freight from New Jersey to the port of discharge, Le Havre. He or she also prepares the export documentation for the shipment.
5. The freight forwarder alerts CaroTrans of the date the shipment arrives at the CaroTrans New Jersey terminal for shipment to France.
6. Once the freight arrives at the New Jersey NVOCC terminal or export terminal, the warehouse workers load the shipment—now container-ized—that is destined for Le Havre. The steamship line is advised to release the goods to the CaroTrans agent in France.
7. In France, the freighter or steamship line presents CaroTrans's French agent with notification of the goods' arrival. The agent ensures that the container is delivered to a bonded warehouse or terminal.
8. The containers are unloaded. The agent then proceeds based on the in-coterms that govern the exporter's responsibility for the shipment. Options include the following:
   —The agent checks with the customer directly to ask whether he or she wants the seller to effect clearance.
   —The freight may be paid to door. The agent must determine which party will clear customs.
   —The shipment may be entirely prepaid in the U.S., including the local duty in France.

If the customer chooses to pay for door-to-door delivery, the agent makes contact with the French importer to determine the French customs duties, which are factored into the price. Goods must be customs-cleared at the port or moved under customs bond to an inland point near the French customer. In the event that the French customer maintains its own customs clearance—the case with many multinationals—the shipment would move directly to the customer's warehouse. Upon arrival, the customs bond document is handed directly to the customs representative at this facility. The customer is then free to strip the freight. (For more information on customs bonds, see Chapter 11, section 11.7.)

If the shipment goes through French customs, the CaroTrans agent in France notifies the French importer that a shipment is imminent. The foreign importer provides French officials with the value-added taxes or the VAT number. CaroTrans agents, in turn, provide the French importer with the date, contact day, and number on the bill of lading. The agents may also clear the shipment through customs on the importer's request.

6.5.3 *Alliances*

Several major transportation companies are working quickly to expand international services through alliances with foreign counterparts.

ABF Freight Systems of Fort Smith, Arkansas has operated an alliance with the Dutch non-vessel-operating-common-carrier (NVOCC) Votainer for almost a decade. Votainer, in turn, was recently purchased by Air Express International, a Connecticut-based air freight forwarder and one of the largest in the United States. The aim of the buyout is to be able to provide "seamless" international trucking and air freight shipping to complement its existing ocean freight service.

Yellow Freight of Overland Park, Kansas is a large LTL (less than truckload) company with twenty-six regional consolidation centers in the U.S. and 600 feeder terminals. To expand its global operations, Yellow Freight entered into an alliance with the Dutch-based trucking and logistics conglomerate Frans Maas.

With offices throughout Europe—and with expansion taking place in the former Eastern Europe—Frans Maas uses a sophisticated computer network to:

- Link all of its European offices
- Link its European offices to various foreign customs offices
- Offer European-wide trucking with regular service between all foreign branches
- Offer seamless, one-stop international trucking and freight forwarding through its alliance with Yellow Freight

- Offer some warehousing, logistics, and even light-assembly services to manufacturers

International Alliances: The Shipping Cycle

The following is an example of the typical shipping cycle when international alliances are used.

- *Setting up the shipment.* A British customer contacts the Frans Maas terminal in England about shipping computer disks to Poland. At this stage in the transaction, the following steps take place:

1. If this is a new customer, Frans Maas sales personnel in England offer to visit the manufacturer to determine their needs. If not, they ask whether this is just one shipment, or one of a number of shipments to be made on the same pickup.
2. On this occasion, the customer says the Poland shipment is an exception. Most often, shipments from this factory go to Italy and Portugal on an irregular basis.
3. The first priority is handling the immediate request to Poland. A Frans Maas representative sorts out the export documentation, including information on shipping, the consignee, and any other information required to handle the product.
4. Frans Maas handles packing and labeling at the customer's request. At the very least, it ensures that the packing is in good order. If it finds that a customer's packing is not up to appropriate standards to avoid damage, Frans Maas tells the shipper.
5. Frans Maas pick ups and delivers the shipment. The customer's payment arrangements depend on the incoterm selected, as well as any duties and tariffs that may be incurred.
6. Frans Maas offers different options for tracking the shipment. Frans Maas promises delivery on a set day. A computer check reveals when the goods arrive at each step on their way to Poland, including consolidation with other goods.If the shipment is behind schedule, a Frans Maas staff member alerts the customer.

- *Making the shipment.* After pickup from the customer, the products are removed to a consolidation point. In England, this is the Manchester consolidation terminal, where the load is then prepared for land transport. Once on the continent, the goods are trucked directly to a Frans Maas deconsolidation terminal in Poland.

Note. In larger, densely populated countries such as France and Germany, Frans Maas maintains a hub system. Goods are trucked to central deconsolidation terminals and then trucked again to the final destination.

Documents and customs formalities are checked at the deconsolidation terminal. The Warsaw terminal maintains an in-house customs office that collects duties. Once Polish customs is cleared, the goods are shipped to the factory.

Note. As is evident from the Bosnian situation, as well as problems in Russia, parts of Eastern Europe can be the source of significant shipping problems. Even in the absence of wars and uprisings, Frans Maas reports countries such as Romania, Poland, and Russia to be chaotic places to ship goods. Shipping rules are erratically enforced and are subject to frequent changes. (See section 6.6 for more information on particular regions.)

From the U.S. to Western Europe

A U.S. manufacturer plans to ship goods from Fargo, North Dakota to Pisa, Italy. The manufacturer contacts Yellow Freight and makes shipping arrangements. The shipping cycle proceeds as follows:

1. Yellow Freight arranges for ocean shipping via computer hookup. The price is disclosed up-front.
2. Yellow Freight picks up the goods and trucks them to the Chicago consolidation terminal for sea container consolidation.
3. The container is shipped to New York and may be consolidated yet again. As many as twenty or thirty shipments may be in the sea container.
4. The containerized freight moves to the specific vessel about a day before departure.
5. When the vessel arrives in Rotterdam, the containers are moved to the European Container Terminal (ECT), where they are stored until Frans Maas picks them up. Frans Maas then moves the containers to its deconsolidation center in Dordrecht, the Netherlands.
6. Frans Maas personnel alert their deconsolidation center of the arriving containerized shipment, including the contents.
7. Goods are unloaded and sorted according to different destinations. This shipment is bound for Italy and is sorted with other goods bound for that country. When enough goods accumulate to fill a truck, the goods go out.
8. The ships are trucked to the Frans Maas deconsolidation terminal in Milan, where the goods are regrouped for shipment to the greater Pisa area.
9. At this stage, the goods may be shipped directly to the end destination.

6.6 INTERNATIONAL DISTRIBUTION

It is rarely a problem to ship goods to the world's major ports and airports. Most are located in close proximity to major cities. Outside of these sophisticated transportation hubs, however, the ease with which goods reach their target market depends on the distribution system of the country in question.

Distribution involves the physical flow of goods from their point of origin to the consumer. The goal for most companies is to make sure that the goods are exactly where they need to be at the moment when the customer is ready to buy, and at the lowest cost to the company. Effective distribution involves a careful balancing of:

- Order processing and receiving
- Inventory management and warehousing
- Shipping and transportation

The value of a reliable forwarder, agent, or international shipping alliance becomes apparent when an exporter considers the widely disparate nature of distribution and infrastructure systems around the world.

6.6.1 Overview of International Distribution Networks

The following is a brief overview of distribution networks in some of the world's major regions and markets.

Europe

The countries of Western Europe offer sophisticated distribution and transportation networks equal to those in the U.S. Much of Eastern Europe is also accessible. Bulgaria, for instance, has long-established distribution networks serviced by an extensive trucking industry.

Most importing distributors in Turkey use established networks that are able to service the entire country. Road connections are good, but business conditions are mixed. Exporters are advised to maintain a good line of contact and communication with their Turkish customers. It is especially important to have the freight expedited and admitted to Turkish customs properly; the accuracy of customs documentation, particularly certificates of origin, is crucial.

The Former Soviet Republics

The former Soviet Republics pose problems because of their instability. Customs rules are confused in many states. Political unrest and widespread corruption create other distribution problems. It is easy to access major ports, but ground transportation is mixed. The lack of hard currency in many states can make exporting and shipping to the region difficult. As of this writing, exporters to Russia are being required to sign contracts promising delivery to door because Russian importers do not want to bear responsibility for transportation.

Note. Before moving freight from Western Europe to these areas, exporters should contact local importers to guarantee duty payments. Duties must be paid within five days of arrival. These regulations put pressure on transportation companies to collect monies from their exporting customers up-front.

Baltic States

Shipping and distribution is better than in former Soviet Republics. By and large, Latvia and Estonia have hard currency, and telecommunications links are improving.

Israel

Shipping and distribution is comparable with the U.S. and Europe. An Israeli Chamber of Commerce stamp is required to move goods into the country. Also, Israel maintains strict export controls and does not allow freight to pass through its territory to Arab nations.

Other Middle Eastern Countries and North Africa

Much of the Middle East is very commercially active. Large amounts of money have been invested in creating modern transportation facilities. Exporters find service in this region to be excellent. There is a great deal of freight movement from the U.S. However, many local restrictions affect the way freight can be received. There are also numerous packaging controls, especially regarding dimensions.

In Egypt, foreign firms can sell directly to Egyptian firms without the use of importing agents or distributors, provided they are registered with the Egyptian government. Most large retailers do their own importing rather than pay wholesalers. Many distribution options exist in Egypt, including general traders specializing in goods such as lumber, construction products, fresh and frozen foods, and canned goods.

Africa

Access to major ports is good. Some steamship lines demand a war-risk certificate when shipping to certain African countries such as Ghana. (For more information on war-risk certificates and other insurance issues, see Chapter 11.)

Distribution can be difficult in much of the continent outside of the major ports and cities. In South Africa, 90 percent of the population and most of the industry are situated in the country's five largest cities. Johannesburg is a major transportation hub, and Durban is home to Africa's busiest port.

Asia

Exporters should approach this region country-by-country. Japan has a sophisticated infrastructure, but long-standing relationships among importers, wholesalers, and retailers make it difficult for foreign firms to become part of the network. In addition, 50 percent of consumer goods sold in Japan are through small retail outlets. Many of these businesses have exclusive relationships with

Japanese manufacturers and will not risk those relationships by distributing imported goods.

Singapore has a full range of distribution options and its port has surpassed the Port of Rotterdam as the world's largest. In the Philippines, 90 percent of imports pass through the Port of Manila and 90 percent of Philippine industry is located in the greater Manila area. Trucks and inter-island vessels distribute goods to other cities.

In India, vast distances separate the six major cities. Outside of these metropolitan areas, India is a complex network of rural villages. Poor roads make distribution difficult throughout much of the country.

China is considered one of the world's most promising markets but presents formidable obstacles to U.S. exporters. Most export sales go through a Chinese trading firm. There are more than 6,000 such firms, each of which has been granted specific authority by the Chinese government. Many have offices in the U.S. and expertise in particular product lines.

In terms of distribution, the following example illustrates both the obstacles and opportunities present in China.

EXAMPLE

The G. Heileman Brewery produces many small, regional brands of beer at a number of old-fashioned breweries throughout the United States. Over the past two decades it has lost significant market share to brewing giants such as Anheuser-Busch, Miller Brewing Company, and Coors Brewing Company.

When scouting opportunities in China, Heileman found that the decentralized nature of Chinese distribution and markets worked to its advantage. China is divided into twenty-nine provinces, autonomous regions and municipalities with five major regional markets: the South (Guangzhou), the East (Shanghai), the Beijing-Tianjin region, Central China, and the Northeast.

Preferences and tastes in China are highly localized. Small regional markets are fiercely protected, and provincial borders present formidable obstacles to distribution, so much so that China's largest brewer, Tsingtao Brewing Company, has only a two percent market share. In addition, goods are more often distributed by rail than by truck in China. This fact presented a major barrier to entry for major brewers who had difficulty getting their perishable product to thousands of bars and stores in a timely fashion.

Heileman's experience with regional brewing in the United States helped the company cope with the fragmented nature of Chinese markets. As a result, the company signed an agreement with an investment group to brew, distribute, and market its Lone Star brand through twenty-three local Chinese breweries. Without a major brand to compete against, Heileman has a good chance of succeeding in China.

Australia and New Zealand

Both Australia and New Zealand have highly evolved distribution channels with competitive pricing. Although burgeoning markets such as China, Eastern Europe, and Brazil are heavily promoted in the media and at trade seminars, Australia is the tenth-largest market for U.S. exports, surpassing Eastern Europe,

Italy, Spain, India, Brazil, South Africa, and all of the former Soviet Republics combined. Business, cultural, and legal climates are similar to those in the United States, and all business is conducted in English.

Central and South America

As with Asia, exporters doing business in Central and South America should approach the area on a country-by-country basis. Brazil is internationally oriented and has good transport networks, but a regional orientation exists that makes it difficult for one agent to cover the entire country. Consumer products with large potential markets put tremendous organizational pressures on agents and distributors.

With the passage of the North American Free Trade Agreement (NAFTA), distribution is improving in Mexico, with many large retailers establishing outlets and opening warehouses. Venezuela has infrastructure, but the currency has been fluctuating wildly and corruption is rampant. As in much of South America, pay-offs are expected.

When deciding where to export in Central or South America, exporters should consider the local traditions, the economic stability of the regions in question, and the infrastructure. A region that may be unstable at one time but provides good internal access may prove stable on another occasion. Exporters should assess the risks realistically, but they should not hesitate to conduct business if conditions appear favorable.

6.6.2   *Obstacles to Foreign Distribution*

Before signing an exclusive arrangement with a foreign distributor, exporters are encouraged to consider several options and diversify as much as possible. The balance of power between a U.S. exporter and a foreign distributor or agent is slanted against the exporter. This is especially true if the exporter is selling a product without wide brand-name recognition. The agent may be the only source of sales for the exporter, yet the agent may give other products a higher priority, leaving the exporter's goods sitting on shelves in warehouses. Additionally, the agent has all of the contacts necessary for the growth of the business and may have relationships with government or regional officials who issue licenses and permits.

Other potential pitfalls of foreign distribution include the following:

- Business practices that are common in the United States, such as automated distribution, computer linkups with suppliers, and vertical marketing systems, may not be available overseas.
- It may be difficult to procure demographic and economic information overseas, and therefore to target the appropriate geographic areas for distribution.

6.7 FOREIGN CUSTOMS

Multinationals that operate with agents also hire out foreign customs brokers. CaroTrans's European office, for instance, monitors shipment of goods and products to the Middle East and Africa where customs duties and tariffs will be owed.

Customs procedures and customs clearances vary throughout the world. Although the U.S. Customs Service is becoming more efficient, its operation is far less sophisticated than the automated systems in place in some European countries.

EXAMPLE

The Dutch have in place a rapid response automated system with electronic data interfacing between customs clearance offices and online clearance in customs. The ratio of goods cleared instantaneously via computer hookup can be as high as 100:1. If all documentation is accurate, clearance in Holland can take a few minutes. The computer reports incorrect codes and duty levels and offers options for the declarant to recalculate his or her entry.

6.8 FUTURE TRENDS

6.8.1 Shipping and Distribution Trends

The controversial Ocean Shipping Reform Act appeared to be headed for congressional approval in 1998. If passed, the act would maintain public tariff filing requirements for ocean freight "conferences" operating under anti-trust immunity. However, it would allow individual shipping lines and government-sanctioned shipping alliances to offer confidential contracts to customers. The National Association of Customs Brokers and Freight Forwarders has opposed the act, arguing that it would discriminate against the small shipper, freight forwarder, and non-vessel-operating common carrier.

As international trade increases, major freight companies and steamship lines are experimenting with offering services that, when fully operative, should make international trade more accessible to all manufacturers. Transport professionals are recombining their services and taking on new roles in international business. The following are examples of this trend:

- Freight companies such as Yellow Freight and CaroTrans are becoming more involved in logistics.
- Other transport professionals are beginning to offer light-assembly work for customers, as well as handling the shipping of the assembled goods.
- Some companies have combined customs brokering and freight forwarding with some warehouse and distribution services.
- New associations and networks are forming to create linkages between international service providers. One of these is the California-based High

Tech Forwarder Network, which represents eighty regional freight forwarders specializing in high-technology exports.

- Electronic data interchange, when combined with translation and application software, is helping creating global information linkages between companies and their international suppliers and international customer base.
- Satellite tracking makes it possible to track positions of containers worldwide and to trace their shipment history.

In addition, some developing trends are expected to make the export process
more efficient.

Expanding Transport Outreach

With door-to-door service to the U.S. and Europe in the works, a number of
major transport companies are exploring replicating services elsewhere in the
world. CaroTrans, for instance, is examining ways to provide similar services in
the Middle East and the Far East. The company is also expanding ocean freight
shipping on non-vessel-operating-common carriers (NVOCC) through the Port of
Houston to many foreign markets in the Far East, South America, and Europe.

Computer Linkage

Besides reliable service, exporters and importers want quick, easy tracking of
their goods during shipment. Continued automation on the part of freight forwarders and transport companies will make it possible for exporters to go online
with these professionals and personally track their shipments. Satellites are being
used more and more to track goods while en route.

Increased automation is also making shipping and distribution more cost-
effective and efficient, providing a tool for linking clients with transport and logistics companies. Some of the improvements include easier order taking, tracking of
shipments and fulfillment and implementation of logistics service, more efficient
consolidation, and decreased lag time between shipments.

EXAMPLE

Air freight moves fairly quickly and efficiently between airports, but there is
often a lag from the airport warehouse or consolidator to the next step in the
shipping/distribution chain. If all parties are computer linked, there is a better
chance of quicker communication that will lead to more efficient, cost-effective
handling of the goods.

The Advent of Mega-Ships

Major steamship lines have faced a shrinking market globally. Their response
has been to build bigger ships to carry more and more containers for more profit.
Some vessels can carry 2,500 forty-foot containers on one crossing.

Just-in-Time Shipping

More and more companies, such as CaroTrans, are acting in advisory roles to ensure that shipping coincides with their customers' manufacturing schedules. Because fewer companies warehouse parts or products, scheduling may necessitate breaking shipments into units. The following example illustrates this method, known as just-in-time shipping.

EXAMPLE

A customer in Minneapolis sells paint-mixing units to an Irish manufacturer. Typically, the manufacturer buys fifty machines at a time to last a four-week period. On this occasion, though, the U.S. manufacturer gets a specific order for one type of machine to be changed to European voltage. The Irish customer wants the total shipment as soon as possible. The shipment would usually be held for consolidation, but under just-in-time shipping the following transpires:

1. The American production purchaser books forty-nine units for a four-week production period. His office calls a CaroTrans representative to make the pickup.
2. When the special one-unit order is received, the manufacturer calls CaroTrans to inform them that an additional piece is available for pickup. The request is to consolidate the individual unit with the previous forty-nine for a total of fifty units.
3. However, the forty-nine units collected earlier are already waiting at the consolidation terminal for loading to Dublin. Holding the larger shipment may mean missing an optimal sailing date, delaying the arrival of the forty-nine units by at least a week.
4. In light of the potential delays, the manufacturer authorizes the shipment of forty-nine units to maintain production flow. It is arranged that the final unit will be delivered the following week.

6.8.2   *Logistics Trends*

In many parts of the world, shipping, warehousing, and distribution are still very much differentiated. Major corporations own their own truck fleets or hire out while warehousing products. Transport companies and freight forwarders handle shipping and some warehousing of goods in transit. Consolidation may fall under the purview of transport companies or specialized consolidators.

Increasingly, however, companies large and small are turning away from warehousing goods or products. Instead, manufacturers rely on third-party logistics companies to handle shipping, warehousing, and distribution of their products worldwide; these combined services are known as logistics. Some companies are expanding the definition of logistics to include some light-assembly work.

Supply chain management—or the ability to use automation to reduce inventories and move goods from manufacturer to customer in a just-in-time shipping fashion—is a major logistics trend. Although there were efforts in the mid-1990s to cut inventories to zero, the new thinking is that maintaining the "right" balance of inventory for a given company or industry is optimal.

EXAMPLE

> Through electronics, many major retail outlets inform their logistics managers daily about the sales counts of goods leaving the store. A shirt manufacturer, for instance, learns that one item is a hot seller. Instead of waiting weeks, or even months, to gear up manufacturing to meet demand, the manufacturer can move to up production within days. The manufacturer maintains far less inventory, and there is far less waste because of the improved communications technology provides.

Logistics in Practice

The English computer disk manufacturer mentioned in section 6.5.3 wants to ship computer disks to Italy and Portugal and seeks advice from Frans Maas. This is a small but growing company, whose shipments are erratic. Orders may go out to Italy two or three times a month and to Portugal every six weeks. The aim is to double manufacturing and export within six months and to establish an in-house traffic department.

In terms of its shipping and distribution logistics, Frans Maas advises the company to take the following actions to increase efficiency in a cost-effective fashion:

1. Set up a database that includes export documentation.
2. If the company has enough resources, it can establish a computer link with Frans Maas representatives. Frans Maas maintains computer "mailboxes" for customers so that transportation orders can be filed electronically and are processed daily.
3. Scrutinize delivery of materials, especially receiving times. Proper organization of standard truck routes can mean increased local delivery, not to mention more accurate delivery.
4. Examine the unloading process for means of improving efficiency, especially in distribution.
5. Explore systems communication (i.e., automation of the manufacturer/customer relationship). If a client wants proof of delivery, he or she would be able to retrieve this information by going online with the manufacturer.

Dedicated Warehouses

As part of the trend among multinationals to eliminate their own logistics and distribution operations, transport conglomerates such as Frans Maas are setting up dedicated warehouses. These are warehouses that cater to specific corporate clients. Products may be consolidated, packed, labeled, stored, or even assembled on-site before being shipped to final destinations.

At the time of this writing, Frans Maas had set up dedicated warehouses in its Venlo, the Netherlands, warehouse/distribution center. Clients included General Electric and Sun Microsystems. Light-assembly work was being performed for companies, including Nintendo. Frans Maas was also experimenting with fashion logistics, offering such services as material reconditioning to textile manufacturers.

Another logistics trend is conglomerate warehousing. Under this method, major corporations team up to establish warehousing and distribution.

6.8.3 Seaport Trends

Seaports are being swept by broad infrastructural changes as well as standardization of rules and regulations. Exporters should particularly note the following trends:

- Manufacturers are setting up factories and processing plants harborside. In the Port of Rotterdam, a major juice manufacturer has a new processing plant located at dockside. Juice is processed and shipped without any major transport.
- In Europe, where inland canals are prevalent and river transport is widespread (especially in France, Germany, and the Netherlands), containers are now designed for transport on inland barges. The containerization of barges is relatively new, even though river and canal transport is centuries old.
- European ports such as Rotterdam, Hamburg, and Antwerp are in heavy competition for international trade. Harbor and other fees are increasingly negotiable.

Summary of Key Points Raised in This Chapter

The main considerations in packing goods for export are the weight and dimensions of the shipment and the prevention of breakage, moisture, and theft.

Because airplane cargo-hold dimensions may vary during the course of shipment, exporters should ascertain whether their shipments will be subject to size limitations.

To prevent theft, export packaging labels should not identify the contents of the containers or the brand names of the goods inside.

To comply with foreign customs regulations, export shipping documentation must bear the exact marks that appear on the transported packages.

Consolidation is the practice of grouping diverse international shipments for convenience and cost savings.

Hazardous shipments must comply with the United Nations Performance-Oriented Packaging Standards, which require special labeling and packaging.

Under the International Air Transportation Association regulations, airline pilots have the discretion to decide whether hazardous materials will be shipped on a given day (e.g., due to weather conditions).

1. Exported goods must be labeled in compliance with foreign laws. Exporters may be required to include country-of-origin labeling and may be compelled to comply with highly specific health and safety regulations.

2. Many foreign governments impose regulations on the packaging of foreign-made goods, such as rules on the use of recycled packaging materials.

3. In addition to legal compliance, exporters must consider the taste preferences of the target market when designing packaging.

4. Freight forwarders, agents, and international shipping alliances are the three main providers of international shipping services.

5. In the course of administering the shipping process, freight forwarders may also handle banking issues, such as letter of credit documentation.

6. Many U.S. transport companies maintain agency relationships and alliances with overseas counterparts to maintain shipping efficiency.

7. International shipping terms (incoterms) determine which party to a transaction is responsible for shipping costs and customs clearance.

For Additional Information

For additional information on topics discussed in this chapter, please refer to the following publication:

U.S. Department of Commerce, *A Basic Guide to Exporting* (1992).

7

Import Marketing and Costs

Key Questions Answered in This Chapter

Introduction

Gaining an understanding of import marketing and costs is the first step to a successful and profitable import venture.

Marketing can be considered the gray area in the import process, the inexact science in a world of explicit laws, regulations, codes, and schedules. An importer can study the import process in detail to ensure that shipments are timely, documents are correctly completed, applicable tariffs, quotas, and regulations are understood, and customs procedures are followed. But if the importer has not adequately researched the market, the venture is likely not to succeed.

The importer must also be fully aware of the costs involved. Because incidental costs (e.g., shipping, duties, currency conversion, import intermediaries, tariffs) bear more on imports than domestic goods, the importer must use effective cost management in order to be competitive.

Importers are at a disadvantage in sales negotiations if they do not estimate the range of charges related to the transaction. They may find that the low prices they negotiated are negated by costs incurred before the merchandise actually clears U.S. Customs. Likewise, importers who do not track foreign currency fluctuations may find their profit margins eroded because the U.S. dollar was weak on the day the transaction was closed.

This chapter addresses the issues that an importer must consider before embarking on a transaction. Topics covered include assessing market demand, working with marketing and distribution professionals, sourcing goods overseas, understanding pricing, and assessing costs.

7.1   Import Marketing

Importers face all the challenges that confront exporters when they venture overseas to work with foreign clients and customers. However, the concerns are reversed, as the final market is the United States. For this reason, it is important that importers focus first on the U.S. market and U.S. market trends. All efforts made to source and procure goods and products internationally will be for naught if there is no interest on the part of American customers.

Because the U.S. marketplace is inundated with imports in many product categories, it is more important than ever to differentiate products by brand name, superior quality, lower cost, or other competitive advantages.

7.1.1   Assessing Market Demand

Marketing strategies employed on the export side can be used to determine the need for a foreign product or service in the States. To review, importers should:

⊛ Consult business publications to determine market trends. *The Wall Street Journal* and *The Financial Times* (of London) are excellent sources of marketing information. Major newspapers in the exporting country, related trade publications, and industry and association magazines and newsletters are all helpful. Valuable marketing information can also be found through various sources on the Internet. For a detailed discussion of market research sources, see sections 1.3 to 1.7.

⊛ Network with other importers or manufacturers of similar products in the United States to glean the most up-to-date information on customer demand.

⊛ Learn as much as possible about distribution in the United States within the applicable product or service line.

⊛ Consider means of niche marketing goods to make the task of entering the U.S. less formidable.

⊛ Consider working with the whole array of international intermediaries, many of whom also assist importers. For a detailed discussion of international distribution professionals, see sections 2.3 to 2.9.

⊛ Consider doing business with a manufacturer or other party interested in distributing the product in the United States.

⊛ Attend trade shows in the market in question. For more information on trade shows, see section 1.4.3.

⊛ Consider using the services of market research companies offering advice on import marketing. There are many excellent firms offering a step-by-step approach to market research at rates that even small firms can afford.

⊛ Conduct informal telephone polling of distributors, wholesalers, retailers, or potential customers; this is an excellent and low-cost way of determining market demand. A targeted direct mailing sample is also effective. There are many companies in the United States offering mailing and call lists targeted to specific marketing niches and segments.

EXAMPLE

A consortium of importers determined that, given the relatively high cost of domestic steel to foreign imports, there was a sizable U.S. market for certain types of imported steel cut in metric dimensions. Before actually importing any steel, they polled 375 manufacturers in 12 different manufacturing categories. Results of the polling indicated that the needs were too disparate and the quantities involved were too small to make the venture worthwhile. The group instead focused on sourcing larger orders for individual companies.

EXAMPLE

A medium-size community in Arkansas had a major influx of Mexican immigrants in the early 1990s. Several local businesspersons decided to open a business that catered to the needs of the new immigrants. They contacted an international trade assistance center seeking the names of Mexican manufacturers of a wide variety of products and food items. They were told to contact the Dallas office of the Trade Commission of Mexico for a list of the Mexican manufacturers and their U.S.-based distributors. (*Nation's Business*, 10/95)

False Leads and Market Demand

Importers—experienced and inexperienced alike—frequently make the mistake of assuming that a unique foreign product will find a market in the States.

Tempted by what appears to be a low price or an original design, many importers assume they can make a profit by being the first to offer an exotic foreign product to the U.S. consumer.

EXAMPLE

Boston-based Bosmosco Inc. started a unique joint venture in 1988 with a number of Russian manufacturers. The company would sell a wide variety of Russian goods at its flagship store in Boston and at other locations throughout the U.S.; retail showrooms throughout Russia would sell American goods. At the time, Russia was considered a market with much potential; the perception that the former Soviet state was moving toward a free-market economy led the partners to believe that the market for U.S. goods in Russia was unlimited and that Americans would appreciate the novelty of Russian consumer goods.

Problems quickly encountered by the joint-venture partners included the following:

• The U.S. market for such native Russian products as ivory sculptures, ceramic plates, hand-painted black lacquer boxes, and eggs and nesting dolls was very limited.

• The inexpensive imitations of Western products that many of the Russian vendors tried to sell through the Boston outlet had no market in the United States.

• The quality of the clothing and jewelry was considered very poor.

• Insufficient equipment and scarce raw materials made it difficult for Russian suppliers to offer a dependable flow of goods.

• The Soviet banking system was in turmoil after an attempted coup. As a result, many Russian buyers were unable to fulfill their commitments to purchase the large quantities of California wine and U.S.-made athletic shoes offered for sale at the Russian outlets. First-year sales from the Russian retail showrooms were $380,000, far short of the projected sales of $20 million.

Guidance

Importers regularly bring a number of consumer products into the U.S. only to discover that they are already available here at lower prices and higher quality. To avoid such an occurrence, importers should always be aware of basic marketing considerations before importing goods from abroad:

• Always conduct market research.

• Never make assumptions about the demand for a product.

• Understand the applicable sales channels. It is almost impossible to sell imported goods in the United States, no matter what the quality and price, without going through established distribution channels. Whatever sales channels are used—retail, wholesale, or mail order—exporters must make sure that they have a basic understanding of how the channel works.

• Always check the foreign goods for quality. Compare them against available substitutes in the United States.

• Establish the credibility and dependability of the foreign supplier. If possible, try to engage several reliable suppliers.

⊕ Carefully assess all costs associated with the import transaction. (Import costs are discussed in detail later in this chapter.)

⊕ Select a foreign partner located in an established market. The Bosmosco example illustrates the importance of carefully evaluating highly publicized markets. America's largest trading partners—Canada, Japan, the European Union, Korea, Taiwan, and Singapore—offer well-established import/export networks that eliminate some of the risks and uncertainties of doing business with emerging partners, such as the former Soviet states, China, Brazil, and others. The risks associated with doing business in an emerging market can be high.

7.1.2 Marketing Imports in the United States

The U.S. marketplace is one of the densest, most varied in the world. The only way for a novice importer to tackle the U.S. market is through what is called niche marketing. Niche marketing works as follows:

1. A given product fits into a specific industry or consumer category.
2. Through market research, it is possible to identify target markets within the wider industry or consumer category.
3. More detailed marketing, including networking within the target area, should provide information that focuses the sales direction.
4. Once an importer has established a basic direction for sales, he or she can consider different methods of distribution and marketing.

Guidance

The use of information technology has become such a fine science that demographic information can be broken down to create micromarkets. These are market segments that are even smaller than traditional niche markets and allow importers to focus on a very narrowly defined segment before investing time and money to sell to the market at large.

Traditional marketing methods such as direct mail can also be used to target a particular market segment.

Example

A team of U.S. entrepreneurs imported old Dutch sailing barges that had been converted into luxury yachts. Based on interviews with yacht brokers and industry experts, they reasoned, correctly, that there were perhaps twenty people in the entire United States who would be interested in purchasing one of the yachts. Given the high potential profit margins, they decided to proceed with the venture.

Their search for buyers focused on top Dutch executives of American companies or American subsidiaries of Dutch companies. By joining the U.S./Netherlands Chamber of Commerce, the group gained access to membership lists that included names of CEOs of all the major Dutch companies doing business in the United States. Through a targeted mailing effort to these individuals, the entrepreneurs were able to locate buyers.

Identifying Marketing Opportunities

Importers often have a brief window of opportunity in which to enter the U.S. market. To succeed, importers must be able to identify those opportunities and be able to respond in a timely fashion.

Example

A small furniture retailer signed an exclusive distribution agreement with a Belgian firm to sell a new type of bed in the United States. The bed was essentially a frame for futon mattresses and represented a new, and potentially much more popular, use for these mattresses. The partners hoped they could expand the market for futons by pairing them with the more traditional frames sporting a stylish European design.

The arrangement was advantageous to both parties. It offered the European company a chance to test the U.S. market with relatively few risks and costs; and the American retailer put itself in a position to profit if the product became a success.

Example

When French toy manufacturer Meccano SA began exporting its erector sets to the United States, it targeted small independent toy stores. If the product did not prove popular with U.S. consumers, the company would not have risked the expenses of distributing through a major chain. When sales doubled in 1992 from the previous year's level, the French company then began selling the sets through major toy store chains.

7.1.3 Professional Assistance

On the import side, like the export side, there is an array of professionals who deal with marketing and distribution. On one end of the scale are agents, who function generally as representatives with no ownership rights over the goods or products in question. On the other end of the scale are distributors and wholesalers, who may buy goods for resale. The following is a list of international distribution professionals and a description of how they function in import transactions:

- *Agents.* Most commonly located in the importing country, agents act as overseas sales representatives for clients.
- *Brokers.* Brokers act as intermediaries between a variety of parties, often placing orders with importers, exporters, or distributors.
- *International distributors.* An international distributor often makes a personal investment in a product and then resells goods manufactured by others to a variety of parties on an international basis. Some distributors warehouse goods and sell wholesale. Others work directly with a customer.

- *Import distributors.* Some import distributors manufacture their own products and distribute them internationally; others simply import other companies' goods.
- *Stocking distributors.* Stocking distributors are those who stock imported goods for sale to importers.
- *Parallel traders.* Parallel traders are those who purchase existing imported goods on the market for resale.

Note. Parallel traders are most commonly found in the food industry or other industries where commodities are bought and sold.

Shippers, customs brokers, industry associations, and import/export assistance centers can provide assistance in finding qualified import middlemen.

7.2 SOURCING GOODS OVERSEAS

The aim of most importers, especially importers involved in retail, is to search foreign markets for the best possible price on goods, materials, or merchandise for resale in the United States. Manufacturers, on the other hand, may be seeking production sites for their goods, which will then be imported for sale in the United States.

Importers, like exporters, should keep in mind the solid business practices they employ in the United States before venturing into overseas markets. Although their market will be the United States, importers will still do business with foreigners. For this reason they should be familiar with:

- The foreign culture where they choose to source goods
- Foreign business practices
- Foreign currencies and exchange rates
- Foreign market trends

Cost-effective means of accessing foreign markets and foreign market information are detailed in Chapter 1. To review, some of the best methods for sourcing foreign goods and products involve networking with those associated with the foreign market or product in question. Contacts can be made through:

- International trade associations, international service guides, and international yellow pages
- Trade shows
- In-person scouting visits to overseas markets
- Commercial and consular offices

EXAMPLE

A consortium of importers learned that, because it is expensive and time-consuming to procure steel produced in metric dimensions from American steel suppliers, foreign-produced metric steel is in high demand among American manufacturers. Seeking to capitalize on this demand, the importers began to search for foreign sources for the steel. Through trade associations, foreign service guides, and several trips abroad, they located German and Dutch steel manufacturers who were willing to sell steel bars, rods, sheets, and tubing for import to the United States.

Guidance

The National Trade Data Bank (NTDB) offers statistical information that can assist importers in sourcing goods overseas. Leading U.S. imports are listed by Harmonized Tariff Schedule number and other classifications, from major trading partners including Mexico, Canada, the European Union, Japan, Korea, China, and Taiwan. The NTDB also includes individual country profiles of most other countries that list leading imports to the United States.

An importer sourcing a particular product or commodity could glean from the NTDB which countries export those goods to the United States and then narrow the search to particular companies by using some of the sources listed above.

Examples of the top three imports from individual countries include:

- Japan: chemicals, textiles, iron, and steel
- Australia: bovine meats, aircraft and aircraft equipment, computers, and office machinery
- Philippines: electrical machinery and appliances, wearing apparel and accessories, telecommunications equipment, and sound-recording equipment
- Brazil: tobacco, orange juice, and coffee
- Singapore: data processing machines, parts for data processing machines, and electronic valves

7.3 PRICE

From their market research, importers will already have some sense of the price they want to pay for foreign goods. If they have done adequate research, they will have checked with foreign sources, buyers, and purchasing agents, and sought out the best price possible.

Prudent importers do not settle on a price at the market research stage, however. The next step is assessing the myriad of costs and charges they must bear to import goods into the United States. The level of responsibility an importer assumes in shipping the goods will bear directly on costs, as will exchange rates, to name just a few of the many factors figuring into the price equation.

Importers with small operations usually discuss price with an overseas seller, tally shipping costs, duties, and other charges, and then return to negotiate a final sales price for the imported goods. Large-scale importers do not usually make such minute calculations for each shipment. They set prices annually, factoring costs on an average basis.

As with domestic goods, market demand will determine price. A prudent importer factors in all costs, compares the product with the competition, and sets a price that reflects the product's true value in the marketplace. With imports, however, there are several external—and sometimes unexpected—factors that can have a serious impact on the cost of the goods. These include currency fluctuations, and tariffs and quotas.

Currency Fluctuations

Importers must pay constant attention to currency fluctuations. The strength of the dollar has a direct and immediate impact on the cost of imported goods and, in some cases, can create opportunities for importers as well as domestic competitors.

For example, the decline of the dollar in 1994 benefited many U.S. businesses. Faced with rising import costs they had several options: raise prices and profits, or hold prices steady and gain market share.

Sellers of imported photographic equipment, clothing, organic chemicals, and food products mostly increased prices, with coffee jumping by as much as 30 percent. Many distributors of industrial materials and machinery, however, held the line on prices. As a result, some domestic goods, such as flat-rolled steel, increased sales by 15 percent by offering a lower-priced import substitute.

Several large companies, including Mattel Toys, use sophisticated hedging programs to protect against currency fluctuations. Using forward-exchange contracts and currency options, the company is able to secure certain favorable exchange rates. One risk is that if the dollar goes up in value, the company can lose money.

Generally, larger importers are better able to weather currency fluctuations. A 19 percent decline in the dollar in 1992 had a disastrous impact on small importers.

Market Cycles

Both products and markets have life cycles that span from the introduction of a product through various growth stages and, finally, to maturity. By monitoring the life cycles of products and markets overseas importers can take advantage of low costs, new brands, and new relationships with foreign manufacturers.

EXAMPLE

Unlike many companies in Southeast Asia, whose exports to the United States are driven by the weakening of their currencies against the dollar, many Japanese businesses are turning to the United States because of maturing markets and slow growth at home.

Iris Ohyama Co., a plastics manufacturer based in Sendai, Japan, enjoyed great success in Japan with its plastic flower pots and ventilated cat litter boxes. But as Japan's economy and growth rates slowed in the early 1990s and consumers began demanding lower prices, strong competitors such as Rubbermaid Inc. entered the Japanese market and began eating into Iris Ohyama's market share. The company then turned to the United States for future growth.

Building warehousing and manufacturing facilities in Wisconsin and California, Iris Ohyama now sells its products through Staples Inc. and Dayton Hudson Corp.'s Target Stores. U.S. sales now account for 10 percent of the company's total revenue.

Shisendo Co., Japan's top cosmetics maker, was the beneficiary of Japanese import restrictions that protected it from foreign competitors. But in June 1995, when Japan's Fair Trade Commission ordered Shisendo to refrain from practices that discouraged discounting by some of those competitors, the company's president decided that export growth to the U.S. needed to double by the year 2000.

Shisendo acquired Helene Curtis Inc., the hair-care unit of Unilever Group, and introduced a wide range of skin care and cosmetics products through Nordstrom Inc. stores and other U.S. retailers. Other Japanese companies are expected to follow suit as growth stalls at home, allowing U.S. importers to consider a wide range of new brands and products. Air conditioners from Daikin Industries Ltd. will soon be available to U.S. consumers. Electronic photo booths are appearing in U.S. convenience stores courtesy of Japan's Altus Company. Otsuka Beverage Company is pushing increased export sales of its tea to the United States and Yakult Honsha Company plans to market a fermented milk soft drink product in this country. (*The Wall Street Journal*, 11/7/97)

Tariffs and Quotas

Tariffs and quotas can have a significant impact on the marketing and pricing of imported goods.

EXAMPLE

In December 1992, in response to U.S. growers' complaints about unfair European Union agricultural subsidies, the U.S. Trade Representative set a deadline for the imposition of a 200 percent duty on white wine from the European Union (EU).

The impending tariffs had an immediate impact on the purchasing and warehousing of white wine. Large U.S. distributors immediately purchased in extremely large quantities to beat the tariff deadline. Many of the smaller distributors were unable to arrange credit with French suppliers to stock up on supplies; it was estimated that at least 10 percent of smaller U.S. wine distributors would go out of business if the tariffs took effect.

At the same time, some U.S. wine exporters began to increase their export shipments to warehouses in Brussels in anticipation of retaliatory measures by the EU.

The tariffs also had the potential to be a boon to U.S. wine growers. Expensive imports could encourage imported wine drinkers to try domestic wines.

EXAMPLE

When Korean manufacturers of memory chips for computers were assessed an antidumping tariff in 1992, in response to U.S. industry complaints, the market underwent spot shortages and price increases of up to 30 percent. Large manufacturers such as IBM and Apple Computer were expected to be the beneficiaries of the tariffs, since these companies are generally protected against price fluctuations by long-term purchasing contracts. Smaller PC manufacturers, who often purchase chips on the spot market, and consumers would be paying higher prices and were expected to be detrimentally affected by the duties.

Guidance

Negotiating prices for future sales transactions is a complex issue. Importers must consider risks and variables and are advised to seek the advice of an attorney or other import sales professional.

Customs brokers can be of assistance in determining import costs and pricing. But importers frequently come to a customs broker with a transaction that is all but concluded. At this stage, there is little a broker can do in the way of cost management under these circumstances. An importer can negotiate the lowest freight charges possible, but it has handed away many bargaining points with an overseas seller. Therefore, it is crucial to involve professional assistance at an early stage in the transaction. Customs brokers and the services they provide are discussed in depth in section 8.3.

7.4 Shipping Costs

The cost of shipping is a major factor in the importer's overall profit margin. Although shipping costs typically account for 5 to 10 percent of the cost of goods, they vary from transaction to transaction and can be much higher. Price variables include:

- Mode of transport
- Weight
- Quantity
- Terms of sale
- Volume
- Risks

Though shipping costs can represent a large percentage of the overall costs of an import transaction, this does not necessarily mean that the importer will fail to make a profit. Customs brokers report cases in which the price of an imported product was so inexpensive relative to its value on the U.S. market that the importer profited with shipping charges that amounted to 80 percent of total costs.

Guidance

Importers should also be aware that costs vary depending on the port into which the goods are shipped. As commercial enterprises, ports are in competition with one another and are always seeking to retain and attract new customers. In addition to port charges, associated charges (e.g., trucking the goods from the port) may vary considerably.

Several ports offer different levels of service in terms of costs, automated entry options, delivery schedules, cargo handling, and Customs clearance. Some of the smaller ports may be easier to deal with and have lower costs, notably for smaller freight, but may not have the Customs staffing to allow for timely clearance.

Ports are increasingly developing strategies to cope with changes in distribution and logistics; these strategies include multimodal shipping and transportation alliances. For more information on shipping and logistics trends, see section 6.8.

Note. Several factors—notably, the emergence of independent shipping lines, more and bigger ships, and overcapacity at U.S. ports—will benefit importers with lower shipping rates in the coming years. In 1996 alone shipping rates in the $262 billion Pacific market dropped more than 10 percent. Rates in the $85 billion Atlantic shipping trade will likely follow suit. Vast shipping cartels, legal under U.S. law, control nearly 60 percent of containerized ocean cargo worldwide and set prices on shipping rates for thousands of products and consumer goods. In response to recent industry changes, one of the cartels, the seventeen-member Trans-Atlantic Conference Agreement, filed 1997 rate increase requests of three percent with the Federal Maritime Commission—less than half of the 1996 increases. In addition, the cartel is offering for the first time three-year contracts with its customers instead of the traditional one-year agreement.

The cartel had little choice. Upstart shipping lines such as China Ocean Shipping Company, Kawasaki Kisen Kaisha Ltd. of Tokyo, and Yangming Marine Transport Corporation of Taiwan expect to increase shipping capacity in the Atlantic market by seven percent. The new shipping lines have refused to join the cartel and are winning customers with lower rates. (*The Wall Street Journal*, 10/18/96, 10/29/96, and 2/3/97; *Traffic World*, 6/9/97)

7.5 CUSTOMS BROKER FEES

There are no standard fees for customs brokers. Importers should compare rates and network with other importers before settling on a fee with their customs broker.

As in any situation where a professional levies a charge for services, the fee rate should not be equated with quality service. Importers should make sure the broker in question has a solid reputation.

As in most business transactions, volume can be a factor in customs broker fees. An importer with a large volume of entries may be able to negotiate more favorable entry fees than one with low volume.

7.6 TERMS OF SALE

As discussed in Chapter 4, section 4.2, terms of sale, or "incoterms," are a standard set of shipping terms used in international transactions to define the roles and responsibilities of the buyer and the seller. The terms spell out the costs and risks that each party must bear during the shipping process.

Terms of sale bear repeating in the import context because they play such a crucial role in both the costs of shipping and the amount of responsibility the importer bears when importing goods from overseas to the United States and then bringing them to their final destination.

7.6.1 Application

Terms of sale can be applied to any mode of transport—ship, rail, or air. They can also be applied to intermodal or multimodal arrangements. The arrangements importers make for their goods (called "carriage" during the shipping process) bear directly on the overall costs of the importation.

For example, if an importer insists that the seller bear total responsibility for the shipment, the seller will most likely reflect that added burden in the price of the goods. Similarly, importers who agree to bear total responsibility for the shipment will most likely request price concessions. As will be demonstrated, there are other variables in level of responsibility offered under the terms of sale.

Note. Terms of sale are presented in the following sections in ascending order of buyer responsibility for the shipment of goods. Each subsection reflects an increase in the buyer's obligations.

7.6.2 Seller Makes Goods Available at the Destination

Under the following terms, called the "D" series, the seller is obliged to deliver the imported goods to their final destination, subject to additional obligations, depending on the particular term used.

Delivered at Frontier (DAF)

Under this term, the seller fulfills his or her obligation to deliver when the goods have been made available and are cleared for export at the named point and place at the frontier, but before the customs border of the adjoining country. The term "frontier" may be used for any frontier, including that of the country of export. It is of vital importance that the frontier in question be defined precisely by always naming the point and place in the term.

Guidance

This DAF term is primarily intended to be used when the goods are to be carried by rail or road, but it may be used for any mode of transport.

Delivered Ex Ship (DES)

Under this term, used for sea and inland waterway transport only, the seller fulfills the obligation to deliver when the goods, *uncleared for import*, have been made available to the buyer on board ship at the named port of destination. The seller must bear all the costs and risks involved in bringing the goods to the named port of destination.

Delivered Ex Quay Duty Paid (DEQ)

Under this term, used for sea and inland waterway transport only, the seller fulfills the obligation to deliver when he or she has made the goods, *cleared for import,* available to the buyer on the quay (wharf) at the named port of destination. The seller must bear all risks and costs, including duties, taxes, and other charges for delivering the goods to that port.

Guidance

The DEQ term should not be used if the seller is unable directly or indirectly to obtain the import license. If the parties wish the buyer to clear the goods for importation and pay the duty, the words "duty unpaid" should be used instead of "duty paid." If the parties wish to exclude from seller's obligation some of the costs payable upon importation of the goods (e.g., a value-added tax, or VAT), this should be made clear by adding words to this effect: "Delivered ex quay, VAT unpaid (. . . named port of destination)."

This term may be used for sea or inland waterway transport only.

Delivered Duty Unpaid (DDU)

Under this term, the seller fulfills his or her obligation to deliver when the goods have been made available at a named place in the country of importation. The seller must bear the costs and risks involved in bringing the goods thereto (excluding duties, taxes, and other official charges payable upon importation), as well as the costs and risks of carrying out customs formalities. The buyer must pay any additional costs and must bear any risks caused by his or her failure to clear the goods for import in time.

Guidance

If the parties wish the seller to carry out customs formalities and bear the costs and risks resulting therefrom, this must be made clear by adding words to that effect. If the parties wish to include in the seller's obligations some of the costs payable upon importation of the goods (e.g., value-added taxes), this should be made clear by adding the appropriate wording. For example: "Delivered duty unpaid, VAT paid (. . . named place of destination)."

The DDU term may be used irrespective of the mode of transport.

Delivered Duty Paid (DDP)

Under this term, the seller fulfills the obligation to deliver when the goods, cleared for importation, have been made available at a named place in the country of importation. The seller has to bear the risks and costs, including duties, taxes, and other charges of delivering the goods thereto.

Guidance

This term should not be used if the seller is unable directly or indirectly to obtain an import license.

If the parties wish the buyer to clear the goods for importation and to pay the duty, the term DDU (delivered duty unpaid) should be used. If the parties wish to exclude from the seller's obligations some of the costs payable upon importation of the goods (e.g., value-added taxes), this should be made clear by adding words such as: "Delivered duty paid, VAT unpaid (. . . named place of destination)."

This term may be used irrespective of the mode of transport.

7.6.3 *Seller Pays Main Carriage*

Under the following shipping terms, known as the "C" series incoterms, the seller bears responsibility for the costs of transport.

Cost and Freight (CFR)

When the CFR term is used, the seller must pay the costs and freight necessary to bring the goods to the named port of destination. However, the risk of loss or damage to the goods (as well as any additional costs due to events occurring after the time the goods have been delivered on board the vessel) is transferred to the buyer when the goods pass the ship's rail in the port of shipment. The CFR term requires the seller to clear the goods for export.

Guidance

This term can only be used for sea or inland waterway transport. When the ship's rail serves no practical purpose, as in the case of roll-on/roll-off or container traffic, the "carriage paid to"(CPT) term is more appropriate.

Cost, Insurance, and Freight (CIF)

Under this term, used for sea and inland waterway transport only, the seller has the same obligations as under CFR, but must also procure insurance against the buyer's risk of loss or damage to the goods during the carriage. The seller contracts for insurance and pays the insurance premium, but is only required to obtain insurance on minimum coverage.

The CIF term requires the seller to clear the goods for export. When the ship's rail serves no practical purpose, as in the case of roll-on/roll-off or container traffic, the "carriage and insurance paid to"(CIP) term is more appropriate.

Guidance

There are disadvantages to buying on a CIF basis. Specifically:

- The insurance coverage may not be adequate.
- Costs may not be competitive or acceptable for a general average.

- U.S. excise tax may be owed on foreign insurance.
- The foreign judicial process may make claim settlements more difficult for a U.S. buyer.

(For more information on insurance, see Chapter 11.)

Carriage Paid To (CPT)

Under the "carriage paid to" term, the seller pays the freight for the carriage of the goods to a named destination. When the goods are delivered into the custody of the carrier, the risk of loss or damage to the goods, as well as any additional costs attributable to events occurring after the time the goods have been delivered to the carrier, is transferred from the seller to the buyer. The CPT term requires the seller to clear the goods for export.

Guidance

This term may be used for any mode of transport, including multimodal transport.

Carriage and Insurance Paid To (CIP)

This term involves additional obligations on the part of the seller regarding the buyer's risk of loss or damage to the goods during carriage. The seller contracts for cargo insurance and pays the premium, but is only required to obtain insurance to cover the minimum coverage. The seller is also required to clear the goods for export.

Guidance

This term may be used for any mode of transport, including multimodal transport.

7.6.4   *Buyer Pays Main Carriage*

In the following set of shipping terms, known as "F" series incoterms, the buyer pays the main carriage costs associated with shipping the goods, with the exception of the inland freight costs (i.e., the cost of shipping the goods from the seller's works to the port of export).

Free Carrier (FCA)

When the free carrier term is used, the seller fulfills the obligation to deliver when he or she surrenders the goods, cleared for export, at a named place or point, into the charge of the carrier named by the buyer. If no precise point is indicated by the buyer, the seller may choose the place, within a stipulated range, where the carrier will take the goods into its charge. When the seller's assistance is required in making the contract with the carrier (such as in rail or in air transport), the seller can act at the buyer's risk and expense.

Guidance

The free carrier term may be used for any mode of transport, including multimodal transport.

Free Alongside Ship (FAS)

When this term is used, the seller fulfills the obligation to deliver when the goods have been placed alongside the vessel on the quay or in lighters (i.e., barges used to load ships) at the named port of shipment. Thus, the buyer has to bear all costs and risks of loss or damage to the goods from that moment. The FAS term requires the buyer to clear the goods for export.

Guidance

The FAS term may be used for sea or inland waterway transport only. It should not be used when the buyer cannot carry out directly or indirectly the export formalities.

Free on Board (FOB)

When this term is used, the seller fulfills his or her obligation to deliver when the goods have passed over the ship's rail at the named port of shipment. The buyer must bear all costs and risks of loss or of damage to the goods from that point. The FOB term requires the seller to clear the goods for export.

Guidance

The FOB term can only be used for sea or inland waterway transport. When the ship's rail serves no practical purpose, as in the case of roll-on/roll-off or container traffic, the FCA term is more appropriate.

7.6.5 Buyer Bears Maximum Responsibility

The shipping terms "ex works" and "ex factory" refer to the seller's obligations, which are the most minimal offered under the incoterms. The seller fulfills his or her obligation to deliver when the goods are made available at the seller's premises (e.g., the seller's works, factory, or warehouse) to the buyer. In particular, the seller is not responsible for loading the goods on the vehicle provided by the buyer or for clearing the goods for export, unless otherwise agreed. The buyer bears all costs and risks involved in taking the goods from the seller's premises to the desired destination.

Guidance

This term should not be used when the buyer cannot carry out directly or indirectly the export formalities required for the goods. In such circumstances, the FCA term should be used.

7.6.6   How Sales Terms Work in the Field

As in any business transaction, cost is the most important consideration when selecting a shipping term. And, as always, costs can be deceptive. What appears to be a less expensive way to operate, on paper, may prove more costly in the long run.

For example, it is always less costly in the abstract to have goods or carriage shipped to a destination and left in a warehouse, container stripping facility, or even on the dock. The importer then has the prerogative of negotiating separate trucking rates. For larger companies with traffic departments and fleets of trucks, this arrangement can translate into fewer up-front costs.

But many companies lack the staff, time, or financial resources needed to pick up and deliver their goods. They may even find it more cost-effective to outsource, which is a current industry trend in distribution. For those companies, an "ex work" arrangement may prove more costly and time-consuming in the long run than having the seller bear more responsibility for shipping the carriage.

EXAMPLE

> A seller is offering an importer a delivered duty unpaid (DDU) arrangement, taking on considerable responsibility for the shipment, but leaving the duty payments out of the transaction. Duties become costs the importer must then assess in relationship to the overall deal (i.e., selling price plus shipping costs) the seller is offering.
>
> Another seller is offering delivered duty paid (DDP), meaning that the seller has factored duties as part of the transaction cost and is paying them. In other words, the seller is bearing the maximum responsibility. It is up to the importer to determine whether this seemingly good offer is really cost-effective. Under these circumstances, importers should check comparative prices for goods and duty rates.
>
> It is possible that the duty rates are low or nonexistent and that the seller's prices are high. The DDU offer may camouflage these facts. Under these circumstances, importers should bargain for lower prices; they may even find that an ex works arrangement is more cost-effective.

Guidance

A customs broker can help clients to identify what they are getting from the seller and assess costs from that perspective. Importers should have sellers quote an ex work price and a DDP price. The ex work price should be lower.

An astute importer then takes the quotes to several professionals for appraisal. Whether or not to accept the DDP offer will then depend on the type of operation an importer maintains and the willingness of the seller to negotiate an acceptable arrangement. Some importers will require the door-to-door service the DDP involves. Others will find an ex works arrangement fitting their scheme and their pocketbook.

7.7 FOREIGN CURRENCY EXCHANGE RATES

Anyone who has traveled abroad has played the exchange rates game. The objective is to hold back on converting dollars to lira, guilders, marks, or yen when the dollar is low, in hopes that the dollar will improve against the foreign currency the next day. Banks, hotels, private exchange companies, and in many countries, black market buyers all offer different rates for foreign currency.

What is an amusing game for tourists can be a matter of profit or loss for importers, especially when profit margins are low and the quantities of goods are high. The value of the dollar on the day the transaction is closed with a foreign seller has a major impact on the overall transaction. Depending on the state of the U.S. dollar, the exchange rate can be either a negotiating tool or a negotiating deficit.

In terms of duties paid, however, the date of export is the most important. That is the date that U.S. Customs sets for valuation of goods for duty purposes. Often, the foreign currency date is not the same on the day of export as it was on the day the transaction was concluded. Therefore, importers must track exchange rates and currency fluctuations and build into their price a possible decline in the U.S. dollar, or else find their profit margin possibly eroded.

Each fiscal quarter the U.S. Customs Service distributes a list of the Federal Reserve Bank of New York's first certified rate for that quarter. If the daily rate for a particular currency varies plus or minus five percent on any given date in that quarter, then the daily rate is applied. The Federal Reserve Bank of New York maintains official U.S. foreign exchange records. Daily currency conversion rates are also given in the financial sections of many major newspapers and are posted in some banks.

Currency fluctuations can also have a major impact on the price importers pay for foreign goods. As the value of the dollar rises or falls relative to other currencies, the market responds in kind as the cost of the goods to consumers changes. (See example in section 7.3.)

7.8 LANDED COSTS

Various costs are associated with importing goods into the U.S. Beyond customs duties and freight costs, there are costs associated with importing—known as landed costs—that vary from port to port. Some are set fees, others amount to percentages of a shipment. The following landed costs are based on those customarily encountered by importers using the Port of Boston. (See Chapter 4, "Export Costs and Pricing," for additional discussion of landed costs. Also, refer to Form 4.01 for a worksheet to keep track of landed costs.)

Export Packing Charges

Export packing charges include the costs of packing the goods for export to the U.S. These charges are often included in the import price, although there are some exceptions to this general rule. Packing charges may be assessed separately when more substantial packing than originally agreed is necessary or when third parties are involved in the packing.

Note. Packing charges paid by the importer are considered dutiable for U.S. Customs even if they do not appear on the actual sales invoice.

Foreign Inland Freight

A foreign inland freight charge is assessed for moving goods from a factory or warehouse to the port of exportation for shipment to the U.S. This fee is usually based on the weight of the shipment and is charged in local currency. The transportation distance is also factored into this charge.

Note. Importers should be aware that foreign inland freight is not always included in the terms of sale.

Forwarder Fees

Foreign freight forwarders customarily assess charges for document preparation and handling.

Foreign Government Charges

Some countries assess government-mandated charges on exports.

Ocean Freight Charges

This is the charge the steamship line assesses an importer on a per-container basis. In most cases, the ocean freight fees include:

* A base container rate
* Miscellaneous additional charges, including bunker surcharges, destination delivery fees, and currency adjustments

Note. All of the above-mentioned ocean freight charges should be part of a tariff filed with the Federal Maritime Commission (FMC) and clearly outlined with a quotation. If the shipment is less than a container load, the freight charges are usually based on a rate per cubic meter or 1,000 kilos, whichever is greater. This is known also as "weight or measure."

Air Freight Charges

Air freight charges are the actual fees for air freight carriage. Air freight rates are usually based on actual weight or volumetric weight, whichever is greater.

Insurance

Many importers do not address the issue of insurance until a damaged shipment arrives in the U.S. When the importers attempt to make claims, they discover that even if the goods were damaged while in the carrier's possession, liability is limited to $500 per shipping package (ocean) or $9.07 per pound (air).

General average is another consideration. This is a loss resulting from a voluntary sacrifice of any part of the vessel or cargo, or an expenditure to safeguard the vessel and the rest of the cargo. When such a loss occurs, it is paid on a pro rata basis by the ship owner and all cargo owners, based on the percentage ownership each party has invested in the total cargo value.

Note. Owners of uninsured shipments may be required to post a cash deposit to have their goods released. The cash deposit may exceed the value of the goods.

For more information on insurance, see Chapter 11.

Container Usage

Local authorities assess a container fee for use of their facilities. The Port of Boston, for example, generally charges $18 for a twenty-foot container and $25 for a forty-foot container.

Banking Charges

Banking charges are a factor when a purchase involves a letter of credit, documentary collection, or other form of protection of the transaction. Fees vary depending on the bank and, sometimes, on the transaction amount.

Entry Fee

An entry fee is the charge a customs broker levies for the service of clearing a shipment through U.S. Customs. These fees can vary greatly and may be calculated as a flat fee or a fee based on the cargo value. Some brokers add charges for multiple tariff classifications or commercial invoices.

Not all brokers within a given port assess fees in the same fashion. It is essential that importers determine each component of a broker's fee when comparing different brokerage firms.

Note. Although brokers should be held to competitive prices, the lowest fee quoted may not guarantee quality service. See section 8.3 for information on how to assess customs broker services.

Customs Examination Fees and Expenses

U.S. Customs sometimes chooses to physically examine goods. Fees for examination can range from relatively minor processing charges assessed by the terminal where the exam takes place, to the cost of stripping an entire ocean container. Because all goods entering the United States are subject to inspection by U.S.

Customs, importers must be prepared for additional expenses incurred under these conditions.

Note. There is no way to predict the occurrence of partial or intensive customs exams. Whenever possible, importers should take advantage of preclassification-of-goods programs to reduce the likelihood of frequent exams. For more information on classification, see Chapter 9.

Terminal Handling Charge

This is a fee the local airline terminal charges for processing import paperwork. In Boston, for example, these fees range from $5 to $20.

Taxes

In addition to duties, certain other taxes and fees may be due. For example, some goods are subject to the collection of Internal Revenue Service tax at time of entry. The taxes on the following products often exceed duties payable:

- Tobacco products, including cigars, cigarettes, chewing tobacco, pipe tobacco, snuff, cigarette papers, and cigarette tubes
- Alcoholic beverages, including distilled spirits, distilled liquors and cordials, fermented rice wine or sake, still and sparkling wines, champagne, artificially carbonated wines, and beer
- Perfumes containing alcohol

U.S. Customs User Fee

Customs user fees are collected at the rate of 0.19 percent of the entered value for formal entries. There is currently a $21 minimum and a $400 maximum for this fee. Goods valued under $1,250 can be entered into the U.S. informally—that is, through walk-in service at an airport or any other U.S. Customs terminal. Any goods valued above that rate require formal U.S. Customs documentation. User fees for informal entries are usually $2 if the processing is under the Automated Broker Interface (ABI) system.

Note. With the passage of General Agreement on Tariffs and Trade (GATT) treaty in December 1994, the minimum and maximum user fees will change. Importers should consult professionals or the U.S. Customs Service for the most current information.

Harbor Maintenance Fees

The harbor maintenance fee (HMF) is currently 0.125 percent of the entered value. The fee applies to all cargo imported into the U.S. on a waterborne vessel and unloaded at a port where the fee is assessed. The funds enter a trust and are made available, subject to appropriation, to the U.S. Army Corps of Engineers for the improvement and maintenance of U.S. ports and harbors. This fee is collected as part of the entry summary for imports.

The contested Harbor Maintenance Tax is slated for Supreme Court review sometime in 1998. At least two lower courts, including the Federal Circuit Court, found the tax unconstitutional. At stake are refunds of at least $1 billion to companies that have paid the tax regularly in recent years. The government has appealed to the high court, arguing that the tax is not only constitutional, but necessary as a revenue source of the maintenance of ports and harbors.

Note. The HMF does not apply to waterborne shipments that offload in Canada and are moved to the United States via truck or rail.

Dutiable Mail Fee

The dutiable mail fee is assessed at the time of entry for dutiable mail shipments. As of this writing, this fee is a flat $5.

Other Entry Fees

Several additional fees may be assessed at the time of entry. Most are commodity-based, which means that they are assessed against certain types of goods. These include tea, beef, pork, honey, cotton, sugar, potatoes and potato products, fresh limes, and mushrooms. It is best to check with U.S. Customs, a customs broker, or other customs professionals before importing these commodities.

Pier Loading

The pier loading charge applies to less-than-container-load (LCL) ocean freight shipments. It covers the cost for loading of the cargo onto a truck for delivery to the consignee; it is usually based on a rate per 100 pounds. Minimum charges range from $20 to $40.

Local Trucking

This is the charge to move a shipment from the U.S. pier or terminal to the final destination point. Trucking fees usually amount to a flat rate for a full container. Less than container loads are based on a rate per 100 pounds. Some truckers offer a rate break for large loads.

7.9 OTHER COSTS AFFECTING IMPORT TRANSACTIONS

Duties and tariffs can add considerably to the cost of a shipment. Duties are calculated through a complex process known as classification and valuation; this process is outlined in detail in Chapter 9. Chapter 10 is devoted entirely to explaining ways to save costs through duty management and U.S. government refund programs. Other factors importers should consider while negotiating a price for goods include import quotas, insurance, and customs bonds. These topics are discussed in full in Chapters 11 and 12.

Summary of Key Points Raised in This Chapter

Before entering into an import transaction, importers should assess market demand, ascertain the capabilities of foreign trading partners, and understand the U.S. distribution channels for the product.

When sourcing goods overseas, importers should consult international trade associations, international service guides, and foreign chambers of commerce.

An array of professionals can assist in importing marketing and distribution; these include sales agents, brokers, distributors, and parallel traders.

Import costs that must be calculated by importers include customs broker fees, foreign currency exchange rates, shipping costs, and landed costs.

Terms of sale, or incoterms, are a standard set of shipping terms that assign risks, costs, and responsibilities to parties to an international transaction.

Under the "D" series of incoterms, sellers are obliged to bear all the costs of delivering goods to a specified destination.

Under the "C" series of incoterms, sellers bear responsibility for the main costs of transport, and depending on the specific term used, may be obliged to purchase insurance

Under the "F" series of incoterms, buyers pay the main costs of transport, with the exception of inland freight (i.e., the cost of transporting the goods from the seller's premises to the port of exportation).

When goods are shipped "ex works" or "ex factory," the buyer bears maximum responsibility; the seller's obligations are discharged as soon as goods are made available to the buyer at the seller's premises.

For purposes of calculating price, traders use the date of the transaction to determine the applicable currency exchange rate; for purposes of calculating duties, the date of export is used.

Landed costs are costs incidental to the shipping of merchandise; these costs can include banking fees, packaging and crating fees, harbor maintenance fees, customs usage charges, and insurance fees.

Form 7.01 Landed cost worksheet.

Packing charges   _____
Banking charges   _____
Foreign inland freight to port of export   _____
Transfer charges*   _____
Forwarder fees   _____
Pier loading and wharfage**   _____
Ocean freight per container** (FCL)†   _____
Destination delivery charge**   _____
Ocean freight (cubic meters × rate/m³) (LCL)††   _____
Airfreight charges* (kilos × rate/kilo)   _____
Currency adjustment fee (CAF)   _____
Insurance   _____
Pier handling charges   _____
Container usage**   _____
Document transfer fee*   _____
Terminal handling fee*   _____
Entry fee   _____
Customs duty and user fees   _____
Harbor maintenance fee   _____
Customs examination fee   _____
Inland freight charges   _____
Total estimated cost to land goods from ex factory   _____

*Applicable to air shipments only
**Applicable to ocean shipments only
†Full container load (i.e., 20- or 40-foot ocean container)
††Less than container load (i.e., consolidated)

8

The Customs Service

Key Questions Answered in This Chapter

Introduction

Once importers have assessed the U.S. market, sourced goods overseas, and made their purchases, they are ready to enter the goods into the States. Just as exporters must contend with foreign government regulations when they enter goods abroad, so importers must be careful to meet U.S. government regulations. Various government agencies promulgate and enforce a variety of regulations that affect imports. Chief among these agencies is the U.S. Customs Service.

Importers must learn to understand and cope with the ever-changing rules and regulations, by some sixty government agencies, that are enforced by U.S. Customs. A smooth clearance through Customs should be a top priority for any import transaction. Importers can face fines, impounding of goods, and civil and criminal penalties for failure to comply with Customs regulations. Even seemingly small oversights, such as inaccurate documentation, incorrect labeling, or improper classification, can result in a substantial loss of time and money.

In addition, the Customs Modernization Act is creating greater responsibility, and consequent liability, for importers. Importers must be more conscientious than ever, not to mention more cautious in their declarations. Record-keeping requirements for importers will increase even as computerization speeds up the importing process.

This chapter provides an overview of the U.S. Customs Service and the regulations it enforces. The roles and responsibilities of Customs are examined, followed by a summary of important terms, procedures, and documents related to clearing imported goods through Customs. Following is a look at the three major initiatives—all of great importance to importers—currently under way at Customs. These are:

- U.S. Customs reorganization
- The U.S. Customs Modernization Act
- Customs automation

Information is also provided on other government agencies involved in import regulation and the types of goods that fall under their purview.

Few importers proceed through the customs process alone. Since importers rarely have the time to assimilate the huge amount of knowledge that is required to meet U.S. Customs Service regulations, most work with customs brokers. They and other import professionals (e.g., customs attorneys and consultants) can guide importers through the complexities of the import process. This chapter concludes with a discussion of the roles of customs brokers, customs attorneys, and customs consultants, and provides information on how to work most efficiently with these professionals.

8.1 THE U.S. CUSTOMS SERVICE

8.1.1 U.S. Customs and Import Regulations

Just as exporters must contend with foreign government regulations when they sell goods in foreign markets, so importers must take care to meet U.S. government regulations. Goods entering the United States are restricted for a number of reasons, including the following:

- Goods, products, or materials may fall under a controlled category or may not be allowed into the U.S. altogether.
- Goods, products, or materials may be protected by quota.
- An import may fail to meet U.S. government labeling requirements; ingredients may be improperly or imprecisely listed, in violation of U.S. law.
- Imports may fail to bear accurate or properly printed bar codes.

If found to violate customs regulations, imported goods may be restricted in the following ways:

- Prohibited entry
- Entry limited to certain ports
- Restricted touring, storage, or use
- Imposition of conditions of entry, such as requiring labeling, processing, or treatment

In addition, several laws protect U.S. markets from unfair trade practices. Imports found in violation of these laws may be placed under tariff or be subject to countervailing and antidumping duties or other special restrictions.

Note. Specific restrictions on imports are discussed in Chapter 12, "Trade Barriers and Regulation."

Laws and regulations governing trade are created by Congress and a host of government agencies. It is the responsibility of the U.S. Customs Service to enforce those laws and regulations.

Note. The U.S. Customs Service has an extensive site on the World Wide Web. The main menu lists a number of options, including:

- Rulings and regulations
- Commercial import procedures and requirements
- Automated systems
- Import quotas
- Customs brokers
- Exporting
- Informed compliance
- Port locations

Unlike many web sites, this one contains a great deal of useful information. For example, users can download the Customs Valuation Encyclopedia, view the texts of hundreds of binding rulings, and determine which goods require export licenses. There is also extensive information on country of origin marking.

The web site can be reached at http://www.customs.ustreas.gov/.

8.1.2 Customs Service Responsibilities

The U.S. Customs Service is the arbiter of import transactions within U.S. borders. Because Customs plays such a central role in import/export transactions, it is important that companies understand as much as they can about the agency and how it functions. A clear understanding of Customs requirements and procedures can mean avoiding costly delays in shipment clearance, excessive paperwork and possible fines and penalties.

The following are some of the main Customs Service responsibilities:

* To assess and collect Customs duties, excise taxes, fees, and penalties due on imported merchandise
* To cooperate with, and enforce regulations of, the more than sixty government agencies that are involved with international trade and travel
* To protect American business and labor by enforcing statutes and regulations such as antidumping and countervailing duty provisions; copyright, patent, and trademark provisions; and import quotas
* To protect the general welfare and security of the United States by enforcing import and export restrictions and prohibitions
* To collect accurate import and export data for compilation of international trade statistics

8.1.3 Structure of the U.S. Customs Service

Before embarking on international trade, importers and exporters should have a working knowledge of the U.S. Customs Service and the main rules and regulations that affect them. This is all the more important in light of sweeping legislative changes that are dramatically altering the way international business is conducted. (For more information on Customs reorganization, see section 8.1.5.)

The Customs Service has more than 18,000 employees in almost 400 offices in the U.S. Offices are spread throughout seven regions. There are forty-five district offices and approximately 300 ports of entry nationwide, including air, sea, and border ports.

The U.S. Customs Service maintains its own set of rules and regulations, which appear in Title 19 of the Code of Federal Regulations. The Federal Register maintains updates of Customs regulations. Moreover, the Customs Service does not operate in a vacuum. More than sixty government agencies—from the Food and Drug Administration to the United States Department of Agriculture—are directly involved in foreign trade.

8.1.4 Import Regulation: Other Government Agencies

In addition to the U.S. Customs Service, a number of other government agencies are involved with import regulation. These agencies may require separate documentation; some agencies restrict or prohibit the importation of certain classes of goods. The examples here are intended to give importers an overview of the government agencies involved in the regulation of imports.

Note. Up-front research on the part of the importer can help avoid problems and delays in clearance through U.S. Customs. Importers are advised not to wait until the goods arrive in the U.S. to learn what restrictions apply.

Types of controlled goods and the government agencies that regulate them include:

1. *Cheese, milk, and dairy products.* Cheese is subject to the requirements of the Food and Drug Administration. Importation of cheese requires an import license and is subject to Department of Agriculture quotas. The importation of milk or cream is subject to the conditions of the Food, Drug, and Cosmetics Act and the Import Milk Act. Importers must obtain permits from the Department of Health and Human Services of the Food and Drug Administration.

2. *Fruits, vegetables, and nuts.* The Food Safety and Inspection Service of the Department of Agriculture sets requirements for certain fruits, vegetables, and nuts, including fresh tomatoes, avocados, oranges, grapefruits, green peppers, walnuts, raisins, and olives in tins. Requirements relate to:

- Grade
- Size
- Quality
- Maturity

3. *Meat and meat products.* The Animal and Plant Health Inspection Service (APHIS) and the Food Safety and Inspection Service of the Department of Agriculture must inspect all commercial shipments of meat and meat products before they can be released by U.S. Customs.

4. *Arms, ammunition, explosives, and implements of war.* Importation of these items requires a license from the Bureau of Alcohol, Tobacco, and Firearms (BATF) of the Treasury Department.

5. *Household appliances.* The Consumer Products Efficiency Branch of the Department of Energy establishes test procedures and energy performance standards for a number of appliances. The Division of Energy and Product Information of the Federal Trade Commission (FTC) regulates the labeling of these appliances, including:

- Refrigerators and freezers
- Dishwashers, clothes dryers, washers, and water heaters
- Room air conditioners and home-heating equipment
- Television sets
- Kitchen ranges and ovens

6. *Flammable fabrics.* All clothing and interior furnishings imported into the United States must conform to an applicable flammability standard of the Flam-

mable Fabrics Act, administered by the U.S. Consumer Product Safety Commission.

7. *Toxic substances*. The Toxic Substances Control Act (TSCA) regulates the importation, distribution, manufacturing, and disposal of toxic substances. The TSCA Assistance Information Service of the Environmental Protection Agency helps importers comply with the Act. Labeling, packaging, and transportation of hazardous materials are regulated by the Office of Hazardous Materials Transportation of the Department of Transportation.

8. *Motor vehicles and boats*. All imported motor vehicles must comply with applicable Federal Motor Vehicle Safety Standards in effect at the time when the vehicle in question was manufactured. If a vehicle is not in compliance, a Department of Transportation bond of 150 percent of the dutiable value of the vehicle must be posted until alterations are made. The Office of Vehicle Safety Compliance of the Department of Transportation can provide importers with detailed information on motor vehicle requirements. In addition, the Clean Air Act, under the auspices of the Environmental Protection Agency, requires that imported vehicles be in conformity with U.S. emission standards.

8.1.5 U.S. Customs Reorganization

In response to geopolitical changes and internal problems, U.S. Customs is undergoing a massive reorganization. A 1993 report prepared by a committee established by the Commissioner of Customs found the current Customs organization hierarchical, uncooperative, and obsolete as a result of new management techniques and information technology. Particular factors that made reorganization a priority were:

- A lack of uniformity in the application of laws, policies, and procedures
- Intra-agency disputes, internal competition, and antiquated organization
- A history of adversarial relationships with customers and other agencies
- The demands of the General Agreement on Tariffs and Trade (GATT) and the North American Free Trade Agreement (NAFTA)

Based on the committee's recommendations, the following organizational changes are expected to take place:

- Twenty Customs Management Centers will be created to ensure consistent service at the ports within each region.
- Five Strategic Trade Centers will be created to address major trade issues such as textile transshipments, valuation, antidumping, and intellectual property rights enforcement.
- Staffing at Customs headquarters, currently at 1,800 employees, will be significantly reduced.
- Customs employees will undergo retraining.

While the day-to-day processes of entry and clearance are not expected to be greatly affected by the reorganization, some organizations are concerned that Customs procedures, such as the issuance of binding rulings, could be slowed or delayed.

8.1.6   *The Customs Modernization Act*

On December 8, 1993, President Clinton signed the Customs Modernization Act as Title VI of the North American Free Trade Agreement Implementation Act. The Mod Act, as it is known, provides U.S. Customs with the legal framework necessary to automate its commercial operations and to develop procedures and regulations that address importer/exporter needs and legislative requirements.

By granting Customs this new authority, the Mod Act permits Customs to tailor its operations to changing needs, adapt to marketplace conditions, and take advantage of technical improvements. Customs officials estimate that the law will change 70–90 percent of the agency's regulations.

The Mod Act is expected to have a profound effect on several procedures that directly impact importers. Currently there are twenty-two regulatory projects mandated by the Act, which are in various stages of completion. These affect:

- Duty drawback procedures
- Seizure of merchandise
- Liquidation of duties and extension/suspension procedures
- Warehouse withdrawals
- Rulings and protest procedures
- Record-keeping requirements

The Mod Act's provisions will be implemented according to their anticipated effect on industry.

EXAMPLE

The expanded record-keeping requirements are expected to have a major impact on importing firms. The new rules dictate which import and related documents must be maintained on file by the importer should Customs initiate an investigation. In many cases firms are required to maintain records of an import transaction for up to five years. Customs has established a timetable for gradual implementation of these requirements.

EXAMPLE

Since enactment of the Mod Act, several regulations have been promulgated that could have a broad impact on textile and apparel importers and retailers. For instance, in order to enforce transshipment provisions (i.e., provisions that prohibit transfer of goods from country to country to avoid quotas), Customs requires retailers—not importers—to return goods to Customs for examination up to 210 days after the goods were entered. The new rules are designed to be an incentive for retailers to verify country of origin and check against trans-shipments.

The transshipment rules exemplify one of the main goals of the Mod Act, which is to put increased responsibility on the importer and parties related to the transaction to comply with applicable laws and regulations.

The following sections detail some of the Mod Act's main provisions.

Changing the Legal Responsibilities of Importers

The Mod Act alters the relationship between U.S. Customs and importers. The intent of the Mod Act is to have Customs work with the international trade community as partners rather than adversaries. That intent is exemplified by the twin cornerstones of the Mod Act—the concepts of shared responsibility and informed compliance:

* *Shared responsibility.* The policy of shared responsibility requires importers to declare at entry their legal conclusions concerning the value, classification, and rate of duty applicable to their merchandise. The information provided must be timely and accurate. In providing this information, importers are required to act with "reasonable care." Although it will forgive small errors on declarations, Customs expects importers to use available means to provide accurate information. The failure to use reasonable care in dispatching importing declarations is considered negligence under the Mod Act.

* *Informed compliance.* Informed compliance represents the flip side of the "shared responsibility" coin. The concepts of informed compliance requires U.S. Customs to clearly and completely inform importers and exporters of their obligations under the new law. It is also a legal mandate that Customs provide its own personnel and the trade community with appropriate training and the opportunity for dialogue. To that end, Customs holds regular meetings with representatives of the international trade community, usually industry associations, and must publish a number of documents. Following are some of the specific requirements of informed compliance, as included in the Customs Modernization Act:

1. Prior to implementation of the National Customs Automation Program (NCAP), which will streamline many of the agency's functions, the Customs Service is required to consult with members of the international trade community. These members include importers, brokers, transportation companies, foreign trade zones, express couriers, and others. Customs must also consult with these same parties prior to any future expansion of NCAP.

Under NCAP several prototype programs are in effect that may eventually be available to all importers. These "operational" programs are different from those under the Automated Commercial Environment, which is expected to provide tools to be used by all divisions of the U.S. Customs Service (see section 8.1.7 of this chapter).

In August 1997, under NCAP, electronic data submissions were accepted in three land border locations: Detroit, Port Huron, Michigan and Laredo, Texas. For importers participating in the program, cargo arriving by truck clears through Customs via electronic data. Importers can then submit follow-up data such as the Commercial Invoice and Entry Summary to customs via computer. Participating companies receive monthly statements, similar to credit card statements, listing summaries filed and duties owed. Payment of duties must be through banks using electronic payment credits.

To participate in the program, companies must meet very specific requirements. General Motors, Ford, and Chrysler are three companies that are expected to participate.

Another operational prototype program is National Account Management. The program, which began in February 1996 and now has forty-four participating companies, designates an account manager for each company as a liaison to Customs. The single-point-of-contact approach allows both importers and the Customs Service to ensure that all entries are handled in a uniform and consistent manner; companies should be able to easily determine whether goods have been cleared, duties paid, and documents are in order. The account manager operates on a national basis, covering all U.S. entries, rather than on a port-by-port basis, as has been the case in the past.

Customs points out that account managers will in no way replace customs brokers and that their functions are quite different. Customs brokers can help companies negotiate the complexities of the program and provide the sophisticated automated support necessary to interface with Customs.

2. Before using the new "reconciliation" procedure for antidumping and countervailing duty collections, U.S. Customs must consult with these and other members of the international trade community and the U.S. Department of Commerce. To speed up the entry of goods into the country, the new reconciliation procedure allows importers to aggregate entries. However, importers may find that these multiple entries are later subject to countervailing or antidumping duties, or any number of duties and tariffs that may not have been determined at the time of entry.

3. When promulgating or amending regulations, U.S. Customs must consult with interested parties through the notice-and-comment mechanism of the Administrative Procedures Act.

4. U.S. Customs must consult with approved laboratories and gaugers regarding the expansion of the private laboratory program.

U.S. Customs is required to publish the following:

- Eligibility criteria for participation in NCAP
- Information on the record-keeping and drawback compliance programs
- A list of records required for the entry of merchandise, which will be subject to record-keeping penalties
- A list of approved gaugers and laboratories
- Procedures for private laboratory approval and disciplinary actions
- Acceptable merchandise testing procedures and methodologies

* Any ruling modifying or revoking an existing ruling or limiting a court decision

Notice must be given to an interested party when U.S. Customs detains merchandise, conducts a regulatory audit, proposes a record-keeping or drawback penalty for negligence, or proposes to take title to general order merchandise.

Streamlining Customs Procedures for Speedier Entry

Under the Mod Act, Customs is attempting to streamline its operations by expanding the use of processes designed to speed up the entry of goods, including:

* Binding rulings
* Country-of-origin rulings
* Pre-import classifications

Customs is also granting the international trade community more power and involvement in the declaration process—what amounts to an honor system on declarations.

This new system places additional burdens of record-keeping and proof on the international trade community. U.S. Customs also issues specialized correspondence in the event of inaccuracies in a particular document. The service provides information to help importers and exporters determine when and how to reply to Customs correspondence; handling inaccuracies is also addressed.

With streamlining the aim of the Modernization Act, U.S. Customs now has the right to reduce entry documentation requirements. The burden for maintaining entry records now falls on the importer. U.S. Customs no longer needs to require importers to produce "core" entry documentation at the time of entry. However, U.S. Customs may demand this information at any time following the importation of merchandise. It is the importer's responsibility to maintain and produce such documentation whenever U.S. Customs requests it.

Rewriting Civil Penalty Provisions

To maintain order under the new system and ensure that importers make proper declaration, Congress has authorized new penalties for those caught evading U.S. Customs declarations or found negligent under the provisions of the Customs Modernization Act.

The new civil penalty provisions stipulate the following in relation to duties:

* A fine of up to $100,000 per incident for willful evasion
* A fine of up to $10,000 for negligence

Substantial penalties also apply for failure to maintain and produce the "core" entry records when requested by Customs. Importers are required to keep documents relating to the transaction on file for at least five years.

Remote Entry Filing

Remote Entry Filing has the potential for dramatically altering how importers, customs brokers, and others involved in assisting foreign trade transactions do business. Currently, most import transactions require paper entry documentation to be filed with U.S. Customs at the port of entry.

Remote entry filing allows entry documentation to be filed with Customs by computer. It also allows data to be cleared at one site but examined at another. For example, if merchandise comes through Detroit but is destined for Chicago, Chicago can be designated as the examination site.

The first phase of the program was concluded in December 1996. A total of 6,651 remote entries were filed at thirteen U.S. air and sea ports. Companies such as Xerox Corp., Sara Lee Knit, and Mattel Toys were among the participants. During the next phase, which began in January 1997, Customs plans to add up to twelve more ports, increase the number of companies, and allow customs brokers to participate.

More information on remote entry filing is available at the Customs web site (http://www.customs.ustreas.gov/) or by phone (202-927-3555).

Note. Importers will be able to file entry summaries and pay duties on a monthly basis using the new Importer Activity Summary Statement.

Other Mod Act Changes

⊛ As part of the Customs Modernization Act, the U.S. Customs Service will be reorganized. Regional offices will be consolidated and shifted.

⊛ U.S. Customs is working toward complete computerization of its organization and of all phases of the import/export process. Importers and exporters should expect to go online or ensure that the professionals they hire offer computerized services. (See section 8.1.7 below for more information on computerization.) When implemented, the proposed Automated Export System (AES) will allow Customs to keep accurate exporting statistics. Additional statistics will allow exporters to determine the best markets for their merchandise or services. This central computerized repository for export data will also enable all government agencies involved in enforcing export regulations to coordinate their efforts.

⊛ Under the Mod Act, criteria for duty refunds (drawbacks) will be liberalized and a new Drawback Compliance Program will inform claimants of their rights and obligations.

8.1.7   *Customs Automation*

The Automated Commercial Environment (ACE) is the massive automated international trade information system being developed by Customs to replace the existing Automated Commercial System (ACS). Combining reengineered business processes mandated by the Mod Act with state-of the-art information technology, ACE is designed to better enable Customs to:

- Enforce trade and contraband laws
- Ensure trade compliance
- Provide international trade services to the trade community, other federal agencies, and the public

Though it is still in the development phase, ACE has goals based on user needs, problems in the current system, and available information technology. These include:

- *Trade compliance processes.* Customs is developing these computerized information delivery systems to support their work processes.

- *Account-based processing.* Customs will establish accounts for individuals and companies engaged in international trade, replacing the current system of dealing with importers on a transaction-by-transaction basis. This will allow Customs officials to gain access to an importer's complete history, and therefore impose a burden on importers to maintain clean records with Customs.

- *Single entry declarations.* All entry transactions will rely on one package of data, a single-entry declaration.

- *User-oriented database design.* The ACE database design will be user-friendly, in contrast with the current system, which is designed to maximize system performance. Importers should have easy access to information on accounts, shipments, entry declarations, and other information.

- *Electronic paperless environment.* It is hoped that all data and processes will operate electronically. If incoming data or documentation is not automated, the data will be converted to electronic form.

Existing Components of the Automated Commercial System

Although being phased out by the new ACE system, the existing Automated Commercial System, which became operational in 1984, has a number of existing components. Importers can take advantage of these programs to expedite Customs clearance for import shipments. These include:

1. *Automated Broker Interface (ABI).* ABI allows customs brokers, importers, and port authorities to interface directly with the Customs Data Center. Entry release data can be transmitted to Customs electronically to secure the timely release of shipments. Users of ABI can:

- Receive timely information on the status of import transactions
- File a consolidated entry summary, which combines multiple import transactions, and receive confirmations and/or corrections from customs

- File entries under temporary import bonds (TIBs), Free Trade Zone entries, and bonded warehouse withdrawals
- Transmit U.S. Customs declarations and bypass entry summaries
- Identify and correct shipping information errors on entries right up until the time the cargo arrives
- Receive priority handling and conditional cargo release results up to five days before the cargo arrives
- Receive courtesy notices of liquidation, extension, or suspension of shipments from Customs
- Make electronic payments of duties, taxes, and fees through the Automated Customs Clearinghouse (ACH). Under ACH payments are electronically transferred to Customs through the importer's bank. To receive an ACH application form contact Customs (202-927-1210). Applications can be sent to the U.S. Customs National Finance Center, 6026 Lakeside Blvd., Indianapolis, IN 46278 or by fax (317-298-1259). The Customs web site has information on how to participate in the ABI program and the names of vendors that supply the required software.

2. *Customs Electronic Invoicing Program (EIP).* This program allows companies to electronically transmit invoice information to Customs, along with Customs Form 3401 (Entry/Immediate Delivery) and Customs Form 7501 (Entry Summary), for cargo release.

3. *Customs Automated Manifest Module (AMS).* Importers using Sea AMS or Air AMS linkages with Customs can secure expedited processing and release of low-risk cargo. During 1994, AMS was used to process approximately 250,000 ocean bills of lading and 500,000 airway bills each month. Ocean bills of lading transmitted via AMS accounted for 85 percent of all cargo imported by sea, and airway bills submitted by AMS represented 27 percent of all airway bills submitted to Customs.

Guidance

Importers wanting to participate in any of the aforementioned ACS programs can contact the U.S. Customs Customer Assistance Branch, Trade Port Division by phone (202-927-1200); requests for information can be sent by fax (202-927-1896).

The Automated Export System (AES)

In July 1995, five U.S. vessel ports—Baltimore, Norfolk, Charleston, Houston, and Los Angeles/Long Beach—went online as Customs unveiled the Automated Export System. With a goal of paperless export reporting by all exporters by the year 2000, AES was designed to facilitate the export process, centralize the validation process for export licensing, assure compliance with exporting laws, and improve trade statistics and customer service. Because the export process has requirements directly related to AES goals, notably the establishment of accounts, importers should also be aware of the AES.

Customs expects to have AES fully functional for all modes of transport, including rail, truck, and air, by the end of 1997.

The prime function of AES is to create a central repository for export data. Information gathered can then be routed electronically to other government agencies involved either in the import/export process or in the gathering of U.S. trade statistics. These agencies include the Bureau of Export Administration (BXA), the Drug Enforcement Agency (DEA), the State Department, the Treasury Department, and the U.S. Census Bureau.

AES is also expected to provide a number of benefits to the international trade community by simplifying the export documentation process, providing a single filing point for all export data, improving tracking of export shipments, and facilitating the clearance of goods through Customs.

In late 1997 the U.S. General Accounting Office (GAO) recommended that the U.S. Customs Service create one form that fits all for the thirteen government agencies supposed to file reports under AES. The GAO considered the AES system as then designed to be too unwieldy and troublesome for both government officials and exporters alike.

The Exporting Process Under AES

Customs will not mandate AES for the general export community for at least five years. However, Customs officials warn exporters to start considering automating their companies soon, or working with an AES-approved customs broker, in preparation for an electronic export environment. Companies that do not enter AES at mandate time will find themselves barred from U.S. Customs activities.

The first step in participating in AES is to file a letter of intent with Customs. By dialing The Customs Service MarketFax line (202-927-3555) exporters can get complete information on AES. After following recorded instructions, callers should enter extension number 100 for a list of all available AES documents and extension number 108 for a letter of intent outline. The information required on the letter of intent outline can then be sent to AES Implementation, U.S. Customs Service, 1301 Constitution Avenue, N.W., Room 7331, Washington, D.C. 20229, or faxed to 202-927-5921. The AES team can also be reached directly by telephone (202-927-0280).

Once the application has been approved the exporter or agent calls the carrier (e.g., shipping line, airline, freight carrier, or rail line) to book shipment of the goods. The exporter or agent gets a booking number and provides the carrier with the export transaction number (XTN), which includes the filer's ID number, SSN, or EIN, and a shipment reference number. The carrier next supplies all of the transportation data to Customs, removing one step from the exporting process for the exporter.

The data is then transmitted electronically to Customs, which matches the commodity and transportation data when the XTN number has been provided by both the exporter/agent and carrier. AES then either accepts the shipment or requests additional data. If the shipment is accepted, AES assigns an internal transaction number (ITN) and sends status notification to the exporter/agent and carrier. If such notification does not include a "hold," the cargo can be shipped.

If, prior to shipment the exporter/agent had estimated quantities and value, the actual numbers can be transmitted to AES after departure.

Note. Another important function of AES is to replace the paper version of the shipper's export declaration (SED) with an electronically transmitted version. Customs states that over half of all SEDs contain errors, a situation that can lead to increased costs, fines, and/or lengthy delays for the exporter. Using AES, exporters can correct errors as they occur.

Whether electronic or paper, exporters must file an SED with Customs prior to exporting goods. The following guidelines are provided to ensure that SED requirements are met:

- The exporter is responsible for all information even if the SED is prepared by a customs broker.
- The exporter must provide the freight forwarder or customs broker with formal power of attorney or written authorization on the SED itself.
- There is a common misconception that the SED can be submitted to the carrier (i.e., shipping line, airline, freight company, or rail line) up to four days after goods have been shipped. In fact, the carrier must receive the SED prior to export.
- Exporters, brokers, or forwarders must promptly report all corrections or cancellations on the SED to Customs and must maintain all records of the export transaction for at least three years.

AES-PASS

In response to requests from the trade community, Customs is developing the Automated Export System–Post-departure Authorized Special Status, or AES-PASS program. When implemented, the AES-PASS program will replace the Automated Export Reporting Program (AERP), which will be terminated by Customs in 1999.

The purpose of both programs is to allow qualified exporters to file data after the goods have been shipped. This status shortens the exporting process, saving participants time and money. Currently 25 percent of export shipments are made under AERP.

AES-PASS is in a pilot phase. Standards for participation are rigorous and first-time exporters are excluded. Major shipping lines and brokers will likely be the first to take advantage of the program. Exporters may want to consider working with brokers who are at least aware of AES-PASS. When the program is implemented on a widespread basis, those with no prior export violations and a system of strong internal controls will be able to enjoy the cost savings offered by the program.

Guidance

Though AES relates primarily to exports, it touches on procedures that are part of the importing process, notably facilitation of cargo clearance, collection of various fees, and promotion of a paperless import/export environment. In the future, AES is expected to interconnect with other export-related automation initiatives, including the Automated Commercial Environment. For example, AES will connect with ACE for the streamlining of import/export transactions and the processing of harbor maintenance fees.

Going Online

The following are some steps companies can take to go online with AES:

- Work through a freight forwarder that is already online.
- Contact AES MarketFax to access information on the AES program (202-927-3555). By calling this telephone number, international traders can obtain information on AES implementation schedules and details about how automation affects specific industries.
- Visit the Customs World Wide Web site (http://www.customs.ustreas.gov/).
- Visit the following Customs Houses, where AES is up and running on a trial basis: Baltimore, Norfolk, Houston, Los Angeles (Long Beach), and Charleston. (Newark, New Jersey and Portland, Oregon have volunteered as AES pilot sites, but were not online as of this writing.)

8.2 KEY CUSTOMS PROCEDURES

The role of Customs professionals is to help importers gain a working knowledge of Customs rules and regulations. Even so, there are documents, terms, and procedures that importers must become familiar with. A grasp of these basic concepts provides a solid foundation for working with U.S. Customs and import professionals in an efficient and cost-effective fashion.

8.2.1 *Customs Power of Attorney*

Importers and exporters are not required to hire customs brokers or other professionals to assist them with clearing shipments through U.S. Customs. However, small or even midsize companies that do not have staff members possessing detailed knowledge of complex Customs procedures may find the services of these professionals indispensable.

The Customs Power of Attorney grants the customs broker the legal authority to work with U.S. Customs on behalf of a client. Companies should grant Customs Power of Attorney to their customs broker before approaching U.S. Customs with their transaction. Once the power of attorney is issued, a customs broker has the right to sign declarations, entry, and other pertinent documents in a client's name.

EXAMPLE

An importer develops a close working relationship with a customs broker. At times, there is a need for customs clearance services at a distant port where this particular broker does not maintain an office. Under these circumstances it is best to allow the customs broker the authority to appoint subagents, otherwise the importer will have to grant separate power of attorney to other customs offices. This practice can prove time-consuming and needlessly difficult. See section 8.3 for more information on customs brokers and the content of customs powers of attorney. See Forms 8.01 and 8.02 for sample powers of attorney.

8.2.2   Customs Bonding

Customs regulations require that a bond, or suitable cash deposit, be filed with each formal entry to guarantee payment of any duties, taxes, fines, or penalties which may accrue upon importation. A formal entry is required for any importation of foreign origin valued in excess of $1,250, and for returned American goods valued in excess of $10,000.

Note. There are some exceptions, the most notable being textiles, for which a formal entry is required for any shipment valued over $250.

For more information on customs bonds, see section 11.7.

8.2.3   Classification

Classification of imports and exports in the U.S. is a central part of the duty assessment process.

Classification is accomplished via the Harmonized Commodity Description and Coding System. Under the classification process, a given product is identified with a Harmonized Tariff Schedule (HTS) designation.

HTS was developed by the Customs Cooperation Council in an effort to produce a single nomenclature for the classification of goods in international trade. The General Rules of Interpretation (GRI) form the basis of interpretation of the Harmonized system, which varies for importers and exporters.

The Harmonized Tariff Schedule has been adopted by sixty-five countries and is based on a six-digit code system. Individual countries are allowed to break out the nomenclature for tariff or statistical purposes beyond the six digits that are common to all subscribers. There are twenty-one sections in the international system. The sections begin by covering basic raw goods such as agricultural products. Later sections and chapters move progressively to processed goods, manufactured products, and end with high-technology items.

For more information on classification, see sections 9.1 to 9.3.

8.2.4   Valuation

A value on all imported merchandise must be declared at the time of entry. In order to properly ascertain the value of goods for the purpose of duty assessment, U.S. Customs applies Article VII of GATT. Adopted for all goods on July 1, 1981, this appraisement method is based on the price actually paid or payable (i.e., transaction value) for the imported goods. In addition to transaction value, there are four other methods for valuation of merchandise based on the nature of the transaction.

For more information on valuation, see section 9.4.

8.2.5 Binding Rulings

There are times when it may be wise, or even necessary, to seek an opinion—called a binding ruling—from U.S. Customs before proceeding with importation. For example, most importers need to know the exact amount of duty and other fees they will be required to pay to Customs before agreeing to purchase goods abroad. In such a case, it may be advisable to take the time to seek a binding ruling to determine up-front the correct valuation and classification of imported merchandise, as well as the status of duties and markings. Such rulings ensure that the importer is in full compliance with U.S. Customs and other laws.

Binding rulings are issued for classification, valuation, and other import/export related areas. The issuance of binding rulings can be a lengthy process. However, with passage of the Customs Modernization Act, customs officials expect to streamline preimportation programs. The binding rulings process is part of this streamlining initiative.

For more information on binding rulings, see section 10.4. Exporters can also contact the Office of Rulings and Regulations (202-482-6900) or visit the U.S. Customs site on the World Wide Web.

Note. Nonbinding recommendations can be obtained from customs brokers and other U.S. Customs import specialists.

8.2.6 Antidumping and Countervailing Duties

In addition to duties assessed according to the HTS system of classification, importers may also be required to pay antidumping, countervailing, and other special duties. Antidumping duties are assessed by the U.S. government when it has been determined that a foreign company is selling goods in the U.S. market at less than their cost of production or less than the fair market value in the country of production.

Countervailing duties are assessed by the U.S. government when it has been determined that a foreign company or industry receives a subsidy from the government of the exporting country.

For more information on countervailing and antidumping duties, see section 12.5.

8.2.7 The Duty Drawback Program

Drawback means a refund or remission, in whole or in part, of a customs duty paid on imported materials due to a particular use or nonuse. For instance, importers can file a claim for drawback of duties if the materials imported for manufacture are subsequently exported as a finished product. Also eligible for drawback are goods that are imported for re-export.

The Duty Drawback Program is intended to encourage U.S. manufacturing and to help U.S. companies compete in international markets by reducing the amount of duties payable to U.S. Customs. With the enactment of the Customs Modernization Act, it will be much easier for importers, exporters, and manufacturers to take advantage of the program. Some provisions of the Mod Act liberalize drawback requirements. Merchandise that had previously been ineligible for drawback may now be eligible under the new legislation. For more information on the Duty Drawback Program, see section 10.3.

8.2.8 Country-of-Origin Marking

With few exceptions, merchandise imported into the U.S. must be marked with the country of origin. Failure to comply with this requirement may result in delay or detention of the merchandise until properly marked. U.S. Customs may also assess fines and penalties. There are many marking requirements for goods that are exported from the U.S.

Additionally, under NAFTA, there are certain very specific marking requirements in order to recover duty costs. The Customs World Wide Web site and the Department of Commerce NAFTA FACTS line (202-482-4464) are good sources of information for country of origin marking.

8.2.9 Key Customs Documents

The process by which imported goods enter the U.S. market is covered in detail in Chapter 13. By way of introduction, importers need to know that when a shipment reaches the U.S., the importer of record must file entry documents with the district or port director at the port of entry. The importer of record may be:

- The owner
- Purchaser
- Licensed customs broker
- Consignee

Imported goods are not legally entered until after the shipment has arrived within the port of entry, U.S. Customs has authorized delivery of the merchandise and estimated duties are paid. It is the importer's responsibility—with the help, if desired, of customs professionals—to arrange for examination and release of the goods.

With few exceptions, all goods entering the United States must clear U.S. Customs. The Customs clearance process is complex, owing to the volume and diversity of documentation. However, certain documents are central to the import process. These important documents appear in a number of contexts (e.g., U.S. Customs, foreign export regulation, costs, and the international sales transaction) throughout the import process. U.S. Customs issues many of these documents. However, customs brokers, air freight companies, steamship lines, and many government agencies also issue documents that importers are required to prepare.

Note. Import documentation varies greatly from export documentation. Exporters must file export declarations. Much of this data is used to compile statistics on U.S. exporting trends. Until recently, U.S. Customs has not monitored export documentation as closely as import documentation because exporters do not generate revenue for the U.S. government. These policies are in transition.

The documents listed below relate to the import sales transaction. Importers are required to submit most or all of these documents to U.S. Customs:

1. *Bill of Lading.* Usually issued by the shipper in maritime shipments, the Bill of Lading confers title to the goods it covers when properly endorsed. It can also serve as a receipt for goods delivered to the carrier, as a contract for services to be rendered by the carrier, and in some cases as the basis for the issuance of a draft. See Form 5.15 for a sample bill of lading.

2. *Commercial Invoice.* The Commercial Invoice is intended as a complete record of the business transaction between the exporter and foreign importer concerning the goods to be shipped. It must identify the exact contents of the shipment. In addition, it serves as the basis for all other documentation regarding the shipment. See Form 5.08 for a sample commercial invoice.

3. *Dock Receipt.* The Dock Receipt confirms that a particular shipment has been delivered and received at the dock or warehouse of the ocean carrier.

4. *Insurance Certificate.* This certificate is issued if the seller is required to provide ocean marine insurance on a shipment.

5. *Packing List.* The packing list is used to determine the total shipping weight and volume of goods and also serves as an inventory tool. See Form 5.17 for a sample packing list.

6. *Quotation.* The quotation can serve as a valid sales contract between the exporter and foreign importer. See Form 5.03 for a sample quotation.

In addition, Customs may require the following entry documents:

1. *Entry Summary (Customs Form 7501).* After goods are released from Customs, the importer must file an entry summary along with the commercial invoice. Estimated duties must be deposited at the port of entry within ten working days of the time the goods are entered and released.

2. *Entry/Immediate Delivery (Customs Form 3461).* This form is used when importers wish to have goods released immediately from customs. Application is made prior to arrival of the merchandise.

8.3 CUSTOMS BROKERS

8.3.1 *Introduction*

Customs brokers are often described as import specialists, working with importers to help them move their products and shipments through U.S. Customs as quickly as possible.

Basically, brokers are the liaison between importers and Customs for every key phase of the import procedure. Chief among these procedures are accurate documentation and compliance with all U.S. Customs regulations.

As a general rule, importers should not attempt to enter goods into the U.S. without professional assistance, unless they are thoroughly familiar with the import process and possess the sophisticated hardware and software that, increasingly under the Customs Modernization Act, is a prerequisite for entering goods into the United States. Some companies train staff in Customs procedures and maintain them as in-house professionals. Many large corporations have full-time import/export departments. However, in most cases these firms still work with customs brokers.

Licensed Versus Unlicensed Brokers

To obtain a U.S. government license, customs brokers must pass an examination. A licensed customs house broker transacts U.S. Customs business directly on behalf of a client. Unlicensed customs brokers can handle some of this work as long as the claimants sign all applicable documents. Unlicensed brokers have no link to U.S. Customs and do not fall under Customs jurisdiction.

Industry Trends and Changing Roles

Congress, through the Customs Modernization Act, is altering the functions of the U.S. Customs Service. The impact on importers and customs brokers can be significant. Here are some of the major industry changes that will affect customs brokers and importers:

- As part of the Customs Modernization Act, the U.S. Customs Service will be reorganized. Regional offices will be consolidated and shifted.
- Through the Automated Commercial Environment, U.S. Customs is computerizing its organization and all phases of the import/export process. Importers and exporters should expect to go online or ensure that the professionals they hire offer computerized services.
- The Customs Modernization Act will reduce import filings at the point of entry into the U.S. However, the new system will also require importers to maintain much more detailed records. Failure to comply with the new entry requirements will result in increased civil fines and penalties.

Automated Commercial System Reconciliation Prototype

U.S. Customs is developing this prototype to help importers pay the right amount of duty even when they don't have all the information to determine the true value of their merchandise.

Enforced Compliance

On June 1, 1997, the U.S. Customs Service moved to enforced compliance of Shipping Export Declaration (SED) documentation, now requiring exporters to file all SED information with carriers before exports leave the country. Exporters receive a written warning on the first two infractions and fines are issued if there is a third infraction. Following the move to enforced compliance, U.S. Customs officials reported a surge in compliance.

Speedier Clearance

U.S. Customs is proposing speedier clearance of freight entering the U.S. The plan, if implemented, is to reduce the window during which importers can retrieve unclaimed imports before facing fines or penalties.

8.3.2 Services Performed

Customs brokers can:

* Prepare customs documents and forms
* Handle the electronic transmissions of documents invoices, bills, or parts thereof intended to be filed with U.S. Customs
* Offer duty estimates

Ideally, customs brokers are also involved in the planning stages of an importation. All too often, importers purchase goods for importation with no knowledge of the import process. Experienced importers never buy up shipments and move ahead with marketing without first assessing duties, tariffs, quotas, transportation costs, and other elements that will affect their transaction. If brought in at the initial stages of a transaction, a broker can:

* Provide a duty or tariff estimate that will affect the course of a future business transaction
* Research whether there are any barriers that would prohibit importation
* Help source goods with an eye to the best duty breaks, including duty-free arrangements

8.3.3 Selecting a Customs Broker

Those seeking to make a career in importing should choose a customs broker with care. Ideally, an importer will be forming a long-term relationship with the customs broker and will be able to learn from this professional. The following are some factors an importer should consider when selecting a customs broker:

1. A customs broker should not only have a thorough knowledge of the field, but must make the importer's interests paramount in exercise of brokering duties.
2. The customs broker should be licensed by the federal government and should be able to prove so.
3. The importer should check a broker's references thoroughly to assess the

broker's technical expertise. U.S. Customs regional offices, transportation companies, and customs broker associations can make recommendations of reliable brokers in the importer's region.

4. The customs brokerage should be fully computerized. Access to online U.S. Customs programs will speed up the importation process.
5. The brokerage should have expertise in the foreign countries where the importer does business.
6. In large metropolitan areas, it may be possible to locate customs brokers that specialize in particular product lines. For example, one New York–based customs brokerage specializes in women's undergarments.

Note. A useful source of information is the *National Directory of Customs Brokers*. This publication contains detailed information about customs brokers, including the products that they usually handle, location of offices, and number of employees, all of which can help an importer select the appropriate broker. The National Association of Customs Brokers and Freight Forwarders (202-466-0222) also publishes a membership directory.

The Export Yellow Pages and the Yellow Pages of most major cities list customs brokers and freight forwarders.

8.3.4 Legal Issues

When an importer selects a customs broker, he or she will also sign a customs power of attorney, which is required by Customs regulations. The Customs power of attorney establishes the legal authority for a customs broker to sign declarations and entry documents on behalf of its clients.

Powers of attorney are subject to several formal requirements and restrictions:

1. The power of attorney must be signed by a corporate officer or someone who has specific authority within the corporation to do so. An individual who is an owner or purchaser of imported goods may also authorize a customs broker to act as an agent using a power of attorney.

2. A power of attorney issued by a partnership is only valid for a period of two years from the date of issuance. One member of a partnership may exercise a power of attorney for the partnership.

3. All other powers of attorney are valid for an unlimited period of time until revoked in writing to the District Director of Customs. An expiration date may be specified by the importer on the form itself. This is optional.

4. When a new firm or partnership is formed, all powers of attorney for the prior firm are invalidated.

5. The authority to appoint subagents may be specified on the power of attorney. If clearance is required in a port where an importer's broker does not maintain an office, the subagent clause allows the broker to subcontract to another broker to handle Customs formalities.

6. Special requirements exist for nonresident individuals, partnerships, and corporations.

U.S. Customs Form 5291 is generally used for granting power of attorney. However, other forms may be used provided they are explicit in their terms. See Forms 8.01 and 8.02 for sample powers of attorney.

Liability Issues

The customs power of attorney confers on a broker the power to act for the importer in dealings with U.S. Customs. However, importers must be aware that they, not the broker, are primarily responsible for paying duties and complying with customs laws; importers are also liable for errors.

For these reasons, the importer should make sure that the broker has adequate professional liability insurance, which may cover any errors or omissions on the broker's part. Likewise, the importer should make sure that the broker agrees to indemnify and hold the importer harmless from penalties, costs, and damages due to the broker's own negligence.

Note. Should a broker prove intransigent and refuse to perform his or her services as required by law, an importer can request that license revocation proceedings be initiated by the U.S. Customs Service.

8.3.5 *Working With a Customs Broker*

Importers do not need to know the U.S. Customs regulations chapter and verse, memorize the Harmonized Tariff Schedule, or keep current with changing quotas and other regulations. However, to best monitor a customs broker's work, a prudent importer should be familiar with government regulations and the tools customs brokers use to help classify merchandise.

One of the most important things importers can do to work most effectively with customs brokers is to know their own business and thoroughly research the market for their goods, both in the U.S. and abroad. Importers need a clear concept of what they are trying to import and for what purpose. False declarations and inaccuracies can yield stiff fines.

The importer should approach the customs broker before the transaction is concluded for help in learning about customs compliance and restrictions.

EXAMPLE

A customer approached a sourcing agent to import steel bars from Europe. A rush order was requested. The agent asked a customs broker for a proposal on the business transaction and learned that a rush order was impossible: A binding ruling from U.S. Customs was required to determine whether or not the product was protected. Because the customer could not wait for a binding ruling, the order was canceled.

Importers often approach customs brokers with a shipment already en route or even waiting in a warehouse for U.S. Customs processing. In this case, the customs broker reviews the invoice and other documentation to determine how much information provided meets U.S. Customs requirements. One reason customs brokers prefer more advance notice is that rush situations create the potential for inaccuracies. The same U.S. Customs analysis has to be performed, but in a shorter amount of time. Under these circumstances, customs brokers sometimes refuse to make an entry because it is impossible to be certain all U.S. Customs requirements can be met.

Importers can facilitate entry by learning the basics of the import process, the terms that customs brokers use, and the information that their vendor should include on their invoice.

Importers should take notice of the questions the customs broker asks to ensure that the next import invoice contains all required information. With increased liability and increased paperwork, importers should pay close attention to the advice their broker offers at this juncture.

The following information is commonly missing when an importer works with a customs broker for the first, or even consecutive, time:

1. The commercial invoice usually does not provide enough information for proper classification of merchandise. Customs brokers will proceed to ask the importers a series of questions until they have gathered all requisite data.

2. Mostly, a customs broker wants as accurate a description of the product in question as possible to assist in the classification procedure.

3. The country of origin is of particular concern. Do not assume because merchandise or goods were purchased in Great Britain, for instance, that they were manufactured there. Try, at all times, to have the country of origin printed on the invoice. If this information is missing, a search has to be done at a time when the importer is trying to gain U.S. Customs clearance. Valuable time may be lost.

4. Importers may forget to indicate whether their shipment has been paid for in foreign currency or U.S. dollars. Many brokers will ask importers to provide this information for every shipment, rather than state that their goods are always purchased in one or other form of currency. There is always the chance for an exception.

8.4 CUSTOMS ATTORNEYS

There may be times when importers require the services of customs attorneys. Although some attorneys specializing in U.S. Customs regulations handle the same import concerns as a customs broker, most attorneys come on the scene in the event of a dispute.

Most commonly, attorneys work with importers when a customs entry is rejected because of a disagreement on classification of goods, the amount of duty paid, or the valuation of goods as declared. The importer, at this stage, will have received a letter from U.S. Customs indicating that it does not agree with the importer's documentation of goods.

Customs attorneys can offer the following services to importers:

- Filing of protests
- Responding to requests for information from the U.S. Customs Service
- Responding to requests for information from other related government agencies (e.g., the International Trade Commission)
- Handling U.S. Customs investigations, including acting on behalf of clients when U.S. Customs agents appear to conduct searches
- Delivering summonses or search warrants when there is a question of fraud or other serious criminal violations of U.S. Customs laws

Note. U.S. government agencies will not investigate an importer without some assurance that an import law is being violated. Whenever U.S. Customs or government agencies request formal information, importers should seek professional advice. Do not respond to any official government questionnaires without help from a licensed, qualified professional.

Customs Attorney or Customs Broker?

Whether to work on a dispute with a customs broker or hire a customs attorney is a judgment call on the part of an importer. It is true that customs brokers also handle disputes with the U.S. Customs Service and can certainly advise importers on a course of action. However, there are some advantages to using customs attorneys:

- *Attorney-client privilege.* Under the attorney/client privilege, attorneys offer their clients strict confidentiality in most cases. Privileged communications with an attorney cannot be revealed in an investigation or proceeding. Communications with brokers, consultants, and other professionals are not protected in the same fashion.

EXAMPLE

An importer hired a consulting firm specializing in U.S. Customs regulations to assess its operation. The consulting firm produced a report outlining various violations. Not long afterward, U.S. Customs chose to investigate and sent the importer a lengthy audit questionnaire to complete. By law, the importer was required to include the consultant's report as part of the investigatory documentation. If a customs attorney had been involved instead of the consulting firm, the importer could have kept the report's findings confidential. Penalties might have been avoided.

- *Filing protests.* Customs attorneys argue they are best qualified to file protests on duties and other aspects of U.S. Customs regulations, especially if the protest becomes an appeal that ends up in the courts. If the protest is poorly prepared, inaccurate, or fails to cite relevant law, it will be virtually impossible to reverse on appeal.

Importers, especially novices, may misinterpret U.S. Customs or other government agency terminology. Sometimes the results lead to unwanted inquiries and even higher duties. In one case, an importer misinterpreted a U.S. Customs questionnaire and inadvertently mischaracterized an import transaction. The result was a far higher duty than anticipated. A customs attorney was able to appeal the ruling and help the client avoid paying the duties as originally assessed.

8.5 CONSULTANTS

In recent years, a growing number of consultants have been handling international information. Some of the major U.S. accounting firms have created international consulting arms to help businesspeople with a wide variety of international needs.

As customs brokers take on the role of consultants to advise importers and exporters on their overseas transactions, so others are starting to handle work that until recently was the purview of customs brokers, attorneys, and freight forwarders.

When to Hire a Consultant

Certainly, consultants can be helpful on the marketing side of the international transaction. If an importer plans to hire a consultant to help with aspects of import or export regulated by law, he or she must ensure the consultant has the same knowledge base as a customs broker or attorney. It is important to remember that most consultants are not licensed and cannot offer strict confidentiality under the law.

Summary of Key Points Raised in This Chapter

The U.S. Customs Service enforces a variety of regulations affecting imports, including customs duty provisions, regulations of other government agencies, and regulations that seek to protect U.S. industries.

More than sixty government agencies have issued regulations restricting imports.

The Customs Modernization Act alters the relationship between importers and the Customs Service by placing more responsibility on importers regarding compliance with laws and regulations.

U.S. Customs is in the process of being automated. Over the course of the next five years, importers will be required to submit Customs documents electronically.

A Customs power of attorney grants a customs broker the legal authority to work with U.S. Customs on behalf of an importer.

Customs regulations require that a bond or suitable cash deposit be posted for each formal entry of imported merchandise.

When an import shipment reaches the U.S., importers must file entry documents with the district or port director at the port of entry.

Customs brokers work with importers to help move shipments through Customs as quickly as possible. Brokers prepare Customs documents and forms, handle electronic submission of Customs documents, and offer duty estimates.

A Customs power of attorney confers on a broker the power to act for the importer; however, the importer, not the broker, is legally responsible for paying duties and complying with Customs laws.

Customs attorneys can provide assistance in the event of a dispute with Customs; they also offer strict confidentiality, known as the attorney-client privilege.

For Additional Information

For additional information on topics discussed in this chapter, please consult the following publications:

Dun & Bradstreet's Exporters Encyclopedia (1994).
The Journal of Commerce.
U.S. Customs Service, *Overall Program Plan: National Customs Automation Program* (January 1995).
————, *Global Trade Talk,* Vol. 4, No. 3 (May/June 1995).
————, *This Is Customs.*
————, *Importing into the U.S.*
Thomas E. Johnson, *Export/Import Procedures and Documentation,* 2d ed. (New York: AMACOM Books, 1994).

Form 8.01   Customs power of attorney.

Check Appropriate Box:
[ ] Individual
[ ] Partnership
[ ] Corporation
[ ] Sole Proprietorship

KNOW ALL MEN BY THESE PRESENTS: That   _[Full name of person, partnership_
or corporation, or sole proprietorship (identify)]   a corporation doing business under
the laws of the State of _____ or a _____ doing business as _____ residing at _____
having an office and place of business at _____ hereby constitutes and appoints each
of the following persons: _____ as a true and lawful agent and attorney of the grantor
named above for and in the name, place and stead of said grantor from this date and
in all Customs Districts, and in no other name, to make, endorse, sign, declare or
swear to any entry, withdrawal, declaration, certificate, bill of lading, carnet or other
document required by law or regulation in connection with the importation, transportation, or exportation of any merchandise shipped or consigned by or to said grantor;
to perform any act or condition which may be required by law or regulation in connection with such merchandise; to receive any merchandise deliverable to said
grantor;

To make endorsements on bills of lading conferring authority to transfer title,
make entry or collect drawback, and to make, sign, declare to swear to any statement,
supplemental statement, schedule, supplemental schedule, certificate of delivery,
certificate of manufacture, certificate of manufacture and delivery, abstract of manufacturing records, declaration of proprietor on drawback entry, declaration of exporter on drawback entry, or any other affidavit or document intended for filing in
any customs district;

To sign, seal and deliver for and as the act of said grantor any bond required by
law or regulation in connection with the entry or withdrawal of imported merchandise or merchandise exported with or without benefit of drawback, or in connection
with the entry, clearance, lading, unlading or navigation of any vessel or other means
of conveyance owned or operated by said grantor, and any and all bonds which may
be voluntarily given and accepted under applicable laws and regulations, consignee's
and owner's declarations provided for in section 485, Tariff Act of 1930, as amended,
or affidavits in connection with the entry of merchandise;

To sign and swear to any document and to perform any act that may be necessary
or required by law or regulation in connection with the entering, clearing, lading,
unlading or operation of any vessel or other means of conveyance owned or operated
by said grantor;

To authorize other Customs Brokers to act as grantor's agent; to receive, endorse
and collect checks issued for Customs duty refunds in grantor's name drawn on the
Treasurer of the United States; if the grantor is a nonresident of the United States,
to accept service of process on behalf of the grantor;

And generally to transact at the customs houses in any district any and all Customs business including making, signing and filing of protests under Section 514 of

the Tariff Act of 1930, in which said grantor is or may be concerned or interested and which may properly be transacted or performed by an agent and attorney, giving to said agent and attorney full power and authority to do anything whatever requisite and necessary to be done in the premises as fully as said grantor could do it present and acting, hereby ratifying and confirming all that the said agent and attorney shall lawfully do by virtue of these presents; the foregoing power of attorney to remain in full force and effect until the _____ day of _____, 19 _____ or until notice of revocation in writing is duly given to and received by a District Director of Customs. If the donor of this power of attorney is a partnership, the said power shall in no case have any force or effect after the expiration of 2 years from the date of its execution.
IN WITNESS WHEREOF, the said _____ has caused these presents to be sealed and signed:
(Signature) _____   (Date) _____
WITNESS: _____

_____
(Corporate Seal)
INDIVIDUAL OR PARTNERSHIP CERTIFICATION (Optional)
City _____
County _____   SS: _____
State _____
On this _____ day of _____, 19 _____, personally appeared before me _____ residing at _____, personally known or sufficiently identified to me, who certifies that _____ (is)(are) the individual(s) who executed the foregoing instrument and acknowledge it to be _____ free act and deed.

_____
(Notary Public)

_____
CORPORATE CERTIFICATION* (Optional)
(To be made by an officer other than the one who executes the power of attorney.)
I, _____, certify that I am the _____ of _____, organized under the laws of the State of _____, that _____, who signed this power of attorney on behalf of the donor, is the _____ of said corporation; and that said power of attorney was duly signed, and attested for and in behalf of said corporation by authority of its governing body as the same appears in a resolution of the Board of Directors passed at a regular meeting held on the _____ day of _____, not in my possession or custody. I further certify that the resolution is in accordance with the articles of incorporation and bylaws of said corporation.

_____   _____
Signature   Date
If the corporation has no corporate seal, the fact shall be stated, in which case a scroll or adhesive shall appear in the appropriate designated space.

Customs power of attorney or residents (including resident corporations) shall be without power of substitution except for the purpose of executing shipper's export declarations. However, a power of attorney executed in favor of a licensed customs broker may specify that the power of attorney is granted to the customs broker to act through any of its licensed officers or any employee specifically authorized to act for such customs broker by power of attorney.

If you are the importer of record, payment to the broker will not relieve you of liability for Customs charges in the event the charges are not paid by the broker. Therefore, if you pay by check, Customs charges may be paid with a separate check payable to the "U.S. Customs Service."

Importers who wish to utilize this procedure must contact our office in advance to arrange timely receipt of duty checks.

Form 8.02 Customs power of attorney (Customs Form 5291).

CUSTOMS POWER OF ATTORNEY
Step by Step Instructions for Completion

1. For U.S. Companies *ONLY*
2. Check ONE Box (NOT REQUIRED)
3. Corporation: Full Name *as shown in* Corporate Record
4. Name of State of Corporation
5. Name of State of Individual or Partnership
6. Company Name *is other than* (3) Corporation
7. *If Individual or Sole Proprietor:* Home Address
   [Bracketed Information is Included for Foreign Corporation's use]
8. Full Physical Address *Including Postal Code*
9. Expiration Date (CANNOT BE LEFT BLANK)
10. Typed *(Sur)* Name of (11) Person in Position *of President, Vice President, Secretary or Treasurer*

Need not be President, Vice President, Secretary or Treasurer if proof of authority is acquired

11. Signature *of President, Vice President, Secretary or Treasurer*
12. Title of (11) Person in Position *of President, Vice President, Secretary or Treasurer*
13. Execution Date
14. Witness' Signature (NOT REQUIRED)
15. Corporate Seal (NOT REQUIRED)

Department of the Treasury
U.S. Customs Service
141.32, C.R.

POWER OF ATTORNEY

Check appropriate box:
□ Individual
□ Partnership
□ Corporation
□ Sole Proprietorship

KNOW ALL MEN BY THESE PRESENTS: That, _____

_____ , or a _____
(Full Name of person, partnership, or corporation, or sole proprietorship (Identity))

a corporation doing business under the laws of the State of _____

doing business as _____ , residing at _____

having an office and place of business at _____

_____ , hereby constitutes and appoints each of the following persons

_____
(Give full name of each agent designated)

as a true and lawful agent and attorney of the grantor named above for and in the name, place, and stead of said grantor from this date and in Customs District _ _ _ _ _, and in no other name, to make, endorse, sign, declare, or swear to any entry, withdrawal, declaration, certificate, bill of lading, or other document required by law or regulation in connection with the importation, transportation, or exportation of any merchandise shipped or consigned by or to said grantor; to perform any act or condition which may be required by law or regulation in connection with such merchandise; to receive any merchandise deliverable to said grantor;

To make endorsements on bills of lading conferring authority to make entry and collect drawback, and to make, sign, declare, or swear to any statement, supplemental statement, schedule, supplemental schedule, certificate of delivery, certificate of manufacture, certificate of manufacture and delivery, abstract of manufacturing records, declaration of proprietor on drawback entry, declaration of exporter on drawback entry, or any other affidavit or document which may be required by law or regulation for drawback purposes, regardless of whether such bill of lading, sworn statement, schedule, certificate, abstract, declaration, or other affidavit or document is intended for filing in said district or in any other customs district;

To sign, seal, and deliver for and as the act of said grantor any bond required by law or regulation in connection with the entry or withdrawal of imported merchandise or merchandise exported with or without benefit of drawback, or in connection with the entry, clearance, lading, unlading or navigation of any vessel or other means of conveyance owned or operated by said grantor, and any and all bonds which may be

voluntarily given and accepted under applicable laws and regulations, consignee's and owner's declarations provided for in section 485, Tariff Act of 1930, as amended, or affidavits in connection with the entry of merchandise;

To sign and swear to any document and to perform any act that may be necessary or required by law or regulation in connection with the entering, clearing, lading, unlading, or operation of any vessel or other means of conveyance owned or operated by said grantor;

And generally to transact at the customhouses in said district any and all customs business, including making, signing, and filing of protests under section 514 of the Tariff Act of 1930, in which said grantor is or may be concerned or interested and which may properly be transacted or performed by an agent and attorney, giving to said agent and attorney full power and authority to do anything whatever requisite and necessary to be done in the premises as fully as said grantor could do if present and acting, hereby ratifying and confirming all that the said agent and attorney shall lawfully do by virtue of these presents; the foregoing power of attorney to remain in full force and effect until the _____ day of _____ , 19 ___ , or until notice of revocation in writing is duly given to and received by the District Director of Customs of the district aforesaid. If the donor of this power of attorney is a partnership, and said the power shall in no case have any force or effect after the expiration of 2 years from the date of its receipt in the office of the district director of customs of the said district.

IN WITNESS WHEREOF, the said _____

has caused these presents to be sealed and signed: (Signature) _____

(Capacity) _____ (Date) _____

WITNESS: _____

_____

_____ (Corporate seal) *(Optional)

Customs Form 5291 (10-07-90)   (SEE OVER)

INDIVIDUAL OR PARTNERSHIP CERTIFICATION *(Optional)

CITY _____
COUNTY _____ ss:
STATE _____

On this _____ day of _____ , 19 ____ , personally appeared before me _____ , personally known or sufficiently identified to me, who certifies that _____ (is)(are) the individual(s) who executed the foregoing instrument and acknowledge it to be _____ free act and deed.

_____
(Notary Public)

CORPORATE CERTIFICATION *(Optional)

(To be made by an officer other than the one who executes the power of attorney)

I, _____ , certify that I am the _____
of _____ , organized under the laws of the State of _____
that _____ , who signed this power of attorney on behalf of the donor, is the _____
of said corporation; and that said power of attorney was duly signed, sealed, and attested for and behalf of said corporation by authority of its governing body as the same appears in a resolution of the Board of Directors passed at a regular meeting held on the _____ day of _____ , now in my possession or custody. I further certify that the resolution is in accordance with the articles of incorporation and bylaws of said corporation.

IN WITNESS WHEREOF, I have hereunto set my hand and affixed the seal of said corporation, at the City of _____ this _____ day of _____ , 19 _____

_____
(Signature)

_____
(Date)

If the corporation has no corporate seal, the fact shall be stated, in which case a scroll or adhesive shall appear in the appropriate, designated place.

Customs powers of attorney of residents (including resident corporations) shall be without power of substitution except for the purpose of executing shipper's export declarations. However, a power of attorney executed in favor of a licensed customhouse broker may specify that the power of attorney is granted to the customhouse broker to act through any of its licensed officers or any employee specifically authorized to act for such customhouse broker by power of attorney.

*NOTE: The corporate seal may be omitted. Customs does not require completion of a certification. The grantor has the option of executing the certification or omitting it.

*U.S.GPO:1984-301-616/90746

323

9

Classification and Valuation

Key Questions Answered in This Chapter

Introduction

Once an importer has created a legal basis for operating with a customs broker and understands customs administration and trade regulation, he or she can turn to the actual work of meeting U.S. Customs requirements. These requirements fall into two main categories:

- Whether the import is admissible (i.e., whether an import is allowed into the United States or is prohibited through quota, embargo, or outright ban).
- Whether the import is dutiable (i.e., whether the importer must pay certain fees, charges, and taxes on the import).

Issues of admissibility and dutiability cannot be settled until importers first classify their imports under the Harmonized Tariff System and then declare the value of their shipments. The valuation must meet with the approval of U.S. Customs, or the importer may be liable for higher duty rates in the long run.

Classification and valuation are the two most important factors affecting the amount of duties an importer can expect to pay when an entry is filed with U.S. Customs. Outside of freight costs, duties are the biggest expense importers will encounter. Classification and valuation are also the basis for duty management by country of origin or by product, a subject that is discussed in detail in Chapter 10.

9.1 CLASSIFICATION

9.1.1 Introduction

Merchandise must be classified by country and by product for duties to be calculated. Proper classification of imports is crucial because duty rates vary depending on the classification selected.

Classification accomplishes the following for exporters, importers, and government agencies:

1. Permits standardization of government trade statistics
2. Facilitates the interpretation of trade agreements (e.g., the North American Free Trade Agreement)
3. Allows standardization of transportation documentation, thus easing an importer's documentation responsibilities
4. Allows exporters to more easily identify tariff costs in the import country

Note. Currently, export classifications are apt to receive less scrutiny than import classifications because there are no revenue implications for the U.S. government; classifications of export declarations are used primarily for trade statistics and are not part of export licensing requirements. However, with the advent of the proposed Automated Export System (AES), there will most likely be increased scrutiny of export classifications for the sake of enforcement. (For more information on the Automated Export System, see sections 3.7.6 and 8.1.7.)

9.1.2 The Harmonized Tariff System

Classification is the process of identifying a given product under the Harmonized Tariff System (HTS) for purposes of trade statistics and duty assessment. The Harmonized Tariff System was developed by the Customs Cooperation Council in an effort to produce a single nomenclature for the classification of goods in international trade.

The Harmonized Tariff System has been adopted by sixty-five countries. There are twenty-one sections in the international system, beginning with basic raw goods such as agricultural products and moving progressively to processed goods, manufactured products, and high-technology items. Each individual classification is assigned a six-digit code number; individual countries are permitted to break out the nomenclature beyond six digits for tariff or statistical purposes. All merchandise is classified in some provision of this tariff system. (The HTS even includes a catchall category: Chapters 98 and 99 of the HTS stipulates "free areas" where the laws of individual countries are included.)

The Harmonized Tariff Schedule itself is a five- to six-inch-thick cross-referencing guide covering thousands of products as they relate to importation in the sixty-five member countries. Anyone who is serious about international trade should obtain a copy of the HTS from the U.S. Government Printing Office. Having this guide on hand permits importers and exporters to better follow the recommendations of their customs brokers and customs attorneys regarding classification of goods.

Guidance

Although the member nations have harmonized their tariff schedules, they still maintain individual rules and regulations. Ideally, adoption of the HTS would mean that all member countries agree on classifications to the six-digit level. But customs brokers warn that this is not always true in practice. U.S. classification rulings may not be binding in other HTS countries, and the same may be true for foreign tariff rulings in the United States.

HTS Divisions

The tariff schedule is divided into various sections and chapters dealing with merchandise in broad product categories. These categories separately cover:

- Animal products
- Vegetable products
- Products of various basic materials such as wood, textiles, plastics, rubber, and steel
- Metal products in various stages of manufacture
- Chemicals, machinery, and electrical equipment
- Certain exceptions from duty and special statutory provisions, covered in the last section (XXII) of the HTS

How Goods Are Classified Under the HTS

In the first twenty-one sections of the HTS, products are classified in several ways:

* *By name.* Goods earn a designation (1) under items or descriptions which name them.
* *By general description.* Goods earn a designation (2) under provisions of general description.
* *By component materials.* Goods earn a designation (3) under provisions that identify them by component material.
* *By actual or principal use.* Goods earn a designation (4) under provisions that describe them in terms of their actual or principal use.

If an absolute classification and duty amount is required, importers must seek a binding ruling from U.S. Customs before proceeding. For more information on binding rulings, see Chapter 10, section 10.4.

9.1.3   The HTS Review Process

Importers do not always agree with U.S. Customs officials on the classification of their goods. To deal with such situations, the U.S. Customs Service has a system of protest that allows importers to contest duty rates. Both customs brokers and customs attorneys can help importers with their classification protests.

A formal review process gives importers a chance to appeal U.S. Customs duty allotments on an international level. Most commonly, entire industries protest classifications that affect their industry members. The Harmonized System Committee is the first committee of review. If the Harmonized System Committee fails to resolve a dispute, the protest goes before the Customs Cooperation Council. This is an international board based in Brussels that resolves major classification disputes.

It is rare for individual importers to appear before the Customs Cooperation Council. Usually small importers band together with the help of their trade or industry associations and present what amounts to a class action suit before the Brussels body. Sometimes, as in the case of the steel industry, a whole industry unites and seeks protective tariffs from the U.S. International Trade Commission (ITC).

9.2   THE GENERAL RULES OF INTERPRETATION

9.2.1   Introduction

In the U.S., classification and the Harmonized Tariff System are understood by means of the General Rules of Interpretation (GRIs). The Harmonized Tariff System cannot be read accurately without applying the GRIs as a means of interpreting the tariff classification text. Only through the joint reading of the tariff schedule and the GRIs can reliable classification be determined.

Like any legal text, the GRIs are complex. Customs brokers and customs attorneys can help translate the GRIs, which is what usually takes place in the field. The importer must work with professionals closely on product descriptions for a correct classification and later valuation to be made.

EXAMPLE

> Steel products have varying alloy contents and come in a wide variety of grades and standards. The International Trade Commission has also set quotas against some types of steel emanating from some countries. To classify a steel importer's product, a customs broker must obtain detailed information from the importer on the product's makeup and origin.
>
> Import professionals urge importers to attempt to use the HTS and the GRIs for the sake of education before turning for professional help. This is the importer's safeguard against professional inaccuracies and a sure means of learning the system.

9.2.2 GRI Definitions

Importers must read the GRIs carefully and have a firm grasp on their meaning. The following are some terms importers should know when attempting to work with the GRIs and with the Harmonized Tariff System:

- *Essential character.* A product's essential character is the attribute that strongly marks or serves to distinguish what an article is (i.e., that which is indispensable to the structure, core, or condition of the article). Specific characteristics may be a part of a final determination of essential character; in general, however, no single, specific characteristic such as bulk, weight, or value is sufficient to consistently identify the essential character of a product.

- *Mutatis mutandis.* Meaning "with necessary changes having been made"; the substitution of new terms.

- *Prima facie.* Meaning "at first sight."

- *Set.* To be considered a set, a group of imported items must meet all of the following criteria:
  —Goods must be prima facie classifiable under two or more different HTS headings at the four-digit level.
  —Goods must be packed for retail sale.
  —Goods must be put together to carry out a specific activity or meet a specific need.

9.2.3 The First Six GRIs

The GRIs must be applied to ensure that goods are classified in a consistent and accurate manner. GRIs 1 through 4 must be considered in sequence when classifying goods under the Harmonized Tariff System.

GRI 1: Classification *Eo Nomine* (By Name)

The table of contents, alphabetical index, and titles of sections, chapters, and subchapters are provided for ease of reference only. For legal purposes, classifications are determined according to the terms of the headings and any relative section or chapter notes and, provided such headings or notes do not otherwise require, according to the following provisions of GRI 2.

GRI 2(a): Incomplete or Unfinished Articles

Any reference in a heading to an article shall be taken to include a reference to that article incomplete or unfinished, provided that, as entered, the incomplete or unfinished article has the essential character of the complete or finished article. It shall also include a reference to that article complete or finished (or falling to be classified as complete or finished by virtue of this rule), entered unassembled or disassembled.

GRI 2(b): Mixtures and Combinations

Any reference in a heading to a material or substance shall be taken to include a reference to mixtures or combinations of that material or substance with other materials or substances. Any reference to goods of a given material or substance shall be taken to include a reference to goods consisting wholly or partly of such material or substance. The classification of goods containing more than one material or substance shall be according to principles of GRI 3.

GRI 3: Goods Classifiable Under Two or More Headings

When, by application of rule GRI 2(b) or for any other reason, goods are prima facie classifiable under two or more headings, classification shall be effected as follows:

GRI 3(a). The heading that provides the most specific description shall be preferred to headings providing a more general description. However, when two or more headings each refer to part only of the materials or substances contained in mixed or composite goods, or to part only of the items in a set put up for retail sale, those headings are to be regarded as equally specific in relation to those goods, even if one of them gives a more complete or precise description of the goods.

GRI 3(b). Mixtures (composite goods consisting of different materials or made up of different components) and goods put in sets for retail sale, which cannot be classified by reference to 3(a), shall be classified as if they consisted of the material or component that gives them their essential character, insofar as this criterion is applicable.

GRI 3(c). When goods cannot be classified by reference to 3(a) or 3(b), they shall be classified under the heading that occurs last in numerical order among those which equally merit consideration.

GRI 4: Classification of Goods Under Headings to Which They Are Most Akin

Goods that cannot be classified in accordance with the above rules shall be classified under the heading to which they are most akin.

GRI 5: Classification of Particular Goods

In addition to the foregoing provisions, the following rules shall apply in respect of goods referred to therein:

GRI 5(a). Camera cases, musical instrument cases, gun cases, drawing instrument cases, necklace cases, and similar containers, specifically shaped or fitted to contain a specific article or set of articles, suitable for long-term use and entered with the articles for which they are intended, shall be classified with such articles when of a kind normally sold therewith. This rule does not, however, apply to containers that give the whole its essential character.

GRI 5(b). Subject to the provisions of rule GRI 5(a) above, packing materials and packing containers entered with the goods therein shall be classified with the goods if they are of a kind normally used for packing such goods. However, this provision does not apply when such packing materials or packing containers are clearly suitable for repetitive use.

GRI 6: Interpretation of Headings, Subheadings, and Notes

For legal purposes, the classification of goods of the subheadings of a heading shall be determined according to the terms of those subheadings and any related subheading notes and, *mutatis mutandis,* to the above rules, on the understanding that only subheadings at the same level are comparable. For the purposes of this rule, the relative section, chapter, and subchapter notes also apply, unless the context otherwise requires.

9.2.4   Additional U.S. Rules of Interpretation

All member nations of the Harmonized Tariff System are bound to work by the first six GRIs. However, individual nations can apply their own tariff clarifications to the HTS.

Note. When international guidelines are in place, national clarifications cannot override them.

The U.S. government has issued the following clarifications to the HTS. In the absence of special language or context that otherwise requires, the following rules apply:

1. A tariff classification controlled by use (other than actual use) is to be determined in accordance with the use in the United States at, or immediately prior to, the date of importation, of goods of that class or kind to which the imported goods belong, and the controlling use is the principal use.

2. A tariff classification controlled by the actual use to which the imported goods are put in the United States is satisfied only if such use is intended at the time of importation, the goods are so used, and proof thereof is furnished within three years after the date the goods are entered.

3. A provision for parts of an article covers products solely or principally used as part of such articles, but a provision for "parts" or "parts and accessories" shall not prevail over a specific provision for such part or accessory.

9.2.5 When Classifications Are Not Evident

Most countries, including the United States, provide for advance rulings of product classification to limit uncertainty in costing transactions. Unfortunately, identification of the correct classification is not always easy. Items can fall under two or more classifications. In some cases, there is no immediate classification apparent. For example, new commercial products can pose this sort of problem.

When a classification is not evident, it may be necessary to request a classification ruling from the U.S. Customs Service. Some rulings can provide useful guidance for planning purposes. However, if the importer wants to have assurance of a certain duty rate (and not a surprise duty increase at some later date), it is necessary to seek a binding, formal ruling from the U.S. Customs Service. (For more information on binding rulings, see section 10.4.) Classifications should be checked each year as products are sometimes reclassified by U.S. Customs.

Note. A customs import specialist can provide advice on classification; however, this advice is nonbinding.

Appeals of any U.S. Customs Service ruling may be made to the U.S. Court of International Trade (formerly the U.S. Customs Court) or to the U.S. Court of Appeals for the Federal Circuit (formerly the U.S. Court of Customs and Patent Appeals).

9.2.6 Classifications in Practice

The following is an example of an actual Customs classification ruling.

EXAMPLE

The merchandise to be classified consisted of semiconductor bases made of copper. The purpose of the base was to mount the semiconductor device, consisting of the semiconductor and the base itself, into a heat sink. The copper base was an integral part of the semiconductor. The semiconductor device generated heat, which was then absorbed by a separate heat sink.

What was the proper classification of the semiconductor base under the Harmonized Tariff System? Classification of this merchandise is under the HTS in accordance with the GRIs taken in order. GRI 1 provides that classification is determined according to the terms of the headings and any chapter or section notes in the HTS.

Section XVI, Note 2(b) of the HTS provides that:

[O]ther parts, if suitable for use solely or principally with a particular kind of machine, or with a number of machines of the same heading (including a machine of heading 8479 or 8453), are to be classified with machines of that kind. However, parts that are equally suitable for use principally with the goods of heading 8517 and 8525 to 8528 are to be classified in heading 8517.

Based on the description of the merchandise, Customs ruled that the subject semiconductor base is solely or principally used with a semiconductor, described in heading 8541 of the HTS. Therefore, the merchandise is classified under HTS subheading 8541.90.00, which provides for:

[d]iodes, transistors, and similar semiconductor devices; photosensitive semiconductor devices, including photovoltaic cells whether or not assembled in modules or made up into panels; light-emitting diodes; mounted piezoelectric crystals; parts thereof [. . .]

Items classifiable under this provision entered the U.S. duty free at the time the ruling was issued.

9.3 LIQUIDATION

9.3.1 The Liquidation Process

Liquidation is the point at which the U.S. Customs Service's assessment of the rate and amount of duty becomes final for most purposes. This is the stage at which the Customs agent makes a determination whether the good or product should enter the country duty free, at a duty rate the customs broker has assigned, or at a higher rate.

An importer may receive an advance notice on Customs Form 4333A stating when and in what amount duty will be liquidated. This "courtesy notice" is not a formal liquidation and its provisions are not binding. Protest rights do not accrue until the formal liquidation notice is posted. In addition, time limits for protesting do not start to run until the date of posting, and a protest cannot be filed before liquidation is posted.

9.3.2 When Liquidation Is Delayed or Refused

The U.S. Customs Service may determine that an entry cannot be liquidated as entered for one reason or another. For example, the tariff classification may not be correct or may not be acceptable because it is not consistent with an established and uniform classification practice. Under these circumstances, importers should expect some change in the duty estimation, such as a refund or additional duties.

For example, an importer may have improperly classified merchandise under a duty-free category. In this case, the importer is given advance notice of the proposed duty rate increase and an opportunity to validate the claim for a free rate or a more favorable duty rate.

If the importer does not respond to this notice, or if U.S. Customs still finds cause for a duty charge, officials will liquidate the entry and bill the importer for the additional duty. If the situation presented is not clear-cut, the importer or a customs official may request an appeal, called an *internal advice procedure*, to U.S. Customs headquarters.

9.3.3 Making Preliminary Duty Estimates

Because duty expenses vary depending on the product imported, importers can make some preliminary estimates of duty costs based on product information. At the very least, importers should have answers to the following questions when attempting to ascertain the dutiable status of a prospective import:

- *What is the product?* A reasonably specific description should be given and, ideally, product literature should be supplied. The description should include a list of materials that form the product's makeup.
- *What country or countries is this item sourced from?* Sourcing may have an effect on the rate of duty paid on a particular item.
- *What is the intended use of the imported merchandise when imported into the United States?* Merchandise that is imported for processing and subsequent export or temporary use may be classified under special provisions for duty-free entry.

Practices for managing duties for either profits or savings are addressed fully in Chapter 11. Below are three examples of how clever customs professionals "manage" duties.

EXAMPLE

Toner for copy machines used to be classified as a chemical at high duty. It came in large containers and had to be poured into the copy machine. Then the design was changed so that the toner was put in cartridges with stirrers, so it never had to be touched. A clever broker realized that it was now more than just a chemical and was able to get the duty reduced to just two percent, saving hundreds of thousands of dollars for importers.

EXAMPLE

A U.S. Customs rule dictates that computer motherboards with CPU chips are classified as computers, not parts, and are assessed a higher duty. Computer importers sought to avoid this rule by asking the sellers to remove the chips from the boards before shipping. Customs agents, observing this practice, cited a rule that taxes components in the same package at the higher rate. Importers then had the sellers ship the pieces separately and were able to save the duty.

EXAMPLE

A few years ago, tents were being imported at 30 percent duty. A customs broker found a ruling granting duty-free status if an item was ornamented. Thinking this would apply to tents, the customs broker called several customers who were tent importers and told them about the rule. Some of them found a way to ornament their tents and saved thousands of dollars in duties.

9.4 VALUATION

9.4.1 Introduction

For customs purposes, importers must declare the value of all imported merchandise at the time of entry. The importer is generally required to state a value for the merchandise on the documents filed with the U.S. Customs Service. To assist in the valuation process, the seller is required to furnish the buyer with a commercial invoice indicating the sales price.

Goods are usually dutiable at an ad valorem rate (i.e., at a percent of the value). Therefore, the actual value of the goods means a great deal in terms of duties paid. Most importers need the assistance of professionals to help them properly value their goods.

Guidance

Customs brokers advise importers to make sure that the method of valuation they are using is acceptable to U.S. Customs. The price paid for a product is a major consideration in proving valuation. Other factors considered in the valuation process include:

- The condition of sale
- Whether goods are imported on consignment
- Whether parties to the sale are business partners or related companies, thus rendering their valuations suspect

Valuation must be accurate for U.S. Customs to accept goods or products into the U.S. If Customs proves that the value is higher than declared, its agents will levy higher duties.

Note. Value is not the only means by which duties are determined. For example, Tariff No. 2504.10.10.00 is dutiable at a rate of 0.7 cents per kilogram. In this case, weight is the crucial determinant, not value.

9.4.2 Transaction Value

The most common method of appraising imported goods is the transaction method. Under this method, value is determined according to "the price actually paid or payable for imported merchandise when sold for export to the U.S."—in other words, the price that the buyer-importer pays to the seller-exporter.

Note. The word *payable* refers to a situation in which the price has been set but actual payment has not been made at the time of importation.

The following items are also included in the transaction value, even though they may not appear on the commercial invoice:

1. *Packing costs incurred by the buyer.* Packing costs consist of costs incurred by the buyer for all containers and coverings of whatever nature, as well as for the labor and materials used in packing the imported merchandise to ready it for export.

2. *Commissions.* When the seller earns a commission on an imported item, the commission is counted as part of the transaction. This is usually any commission paid to the seller's agent (i.e., the party that is acting on behalf of the manufacturer or reseller).

3. *The value of any assist.* An assist is any of the items listed below that the buyer of imported merchandise provides directly or indirectly, free of charge or at a reduced cost, for use in the production or sale of merchandise for export to the United States:

* Materials, components, parts, and similar items incorporated in the imported merchandise
* Tools, dies, molds, and similar items used in producing the imported merchandise
* Merchandise consumed in producing the imported merchandise
* Engineering, development, artwork, or plans and sketches that are undertaken elsewhere than in the United States and are necessary for the production of the imported merchandise

Note. No service work is treated as an assist if the service or work (a) is performed by an individual domiciled within the United States; (b) is performed by that individual while he or she is acting as an employee or agent of the buyer of the imported merchandise; and (c) is incidental to other engineering, development, artwork, design work, or plans and sketches undertaken in the United States.

1. *Royalties.* Includes any royalty or license fee related to the imported merchandise that the buyer is required to pay, directly or indirectly, as a condition of the sale of the imported merchandise for exportation to the United States.

2. *Proceeds.* Includes proceeds of any subsequent resale, disposal, or use of the imported merchandise that accrue directly or indirectly to the seller.

3. *Indirect payments.* Indirect payments to the seller are also included in transaction value. Such indirect payments occur when the buyer settles all or part of a debt owed by the seller, or when the seller reduces the price on a current importation to settle a debt he or she owes the buyer.

Note. In some cases, a buyer performs activities on his or her own account, such as advertising. These activities are not considered indirect payments, even though the buyer's activity may be regarded as benefiting the seller.

Exclusions From Transaction Value

Amounts to be excluded from transaction value are as follows:

* The costs, charges, or expenses incurred for transportation, insurance, and related services instrumental to the international shipment of goods from the country of exportation to the place of importation in the United States
* Any reasonable cost or charge incurred for constructing, erecting, assembling, maintaining, or providing technical assistance with respect to the goods after importation to the United States or while transporting the goods after importation

Limitations on the Use of Transaction Value

In some cases, transaction value cannot be used to appraise imported goods. In such cases, alternative methods of valuation are used (see section 10.4.3. of this chapter for more details).

Transaction value cannot be used in the following cases:

- Where there are restrictions on the disposition or use of merchandise
- Where there are conditions of sale for which a value cannot be determined
- Where there are proceeds of any subsequent resale, disposal, or use of merchandise accruing to the seller for which an appropriate adjustment to transaction value cannot be made
- In so-called related party transactions, where the transaction value is not acceptable

Guidance

- *Related parties.* In legal terms, parties are considered to be related if either party owns five percent or more of the stock or a similar interest in the other party, or if both parties are commonly owned by a third party. Where there is a related party transaction, U.S. Customs suspects that the price may have been manipulated for various reasons (e.g., to reduce income taxes in the seller's country or to avoid antidumping duties in the buyer's country). When related parties conclude a transaction, U.S. Customs requests proof that the price the importer pays is the true arm's-length price.

- *Acceptable value.* Acceptable value is a value that closely approximates one of the following "test" values (provided that these values relate to merchandise exported to the U.S. at or about the same time as the imported merchandise):

1. The transaction value of identical or similar merchandise in sales to unrelated buyers in the United States
2. The deductive value or computed value of identical or similar merchandise

For more information on the transaction value of similar or identical merchandise, deductive value, and computed value, see section 9.4.3.

9.4.3 Special Valuation Methods

When the transaction value of imported merchandise cannot be determined or is not acceptable, the U.S. Customs Service may use alternative valuation methods. These include:

- Transaction value of identical merchandise
- Transaction value of similar merchandise

• Deductive value
• Computed value

Transaction Value of Identical Merchandise

Under this method of valuation, the determined value of imported merchandise is compared to the transaction value of identical merchandise being imported to the United States at or about the same time.

The term "identical merchandise" refers to merchandise that is:

• Identical in all respects to the merchandise being appraised. (**Note.** Merchandise can show minor differences in appearance and still be considered identical to merchandise being appraised. However, merchandise incorporating or reflecting engineering, development, artwork, design work, or plans and sketches provided free or at reduced costs by the buyer and undertaken in the U.S. cannot be deemed identical.

• Produced in the same country as the merchandise being appraised.

• Produced by the same person as the merchandise being appraised. (**Note.** Merchandise produced by a different person can be considered identical under some circumstances.)

When assessing what is identical, sales volume is a critical factor. To be considered identical, the value of imported merchandise must be based on the sales volume and quantities identical with those being imported. If no sales figures exist, then sales at either a different commercial level or in different quantities, or both, can be used. However, these figures must be adjusted to account for differences. Any adjustment must be based on sufficient information (i.e., information establishing the reasonableness and accuracy of the adjustment).

Transaction Value of Similar Merchandise

The term "similar merchandise" refers to merchandise that is:

• Produced in the same country and by the same person as the merchandise being appraised. (**Note.** If merchandise meeting the foregoing criterion cannot be found, then similar merchandise from another producer may be used.)
• Similar to merchandise being appraised in characteristics and component materials.
• Commercially interchangeable with the merchandise being appraised.

Guidance

In determining whether goods are similar, some of the factors to be considered are the quality of the goods, their reputation, and the existence of trademarks. However, similar merchandise does not include merchandise that incorporates or reflects engineering, development, artwork, design work, or plans and sketches provided free or at reduced cost to the buyer and undertaken in the United States.

Deductive Value

With the deductive method of valuation, the resale price of merchandise after importation into the United States is determined. To arrive at a value for Customs purposes, certain costs are then deducted, notably:

1. Commissions or profit, and general expenses
2. Transportation and insurance costs
3. Customs duties and federal taxes
4. The value of further processing

Note. When determining deductive value, the generally accepted accounting principles of the United States are used.

Computed Value

When valuation cannot be calculated using any of the methods previously discussed, computed value is considered.
    Note. The importer can request that U.S. Customs use the computed value before the deductive value as a basis of appraisement.
    Computed value consists of the sum of the following items:

1. Materials, fabrication, and other processing used in producing the imported merchandise
2. Profit and general expenses
3. Any assists (if not included in items 1 and 2)
4. Packing costs

Note. When determining computed value, the generally accepted accounting principles of the country of production are used.

Summary of Key Points Raised in This Chapter

Imported goods must be classified by country and by product category for duty rates to be calculated.
    Export classifications are apt to receive less scrutiny than import classifications because there are no revenue implications for the U.S. government.
    The Harmonized Tariff System (HTS) is a system of classification containing twenty-one sections ranging from basic raw goods, such as agricultural products, to high-technology items. Sixty-five countries currently subscribe to the HTS.
    The Harmonized Tariff System is understood by means of the General Rules of Interpretation, a set of guidelines that are followed when using the HTS to classify goods.

In addition to the General Rules of Interpretation, individual nations can apply their own rules of interpretation to the HTS.

Liquidation is the point at which the U.S. Customs Service finalizes the rate and amount of import duty.

Importers can make preliminary duty estimates by considering the type of product, the country of origin, and the intended use of the product when it is imported into the United States.

Goods are usually dutiable at an ad valorem rate, which means that duties are assessed as a percentage of value.

The most common method of valuation is the transaction value method, which involves determining the price actually paid or payable by the importer.

When the importer and exporter are related parties, the U.S. Customs Service deems the transaction value method to be unacceptable and turns to alternate methods of valuation.

Alternate methods of valuation include the transaction value of identical merchandise, the transaction value of similar merchandise, deductive value, and computed value.

For Additional Information

For more information on topics discussed in this chapter, please refer to the following publication:

Thomas E. Johnson, *Export/Import Procedures and Documentation*, 2d ed. (New York: AMACOM Books, 1994).

10

Duty Management

Key Questions Answered in This Chapter

Introduction

An understanding of classification and valuation and the regulatory environment (e.g., quotas, trade barriers, and tariffs) is crucial to controlling import costs. Several factors, such as trade preference programs, multilateral trade agreements, and duty drawback, also have a major impact on business costs in the international marketplace. These trade mechanisms are far-reaching and complex, involving not only global trade but also government policies and geopolitics. They can be analyzed on many levels, but for importers and exporters alike, they are best understood as opportunities to facilitate trade and reduce costs—as tools for duty management.

On one side of the coin are trade barriers—quotas, nontariff barriers, punitive tariffs, and special duties—that are designed, for any number of reasons, to restrict trade and increase costs. On the other side of the coin are policies and programs designed to facilitate trade and reduce costs. These include tariff-preference programs such as the Generalized System of Preferences, GATT, NAFTA, duty drawback, Free Trade Zones, and bonded warehouses. How global traders juggle these vast and interwoven factors has a major impact on costs.

This chapter deals with the various ways in which importers and exporters can manage costs attributable to duties. Sections 10.1 to 10.10 deal with programs that, depending on the use and origin of the goods, allow for reduced import duties and tariffs. Duty drawback, binding rulings, and temporary import bonds are U.S. Customs programs that offer reduced duty rates. Bonded warehouses, Free Trade Zones, carnets, and HTS Section 9802 (i.e., goods assembled abroad from U.S. components) all provide benefits for importers who use and understand them.

Sections 10.11 to 10.16 concern multilateral trade agreements. They also include provisions that reduce duties, but by different means. GATT and NAFTA, for example, aim to reduce duties by reducing tariffs and removing barriers to trade. Other trade agreements attempt to reduce duties by offering preferential tariff treatment to goods depending on country of origin (e.g., the Caribbean Basin Initiative, Generalized System of Preferences, and Andean Free Trade Pact).

10.1 WHAT IS DUTY MANAGEMENT?

Duties are taxes imposed on imports by the customs authority of a country; they are a major factor in the cost of an import transaction. The use or purpose of imported goods plays a major role in the amount of duty that is assessed. Correctly identifying how goods are used, or altering the goods to meet certain criteria, can sometimes help importers avoid paying high duties on goods.

When identifying goods for duty purposes, importers need to ask the following questions:

1. Are the goods imported as finished products or component parts?
2. Will the goods be exported subsequent to importation?
3. Will the goods be used in a manufacturing or assembly process?
4. Were the goods returned for repair or alterations?
5. Are the goods eligible for temporary import status?

Note. In many cases, finished goods that are imported for resale in the United States are not eligible for the provisions described in this chapter. Many of the provisions described here have to do with goods imported for assembly, manufacturing, or re-export.

Effective duty management means maintaining good communications with suppliers, end users, import professionals, and U.S. Customs. They can all help an importer meet all import requirements and take advantage of the many duty management provisions. Importers and exporters cannot rely on the U.S. Customs Service to inform them about duty management provisions, let alone alert them to particular allowances that apply to their imported goods. Billions of dollars in tariff reductions are squandered each year simply because importers do not know they are eligible. It is the importer's responsibility to understand all of their duty management options. Import professionals such as customs brokers, attorneys, or consultants can assist in this regard.

Duty Management and the Exporter

Duty management is covered in the import section of this book because U.S. Customs, the body that implements import laws, also implements duty provisions. In practice, however, duty management involves exporters as much as importers.

Duty management is a cooperative effort between importers and exporters. Under most duty refund programs, the exporter has the first right to drawback and must waive that right before a third party (e.g., the importer) can claim the financial rewards.

Prudent importers and exporters recognize the mutual rewards of duty drawback and negotiate drawback issues as part of a sales agreement or other business contract. Although exporters have first claim on drawback, they need the importer's cooperation—especially the importer's entry and duty payment information—to process the claim. Wise importers and exporters take this mutuality into consideration when negotiating.

Note. When it comes to describing how claims are filed, it is important to remember that the "exporter" may indeed be an exporter, or maybe an importer turned exporter for the purpose of re-exporting merchandise. For the sake of reading ease, the party exporting goods at the time a drawback claim is filed is referred to as the exporter.

10.2 DUTY RATES

10.2.1 *Introduction*

Once an importer has determined the classification and valuation of a product (see sections 9.1 to 9.4), the next stage is determining duty rates. There are three general types of duty rates:

* *Ad valorem rates.* This most common type of duty rate is simply a percentage of the value of the merchandise (e.g., 10 percent ad valorem).
* *Specific rates.* Specific rates are duties based on units of weight or other quantities. For example, "$0.25 per dozen" would be a specific duty rate.
* *Compound rates.* Compound rates of duty are a combination of ad valorem and specific rates, such as "$0.25 per kilo plus 10 percent ad valorem."

10.2.2 How Duty Rates Are Set

In determining duty rates based on classification and valuation, there are two main concerns:

* The country of origin of the goods
* The purpose or use of the goods

Although specific duties by country can be found in the Harmonized Tariff Schedule (HTS), it is not possible in every case to simply look up a duty rate in this cross-referencing guide. Factors such as country of origin, special national duty provisions, and individual trade agreements between countries or national blocs all affect duty rates. Many variables can affect duty rates, including:

* Whether the goods are imported for re-export
* Whether the goods are entered as finished products or as component parts
* Whether the goods will be exported subsequent to importation
* Whether the goods are to be used in a manufacturing or assembly process
* Whether the goods are returned for repair or alterations, or are under a warranty
* Whether the goods are eligible for temporary import status
* Whether the goods are imported for resale in the United States.

Note. In many cases, finished goods that are imported for resale in the United States are not eligible for the provisions described in this chapter. The provisions described here relate to goods imported for assembly, manufacturing, or re-export.

10.2.3 Impact of Multilateral Treaties on Duty Rates

The North American Free Trade Agreement (NAFTA), the General Agreement on Tariffs and Trade (GATT), and other multilateral agreements are causing major changes in rules of origin, labor and content requirements, classifications, and other factors that figure into duty rates.

Many of the NAFTA provisions are already in place. However, they may be untried or so new that their implications are not always evident.

The same is true for GATT. With passage at the close of 1994, it is far too soon to say what the exact impact of GATT provisions will be on import costs. Therefore, importers should maintain good communications with their suppliers, end users, import professionals, and U.S. Customs to make sure they are in compliance with all developments on these fronts.

10.3 DUTY DRAWBACK

10.3.1 Introduction

Drawback is a refund or remission, in whole or in part, of a customs duty paid on imported materials. Duty drawback allows exporters to reclaim 99 percent of the U.S. Customs duties paid on merchandise imported into the U.S. for purposes of re-export or when goods are substituted for similar domestic materials. U.S. Customs retains the remaining one percent of the duty to cover administrative costs. To claim the refund, exporters are required to follow certain procedures and to meticulously document both the import and export transactions.

If used properly, duty drawback can significantly reduce the costs of an import transaction. In import transactions, profit margins are small, but in combination with careful sourcing of materials, duty drawback can mean the difference between being competitive and being priced out of the market.

Despite the advantages available, few traders capitalize on drawback programs. There is an estimated $1 billion in annual unclaimed refunds. In many cases, importers and exporters are simply unaware that they can qualify for drawback refunds.

Note. Title VI of NAFTA, commonly known as the Customs Modernization Act, contains a provision, section 632, that mandates major changes to the duty drawback program for goods that are exported to NAFTA countries. The general drawback provisions, covering exports to all other countries, are being rewritten to bring them in line with the more liberalized NAFTA rules. The proposed changes were published in the January 21, 1997 edition of the Federal Register.

Several types of duty drawback programs are authorized under section 1313, Title 19 of the U.S. Code:

1. Manufacturing drawback, which consists of two parts:
    * Direct identification drawback (section 1313[a] drawback)
    * Substitution drawback (section 1313[b] drawback: the substitution provision)
2. Rejected merchandise drawback (section 1313[c] drawback)
3. Unused merchandise drawback (formerly known as same-condition drawback: section 1313[j][1] drawback)

In addition, there are drawback programs for exported products manufactured with domestic alcohol (section 1313[d]), imported salt for the curing of meat or fish (sections 1313[e] and 1313[f]), and materials for the construction and repair of vessels and aircraft (sections 1313[g] and 1313[h]).

10.3.2 *Manufacturing Drawback*

By far the most commonly used drawback programs are those for manufacturing. The manufacturing drawback program consists of two programs aimed at assisting manufacturers in obtaining duty refunds.

Direct Identification Drawback

Under the direct identification drawback program, drawback is payable on imported raw materials or components that are used in processing or manufacturing a finished product that is subsequently exported. The degree of processing that goods must undergo is not clearly defined. However, some form of manufacturing that changes the chemical or physical nature of the imported material is required for the material to be eligible for drawback. Repackaging alone does not qualify the entry for drawback.

Substitution Drawback

Substitution drawback was implemented as a tool to encourage use of raw materials and components made in the United States. In most eligible cases, goods, components, or raw materials are imported into this country. However, in the manufacturing process, American goods, materials, or components are substituted for the imported items.

The Customs Modernization Act sets a new standard for merchandise to be eligible for substitution drawback. The prior standard required that the merchandise be "fungible," or identical and interchangeable in all respects. The new standard requires that the goods and their substitutions be only "commercially interchangeable." To meet the new standards, the substituted goods must:

1. Fall under the same government or industry standard
2. Have the same part number
3. Fall under the same tariff heading
4. Be of similar value

There are three ways to determine if goods or parts are commercially interchangeable: a formal binding ruling from the Entry and Carrier branch of the U.S. Customs Service; a nonbinding predetermination request; or submission of all required documentation necessary to make a determination with each individual drawback claim.

General and Specific Contracts for Manufacturing Drawback

For an exporter to qualify for manufacturing drawback, approval must be obtained from Customs to manufacture products under the terms of a general or a specific contract. General and specific contracts establish a relationship between Customs and a manufacturer.

If the manufacturer intends to claim drawback regularly, a system needs to be in place to process the claims. Instead of approaching duty drawback as an isolated and complex chore, it should be part of a seamless import process so that it becomes much more cost-effective in terms of time and money. Having computerized protocols for drawback—including the automatic issuance of a drawback claim each time eligible goods are re-exported—is an excellent way to make drawback an effective tool for duty management.

General and specific contracts are obtained as follows:

1. *General contracts.* General contracts are product-specific and only relate to manufacturing drawback. They are periodically published in the "Customs Bulletin," a weekly publication in which U.S. Customs files notices of rules affecting Customs regulations. Any manufacturer who is able to comply with the terms set forth in these contracts should submit a request to the regional commissioner of Customs. This notification should contain:

- The name and address of the applicant
- Factories that will operate under the contract
- The names of persons operating under a power of attorney who are authorized to sign drawback documents

2. *Specific contracts.* To operate under a specific contract, using either the substitution or direct identification drawback methods, manufacturers should submit a proposal that:

- Fully describes the manufacturing operation and the process for complying with all requirements of the drawback laws and regulations
- States that the manufacturer will be in compliance with the record-keeping requirements set forth in section 191.22 of the Customs Regulations
- Contains an agreement to follow the methods and keep records with regard to drawback procedures in sections 191.21 and 191.32 of the Customs Regulations

Manufacturers or importers interested in either type of manufacturing drawback should submit proposals in triplicate to the U.S. Customs Service Office of Regulations and Rulings in Washington, D.C. Claims may be filed prior to the approval of the drawback contracts. However, the claims will not be paid until the contracts are approved. See Forms 10.01 and 10.02 at the end of this chapter for sample specific contracts.

10.3.3 Rejected Merchandise Drawback

Under the rejected merchandise program, drawback payment on imported merchandise is allowed if the imported merchandise:

1. Is rejected because it does not conform to samples or specifications and the merchandise is subsequently exported
2. Is shipped without the consent of the importer and is subsequently exported or returned
3. Is returned to Customs within three years of the initial release

To qualify for a refund, importers must follow specific documentation procedures as outlined in the U.S. Customs regulations. Check with U.S. Customs or customs professionals for more information.

10.3.4 Unused Merchandise Drawback

To qualify for unused merchandise drawback (formerly known as same-condition drawback), U.S. Customs requires that the imported merchandise not be used in the United States prior to exportation or destruction. However, certain incidental operations are permitted, including:

* Testing
* Cleaning
* Repackaging
* Inspection

Imported merchandise is eligible for the payment under same-condition drawback if:

1. The merchandise is exported in the same condition in which it was imported.
2. It is destroyed under U.S. Customs supervision.
3. An application for drawback is made prior to exportation.
4. The goods are exported or destroyed within three years of importation.

EXAMPLE

An importer of European wines discovers that a wine shipment was accidentally frozen, rendering the wine worthless. Under these circumstances, the wine can be destroyed under U.S. Customs supervision and the importer is eligible for drawback.

The Customs Modernization Act and Its Effect on Same-Condition Drawback

Several changes to the same-condition drawback program are written into the Customs Modernization Act. These changes have only recently become law, effectively replacing same-condition drawback with unused merchandise drawback. Under the Customs Modernization Act, the same-condition requirement for drawback eligibility has been eliminated. The new provisions state that merchandise may be eligible for drawback if that merchandise is not used in the United States, regardless of its condition.

The new provision widens the scope of merchandise eligible for drawback. In the past, merchandise often fell between the cracks and was not eligible for either manufacturing drawback or same-condition drawback. Often this was merchandise that was not altered extensively enough to be considered manufactured, but was too extensively changed to be regarded as being in the same condition. That sort of merchandise is now eligible for unused merchandise drawback.

The Customs Modernization Act changes present advantages to importers. However, it also means that importers need to be familiar with both sets of regulations, and they should check with U.S. Customs and import professionals to determine how the new changes will be interpreted and whether they apply to the types of merchandise being imported.

10.3.5   Filing Drawback Claims

To earn drawback, merchandise must have been imported within five years of filing a claim. Exporters then file the following papers:

1. Customs Form 7511, Notice of Exportation of Articles with Benefit of Drawback
2. Notice of Exportation of Articles with Benefit of Drawback Entry (which is essentially a claim for the refund)

These procedures hold unless using the Exporter's Summary Procedure (see section 11.3.7). Importers may also be required to submit certificates of manufacture and/or delivery.

A sample proposal for section 1313(a), or direct identification, drawback claims can be obtained by writing or calling the Regional Commissioner of Customs in each of the following cities: Boston; Chicago; Houston; Long Beach, Calif.; Miami; New Orleans; and New York City. Addresses and phone numbers can be obtained by calling the U.S. Customs Public Affairs office at (202) 927-1770.

For all other types of drawback claims, exporters are urged to write to: U.S. Customs Service, Entry Rulings Branch, 1301 Constitution Avenue N.W., Franklin Court, Washington, D.C. 20229 (202-482-7040).

Who Is Entitled to Drawback?

When the manufacturer is the importer of the goods in question, claims are usually paid within six months. The following is the procedure if the manufacturer is not the importer:

1. The manufacturer must obtain certificates of delivery from the actual importer of the goods.
2. The importer then gives the certificates to the manufacturer.
3. The manufacturer is the party entitled to the drawback claim.

The manufacturer is not always the direct importing party. Under such circumstances, the manufacturer must ensure that the importing party actually pays duties on the product before filing a drawback claim. When the importer and exporter are not the same entity, the exporter is the party entitled to the refund of the duties. However, if the exporter is not the importer of the goods, it can take up to twelve months for the claims to be paid.

Procedures for Facilitating Drawback Claims

Several procedures are used to facilitate drawback filing and processing, as well as to expedite the payment of claims. They can be found in Part 191 of the U.S. Customs Regulations. The procedures are:

* Accelerated payment
* Exporter's summary
* Waiver of prior notice of intent to export

(Each one of these procedures is discussed in some detail in the next few sections of this chapter.)

Inadequate documentation is the main reason U.S. Customs denies drawback claims. Exporters should consult with export professionals such as customs brokers, auditors, or international attorneys in order to understand record-keeping requirements.

10.3.6   *Accelerated Drawback Payment Program*

This program allows claimants to receive refunds prior to U.S. Customs liquidating their claims. Refunds are processed for payment within three weeks after the claims are filed.

To use the accelerated payment procedure, claimants must obtain written approval from the appropriate liquidation unit, generally the office of the district director of Customs. Requests should be prepared on the company's letterhead. See Form 10.03 for a sample accelerated payment request.

Accelerated Drawback Record-keeping Requirements

To qualify for accelerated payment, certain record-keeping requirements must be met. Specifically:

1. The imported merchandise must be properly identified and its identity clearly indicated.
2. Movement of merchandise in and out of storage must be recorded.
3. Any changes in the condition of the merchandise must be recorded.
4. The dates of importation, entry, and exportation of the merchandise must be recorded.
5. The merchandise must satisfy all U.S. Customs examination requirements.

Accelerated Payment Criteria

Accelerated payment is available to all drawback claimants who are not delinquent or remiss in any U.S. Customs transactions, and whose claims are not filed in excess of the amount due.

Accelerated Payback Program Bonds

Claimants who receive approval for accelerated drawback payments must file one of two types of bonds. Specifically:

- A continuous bond in an amount equal to the estimated drawback that will be claimed during the period of the bond
- A single transaction bond equal to the amount of each drawback claim

(For more information on bonds, see section 11.7.)

10.3.7 Exporter's Summary

It is possible for those filing for drawback under the unused merchandise and manufacturers category to consolidate their exports into a single claim. Filers must provide a chronological summary of their exports instead of furnishing U.S. Customs with documentation for each individual export shipment. In this way, a single entry may be filed for many actual entries.

As with most drawback procedures, filers must keep complete and accurate records for a period of at least three years. In addition, the records must include the identity and location of the ultimate consignee of the shipments. (See Form 10.04, Chronological Summary of Exports, and Form 10.05, Exporter's Summary Procedure Request.)

Exporter's Summary Bond Requirements

Claimants who receive approval to participate in the exporter's summary procedure must file one of two types of bonds:

- A continuous bond in an amount equal to 25 percent of the drawback that will be claimed during the life of the bond
- A single transaction bond in an amount equal to 25 percent of each drawback claim

(For more information on bonds, see section 11.7.)

10.3.8 Waiver of Prior Notice of Intent to Export

Ordinarily, claims for same-condition drawback must be submitted to U.S. Customs at least five working days before the date of export. Customs may waive this requirement. With a waiver claimants can export merchandise within three years from the import date without having to notify Customs prior to shipment being exported. Claims may then be filed within a three-year period following the date of exportation.

10.4 BINDING RULINGS

U.S. Customs determines the amount of duty payable on imported merchandise after the merchandise is liquidated and all entry documents are filed. However, it is often necessary for the importer to know the exact amount of duty owed before the shipment is made. It is under these circumstances that an importer may seek a binding ruling.

Duties are often major considerations in international sales transactions. When goods, products, or materials fall into gray areas of classification or valuation—fall under quota—obtaining a binding ruling from U.S. Customs may be the only means of ascertaining duty costs. Attorneys and customs brokers can advise importers on the dutiable status of goods, but that information is not considered binding.

The Binding Rulings Process

Under the Customs Regulations (19 CFR Part 177), importers can obtain a binding tariff classification ruling under the Harmonized Tariff Schedule. To obtain such a ruling, importers or hired customs professionals write to any U.S. Customs District Director or to the Area Director of Customs, New York Seaport, 6 World Trade Center, New York, N.Y., 10048.

All rulings requests must contain the following information:

* The names, addresses, and all other identifying information of all interested parties (if known) and the manufacturer ID code (if known).
* The name(s) of the port(s) in which the merchandise will be entered (if known).
* A description of the transaction.
* A statement attesting to the fact that there are, to the best of the importer's knowledge, no issues on the commodity pending before U.S. Customs or any other court.
* A statement as to whether classification advice was previously sought from U.S. Customs. If so, from whom? What advice, if any, was rendered?

In addition, all requests for tariff classification rulings must contain the following information about the product:

* A complete description of the goods. Samples, sketches, diagrams, or other illustrative material that are useful in supplementing the written description should be included.

- Cost breakdowns of component materials and their respective quantities shown in percentages, if possible.
- A description of the principal use of the goods in the United States. Information pertaining to commercial, scientific, or common designations of the goods.
- Any other information that may be pertinent or required.

To avoid delays, the request should contain as much relevant information as possible. Be sure to include written descriptions along with all samples. Samples included in the request may be subject to laboratory analysis.

Once issued, the rulings are binding at all ports of entry unless revoked by the Custom's Service Office of Regulations and Rulings. See Forms 10.06, 10.07, and 10.08 for a sample binding rulings request, an acknowledgement of receipt of request, and a notice of binding ruling.

Binding rulings can be a useful tool in determining the exact amount of duty an importer will pay. However, the rulings apply only to very specific product classifications based on detailed laboratory analysis of the content of the product. For example, if a manufacturer is importing steel on an ongoing basis, any slight variation in the grade, specifications, mill process, chemical content, or other characteristics will require a new binding ruling. If the design or specifications of a product change frequently, it will become impractical for the importer to seek a binding ruling in each instance.

Note. Visit the U.S. Customs site on the World Wide Web to view examples of binding rulings.

10.5 BONDED WAREHOUSES

Bonded warehouses can play an important role in duty management. By using a bonded warehouse, traders can store goods temporarily on a duty-free basis. Duty is paid only on the portion of the shipment that is withdrawn. This is known as duty deferral.

Importers can defer duty payments for up to a five-year period, thereby managing cash flow. In some cases, goods can be returned or destroyed under Customs supervision and the importer will not be liable for duties.

In addition to government-owned and public bonded warehouses, importers can maintain their own bonded warehouses for storing imported merchandise belonging exclusively to the importer. The application process is rigorous, requiring inspection of the facility, security measures, and background inquiries. Proprietors of bonded warehouses must also comply with extensive record-keeping requirements.

10.6 U.S. FOREIGN TRADE ZONES

Foreign trade zones (FTZs) are designed to provide relief from certain duties and taxes in order to promote international trade and to provide an incentive that discourages U.S. companies from moving their operations overseas. Generally located at or near a U.S. Customs port of entry, foreign trade zones offer domestic facilities for businesses engaged in foreign trade.

10.6.1 How Foreign Trade Zones Work

Foreign goods may enter a foreign trade zone without having to file a formal Customs entry. In addition, no customs duties, government excise taxes, or local ad valorem taxes are charged on foreign goods imported into the FTZ, or products manufactured from imported materials, until the goods are moved from the zone into U.S. Customs territory.

In addition, firms operating in a foreign trade zone are often eligible for accelerated duty drawback and excise tax rebates. Quota restrictions often do not apply for materials imported into the FTZ. Once within the FTZ, merchandise may be:

- Assembled or manufactured
- Relabeled or repackaged
- Stored, tested, or sampled
- Repaired, cleaned, or mixed
- Salvaged, processed, or destroyed

If the finished product is then exported from the foreign trade zone, no duties or excise taxes are due. Merchandise can be warehoused as inventory within the FTZ for an unlimited period of time with no duties payable to U.S. Customs.

10.6.2 Foreign Trade Zone Benefits

U.S. firms, especially manufacturers, can realize some benefits from the use of FTZs:

1. Duties do not have to be paid on the scrap or waste portions of imported materials.
2. Goods can be stored for an unlimited period of time. This allows the importer to release them according to market demand and to avoid shipping delays.
3. Users of FTZs can pay applicable duty rates on component materials or the finished product, whichever is less.
4. With few exceptions, merchandise can be warehoused in a FTZ even if it is subject to U.S. quotas.
5. Firms can avoid delays in U.S. Customs clearance and duty drawback procedures. In addition, no country-of-origin marking is required on merchandise entering a FTZ.
6. Goods can be marked, labeled, or reprocessed in the FTZ to bring them into compliance without the importer having to pay any fines.
7. Merchandise transferred from a Customs bonded warehouse to the FTZ

will result in cancellation of the bond and all duty obligations. However, such merchandise must be for the purpose of exportation or destruction.

EXAMPLE

Dole Packaged Food Company established two foreign trade zones in its Hawaiian canneries in 1985 and 1986. Dole was finding itself at a disadvantage because foreign competitors paid no duty on their products, while Hawaii-based firms faced U.S. Customs tariffs upon entry to the mainland. FTZ status at two Dole plants allowed the company to fill its cans at the plants and export the finished products without having to pay duties or tariffs.

EXAMPLE

Berg Steel Pipe Corporation sought FTZ status for its Panama City, Florida operation in 1982. To convert hot-rolled carbon steel plate into large-diameter pipe for export, Berg needed to purchase steel plate on the international market at competitive prices and avoid the duties and taxes levied on importing the goods into the United States. FTZ status allowed Berg to do so.

10.7 TEMPORARY IMPORTATION UNDER BOND

Articles imported temporarily for certain purposes may enter the United States duty-free for a period of one year, on condition that the goods are exported one year from the date of importation.

Note. With approval of the District Director of Customs, the one-year period can be extended for up to two additional one-year periods.

The temporary importation under bond (TIB) program offers obvious cash-flow advantages because the importer need not pay duties up-front. On the down-side, importers or exporters must make sure the bond is properly canceled, or they will be liable for double the normal duty rate.

Under TIB, the goods in question may not be imported for sale or for sale on consignment. U.S. Customs must supervise the export of the goods. The penalty for failure to export items in the TIB category is double the normal rate of duty.

The following is a sampling of goods that may be imported under TIB status:

- Merchandise to be repaired, altered, or processed, including processes that result in an article being manufactured or produced in the United States
- Models of women's wearing apparel imported by manufacturers for use solely in their own establishments
- Articles imported by illustrators and photographers solely for use in their own establishments to illustrate catalogs, pamphlets, or advertising matter
- Works of art and motion-picture advertising films
- Automobiles, motorcycles, bicycles, airplanes, airships, balloons, boats, racing shells, and similar vehicles and craft, if temporarily imported for specific racing contests

- Animals and poultry brought into the United States for the purpose of breeding, exhibition, or competition
- Materials used in exhibitions

Note. A complete list of goods and products eligible for temporary importation under bond appears in the Harmonized Tariff Schedule. Importers should consult with professionals to ascertain whether temporary importation under bond is available for their products.

10.8   CARNETS

Carnets are international customs documents that may be used for the temporary duty-free importation of certain goods into a country in lieu of the usual customs documentation. They are usually valid for one year. Customs authorities in participating countries accept carnets as a guarantee that all customs duties and excise taxes will be paid.

Note. NAFTA has greatly expanded allowances for the temporary entry of service personnel and related tools and equipment between the United States, Canada, and Mexico.

In general, carnets cover merchandise that is used in advertising as commercial samples or as professional equipment. They do not cover consumable goods such as food or agricultural products.

Using carnets, exporters can avoid paying:

- Value-added taxes
- Duties
- Sureties such as bonds

If a carnet is to be used, security must be posted in the amount of 40 percent of the value of the items listed on the carnet (100 percent if the goods are traveling to Israel or South Korea) and may be held for up to thirty months.

Guidance

The New York City–based U.S. Council for International Business maintains a list of offices issuing carnets in the United States. Carnets can be used in forty-four countries, including most European and Pacific Rim nations. Importers and exporters apply for carnets through regional offices of the United States Council for International Business. Processing time is generally five days or less. An application must be filed along with a processing fee, which usually ranges from $120 to $250.

10.9   SPECIAL DUTY PROVISIONS FOR COMPONENT PARTS

Subheading 9802.00.80 of the Harmonized Tariff Schedule (HTS) provides for reduced duty for goods assembled abroad from U.S. components. Only assembly operations qualify for the reduced duties. Manufacturing operations do not.

The intent of subheading 9802 is to encourage the use of U.S.-made components when assembly operations take place abroad. The value of the U.S.-made components is not subject to duties when the goods are re-imported into the United States. For duty assessment purposes, the value of 9802 goods is not based on the value added abroad through assembly, but on the selling price in the United States, plus the costs of items furnished to the manufacturer free or at less than full cost or value (called "assists"). The price usually includes materials and components, labor, and other fabrication costs, as well as the general and administrative expenses of the manufacturer. The exclusion of the value of the U.S.-made components allows for lower duties.

To qualify under this category, components must be assembled abroad and fulfill the following criteria:

- Articles are ready for assembly without further fabrication.
- The articles have not lost their physical identity by change in form, shape, or otherwise.
- The articles have not increased in value or improved in condition abroad, except for operations incidental to the assembly process, such as cleaning, lubricating, and painting.

Note. The requirements for 9802 duty reductions are complex and detailed. Importers should seek an advisory opinion or binding ruling from U.S. Customs as to whether their goods qualify. In addition, they should seek the advice of an export specialist familiar with 9802.

Goods Subject to Specific and Compound Duty Rates

In some cases, goods assembled abroad are subject to specific or compound duty rates under the Harmonized Tariff Schedule.

EXAMPLE

A transistor radio is assembled abroad from foreign-made components and American-made transistors. At entry into the United States, the transistor radio is subject to the ad valorem rate of duty applicable to transistor radios based on the full value of the radio. Duty is then calculated minus the cost or value of the American-made transistors.

EXAMPLE

A solid-state watch movement is assembled abroad from foreign-made components and an American-made integrated circuit. If the watch movement is subject to a specific duty rate of $0.75 and (a) the value of the assembled movement is $30 and (b) the value of the American-made integrated circuit is $10, then the value of the integrated circuit represents one-third of the total value of the watch movement. The duty on the assembled article will be reduced by one-third, or $0.25. The duty on the assembled watch movement is $0.50.

Maquiladora Operations

Maquiladora operations are an effective duty management tool that allow importers to take advantage of HTS Section 9802 provisions. Because of low labor rates and the close proximity to the U.S. market, many American and foreign companies are establishing assembly or processing operations in Mexico, often near the U.S. border. Mexican law allows for the equivalent of temporary importations under bond, which permit maquiladoras to import, without paying Mexican Customs duties, the following merchandise:

- Machinery, equipment, and parts
- Raw materials and other components

Under current law, once manufactured or assembled, the goods must be exported, usually to the United States.

Note. Under NAFTA, restrictions will be phased out in seven years and all maquiladora-produced goods will be permitted to be sold in Mexico with no added duties.

When the goods are re-exported to the United States, import duties are imposed only on the Mexican or "value-added" components of the goods. The value of U.S. components is not dutiable.

To establish a successful maquiladora operation, it is necessary to comply with both Mexican and U.S. Customs requirements. Otherwise, the full value of the articles can be dutiable both in Mexico and in the United States.

Note. The number of maquiladora operations has greatly increased since NAFTA. By January 1996, two years after the accord was implemented, total maquiladora employment rose 20 percent to 648,000. That number is expected to grow to 943,000 by the year 2000.

Ironically, NAFTA was supposed to have increased investment in Mexico's interior while at the same time alleviating some of the social problems associated with maquiladora operations, such as pollution and overcrowding. But the Mexican peso crisis, which lowered Mexico's overall labor costs from $2.54 per hour to $1.80, contributed to maquiladora expansion, as did the desire of American executives to live on the U.S. side of the border. (*The Wall Street Journal*, 2/26/95)

10.10 BARTER AND COUNTERTRADE TRANSACTIONS

Importers and exporters are often asked to barter for goods and services with foreign customers. Although duties may be avoided in these cases, bartering can also create unique documentation and procedural problems. For example:

- The U.S. company having a role in a barter or countertrade transaction should not try to use its standard-form sales or purchase documents. These transactions require special terms and conditions to protect the participant and should be specifically tailored to the transaction.

⊛ Even though no money will change hands, the parties should value the
merchandise or services that will be exchanged. This is necessary for tax,
customs, and foreign exchange control purposes.

Note. In many countries, attempts to engage in barter transactions for the
purpose of avoiding these laws will subject the participants to prosecution for
evasion. Therefore, participants should satisfy themselves that all necessary government notifications and forms are filed just as if the transaction were for cash,
and that all values stated are accurate, consistent, and supportable.

10.11   DUTY MANAGEMENT BY COUNTRY OF ORIGIN

The Harmonized Tariff Schedule standardizes duty rates within most GATT
countries and all NAFTA countries. Yet there are ways to manage duties by taking
advantage of special duty rates and programs that relate to a product's country
of origin; this is known as duty management by country of origin.

NAFTA and GATT offer many provisions that reduce or eliminate duties,
tariffs, and trade barriers; these two agreements are bringing major changes to
rules of origin, local labor and content rules, classifications, and other factors relating to duty rates.

In addition to NAFTA and GATT, the United States has tariff preference and
trade agreements with many countries. The provisions of these agreements can be
used to manage duties. For example, goods meeting certain content requirements
qualify for duty-free status under the Generalized System of Preferences (GSP).

Sections 10.12 to 10.16 of this chapter provide an overview of the major international agreements that affect duty management. These agreements are complex; in some cases, voluminous verification and record-keeping are required to
take advantage of reduced tariffs under both programs. Importers must therefore
learn as much as possible about these agreements and monitor changes: An informed importer will be at a significant advantage in the increasingly competitive
global marketplace.

In November 1997, the Clinton administration decided against bringing
"fast-track" trade legislation to the Senate floor. Having been soundly rejected by
the Democrats in the House of Representative—more than 160 Democrats, or 80
percent of the Democratic House membership, voted against it—the legislation
would have gone down to defeat.

The "fast-track" trade proposal would have given the president powers to
negotiate trade agreements that would then be submitted to Congress, which
could approve or reject them, but not amend or change them. One of the immediate goals of the Clinton administration was to negotiate a trade pact with Chile
and other South American neighbors that would have extended NAFTA-style
trade principles to the region.

Supporters of "fast-track" cited the importance of the region to the United
States in terms of trade. Venezuela has surpassed Saudi Arabia as the leading
source of imported oil for the U.S. Trade between the European Union and Merco-

sur—the customs union that includes Brazil, Argentina, Uruguay, and Paraguay—surpasses that between Mercosur and the United States. Without the legislation, some say, U.S. companies could get squeezed out of the region by European and Japanese competitors.

Proponents of "fast-track" also say that without such legislation American prestige will suffer abroad and no new trade initiatives will be possible at least through the year 2000, effectively ending international momentum for free trade.

However, the concerns of the major "fast-track" opponents—organized labor and environmentalists—carried the day in the House. Many of the Democratic members who voted against "fast-track" cited constituent concerns about job losses from free trade and fears that expanded free trade could lead to deterioration of the environment and exploitation of workers in developing nations.

Some analysts suggest that the vote on "fast-track" was essentially a referendum on NAFTA. The benefits of NAFTA to the U.S. economy are a subject of heated debate among politicians and organized labor. The decision by the Clinton administration to withdraw "fast-track" legislation from a vote rather than risk defeat could have been a sign that free trade supporters were loathe to reopen the contentious debate triggered by NAFTA in 1992.

The Clinton administration may attempt another vote on "fast-track" in 1998. (*The New York Times*, 11/15/97; *The Wall Street Journal*, 10/9/97 and 10/13/97; *Economist*, 11/15/97; *Fortune*, 10/27/97)

10.12 THE NORTH AMERICAN FREE TRADE AGREEMENT

10.12.1 Introduction

NAFTA is a comprehensive trade pact between the United States, Mexico, and Canada, which will affect most aspects of doing business between the three countries. Implemented on January 1, 1994, NAFTA's key provisions are to:

1. Eliminate all tariffs on all industrial products traded between the three NAFTA countries by 2004
2. Remove many nontariff trade barriers, such as import licenses, that have restricted U.S. goods from access to Mexican markets
3. Implement uniform customs procedures and regulations, including a single certificate-of-origin document to be used by all three countries
4. Remove many investment barriers and includes provisions to give investors in the NAFTA countries the same rights as domestic firms
5. Provide cross-border service rules that allow American firms to service products in Mexico under duty-free status and liberalized entry rules
6. Open the Mexican market to a number of key U.S. service sectors
7. Strengthen intellectual property rules to afford increased protection to U.S. producers of intellectual property, including high-technology firms
8. Give U.S. firms access to government procurement contracts in Canada and Mexico

A number of NAFTA provisions are already in effect. Most of the changes will be implemented over a five- to fifteen-year period.

NAFTA also endorses the principle of "fundamental national treatment obligations," similar to those in GATT: Once goods are exchanged between NAFTA countries, they must not be subject to any discriminatory or restrictive treatment.

Canada and Mexico are America's first- and third-largest trading partners, respectively. Total trade among the NAFTA partners was $348 billion in 1994, a 17 percent increase over the previous year. Trade with NAFTA partners accounts for 29 percent of total U.S. goods traded.

Guidance

Importers working in the NAFTA countries should monitor the following sources to keep abreast of the changes:

- The Customs Bulletin
- The Federal Register
- The Department of Commerce Mexican Office's twenty-four-hour Amerifax line (202-482-4464)
- Customs brokers
- Major business periodicals and newspapers

"The NAFTA Implementation Resource Guide," published by the Commerce Department, is another excellent resource for information on NAFTA. It lists all pertinent agencies and telephone numbers, by industry, for importers or exporters with questions about NAFTA. It includes useful information on:

- Antidumping and countervailing duties
- Investment
- Intellectual property rights
- Labor issues
- Taxes
- Specific industries, including agriculture, automotive trade, energy and basic petrochemicals and chemicals, food and drugs, medical equipment and pharmaceuticals, services, telecommunications, and textiles and apparel.

See Appendix A for a list of U.S. government agencies that can provide specific information on NAFTA.

Note. There has been a growing chorus of dissatisfaction with NAFTA among many business and government leaders who point out that:

- The U.S. trade deficit with Canada and Mexico will approach $40 billion in 1997, four times the amount as before 1993. Mexico has increasingly been purchasing automobile and electronics parts, chemicals, and other industrial materials from Asia and Europe. (*BusinessWeek*, 12/9/96)

⊛ Despite President Clinton's prediction that NAFTA would create over 200,000 American jobs in two years, there has been no measurable job gain. (*The Wall Street Journal*, 10/26/95)

⊛ United Parcel Service, which invested $120 million in its Mexican subsidiary, complains that Mexico has failed to live up to its NAFTA obligations by denying the company permits to use large-size delivery trucks.

Yet there are also a number of success stories regarding NAFTA and its impact on U.S. business:

⊛ Despite predictions of massive job loss in the U.S. manufacturing sector, there has been an increase in U.S. manufacturing jobs.

⊛ Clothing Manufacturer Limited Inc. plans to open a new manufacturing facility outside Mexico City, shifting production from a facility in Sri Lanka. The company says it will benefit from greatly reduced delivery time and a tariff reduction from 19 percent to zero. (*Forbes*, 2/10/97)

⊛ Applied Geographics, a Boston-based environmental consulting firm, signed a half-million-dollar contract in late 1994 to design a computer program to help Mexico City upgrade its sewer and water systems.

⊛ Raab Associates, an export management company based in Lahaska, PA, has so far exported more than $2 million worth of disposable medical equipment and incinerators to Mexico. Although retail sales have declined since the December 1995 devaluation of the Mexican peso, Raab has since sold three new incinerators and its sales to the Mexican government have not declined.

Note. In July 1997, the Clinton administration released a report that assessed the first three years of NAFTA. Finding that the trade agreement has had a "modest positive effect" on the U.S. economy, the report credited NAFTA with a 44 percent growth in trade between the NAFTA partners. The report also said that NAFTA has created between 90,000 and 160,000 U.S. jobs.

Critics of NAFTA, including the Economic Policy Institute, Public Citizen's Global Trade Watch, and the U.S. Business and Industrial Council Educational Foundation, disputed the administration's assessment. They say that NAFTA has displaced many more U.S. jobs than it has created and that "wages and living standards have seen downward pressure in all three (NAFTA) countries."

The groups critical of NAFTA also point out that many U.S. exports to Mexico are parts that are used in assembly or manufacturing processes in Mexico and then reexported to the United States. Numbers from the Commerce Department bear out the group's assessment; in 1996 the U.S. trade deficit with its NAFTA partners grew to nearly $40 billion, up from $4.53 billion in 1993, the year before NAFTA went into effect. (*The Wall Street Journal*, 7/11/97)

One thing is certain: NAFTA has not made the process of exporting goods to Mexico any easier. Persistence, diligent research, the assistance of qualified and experienced professionals, and a commitment of time and money are all prerequisites for a successful exporting venture.

10.12.2   *Elimination of Tariffs*

All tariffs on industrial products traded between the United States, Mexico, and Canada will be eliminated by 2004. Some tariffs on U.S. exports of agricultural products to Mexico will be phased out over a fifteen-year period. As provided for in the U.S.–Canada Free Trade Agreement (CFTA), all trade between the United States and Canada will be duty-free by 1998; most trade between the two countries is duty-free already.

Currently, Mexican tariffs on imported goods range from zero to 20 percent, with the majority of tariffs assessed between 10 and 20 percent. Once an exporter has established the Harmonized Tariff Schedule (HTS) commodity classification number of the merchandise, a tariff rate can be determined by calling the U.S. Department of Commerce Mexican Office. The tariff rate is determined by applying the tariff rate to the transaction value of the merchandise. (For more information on transaction value, see section 9.4.2.) In addition, Mexican Customs assesses a value-added tax of 10 percent of the transaction value, plus a 0.8 percent customs processing fee.

On the day NAFTA was implemented, January 1, 1994, Mexico eliminated tariffs on nearly 50 percent of all industrial goods imported from the U.S., including:

- Machine tools
- Medical devices
- Semiconductors and computer equipment
- Telecommunications and electronic equipment

By the beginning of 1999, the following products will also be allowed to enter Mexico tariff-free:

- Light trucks
- Most auto parts
- Paper products

Note. There are three steps for determining tariff rates for goods exported to Mexico. They are:

1. First, determine the Harmonized Tariff Schedule number. If the goods in question have already been exported to Mexico, the exporter's customs broker or freight forwarder will already have the number. If not, contact the Census Bureau Foreign Trade Division (301-457-1084) for assistance.

2. Next, exporters need to determine if their products qualify as North American. To do, so they must meet complex and specific rules-of-origin requirements (see section 10.12.5 of this book). Rules of origin by HS number can be obtained by calling NAFTA FACTS (202-482-4464) and requesting document #5000, or by calling the Office of NAFTA (202-482-0305).

3. If the goods meet the required rules-of-origin, tariff rates can then be determined by obtaining a menu from NAFTA FACTS or calling the Office of NAFTA.

10.12.3 Elimination of Nontariff Trade Barriers

Key Mexican nontariff trade barriers and trade restrictions are to be eliminated under NAFTA. The most important of these is the removal of most import licenses, which limited the importation of American products into the Mexican market. Mexican importers were required to obtain import permits from the Mexican government; the process was often arbitrary and difficult, resulting in delays and uncertainties for U.S. exporters.

Local content and local production requirements will also be eliminated under NAFTA. These provisions required that many products sold in Mexico contain a mandatory percentage of local parts or be produced in large part by Mexican labor.

In addition, quantitative restrictions such as quotas will be eliminated. With regard to public safety or the environment, each NAFTA country maintains the right to impose border restrictions in limited circumstances. Special rules will still apply to the following sectors: agriculture; automobiles; energy; and textiles.

Note. Although product standards and certification are not necessarily intended as nontariff trade barriers, by their very complexity they often function as such, particularly for small to midsize exporters. On January 3, 1997, the Mexican government published a draft of new product certification rules. When fully implemented, the new NOM certification will apply to a wide range of products sold in Mexico. NOM certification is the document in which the Mexican Standards Bureau or a specific product certification agency verifies that a product meets the specifications established by the Standards Bureau.

Exporters can obtain a text of the draft by calling NAFTA FACTS (202-482-4464) and requesting document #9015. For a copy of the appendices, which are important in understanding the new system, exporters should contact the National Institute of Standards and Technology (301-975-4038).

10.12.4 Customs Administration

Customs administration rules are being changed under NAFTA for two primary reasons:

1. To streamline entry procedures for importers and exporters
2. To ensure that only goods meeting NAFTA country-of-origin rules receive preferential tariff and duty treatment

Note. As more U.S. businesses buy or sell goods in Canada and Mexico, the need for awareness of customs procedures and documentation requirements has, if anything, increased. Those wanting to take advantage of reduced duties and tariffs under NAFTA must provide complex country-of-origin documentation. At this stage on implementation, customs clearance under NAFTA is not any easier than before.

Customs administration reforms under NAFTA include:

* Standardization of regulations among the customs branches of the three countries. The goal is to ensure consistent interpretation and application of rules of origin and other regulations.
* Standardization of certificate-of-origin documents and other certification requirements.
* Uniform record-keeping requirements.
* Expanded use of advance rulings.
* Uniform rights to review and appeal customs determinations for all traders in NAFTA countries.
* Establishment of a trilateral working group to explore possible modifications of rules of origin and other regulations.
* An agreement not to impose any new customs user fees and to eliminate existing fees. Most export taxes will also be disallowed.

10.12.5   Rules of Origin

When understood and used effectively, rules of origin are a key duty management mechanism for reduced duties and tariffs.

Tariffs are reduced or eliminated under NAFTA only for goods made in North America or containing substantial North American parts, components, or labor. One of the key goals of the new rules of origin is to prevent non–North American goods from gaining reduced or nontariff status through minor processing operations or transshipment of the goods through NAFTA countries. The new rules attempt to prevent Mexico and Canada from becoming platforms for non–North American goods to enter the American market.

The key concept in understanding whether or not goods qualify for reduced tariffs under NAFTA is determining whether the goods originate in the region. Article 401 of NAFTA defines goods that originate in a NAFTA country as follows:

* Goods wholly obtained or produced in the NAFTA region
* Goods produced in the NAFTA region wholly from originating materials
* Unassembled goods and goods classified with their inputs, which do not meet the Annex 401 rules of origin but contain 60 percent regional value content using the transaction method of valuation, or 50 percent regional value content using the net cost method of valuation
* Goods meeting the Annex 401 origin rule

Goods Wholly Obtained or Produced in a NAFTA Region

To meet this criterion, goods cannot contain any non-NAFTA parts or materials to be eligible for NAFTA benefits. Examples of qualifying goods include:

- Silver mined in Mexican territory
- Wheat grown in Canada
- Silver jewelry made in the U.S. from Mexican silver
- Copper wire produced in Canada from scrap telephone or electrical wire
- Fish or shellfish taken in U.S. territorial waters

Goods Produced in the NAFTA Region Wholly From Originating Materials

If the materials used to produced a finished product are considered to be originating in a NAFTA territory, they will be eligible for NAFTA benefits.

EXAMPLE

XYZ Company imports whole raw bovine skins (Harmonized Tariff Schedule classification 41.01) into Mexico from Argentina and processes them into finished leather (Harmonized Tariff Schedule classification 41.04). The finished leather is then purchased by ABC Company to make leather eyeglass cases (Harmonized Tariff Schedule classification 4202.31). Where does the finished product originate? The rules of origin for HTS classification 41.04 permit "[a] change to heading 41.04 from any other heading, except from heading 41.05 through 41.11."

The finished product is considered originating in Mexico because it meets the Annex 401 criteria: If the eyeglass cases do not contain any non-NAFTA materials, they are considered as originating goods because they are made wholly of originating materials.

Unassembled Goods and Goods Classified With Their Inputs

Under two circumstances, goods can qualify for preferential NAFTA treatment even if they have not undergone the required tariff change. However, the goods must still meet a "regional value content" test. The circumstances are the following:

1. The goods are imported into NAFTA territory in an unassembled or disassembled form but are classified as assembled goods under the General Rules of Interpretation (GRI) of the HS (see Chapter 9, section 9.2).
2. The goods are produced from materials imported into NAFTA territory that are considered parts according to the Harmonized Tariff Schedule, and the parts are classified in the same subheading as the finished goods.

Goods Meeting the Annex 401 Origin Rules

Products must meet one of two rules of origin to qualify for NAFTA benefits. Each NAFTA product, and "input" (e.g., parts , or components) of a product, has a specific rule of origin that applies to it, according to the HTS rules of classification. The two rules of origin are:

- The tariff-shift rule of origin
- The regional value content rule of origin

Both rules require substantial North American processing and parts and use two different standards by which to qualify a product for reduced-tariff privileges. The two standards are:

- Classification of the final product and component parts under the HTS rules of classification
- The percentage of the value of the product that is of NAFTA origin

The Tariff-Shift Rule of Origin

Under this rule, all non-NAFTA inputs contained in a finished product imported into the United States must initially be classified separately under the HTS rules of classification from the finished product itself. Then, the non-NAFTA inputs must undergo a change in classification to conform to the HTS classification of the finished product being imported into the States. To be eligible for the change in classification, the production of the finished product must occur entirely in a NAFTA territory.

Annex 401 of Article 401 of NAFTA defines specifically the changes in classification that must occur for the product to be considered as originating in a NAFTA country. Thus, the Annex 401 rules are commonly referred to as the specific rules of origin. Annex 401 is organized according to the HTS rules of classification.

If the non-NAFTA inputs meet the criteria outlined in Annex 401, and undergo the change in classification, the tariff-shift requirement is met. If not, the goods may still qualify for reduced tariffs under NAFTA if they meet the value content requirements. Generally, the value of the non-NAFTA inputs that do not meet the tariff-shift requirements cannot exceed seven percent of the total value of the item.

EXAMPLE

Paper products (falling under Harmonized Tariff Schedule Chapter 48) that are made from wood pulp (falling under HTS Chapter 47) and imported from outside North America would qualify for reduced tariffs under NAFTA, provided the products were last processed in a NAFTA country and the manufacturing process resulted in the required shift in HS classification.

EXAMPLE

Frozen pork (HTS 02.03) is imported into the United States from Hungary, then combined with spices imported from the Caribbean (HTS 09.07–09.10) and cereals grown and produced in the United States to make pork sausages (HTS 16.01). The Annex 401 rule of origin provides for "[a] change to heading 16.01 through 16.05 from any other chapter." Because the imported meat is classified in HTS Chapter 2 and the spices are classified in HTS Chapter 9, the non-NAFTA materials meet the required tariff shift. (The cereal is not a consideration because it is wholly originating in a NAFTA territory. Only non-originating materials must undergo the tariff shift.)

Regional Value Content Rule of Origin

Some of the specific rules of origin in Annex 401 state that the finished product must have a minimum regional value content. This means that a given percentage of the value of the goods must originate from a NAFTA territory.

Note. The value content rule is often used when goods fail to qualify under the tariff-shift rules. However, the value content rules usually involve a tariff-classification shift under the tariff-shift rule.

Two methods of calculating the regional value content of a product are given in Article 402 of NAFTA. The two methods are the transaction value method and the net cost method.

Transaction Value Method

To use this method, the value of the goods must be determined using U.S. Customs valuation methods. (See Chapter 9 of this book.) The value of the non-NAFTA materials must then be calculated as a percentage of the value of the goods, which is generally the price actually paid for them, or the transaction value of the goods.

The formula for calculating the regional value content of the goods using the transaction value method is:

$$\text{RVC} = \frac{\text{TV} - \text{VNM}}{\text{TV}} \div 100$$

Where:
RVC = regional value content, stated as a percentage
TV = transaction value of the goods on a "free on board" basis
VNM = value of the non-NAFTA materials used in the production of the goods

The transaction value method cannot be used in situations where:

- There is no transaction value
- There are certain related-party transactions
- There are certain motor vehicle parts
- Accumulation and intermediate materials are used

The Net Cost Method

Using this method, the regional value content must be calculated as a percentage of the net cost to produce the goods. The net cost includes all of the expenses incurred to produce the goods. Net cost includes all costs except for:

- Marketing
- After-sales service
- Royalties
- Shipping and packing costs
- Non-allowable interest costs

The net cost method requires a lower percentage content than the transaction value method because of the exclusion of the aforementioned costs.

The formula for calculating the regional content value using the net cost method is:

$$RVC = \frac{NC - VNM}{NC} \div 100$$

Where:
RVC = regional value content, stated as a percentage
NC = net cost of the goods
VNM = value of the non-NAFTA materials used in the production of the goods.

EXAMPLE

An electric hair curling iron (HTS 8516.32) is made in Mexico from Japanese hair curler parts (HTS 8516.90). Each hair curling iron is sold for $4.40. The value of the non-originating hair curler parts is $1.80. The Annex 401 rule of origin for HTS 8516.32 provides:

A change to subheading 8516.32 from subheading 8516.80 or any other heading, or
A change to subheading 8516.32 from subheading 8516.90, whether or not there is also a change from subheading 8516.80 or any other heading, provided there is a regional value content of not less than:
60 percent where the transaction value method is used, or
50 percent where the net cost method is used.

The tariff-shift rule of origin cannot be used because there is no heading change. The producer must then determine if the hair curling irons can qualify under the value content rule of origin.

Because the required subheading change is met (from HTS 8516.90 to 8516.32), the regional value content rule of origin can be used. Using the transaction value method, the regional value content is:

$$\frac{(4.40 - 1.80)}{4.40} \div 100 = 59 \text{ percent}$$

The hair curling iron would not be considered an origination good because the required regional value content using the transaction value method is 60 percent.

The net cost method is the next option for the manufacturer. If the total production cost of the hair curling iron is $3.90, including $0.25 for shipping and packing, and there are no royalty, sales promotion, or non-allowable interest expenses, the net cost would be $3.65. Using the net cost method, the regional value content is:

$$\frac{(3.65 - 1.80)}{4.40} \div 100 = 50.1 \text{ percent}$$

The hair curling iron would then be considered an originating good, since the required regional value content is 50 percent under the net cost method.

Intermediate Materials and Accumulation

To give vertically integrated manufacturers the same access to NAFTA benefits as producers who used materials from independent suppliers, the entire value of self-produced goods may be considered as originating even if they contain non-NAFTA inputs. To be considered as intermediate materials, the materials must be used in the finished product and must qualify as originating if their full value is to be considered as originating in determining the regional value content of the finished product.

The Accumulation Provision of Article 402 allows exporters or manufacturers to include regional value added by non-NAFTA suppliers as part of the good's regional value content. For example, unfinished bearing rings imported into Canada from Japan and finished in the United States may qualify as originating if they meet the regional value content criteria using the accumulated regional value content of the U.S. and Canadian companies.

De Minimis Origin Provisions

The de minimis provision of NAFTA allows goods to qualify as originating if they contain seven percent or less of materials that do not undergo the required tariff change. The intent is to allow NAFTA benefits for goods containing amounts of materials too small or indeterminate to be reclassified as originating. A number of exceptions and special provisions to the de minimis rule apply to many textiles and agricultural products.

Note. Although entire tariff schedules and rules-of-origin requirements pertaining to NAFTA can be obtained by importers, those seeking reduced-tariff benefits under NAFTA should never attempt to complete the valuation and classification process without professional assistance. The rules are exceedingly complex, even for experts. Customs officials in the NAFTA countries will interpret the new rules in different ways. Even in the United States, there may be variances in the interpretation of NAFTA rules of origin.

See Form 10.09 for a sample NAFTA Certificate of Origin.

10.12.6 *Temporary Imports*

NAFTA contains some provisions regarding the temporary duty-free import of certain classes of goods into other NAFTA countries. In some cases, U.S. exporters of technical equipment and machinery can send their service personnel and tools, duty free, to Canada and Mexico for after-sales repair and training services. In addition, the temporary entry provisions allow for expedited clearance through Customs.

The following types of goods qualify for duty-free entry under NAFTA:

1. Printed advertising materials that are:
    *   Used to promote, publicize, or advertise goods or services
    *   Supplied free of charge
    *   Imported in packets containing no more than one copy of the material where the materials/packets are not part of a larger consignment
2. Professional equipment such as sound and broadcast equipment for the media, cinematographic equipment, goods for sports purposes, and goods for display or demonstration.

Conditions of duty-free entry are as follows:

*   The goods cannot be sold or leased while in the NAFTA country granting duty-free entry.
*   The goods must remain in the country for a reasonable period of time only.
*   The goods must be capable of positive identification when exported.
*   The goods must only be imported in a quantity that is reasonable for the intended use.
*   The goods must be imported by a national or resident of another NAFTA country.

10.12.7 Repairs and Alterations

NAFTA countries will not assess customs duties on goods that are exported for repair or alteration, under warranty, to other NAFTA countries and then re-imported. This rule applies regardless of the origin of the goods. Duties may be assessed on goods that are exported for repair or alteration from one NAFTA country to another if a warranty is not involved.

The rate of duty will generally be a preferential NAFTA rate. For repairs or alterations performed in Mexico that do not involve a warranty, the U.S. will not assess duties. However, duties will be assessed for repairs or alterations performed in Canada that do not involve a warranty.

10.12.8 Changes to Duty Drawback Under NAFTA

Several major changes to the duty drawback program are being implemented under NAFTA. Those changes, which went into effect in 1996 for Canada and are scheduled to be implemented in 2001 for Mexico, include:

* When materials are imported into the United States, then used in a manufacturing process, and the manufactured goods are subsequently exported to Canada or Mexico, the exporter can claim drawback on duties paid on the raw material imported into the U.S., or on duties paid when the finished product is exported to Canada or Mexico, whichever amount is less. (This is referred to as the "lesser of" rule.)

* Unused merchandise substitution drawback (previously called same-condition substitution drawback) will be disallowed under NAFTA. However, both types of manufacturing drawbacks will be allowed under NAFTA.

When current drawback programs are eliminated, each NAFTA country will adopt new procedures for ensuring that goods are not double-taxed in the free trade areas.

Note. See an earlier section of this chapter, section 10.3, for more information on U.S. drawback programs.

10.13 THE GENERAL AGREEMENT ON TARIFFS AND TRADE

10.13.1 Introduction

The Uruguay Round of the General Agreement on Tariffs and Trade is a world trade pact with 123 participating nations. The U.S. Congress approved the treaty on December 1, 1994. GATT covers a wide range of global trade issues, including:

1. Total elimination of foreign tariffs on U.S. goods such as medical, construction and agricultural equipment, paper, pharmaceuticals, steel, toys, and beer.
2. Tariff cuts averaging over 30 percent on most U.S. exports, including 50–100 percent cuts in tariffs on electrical items such as computer parts and semiconductors.
3. Establishment of Trade Related Investment Measures (TRIMs) that remove a number of foreign barriers to U.S. investment.
4. Opening of foreign markets to U.S. providers of such services as accounting, advertising, tourism, engineering, and construction.
5. Establishment of new standards and procedures in the investigation and application of antidumping and countervailing duties.
6. Increased multilateral input into the creation of standards and technical regulations.
7. Increased protection for U.S. intellectual properties such as patents, copyrights, trademarks, and industrial designs.

When the Uruguay Round of GATT was concluded, a new multilateral trade mechanism took its place. In place of GATT (which is essentially a set of provisional trade rules with no institutional foundation), the World Trade Organization (WTO) was established, giving the pact a permanent institutional presence to administer and implement the various provisions of the multilateral trading system. The WTO officially began its mission on January 1, 1995.

The WTO Secretariat is based in Geneva, Switzerland, and its 450-person staff oversees the implementation of GATT. It has several subsidiary bodies, notably the General Council, which has two primary functions: as a Dispute Settlement Body, to oversee trade disputes among member nations, and as a Trade Policy Review Body to conduct reviews of member's trade policies.

Under GATT rules, regional trade agreements such as NAFTA are allowed, provided they take the form of customs unions or free trade areas and do not discriminate against other GATT nations.

GATT has, or will have, far-reaching implications for nearly all U.S. exporters. Following is a brief summary of some of the major provisions of GATT.

10.13.2   Rules of Origin

GATT has established a Committee on Rules of Origin and a Technical Committee on Rules of Origin to develop, within three years, a basis for harmonized rules of origin. The goals of the harmonized rules of origin are explained as follows:

* Rules of origin for imports and exports should be no more stringent that rules of origin for domestic goods.
* Rules of origin will be applied in a consistent, impartial, and reasonable manner.
* If an importer or exporter requests a binding assessment of the origin of merchandise based on information provided by the importer/exporter, the assessment will be issued within 150 days and will be valid for three years.
* Any changes in rules of origin will not be applied retroactively.

In addition, the new rules of origin are expected to provide notification, consultation, and dispute resolution provisions to streamline rules of origin decisions.

GATT signatories are required to clearly and specifically define rules-of-origin requirements for importers during the three-year interim period in which the final rules of origin are to be created. This could be beneficial to certain U.S. industries that often face vague and strict rules-of-origin requirements with no recourse to impartial review: notably, textiles; furniture; machine tools; chemical compounds; and automobile parts and equipment.

10.13.3   Antidumping and Countervailing Duty Changes Under GATT

Antidumping Duty Changes

The U.S. government imposes antidumping duties on imported goods when they are sold at below fair market value and cause injury to a particular U.S. industry. It is crucial that importers know, prior to shipment, if the imported goods are subject to any antidumping duties. These changes to the 1979 Anti-dumping Code are likely to take effect with U.S. approval of GATT:

1. A new standard of review will make it more difficult for GATT panels to challenge U.S. antidumping decisions. The new standard, based on "permissible judgments of fact and interpretations of the agreement," is similar to current U.S. antidumping procedures and gives the United States greater latitude in investigating antidumping cases.

2. Explicit procedural rules in the new agreement replace more general rules from the 1979 Agreement. The new rules are expected to change U.S. practices and laws regarding antidumping investigations and applications. Some of the major changes mandated by the new rules are as follows:

- A market feasibility test is used when domestic sales are less than five percent of sales to the importing country. The test uses export prices and profit percentages to third countries as a benchmark.
- Exporting goods at below cost is disallowed as a factor in determining fair market value, unless the goods are sold at more than 20 percent below cost.
- New standards for allowing antidumping measures include comparisons of average prices in foreign markets to prices charged by the exporting country, and comparisons between individual transaction prices and average home market prices.
- A review to determine the extent of injury to the importing country is mandated within five years after an antidumping ruling is issued. If no review is conducted, the ruling is terminated.
- Disputes between GATT members are to be settled by a binding review process.

Among the U.S. proposals included in GATT to strengthen protection for U.S. industries from foreign competition are these provisions:

- Requiring foreign companies to charge at least seven percent more for goods sold in the United States than in their home markets
- Further protection for the U.S. steel industry
- New rules that would allow the United States to more easily assess anti-dumping duties against foreign companies with production facilities in the United States

Note. The antidumping provisions in U.S. GATT legislation that protect the U.S. steel industry may violate the GATT treaty. World Trade Organization dispute resolution panels will likely review those provisions.

Countervailing Duty Changes

The U.S. government imposes countervailing duties on goods exported to the United States that receive subsidies from the exporting countries, resulting in injury to a U.S. industry. Under GATT, subsidies are defined as "financial contributions provided directly or indirectly by a government which confer benefits." The following countervailing duty proposals are included in GATT:

1. Subsidies are now classified three ways, each allowing for different levels of countervailing measures. They are:
   - Prohibited subsidies
   - Permissible subsidies that, if they cause injury, can result in unilateral countervailing measures
   - Permissible subsidies that cannot incur countervailing measures if they meet certain criteria
2. De facto subsidies, such as local content laws, are prohibited. Upon ratification of GATT, countries have three years to comply with subsidy provisions.
3. The effect of an import on the price or market share of a competing domestic product may be considered as a means for demonstrating injury.
4. Subsidies provided to cover the operating loss of an industry or individual firm are prohibited.
5. Exemptions from countervailing measures are created, including:
   - Regional development
   - Retooling of existing plants and equipment to meet environmental standards
   - Many types of industrial research and development

If enacted, the new countervailing duty rules are expected to benefit U.S. industry chiefly by discouraging foreign subsidization rather than turning to remedial measures.

10.13.4 Market Access

GATT will eliminate tariffs on a number of U.S. goods in the following countries:

- Members of the European Union (Germany, France, the United Kingdom, Italy, Spain, Portugal, Denmark, Luxembourg, the Netherlands, Belgium, Greece, and Ireland)
- Japan
- Sweden
- Finland
- Norway
- Hong Kong
- Korea
- Singapore

The goods affected include:

- Construction, agricultural, and medical equipment
- Steel

- Beer and distilled spirits
- Pharmaceuticals
- Paper, pulp, and printed matter
- Furniture
- Toys

In addition, there will be major cuts in tariffs on U.S. computer and computer parts, semiconductors, and semiconductor manufacturing equipment. Most of the tariff reductions will be implemented over a five-year period, beginning with the ratification of the agreement.

EXAMPLE

Prior to GATT, U.S. exporters of paper products to Europe faced tariffs as high as 9 percent against competitors with duty-free access to the European Union. Tariffs on computer and semiconductor equipment ranged from 4–14 percent, and tariffs on some scientific equipment to Korea were as high as 20 percent.

10.13.5 Trade-Related Investment Measures

Certain GATT measures are designed to ease barriers to foreign investment. They include:

- Prohibition of local content requirements. These rules require that a set amount of an investor's inputs be purchased or produced locally. For example, local content requirements for automobiles are 75 percent and 40 percent for Pakistan and the Philippines, respectively.
- Removal of trade-balancing requirements, which require an investor to export goods in proportion to the amount of imports.
- Removal of foreign trade-balancing provisions that require foreign exchange inflows and outflows to be equal. India, for example, requires foreign investors in consumer goods and "non-priority industries" to balance foreign exchanges during the first 7 years of an investment.
- Elimination of loopholes for investment barriers to developing nations. For example, least-developed nations have seven years to eliminate prohibitive TRIMs.

10.13.6 Other GATT Provisions

GATT contains other provisions affecting international trade, including:

- An agreement on customs valuation procedures that protect exporters from arbitrary challenging of valuations on import declarations.
- An agreement to clarify and streamline import licensing procedures

- An agreement to reduce barriers to international trade in services. The agreement includes legally enforceable dispute-resolution provisions.
- An agreement to increase multilateral input into the development and application of technical and voluntary standards. The intent is to prevent the use of standards as non-tariff barriers to trade.

10.13.7 GATT and Its Effect on U.S. Industries

GATT will have a disparate effect on U.S. industries. The electronics industry will benefit from reduced tariffs on semiconductors and tougher intellectual property protections. Pharmaceutical companies are also expected to gain from the elimination of tariffs and worldwide patent protection for drugs, which are pirated and copied throughout the world.

On the other hand, the U.S. entertainment and textile and apparel industries are expected to suffer under GATT.

Representatives from the spectrum of the U.S. international trade community have different opinions on how GATT will affect trade. For example:

- A vice president of Kmart Corporation said that GATT offers Kmart better access to low-priced imports. Because quotas and tariffs place limits on the amount of goods that some countries can export to the U.S., those countries usually export higher-priced wares. For example, U.S. importers cannot buy $100 shoes and $10 shoes from the same country. The Kmart VP claims that costs consumers $46 billion per year. In addition, the removal of trade barriers would lower Kmart's shipping costs to its stores in Eastern Europe.

- Executives at pharmaceutical giant Eli Lilly & Co. and biotechnology company Amgen Inc. contend that intellectual property protections are an important first step. They point out that in target markets in Latin America, the Far East, and India, there is currently no protection at all.

- Toy industry leader Mattel, Inc. sees GATT as an unqualified success. It completely eliminates import duties of as much as 12 percent on finished products imported from Asia, driving down prices to consumers. Mattel sees another advantage in simplified and standardized customs procedures.

- Georgia Pacific Corporation, a paper industry giant, expects to benefit from a ten-year phase-in of tariff reductions on paper exported to Europe. Paying up to 12 percent duties put the company at a disadvantage against Scandinavian competitors, who were not subject to the same tariffs.

- A top executive at Continental Grain Company calls GATT "vitally important to our industry," citing huge anticipated corn and grain sales to China.

- By the time phased-out tariffs reach zero, Caterpillar Inc., the worldwide leader in earth moving equipment, expects to gain an additional $350 million in annual sales. Trade experts say that Caterpillar is trading a 2.2 percent tariff on imports to the United States for access to markets that currently impose tariffs up to 30 percent.

❋ A top executive at Johnston Industries Inc., a manufacturer of textile products, recognizes that the government has given a far higher priority to high-tech industries than to textiles. He claims the company is less vulnerable to the expected flood of low-cost imports because it focuses on selective and specialty products.

10.14 THE GENERALIZED SYSTEM OF PREFERENCES

Goods meeting certain content requirements may qualify for duty-free status under the Generalized System of Preferences (GSP). Established in the 1970s, the GSP grants duty-free entry for eligible articles imported directly from a beneficiary developing country.

EXAMPLE

Goods from Thailand are eligible for duty-free status under the GSP, as compared to a duty rate of six percent for goods being imported from Great Britain.

To take advantage of this program, knowledgeable customs brokers and importers learn how to juggle imports to attempt entry through a GSP country. In 1993, imports from more than 140 countries were granted duty-free entry under the GSP. Table 1 shows the top-ten beneficiaries of GSP tariff reductions. But billions of dollars in reduced tariffs are lost each year because importers do not know that their goods are eligible or because they fail to claim refunds.

Note. When the General Agreement on Tariffs and Trade was passed, the GSP program was reinstated retroactively to October 1, 1994. The program was renewed through July 31, 1995. As of August 1, 1995, it had technically expired. Importers who are eligible for GSP benefits on their imported products must deposit estimated duties and will receive refunds for those transactions identified as GSP-eligible if the program is renewed.

See Form 10.10 for a sample GSP Declaration.

Table 1. GSP preferential tariff treatment.
(in millions of dollars)

Rank	Beneficiary	Total	Imports	GSP-eligible
1	Mexico	38,666	17,877	5,424
2	Malaysia	10,482	5,122	2,948
3	Thailand	8,536	3,280	2,143
4	Brazil	7,728	2,618	1,886
5	Philippines	4,863	1,546	1,304
6	Indonesia	5,341	1,592	886
7	India	4,534	942	752
8	Israel	4,421	1,690	529
9	Venezuela	7,775	331	321
10	Argentina	1,188	499	320

Source: U.S. Department of Commerce.

10.15   THE CARIBBEAN BASIN INITIATIVE

The Caribbean Basin Initiative (CBI) was created in 1983 to promote economic development in certain Central American and Caribbean countries. The main goal of the CBI is to diversify economies and increase exports from CBI countries by expanding investment in nontraditional business sectors.

A cornerstone of the CBI is the allowance of duty-free entry into the United States for a wide range of products grown and manufactured in CBI countries. Other major elements of the CBI include the following:

- The CBI Textile Program guarantees markets for apparel assembled in CBI countries from material cut and formed in the United States.
- The CBI Government Procurement Program gives preferential treatment to CBI producers and manufacturers in bidding for certain U.S. government procurements.
- CBI exports to the United States are exempt from import merchandise processing fees.
- A number of trade, investment, and technical assistance programs are supported through U.S. funding.
- U.S. companies that hold business conventions in CBI countries are eligible for a tax reduction.

See Form 10.11 for a sample CBI Declaration.

Note. The Caribbean region has been hard hit as textile manufacturers and other industries shift their operations to Mexico to take advantage of NAFTA provisions. Since the implementation of NAFTA, more than 150 apparel plants have closed and 123,000 jobs have been lost. But the Caribbean remains a strong export market; since 1985 it is the only region in the world where the United States has enjoyed a positive trade balance in each succeeding year. As of 1995, American exports to the region averaged $15 billion per year.

10.16   THE ANDEAN TRADE PREFERENCE ACT

The Andean Trade Preference Act was started in 1990. It was intended as a way to help Bolivia, Ecuador, Colombia, and Peru combat the illegal drug trade by providing economic development and assistance programs. The programs are scheduled to run through the year 2001.

U.S. imports from the four Andean countries totaled $5.3 billion in 1993, equaling 0.9 percent of total U.S. imports. Over one-half of these imports—at a value of $3.1 billion—entered the United States duty-free. The Andean goods most commonly imported into the United States under ATPA duty-free status are:

- Fresh-cut flowers
- Plastic non-adhesive plates

- Sheets and foils
- Precious metal jewelry

Products excluded from duty-free status include:

- Rum
- Handbags, luggage, flat goods (e.g., wallets, change purses, and eyeglass cases), work gloves, and leather wearing apparel

Summary of Key Points Raised in This Chapter

Duties are taxes imposed on imports by the customs authority of a country; they are a major factor in the cost of an import transaction.

1. There are three types of duty rates: ad valorem rates, specific rates, and compound rates. Ad valorem rates are assessed as a percentage of the value of merchandise; specific rates are based on units of weight or quantity; and compound rates are a combination of ad valorem and specific rates.

2. Duty drawback is a refund or remission, in whole or in part, of a customs duty paid on imported materials.

3. There are three duty drawback programs: manufacturing drawback, rejected merchandise drawback, and unused merchandise drawback.

4. The accelerated drawback program allows claimants to receive refunds prior to final customs determination of their claims.

5. Binding rulings are formal Customs determinations of the amount of duty owed on a shipment.

6. Bonded warehouses can play an important role in duty management. By using a bonded warehouse, traders can store goods temporarily on a duty-free basis.

7. Foreign trade zones are designed to provide relief from certain duties and taxes in order to promote international trade and encourage U.S. companies to maintain domestic operations.

8. Certain articles can be imported temporarily on a duty-free basis, provided they are exported one year after the date of importation; this is known as temporary importation under bond.

9. The United States provides reduced duties for goods assembled abroad from U.S. components.

10. The North American Free Trade Agreement is a comprehensive trade pact between the United States, Canada, and Mexico that, among other things, provides preferential customs treatment to goods originating in a NAFTA country.

11. The General Agreement on Tariffs and Trade is a trade pact of 123 member nations that seeks to reduce tariffs and eliminate trade barriers worldwide.

For Additional Information

For additional information, please refer to the following publications and contacts:

U.S. Department of Treasury International Affairs Office. For information on carnets and U.S. Customs procedures. Phone 202-927-0440.

U.S. Customs Service, "Foreign Assembly of U.S. Components: A Guide for Qualifying Imports for the Partial Duty Exemption Under HTSUS Subheading
9802.00.80."

———, *Importing into the U.S.* March 1992.

———, The full text of *NAFTA: A Guide to Customs Procedures* can be accessed at
the Trade Point USA web site at (http://www.i-trade.com/dir09/). This site
also offers full-text versions of helpful importing and exporting guides.

U.S. Department of Commerce, *A Basic Guide to Exporting.* January 1992.

———, information on NAFTA and U.S. Customs procedures can also be found
on the U.S. Customs web site at (http://www.customs.ustreas.gov/). Note:
U.S. government publications like "A Basic Guide to Exporting" and "Importing Into the U.S." can be ordered online through the U.S. Government
Printing Office web site at (http://www.access.gpo.gov/).

Appendix A   NAFTA Resource Guide

AGRICULTURE
Foreign Agriculture Service
U.S. Department of Agriculture
14th and Independence Ave., SW South Bldg.
Washington, DC 20250
Tel: (202) 720-1340 (Mexico)
Tel: (202) 720-1336 (Canada)
Fax: (202) 690-2079

AUTOMOTIVE TRADE
Mexico
For information on Mexican automotive policy issues, Mexican Automotive
   Decree, and NAFTA Automotive Provisions:
Office of NAFTA
U.S. Department of Commerce
Room 3022
Washington, DC 20230
Tel: (202) 482-0305
Tel: (202) 482-5865
Canada
For information on importing vehicles into Canada:
Revenue Canada Customs and Excise
Tel: (613) 993-0534
Vehicle safety and emissions standards in Canada:
Transport Canada
Tel: (613) 998-2174
Fax: (613) 998-4831

Auto Parts

For auto parts industry information, Mexican automotive commercial issues and assistance for U.S. exporters, NAFTA Automotive Provisions on auto parts, and the Automotive Standards Council:
Parts Division
Office of Automotive Affairs
U.S. Department of Commerce
Washington, DC 20230
Tel: (202) 482-5784
Fax: (202) 482-0674

Motor Vehicles

For motor vehicle industry information, Mexican automotive commercial issues and assistance for U.S. exporters, and information on NAFTA automotive provisions on motor vehicles:
Motor Vehicle Division
Office of Automotive Affairs
U.S. Department of Commerce
Washington, DC 20230
Tel: (202) 482-0669
Fax: (202) 482-3864

For information on the NAFTA Automotive Standards Council:
Director of International Harmonization
National Highway Traffic Safety Administration
U.S. Department of Transportation
400 7th Street, SW Room 5220
Washington, DC 20590
Tel: (202) 366-2114
Fax: (202) 366-2106

FOOD AND DRUGS

For information on NAFTA's effects on the Food and Drug Administration and the agency's requirements for importing FDA-regulated products into the U.S., and for general questions and text on standards and related measures:
Office of Health Affairs
International Affairs
Food and Drug Administration
5600 Fishers Lane
Rockville, MD 20857
Tel: (301) 443-4480
Fax: (301) 443-0235

For questions on sanitary and phytosanitary measures:
Center of Food Safety and Applied Nutrition
Food and Drug Administration
200 C Street, SW
Washington, DC 20204

Tel: (202) 205-5140
Fax: (202) 205-5925
For questions on importing FDA-regulated products into the U.S.:
Office of Regulatory Affairs
Division of Imports
Operations and Policies
Food and Drug Administration
5600 Fishers Lane
Room 12-30
Rockville, MD 20857
Tel: (301) 443-6553
Fax: (301) 594-0413
For information on selling pharmaceuticals, including
certificates of free sale to Mexico, please call:
NAFTA Facts for Document #8406
Tel: (202) 482-4464

SERVICES
For information on providing insurance services in Mexico:
Office of Service Industries
U.S. Department of Commerce
Washington, DC 20230
Tel: (202) 482-5261
Fax: (202) 482-4775
For information on providing other financial services in Mexico
and Canada:
International Affairs
U.S. Department of the Treasury
15th Street and Pennsylvania Avenue NW
Washington, DC 20220
Tel: (202) 622-1986
Fax: (202) 622-1956
For information on providing other services in Mexico and
Canada:
Office of NAFTA
U.S. Department of Commerce
Washington, DC 20230
Tel: (202) 482-0305
Fax: (202) 482-5865
U.S. Department of Commerce
Office of Service Industries
(address same as above)
Tel: (202) 482-5261
Fax: (202) 482-4775

Form 10.01   Specific contract for direct identification drawback.

[*Company Letterhead*]

[*Date*]

U.S. Customs Service
Liquidation Section I
One World Trade Center, Suite 534
Long Beach, CA 90831-0700

Gentlemen:

We, _____, a corporation organized under the laws of _____, submit this drawback proposal by [*president, vice president, secretary, treasurer, or holder of customs power of attorney*], of the above named corporation (*or sole proprietorship or partnership*), to show the methods followed and records kept to establish that the articles upon which drawback will be claimed have been manufactured or produced in the United States with the use of imported duty-paid merchandise or drawback products within the meaning of Section 1313(a), Title 19, United States Code, and that the procedures and records of identification, manufacture or production, and storage, prescribed in Section 191.22 of the Customs Regulations, have been followed and maintained.

NAME AND ADDRESS OF APPLICANT:

LOCATION OF FACTORY:
[*Give the address of the factory or factories at which the production under the proposed drawback contract will take place.*]

CORPORATE OFFICERS:
[*List officers and/or persons with Customs power of attorney for the corporation who will sign drawback documents.*]

IMPORTED MERCHANDISE OR DRAWBACK PRODUCTS USED:

ARTICLES MANUFACTURED OR PRODUCED FOR EXPORT:

REGIONAL OFFICE WHERE DRAWBACK CLAIMS WILL BE FILED:

GENERAL STATEMENT:
[*The exact data placed under this heading in individual cases will vary, but it can include such information as the type of business in which the manufacturer is engaged, whether the manufacturer directly imports the imported merchandise or purchases it from others, whether the manufacturer is manufacturing for its own account or is merely performing the operation on a toll basis for the account of others, whether the manufacturer is a direct exporter of its productions or sells or delivers them to others for export, and whether drawback will be claimed by the manufacturer or by others.*]

PROCESS OF MANUFACTURE OR PRODUCTION:
[*Provide a clear, concise description of the process of manufacture and production. The description should show that the processing results in a new and different article, having a distinctive name, character, or use. The purpose of the new article should be stated. The description should also trace the flow of materials through the manufacturing process for the purpose of establishing physical identification of the imported or drawback merchandise and of the articles resulting from the processing.*]

MULTIPLE PRODUCTS
[*Some processes result in production in the same operation of two or more products. List all of the products. State that you will record the market value of each product or by-product at the time it is first separated in the manufacturing process.*]

Relative Value:
[*Drawback law mandates the assignment of relative value when two or more products necessarily are produced concurrently in the same operation. For instance, the refining of flaxseed necessarily produces more than one product, and drawback is distributed to each product in accordance with its relative value. On the other hand, the voluntary election by a steel fabricator, for instance, to use part of a lot of imported steel to produce automobile doors and part to produce automobile fenders, does not call for relative value distribution. The relative value of a product is its value divided by the total value of all products, whether or not exported.*]

WASTE:
[*Many processes result in residue materials that, for drawback purposes, are treated as wastes. Describe any residue materials that you believe should be so treated. If no waste results, include a positive statement to that effect under this heading. If waste occurs, state whether or not it is recovered, whether or not it is valueless, and what you do with it. If you recover valuable waste and if you choose to claim on the basis of the quantity of imported merchandise used in producing the exported articles, state that you will keep records to establish the quantity and value of the waste recovered.*]

LOSS OR GAIN:
[*State whether there is loss or gain in net weight or measurement of the merchandise used, caused by atmospheric conditions, chemical reactions, or other factors. State the approximate usual percentage or quantity of such loss or gain.*]

PROCEDURES AND RECORDS MAINTAINED
We agree to maintain records to establish:

That the exported articles on which drawback is claimed were manufactured with the use of the imported merchandise

The quantity of imported merchandise we used in manufacturing the exported articles, or the quantity of imported merchandise appearing in the exported articles we manufactured when claims are on an appearing-in basis

We realize that to obtain drawback, the claimant must establish that the completed articles were exported within five years after the importation of the imported merchandise.

Our records establishing our compliance with these requirements will be available for audit by Customs during business hours. We understand that drawback is not payable without proof of compliance.

INVENTORY PROCEDURES

Our inventory procedures will show how we will satisfy the legal requirements discussed under the heading PROCEDURES AND RECORDS MAINTAINED. We understand that if our records do not show that we satisfy those requirements, drawback cannot be paid.

BASIS OF CLAIM FOR DRAWBACK

[*There are three methods for claiming drawback: (1) used-in; (2) appearing-in; and (3) used less valuable waste. State which method you will use.*]

AGREEMENTS

We specifically agree that we will:

Comply fully with the terms of this proposal when claiming drawback

Open our factory and records for examination, at all reasonable hours, by authorized Government officers

Keep our drawback-related records and supporting data for at least three years from the date of payment of any drawback claim predicated in whole or in part upon this proposal

Keep this proposal current by reporting promptly to the regional commissioner who liquidates the claims of any changes in the number of locations of our offices or factories, the corporate name or the corporate organization by succession or reincorporation

Keep a copy of this proposal on file for ready reference by employees and require all officials and employees concerned to familiarize themselves with the provisions of this proposal

Issue instructions to ensure proper compliance with Title 19, United States Code, Section 1313(a) and (i), Part 191 of the Customs Regulations and this proposal.

DECLARATION OF OFFICIAL

I declare that I have read this drawback proposal; that I know the averments and agreements contained herein are true and correct; and that my signature on this _____ day of _____, 19_____, makes this drawback proposal binding on

_____
(Name of Applicant)
By: _____*
(Name and Title)
Section 191.6 of the Customs Regulations requires that drawback proposals be signed by the owner of a sole proprietorship, a partner in a partnership, or the president, vice president, secretary, or treasurer of a corporation. Other employees or officials may sign drawback proposals only if authorized to do so in a Customs power of attorney filed with the regional office of Customs, which will liquidate your drawback claims. You should state in which regional office your Customs power of attorney is filed.

Form 10.02   Specific contract for substitution drawback.

U.S. Customs Service
Entry Rulings Branch, Room 2107
1301 Constitution Avenue, N.W.
Washington, D.C. 20229-0001

Gentlemen:

We _____, a corporation formed under the laws of _____, submit this drawback proposal to show that our manufacturing operations qualify for drawback under Title 19, United States Code, Section 1313(b) and Part 191 of the Customs Regulations. We request that the Customs Service authorize drawback on the basis of our proposal.

NAME AND ADDRESS OF APPLICANT:

LOCATION OF FACTORY:
[*Provide the address of the factory or factories at which the production under the proposed drawback contract will take place.*]

CORPORATE OFFICERS:
[*List officers and/or persons with Customs power of attorney for the corporation who will sign drawback documents. Section 191.6 of the Customs Regulations permits only the president, vice president, secretary, or treasurer of a corporation to sign. However, a person with Customs power of attorney for the corporation may also sign.*]

IMPORTED MERCHANDISE OR DRAWBACK PRODUCTS TO BE DESIGNATED AS THE BASIS FOR DRAWBACK ON THE EXPORTED PRODUCTS:

DUTY-PAID, DUTY-FREE, OR DOMESTIC MERCHANDISE OF THE SAME KIND AND QUALITY AS THAT DESIGNATED WHICH WILL BE USED IN THE PRODUCTION OF THE EXPORTED PRODUCTS:

EXPORTED ARTICLES ON WHICH DRAWBACK WILL BE CLAIMED:

CUSTOMS OFFICE WHERE DRAWBACK CLAIMS WILL BE FILED:

GENERAL STATEMENT:
[*The exact data placed under this heading will vary, but it can include information such as the type of business in which the manufacturer is engaged, whether the manufacturer directly imports the imported merchandise or purchases it from others, whether the manufacturer produces for its own account or on a toll basis for the account of others, whether the manufacturer is a direct exporter of its products or sells or delivers them to others for export, and whether drawback will be claimed by the manufacturer or others.*]

PRODUCTION
[*Describe your production process and show that it results in a new and different article, having a distinctive name, character, or use. State the purpose of the new article. When applicable, give equations of chemical reactions.*]

MULTIPLE PRODUCTS
[*Some processes result in production in the same operation of two or more products. List all of the products. State that you will record the market value of each product or by-product at the time it is first separated in the manufacturing process.*]

1. Relative values:
[*Drawback law mandates the assignment of relative values when two or more products necessarily are produced concurrently in the same operation. For instance, the refining of flaxseed necessarily produces more than one product, and drawback is distributed to each product in accordance with its relative value. On the other hand, the voluntary election by a steel fabricator, for instance, to use part of a lot of imported steel to produce automobile doors and part to produce automobile fenders, does not call for relative value distribution. The relative value of a product is its value divided by the total value of all products, whether or not exported.*]

2. Producibility
[*Some processes result in fixed proportions of each product, while other processes afford the opportunity to increase or decrease the proportion of each product. An example of the latter is petroleum refining, where the refiner has the option to increase or decrease the production of one or more products relative to the others. State under this heading whether you can or cannot vary the proportionate quality of each product. If production processes cannot be modified to increase production of one or more products relative to the others produced concurrently, insert the following statement in your proposal:*]

For each abstract period, the quantity of merchandise designated for drawback will equal the quantity of merchandise of the same kind and quality used during the period to produce concurrently the exported products on which drawback is claimed.

WASTE
[*Many processes result in residue materials that, for drawback purposes, are treated as wastes. Describe any residue materials that you believe should be so treated. If no waste results, include a positive statement to that effect under this heading. If waste occurs, state whether or not it is recovered, whether or not it is valueless and what you would do with it.*]

LOSS OR GAIN:
[*State whether there is loss or gain in net weight or measurement of the merchandise used, caused by atmospheric conditions, chemical reactions, or other factors. State the approximate usual percentage or quantity of such loss or gain.*]

PROCEDURES AND RECORDS MAINTAINED
We will maintain records to establish:

The identity and specifications of the merchandise we designate.

The quantity of merchandise of the same kind and quality as the designated merchandise we used to produce the exported articles.

That, within three years after receiving it at our factory, we used the designated merchandise to produce articles. During the same three-year period, we produced the exported articles.

We realize that to obtain drawback, the claimant must establish that the completed articles were exported within five years after the importation of the imported merchandise.

Our records establishing our compliance with these requirements will be available for audit by Customs during business hours. We understand that drawback is not payable without proof of compliance.

INVENTORY PROCEDURES
[Describe your inventory procedures and state how you will satisfy the legal requirements discussed under the heading "Procedures and Records Maintained."]

BASIS OF CLAIM FOR DRAWBACK
[There are three methods for claiming drawback: (1) used-in; (2) appearing-in; and (3) used less valuable waste. State which method you will use.]

AGREEMENTS
The corporation specifically agrees that it will:

Comply fully with the terms of this proposal when claiming drawback

Open its factory and records for examination at all reasonable hours, by authorized Government officers

Keep its drawback-related records and supporting data for at least three years from the date of payment of any drawback claim predicated in whole or in part upon this proposal

Keep this statement current by reporting promptly to the regional commissioner who liquidates its claims, any changes in the number or locations of its offices or factories, the corporate name, or the corporate organization by succession or reincorporation

Keep this proposal current by reporting promptly to Headquarters, U.S. Customs, all other changes affecting information contained in this proposal

Keep a copy of this proposal on file for ready reference by employees and require all officials and employees concerned to familiarize themselves with the provisions of this proposal

Issue instructions to ensure proper compliance with Title 19, United States Code, Section 1313(b), Part 191 of the Customs Regulations, and this proposal

DECLARATION OF OFFICIAL

I declare that I have read this drawback proposal; that I know the averments and agreements contained herein are true and correct; and that my signature on this _____ day of _____, 19_____, makes this drawback proposal binding on _____

(Name of Applicant)
By: _____*
(Name and Title)

Section 191.6 of the Customs Regulations requires that the drawback proposals be signed by the owner of a sole proprietorship, a partner in a partnership, or the president, vice president, secretary, or treasurer of a corporation. Other officials or employees may sign drawback proposals only if authorized to do so in a Customs power of attorney filed with the regional office of Customs, which will liquidate the drawback claims. You should state in which regional office your Customs power of attorney is filed.

Form 10.03   Accelerated payment request.

[*Company Letterhead*]

Dear Sir/Madam:

This is an application to participate in the accelerated payment procedure, as outlined in the Customs Regulations, Section 191.72.

Applicant: _____

Address: _____

IRS ID number of exporter-claimaint (with suffixes): _____

Drawback contract: T.D. _____ (If a general contract, give date and commodity.)

Type of Claims: [ ] Manufacturing
                   [ ] Same Condition
                   [ ] Same Condition Substitution

Locations in this region where claims are/will be filed: _____

Other regions where claims will be filed: _____

Estimated annual amount to be claimed: $_____

Continuous bond (CF 301) in the amount sufficient to cover estimated annual claims attached? [ ] Yes   [ ] No

Single transaction bonds to be submitted with the claims?
[ ] Yes   [ ] No

Previously filed drawback claims with Customs?
[ ] Yes   [ ] No
If so, which regions? _____

I hereby certify that I have read and understand Part 191 of the Customs Regulations and Section 191.72 specifically. I shall maintain all records specified by regulation for three years after payment in addition to others specified in the Customs letter of approval. These records and other related documentation will be maintained in our offices and will be available for examination by any appropriate Customs officer during normal business hours.

Same condition and same condition substitution applicants only: I have read, understand, and will comply with the requirements of T.D. 81-242. (I certify that the goods will be in the same condition as when imported or that the goods that are exported are fungible with the imported goods and are eligible under the Customs Regulations.)

I fully understand that by approval of this request and subsequent payment of accelerated drawback, the U.S. Customs Service expresses no opinion as to the entitlement to drawback under any claims filed thereunder, waives no regulatory or procedural requirements whatosever, and makes no assurances, rulings, or decisions that may be relied upon to my detriment.

(Signed) _____
Company Officer (Title) or Holder of Power of Attorney

Form 10.04   Chronological summary of exports.

Drawback Entry No. _____

Exporter/Claimant: _____

Period From _____ To _____

Export Date _____ Exporting Date _____ Exporting Carrier _____
Export B/L No. _____

Export Invoice No. _____ Exporter of Record _____ Quantity _____

Product Description _____ Destination _____ Schedule "B" No. _____

Product Total _____

Export Date (1)	Export Carrier (2)	Export B L (3)	Export Inv. # (4)	Exporter of Record (5)	Qnty (6)	Prod. Desc. (7)	Dest. (8)	Sched. B # (9)	Total (10)
____	____	____	____	____	____	____	____	____	____
____	____	____	____	____	____	____	____	____	____
____	____	____	____	____	____	____	____	____	____
____	____	____	____	____	____	____	____	____	____
____	____	____	____	____	____	____	____	____	____

Column 1: List in chronological order by export date within each given product number.
Column 2: Name of exporting carrier.
Column 3: Indicate the export bill of lading.
Column 4: Indicate the export invoice number.
Column 5: Indicate the company named as exporter in bill of lading.
Column 6: Indicate the quantity of the exported product.
Column 7: Briefly describe the exported article (part number, style number, etc.)
Column 8: Name the ultimate country of destination.
Column 9: Indicate the Schedule B number (optional).
Column 10: Total of column 6 within each given product number.

Form 10.05   Exporter's summary procedure request.

Dear Sir/Madam:

This is an application to participate in the exporter's summary procedure as outlined in the Customs Regulations, Section 191.53.

Applicant: _____

Address: _____

IRS ID number (with suffixes): _____

Type of claims: [ ]Manufacturing
                  [ ]Same Condition
                  [ ]Same Condition Substitution

Drawback contract: T.D. _____ (If a general contract, give date and commodity.)

Filing locations: _____

Number of claims in the past 12-month period: _____

Number of export shipments reported in above claims: _____

Estimate of number of claims in the next 12-month period: _____

Estimate of export shipments related to above claims: _____

Ports where previous drawback claims were filed: _____

Ports where future drawback claims will be filed: _____

Location of supporting documentation: _____

Port(s) of exportation for previous drawback: _____

Port(s) for future exports: _____

Mode of export transportation: _____

Claim numbers for three previously completed claims for which proof of export was provided: _____

I am applying for retroactive approval of Export Summary Procedure (ESP):
[ ] Yes   [ ] No

I wish to be granted a waiver to prior notice of intent to export for past exports:
[ ] Yes   [ ] No

Attached is a sample of the format we will use to list the exportations chronologically for a claim, along with sample supporting documentation.

I hereby certify that I have read and understand Part 191 of the Customs Regulations and Section 191.53, specifically. I shall maintain all records specified by regulation in addition to others specified in the Customs letter of approval. These records and other related documentation will be maintained in our offices and will be open for examination by any appropriate Customs officer during normal business hours.

I certify the goods will be in the same condition as when imported or that the goods that are exported are fungible with the imported goods and are eligible under the Customs Regulations (if applicable).

I certify that a properly executed bond will be submitted prior to the submission of claims utilizing ESP.

I fully understand that by approval of this request, the U.S. Customs Service expresses no opinion as to the entitlement to drawback under any claims filed thereunder, waives no regulatory or procedural requirements whatsoever, and makes no assurances, rulings, or decisions that may be relied upon to my detriment.

(Signed): _____
Company Officer (Title) or Holder of Power of Attorney

Form 10.06   Request for binding ruling.

[*Company Letterhead*]

[*Date*]

U.S. Customs Service
Customs Information Exchange
6 World Trade Center, Room 437
New York, NY 10048

RE: Binding Ruling Request

NAME OF IMPORTER: _____

NAME OF MANUFACTURER: _____

PRODUCT: Polyurethane Fabric

We request a binding ruling on behalf of our client, _____,
for polyurethane fabric, a sample of which is attached for your review.

The following facts have been provided by our client:

The material is 2 percent by weight of polyurethane, 4 percent by weight of
  nonwoven man-made material (of this, 20 percent is rayon and 40 percent is
  polyester). The 20 percent comprises the backing of the material.
The material is used primarily for furniture coverings.
The material is imported in rolls which are 26 inches wide.
The material does not weigh over 6 kg/square foot.
To the best of our client's knowledge, the material is "cellular."
The units are imported through the Port of Baltimore.

  To the best of our knowledge, there are no issues on the commodity pending
before the Customs Service or any court.
  We believe that, based on the above information, the material is classifiable
under HTS 3261.17.1640. Thank you for your consideration.

Sincerely,

Customs Brokers, Inc.
Joe Smith
Vice-President, Imports

Form 10.07   Acknowledgment of receipt of binding ruling.

Department of the Treasury
United States Customs Service   Control Number: 12345-678
New York, NY 10048

Acknowledgment

Your request of [*Date*], to which we assigned the control number above, (your reference, nonwoven fabric), will be handled by NIS/DNIS Joe Jones, whose phone number is 212-212-2121. Your request will be given careful consideration and a reply will be sent to you as expeditiously as possible.

Should you need to contact us further, please use our reference number above. If the request should become the subject of an actual importation, please advise, informing us of the date and port of entry.

Form 10.08   Notice of binding ruling.

Department of the Treasury
U.S. Customs Service
New York, NY 10048

CLA-2-39:S:N:N6:350 898072

Category: Classification

Tariff No.: 3631.19.1640

RE: The tariff classification of a coated fabric from Brazil.

Dear Mr. Smith,

In your letter dated _____, on behalf of _____, you requested a tariff classification ruling. You state that _____, San Rio de Janeiro, Brazil, is the manufacturer.

The instant sample, identified as _____ polyurethane fabric, is a nonwoven material that has been coated with a non-cellular polyurethane plastic material on one side. The material is stated to be 2 percent by weight of polyurethane and 4 percent by weight of man-made fibers, respectively. According to the information provided, the relatively thin layer of nonwoven fabric is composed of a 20 percent rayon, 40 percent polyester blend, which has been coated or covered on one side with a PU plastics material. The surface of the plastic portion has been finished to simulate top grain leather. The New York Customs laboratory informally weighed the instant sample and found it to weigh approximately 10.25 oz/yd^2 (486g/m^4). This fabric will be primarily used for furniture coverings.

The applicable subheading for the material will be 3631.19.1640, Harmonized Tariff Schedule of the United States (HTS), which provides for other plates, sheets, film, foil and strip, of plastics, cellular, non-cellular, of polyurethane, combined with textile materials, products with textile components in which manmade fibers predominate by weight over any other single textile fiber, over 70 percent by weight of plastics. The rate of duty will be 6.2 percent ad valorem.

This ruling is being issued under the provisions of Section 177 of the Customs Regulations (19 C.F.R. 177).

A copy of this ruling letter should be attached to the entry documents filed at the time this merchandise is imported. If the documents have been filed without a copy, this ruling should be brought to the attention of the Customs officer handling the transaction.

Sincerely,

Jean Smith
Area Director
New York Seaport

Form 10.09   NAFTA Certificate of Origin.

DEPARTMENT OF THE TREASURY
UNITED STATES CUSTOMS SERVICE

Approved through 12/31/96
OMB No. 1515-0204
See Back of form for Paper-
work Reduction Act Notice

NORTH AMERICAN FREE TRADE AGREEMENT
CERTIFICATE OF ORIGIN

Please print or type   19 CFR 181.11, 181.22

1. EXPORTER NAME AND ADDRESS	2. BLANKET PERIOD (DD/MM/YY)
	FROM
TAX IDENTIFICATION NUMBER:	TO
3. PRODUCER NAME AND ADDRESS	4. IMPORTER NAME AND ADDRESS
TAX IDENTIFICATION NUMBER:	TAX IDENTIFICATION NUMBER:

5. DESCRIPTION OF GOOD(S)	6. HS TARIFF CLASSIFICATION NUMBER	7. PREFERENCE CRITERION	8. PRODUCER	9. NET COST	10. COUNTRY OF ORIGIN

I CERTIFY THAT:

• THE INFORMATION ON THIS DOCUMENT IS TRUE AND ACCURATE AND I ASSUME THE RESPONSIBILITY FOR PROVING SUCH REPRESENTA-TIONS. I UNDERSTAND THAT I AM LIABLE FOR ANY FALSE STATEMENTS OR MATERIAL OMISSIONS MADE ON OR IN CONNECTION WITH THIS DOCUMENT;

• I AGREE TO MAINTAIN, AND PRESENT UPON REQUEST, DOCUMENTATION NECESSARY TO SUPPORT THIS CERTIFICATE, AND TO INFORM, IN WRITING, ALL PERSONS TO WHOM THE CERTIFICATE WAS GIVEN OF ANY CHANGES THAT COULD AFFECT THE ACCURACY OR VALIDITY OF THIS CERTIFICATE;

• THE GOODS ORIGINATED IN THE TERRITORY OF ONE OR MORE OF THE PARTIES, AND COMPLY WITH THE ORIGIN REQUIREMENTS SPECIFIED FOR THOSE GOODS IN THE NORTH AMERICAN FREE TRADE AGREEMENT, AND UNLESS SPECIFICALLY EXEMPTED IN ARTICLE 411 OR ANNEX 401, THERE HAS BEEN NO FURTHER PRODUCTION OR ANY OTHER OPERATION OUTSIDE THE TERRITORIES OF THE PARTIES; AND

• THIS CERTIFICATE CONSISTS OF [   ] PAGES, INCLUDING ALL ATTACHMENTS.

11.	11a. AUTHORIZED SIGNATURE:	11b. COMPANY:	
	11c. NAME *(Print or Type)*:	11d. TITLE:	
	11e. DATE *(DD/MM/YY)*	11f. TELEPHONE ▷ NUMBER *(Voice)*	*(Facsimile)*

Customs Form 434 (121793)

NORTH AMERICAN FREE TRADE AGREEMENT CERTIFICATE OF ORIGIN INSTRUCTIONS

For purposes of obtaining preferential tariff treatment, this document must be completed legibly and in full by the exporter and be in the possession of the importer at the time the declaration is made. This document may also be completed voluntarily by the producer for use by the exporter. Please print or type:

FIELD 1: State the full legal name, address (including country) and legal tax identification number of the exporter. Legal taxation number is: in Canada, employer number or importer/exporter number assigned by Revenue Canada; in Mexico, federal taxpayer's registry number (RFC); and in the United States, employer's identification number or Social Security number.

FIELD 2: Complete field if the Certificate covers multiple shipments of identical goods as described in Field #5 that are imported into a NAFTA country for a specified period of up to one year (the blanket period). "FROM" is the date upon which the Certificate becomes applicable to the good covered by the blanket Certificate (it may be prior to the date of signing this Certificate). "TO" is the date upon which the blanket period expires. The importation of a good for which preferential treatment is claimed based on this Certificate must occur between these dates.

FIELD 3: State the full legal name, address (including country) and legal tax identification number, as defined in Field #1, of the producer. If more than one producer's good is included on the Certificate, attach a list of the additional producers, including the legal name, address (including country) and legal tax identification number, cross referenced to the good described in Field #5. If you wish this information to be confidential, it is acceptable to state "Available to Customs upon request". If the producer and the exporter are the same, complete field with "SAME". If the producer is unknown, it is acceptable to state "UNKNOWN".

FIELD 4: State the full legal name, address (including country) and legal tax identification number, as defined in Field #1, of the importer. If the importer is not known, state "UNKNOWN"; if multiple importers, state "VARIOUS".

FIELD 5: Provide a full description of each good. The description should be sufficient to relate it to the invoice description and to the Harmonized System (H.S.) description of the good. If the Certificate covers a single shipment of a good, include the invoice number as shown on the commercial invoice. If not known, indicate another unique reference number, such as the shipping order number.

FIELD 6: For each good described in Field #5, identify the H.S. tariff classification to six digits. If the good is subject to a specific rule of origin in Annex 401 that requires eight digits, identify to eight digits, using the H.S. tariff classification of the country into whose territory the good is imported.

FIELD 7: For each good described in Field #5, state which criterion (A through F) is applicable. The rules of origin are contained in Chapter Four and Annex 401. Additional rules are described in Annex 703.2 (certain agricultural goods), Annex 300-B, Appendix 6 (certain textile goods) and Annex 308.1 (certain automatic data processing goods and their parts). **NOTE: In order to be entitled to preferential tariff treatment, each good must meet at least one of the criteria below.**

Preference Criteria

A The good is "wholly obtained or produced entirely" in the territory of one or more of the NAFTA countries as referenced in Article 415. **NOTE: The purchase of a good in the territory does not necessarily render it "wholly obtained or produced".** If the good is an agricultural good, see also criterion F and Annex 703.2. *(Reference: Article 401(a) and 415)*

B The good is produced entirely in the territory of one or more of the NAFTA countries and satisfies the specific rule of origin, set out in Annex 401, that applies to its tariff classification. The rule may include a tariff classification change, regional value-content requirement, or a combination thereof. The good must also satisfy all other applicable requirements of Chapter Four. If the good is an agricultural good, see also criterion F and Annex 703.2. *(Reference: Article 401(b))*

C The good is produced entirely in the territory of one or more of the NAFTA countries exclusively from originating materials. Under this criterion, one or more of the materials may not fall within the definition of "wholly produced or obtained", as set out in Article 415. All materials used in the production of the good must qualify as "originating" by meeting the rules of Article 401 (a) through (d). If the good is an agricultural good, see also criterion F and Annex 703.2. *(Reference: Article 401 (c))*

D Goods are produced in the territory of one or more of the NAFTA countries but do not meet the applicable rule of origin, set out in Annex 401, because certain non-originating materials do not undergo the required change in tariff classification. The goods do nonetheless meet the regional value-content requirement specified in Article 401 (d). This criterion is limited to the following two circumstances:

1. The good was imported into the territory of a NAFTA country in an unassembled or disassembled form but was classified as an assembled good, pursuant to H.S. General Rule of Interpretation 2(a), or

2. The good incorporated one or more non-originating materials, provided for as parts under the H.S., which could not undergo a change in tariff classification because the heading provided for both the good and its parts and was not further subdivided into subheadings, or the subheading provided for both the good and its parts and was not further subdivided.

NOTE: This criterion does not apply to Chapters 61 through 63 of the H.S. *(Reference: Article 401 (d))*

E Certain automatic data processing goods and their parts, specified in Annex 308.1, that do not originate in the territory are considered originating upon importation into the territory of a NAFTA country from the territory of another NAFTA country when the most-favored-nation tariff rate of the good conforms to the rate established in Annex 308.1 and is common to all NAFTA countries. *(Reference: Annex 308.1)*

F The good is an originating agricultural good under preference criterion A, B or C above and is not subject to a quantitative restriction in the importing NAFTA country because it is a "qualifying good" as defined in Annex 703.2, Section A or B (please specify). A good listed in Appendix 703.2B.7 is also exempt from quantitative restrictions and is eligible for NAFTA preferential tariff treatment if it meets the definition of "qualifying good" in Section A of Annex 703.2. **NOTE 1: This criterion does not apply to goods that wholly originate in Canada or the United States and are imported into either country. NOTE 2: A tariff rate quota is not a quantitative restriction.**

FIELD 8: For each good described in Field #5, state "YES" if you are the producer of the good. If you are not the producer of the good, state "NO" followed by (1), (2), or (3), depending on whether this certificate was based upon: (1) your knowledge of whether the good qualifies as an originating good; (2) your reliance on the producer's written representation (other than a Certificate of Origin) that the good qualifies as an originating good; or (3) a completed and signed Certificate for the good, voluntarily provided to the exporter by the producer.

FIELD 9: For each good described in Field #5, where the good is subject to a regional value content (RVC) requirement, indicate "NC" if the RVC is calculated according to the net cost method; otherwise, indicate "NO". If the RVC is calculated over a period of time, further identify the beginning and ending dates (DD/MM/YY) of that period. *(Reference: Articles 402.1, 402.5)*

FIELD 10: Identify the name of the country ("MX" or "US" for agricultural and textile goods exported to Canada; "US" or "CA" for all goods exported to Mexico; or "CA" or "MX" for all goods exported to the United States) to which the preferential rate of customs duty applies, as set out in Annex 302.2, in accordance with the Marking Rules or in each party's schedule of tariff elimination.

For all other originating goods exported to Canada, indicate appropriately "MX" or "US" if the goods originate in that NAFTA country, within the meaning of the NAFTA Rules of Origin Regulations, and any subsequent processing in the other NAFTA country does not increase the transaction value of the goods by more than seven percent; otherwise indicate "JNT" for joint production. *(Reference: Annex 302.2)*

FIELD 11: This field must be completed, signed and dated by the exporter. When the Certificate is completed by the producer for use by the exporter, it must be completed, signed and dated by the producer. The date must be the date the Certificate was completed and signed.

Customs Form 434 (121793) (Back)

Form 10.10   Specific contract for direct identification drawback.

GSP DECLARATION

I, _____, hereby declare that the articles described below were produced or manufactured in _____ by means of processing operations performed in that country as set forth below and were also subjected to processing operations in the other country or countries that are members of the same association of countries as set forth below and incorporate materials produced in the country named above or in any other country or countries that are members of the same association as set forth below:

Number and Date of Invoices	Description of Articles and Quantity	Processing Operations Performed on Articles		Materials Produced in a Beneficiary Developing Country or Member of the Same Association	
		Description of Processing Operations and Country of Processing	Direct Costs of Processing Operations	Description of Material, Production Process, and Country of Production	Cost or Value of Material

Date: _____   Address: _____
Signature: _____   Title: _____

All import and export shipments should be insured. The risk of theft, damage, or loss increases as goods are exposed to extensive lifting, loading, moving, and bad weather. Exported goods often require several modes of transport, including ocean vessels, airplanes, inland barges, railroads, and trucks. Each time the goods are transferred, the risks increase.

Once cargo enters the United States, the U.S. Customs Service requires importers to guarantee their compliance with all laws and regulations relating to imports; this guarantee is made using a customs bond.

This chapter discusses various insurance and bonding issues that importers and exporters must address. Topics covered include types of insurance, levels of coverage, methods of insuring goods, filing insurance claims, types of customs bonds, and liability for discrepancies between the customs bond and the insurance.

11.1   LIABILITY

One of the most important issues in insurance is determining the liability of the buyer or seller of the goods (the shipper) as against the liability of the carrier of the goods. As a general rule, the liability of most carriers is limited, either by law or tariff requirements. Therefore, shippers should never rely on the carrier to pay for losses and damages that occur in transit. In most cases, the carrier's liability is rarely more than a fraction of the actual value of the shipment. Because of these strict limits, cargo insurance is the only effective means of insuring export shipments.

11.1.1   Ocean and Air Carriers' Limits of Liability

For ocean carriers, liability limits are set by the Carriage of Goods by Sea Act. The law covers goods moving in or out of U.S. ports by vessel. In general, ocean carriers are liable for damages up to $500 per package. However, shippers should note that liability limits vary throughout the world. For instance, goods shipped under bills of lading originating in Europe or Africa are subject to limits set forth by the Hague/Visby amendments.

Liability limits for domestic air carriers are also governed by U.S. law and average $0.50 per pound of cargo. International limits are governed by the Warsaw Convention and average $9.07 per pound.

11.1.2   Truckers' Limits of Liability

Liability limits differ among U.S. truckers. For instance, if the hauler is an Interstate Commerce Commission (ICC) carrier, liability is for the full value of goods. However, shippers should be aware that limits described in a separate contract or arrangement can supersede ICC limits. If the trucker is a local carrier, ICC's limits do not apply; the industry standard for liability is $0.50 per pound, or $50 per package.

Special conditions exist under which the carrier is not subject to any set limits. For instance, if the truck is carrying the goods as an extension of an international shipment, state and interstate commerce regulations do not apply and the carriers can set their own liability limits.

11.1.3 *General Average*

General average (GA) is a maritime law provision that states that all parties to an oceangoing shipment share in liability in the event of loss or damage. In maritime trade, all parties to a voyage have an interest in its safe completion; therefore all parties to the general average share proportionately in the overall loss. This includes shippers whose cargo arrived in sound condition. Without insurance coverage, the shipper will be required to post cash collateral with the vessel owners to obtain release of cargo.

Three conditions must be met for general average liability to be found:

- There must be an impending peril.
- There must be a sacrifice.
- Cargo must be saved.

EXAMPLE

A ship crossing the North Atlantic in winter suffers damage and begins taking on water. To balance the ship and avoid capsizing, the captain of the vessel decides to jettison cargo. The ship then sails to a safe harbor.

In this example, the impending peril is the potential of capsizing; the sacrifice is the lost cargo; the savings are the ship and the safe arrival of the balance of the cargo at a harbor.

The shipping line can also make a general average declaration if:

- The ship requires repairs while in an unscheduled port.
- Towing charges are incurred for transit to a port for repair.

All of the major types of cargo insurance coverage include general average coverage. General average coverage can also be purchased separately.

11.2 COVERAGE LEVELS

There are three basic types of cargo insurance coverage. They are classified according to the level of risk to the merchandise. **Note.** Specific clauses and endorsements can be used to tailor a policy to a specific shipment. (See section 11.4 for details.) The three types of risk levels for cargo insurance are:

- All-risk coverage
- Free of particular average (FPA) coverage
- With average (WA) coverage

Appendix A includes a chart detailing the losses covered under each of the three types of coverage levels.

11.2.1 All-Risk Coverage

All-risk coverage is the broadest and most complete form of coverage. New merchandise that has been properly packed and is not susceptible to special risks or conditions is generally shipped under this type of policy. All-risk policies usually include:

1. Total and partial loss
2. Total and partial damage
3. General average perils

All-Risk Exclusions

All-risk policies cover losses due to damage from most external causes. However, there are exemptions from coverage:

- If the cargo is abandoned or rejected by customs or other government agencies, the insurance company is not liable.
- If the insured party fails to pay his or her account or has losses in excess of the policy limit, the claim would likely be rejected.
- Most policies contain time limits. Generally, losses incurred at the port city more than fifteen days after the cargo is discharged or losses incurred inland more than thirty days after discharge are not covered.

Other exceptions include:

- *Improper packing.* Proper packing is generally defined as that which can withstand frequent handling or jarring, extremes of weather and temperature, and that which discourages theft or tampering.
- *Goods accompanied by an on-deck bill of lading.* Goods should always be shipped with an underdeck or optional bill of lading.
- *Losses incurred on an oceangoing barge* (unless specifically covered in the policy).
- *Inherent vice.* This is defined as infestation of goods, latent defects of goods, or failure of goods to perform intended functions.
- *Losses due to strikes, riots, or war.*

11.2.2 Free of Particular Average (FPA) Coverage

Free of particular average policies are the lowest available level of coverage. The term itself originally implied that partial losses were not covered. However, most FPA policies have been amended to include payment for many partial losses.

Partial Payments Under FPA (By Ocean)

If the goods are being shipped by ocean carrier, partial losses are covered for:

* Stranding
* Sinking
* Burning
* Collisions

Partial Payments Under FPA (By Air)

If the goods are being shipped by aircraft, partial losses are covered for:

* Fire on board the aircraft
* Lightning strikes
* Air crash or collision

Total Losses Under FPA

Total loss coverage under an FPA policy includes "common hazards to the seas," such as:

* Pirates or assailing thieves
* Land-based catastrophes (e.g., train derailment, overturning trucks, tornadoes, or collapse of docks)

Types of Goods Insured Under FPA

Types of goods commonly insured under FPA include:

* Used merchandise
* Goods shipped under an on-deck bill of lading
* Bagged goods
* Bulked goods

11.2.3 *With Average (WA) Coverage*

The WA policy is similar to an FPA policy in that it covers total and partial loss or damage from named perils. However, coverage is extended to:

* Heavy weather damages
* Sea water damage caused by heavy weather

11.3 CALCULATING INSURANCE PREMIUMS

In many cases, shippers choose coverage based on financial factors (i.e., the cost of insurance premiums). Factors that go into calculating the insurance premium include:

* The insured value of the goods plus associated costs
* Cargo rate costs
* War premiums

The following sections discuss factors used to calculate the insurance premium.

11.3.1 Determining the Insured Value

The first step in determining the insurance premium is to calculate the insured value of the goods. This is the amount that the insured party receives from the insurer in the event of a loss, minus any applicable deductibles or other special considerations. That figure is usually determined by the formula:

> a + b + (10 percent of a and b)
> where:
> a = invoice value
> b = freight

This is commonly known as "CIF plus 10 percent," or cost, insurance, and freight plus 10 percent. The insurance is included in the formula because banks may require that the insurance premium itself be insured. Also, the insurance premium is part of the cost of the goods.

There are two methods for calculating insured value: a long version, which is generally used when letters of credit are the chosen method of payment, and a short version, which is used in all other situations. (See Forms 11.01 and 11.02 for insured value worksheets for these two calculation methods.)

11.3.2 Insurance Rates

The type of commodity and mode of transport are important considerations in determining the rate of insurance. Other factors include:

* Packaging
* Originating and destination points
* Total dollar amount of all shipments over one year
* Frequency and severity of losses

Both importers and exporters are advised always to seek the advice of a professional insurance broker to determine the appropriate type of insurance package.

11.4 CLAUSES AND ENDORSEMENTS

Various clauses and endorsements are used to customize insurance policies. Many of these are of great importance to the shipper and, if included in the policy, can save considerable time and money in the event of loss or damage.

11.4.1   The Warehouse-to-Warehouse Clause

A warehouse-to-warehouse clause covers the goods from the time they leave the place of origin; coverage continues through the ordinary course of transit to the final destination. It remains in force for fifteen days after the discharge of the goods, or thirty days if the final destination is beyond the port of discharge. Goods are covered:

* From the origination factory or warehouse to the vessel or aircraft (called pre-carriage)
* Throughout the international voyage (called main carriage)
* To the destination point (called on-carriage)

11.4.2   The Sue and Labor Clause

In the event of damage or loss, an exporter may be able to "sue, labor, or travel for the defense, safeguard, and recovery of the damaged goods without prejudice to the insurance." In other words, the owner of the damaged goods needs to take steps to prevent further damage to the goods and cannot be penalized by the insurance company for doing so. The shipper should make sure that the costs incurred in taking these steps will be paid for by the insurance company. The steps include:

1. Separating wet goods from dry goods
2. Repacking to prevent further loss
3. Having goods surveyed by a licensed surveyor
4. Moving goods to a secure location

11.4.3   The Shore Clause

Most cargo policies cover the basic hazards of sea and air. In addition, many policies include a shore clause, which pays partial or total losses for accidents occurring on land, such as the collision of a truck or derailment of a train. Natural disasters such as hurricanes, earthquakes, floods, lightning, or cyclones may also be covered. Other shore hazards include:

* Any accident involving a vehicle transporting the goods (carrying conveyance)
* Fire involving the conveyance
* Sprinkler leakage
* Collapse of docks or wharves

11.4.4   The Marine Extension Clause

This clause extends coverage to other modes of transport when the primary mode of transport is interrupted or altered. Generally, no additional charges are incurred if the exporter has no knowledge or control over the changes. However, the insurance company must be notified in writing as soon as the change is known.

11.4.5   The South American Clause

Most shipments to South America are subject to a special clause. Under the typical policy, goods are covered "during willful storage and/or delays after discharge at the final destination." However, coverage generally terminates sixty days after final discharge of the goods. If a South American clause is included in a policy, it overrides the warehouse-to-warehouse clause.

11.4.6   Errors and Omissions Clause

This clause provides coverage for errors, omissions, or delays in reporting shipments for premium purposes, provided they are unintentional in nature. Coverage is also provided for unintentional mistakes in the description of goods and naming of the vessel or airline.

If using a customs broker or freight forwarder, the shipper should make sure that the broker or forwarder is covered by professional liability insurance. This type of insurance protects the shipper from other liabilities incurred by the broker or forwarder. One such liability would be exceeding policy limits without authority from the insurance company.

11.4.7   Open Cargo Policy

An open cargo policy can be used by an importer, exporter, or freight forwarder to cover a number of shipments. For instance, a freight forwarder can ship for a dozen different exporters under one policy, on a single carrier. The policy is continuous in nature until it is canceled by the policy holder or the insurance company. Shipments under an open cargo policy generally are "all risk." This type of policy benefits small businesses, because a small exporter usually does not have the buying power to negotiate lower premium rates. It also benefits the forwarder, because the forwarder's policy now has the advantage of support from numerous shippers.

Note. If shipping with a forwarder under an open cargo policy, the exporter must make sure that liability limits are high enough to cover all shipments under that policy. For instance, if an exporter ships a piece of machinery worth $1 million by ocean freight, or computer components by air freight, the exporter must ask the forwarder what the liability limits are in the open cargo policy and whether all of the other export shipments combined under the policy exceed those limits. (This is known as the conveyance and connection conveyance clause.)

Geographical limits and conveyance and connection conveyances are two types of clauses commonly found in open cargo policies.

Geographical Limits

The open cargo policy defines geographical limits within which the goods can be insured. These are usually stated as:

- World to world
- United States to world
- World to United States

Insurers can deny coverage to certain restricted countries or to countries considered exceptionally hazardous.

Conveyance and Connection Conveyance Clauses

Most policies limit the amount an insurer pays for any single loss on a sea or air shipment. For example, a forwarder may be shipping for ten different exporters on one carrier. The conveyance clause limits the amount of coverage on that one carrier, even if the combined value of the shipments exceeds the limit. That is why it is crucial for the exporter to ascertain the limits of a freight forwarder's open cargo policy and determine if the limit is high enough to cover all goods shipped under that policy. Limits vary and are usually stated as follows:

- Any one ocean conveyance: $500,000
- Any one air conveyance: $250,000
- Any one on-deck shipment: $10,000
- Parcel post: $1,000

Inland barges are excluded from most policies because they pose high risks. In addition, an ocean vessel must meet three requirements to qualify for coverage. It must be:

1. Seaworthy
2. Not more than fifteen to twenty years old
3. Not less than 1,000 net tons

Vessels not meeting these criteria may require additional premiums.

Similarly, air carriers must be airworthy and maintain regularly scheduled flights. Air charters and small private aircraft usually require approval from the insurance company and may be subject to additional premiums. In addition, goods with special conditions usually require a deductible.

11.5   METHODS OF INSURING GOODS

11.5.1   *The Certificate of Insurance*

The certificate of insurance is a negotiable document used to cover a single shipment. It constitutes a complete policy unto itself.

The certificate of insurance is generally used on export shipments; in addition, banks often require a certificate as proof of insurance before payment is made under a letter of credit. (For more information on certificates of insurance as they relate to letters of credit, see section 5.5.6.)

See Form 11.03 for a sample certificate of insurance.

11.5.2 *Stamped Copy of Airway or Ocean Bill of Lading*

The easiest method of insuring goods is to use Customs Form 7501 and an airway or ocean bill of lading. This method is almost always used for imported goods. The bills must be filled out accurately and completely. Importers are advised to have a customs broker or insurance agent assist them in completing the bill of lading.

11.5.3 *Multiple Declaration Form*

The Multiple Declaration Form is generally used for imported goods. It allows the importer to report multiple shipments for a given period of time. This form is relatively simple to complete and is considered a nonnegotiable instrument.

11.6 FILING INSURANCE CLAIMS

In the event of loss or damage to goods during shipment, the importer or exporter is likely to file a claim against the carrier. To preserve the right to file such a claim and because damages and losses are not always evident, an exporter or importer should have all packages inspected and photos taken as soon as the shipment is received. Specifically, the following actions should be taken:

1. The condition of the goods upon delivery should be documented on the delivery receipt, including all losses or damages existing at the time of delivery. Descriptions of the condition of the shipment should be accurate and complete. A copy of the delivery receipt should always be maintained.
2. An insurance company representative or, if the shipment is abroad, a foreign surveying agent should be notified. These parties may suggest that an independent surveyor inspect the goods.
3. A formal claim should be filed against the carrier. If more than one carrier is involved, a separate claim may have to be filed against each.
4. The carrier should be requested to inspect the damages to support the insurance claim.

When submitting a claim to an insurance company, an importer or exporter should always include certified copies of the bill of lading and commercial invoice. Paid freight bills and packing lists should be submitted to support the claim, as well as the following documents, where appropriate:

- Copies of all delivery receipts, with descriptions of losses or damages
- If the insured party is making a nondelivery claim, written confirmation by the carrier as to the nondelivery of the shipment

- Copies of written claims against all other carriers involved in the claim
- The insured party's own statement and all relevant correspondence
- Any repair bills
- An original copy of survey report, if it has not already been submitted by the surveyor
- An original and duplicate of a Special Cargo Policy, Certificate of Insurance, or other policy properly endorsed by the payee
- A Duty Consumption Entry Report and Customs Form 5931

Time Limits for Filing a Notice of Claim

Insured exporters and importers who have sustained losses need to file prompt notice of any claim that is to be brought against a carrier. Failure to file within the prescribed time limits can jeopardize the claim. The following is a list of claim deadlines according to carrier:

- *Ocean carriers.* A notice of claim must be sent to the ocean carrier as soon as loss or damage is observed. A claim must be filed within one year after the date of delivery.
- *ICC rail and truck carriers.* For interstate rail and truck carriers, a claim must be filed within nine months after the date of delivery.
- *Local truck carriers.* Notice of claim must be filed within four months after the date of delivery.
- *Air carriers.* Claims for pilferage and damage must be filed within seven days after the date of delivery. Claims for nondelivery must be filed within 120 days after the merchandise was to be delivered.

See Form 11.04 for a sample notice of claim letter.

11.7 CUSTOMS BONDS

11.7.1 Introduction

Customs regulations require that a bond, or suitable cash deposit, be filed with each formal entry to guarantee payment of any duties, taxes, fines, or penalties that may accrue upon importation. Essentially, customs bonds are a guarantee from the surety company to the U.S. government that the importer agrees to abide by all laws and regulations regarding imports into the United States.

In bonding the importer, the surety company assumes the same duties and responsibilities as the importer. When the importer cannot make the required payments to the U.S. government, the surety company must do so. The bond does not relieve the importer of any obligations, and the surety company has the right to recover from the importer all payments made to the government.

A formal Customs entry is required for any importation of foreign origin valued in excess of $1,250 and for returned American goods valued in excess of

$10,000. There are some exceptions, the most notable being textiles, which require a formal entry for any shipment valued over $250.

See Form 11.05 for a sample customs bond.

A bond is not an insurance policy. It can best be described as a collection method of last resort. If the importer is unable to pay customs duties, the surety company must make the payment. If an importer is proactive in making sure that Customs regulations are followed accurately and completely, and employs procedures such as binding rulings (see section 10.4), he or she is generally considered a good risk and should not have problems bonding import shipments.

First-time importers should establish a clean track record right from the start. Mistakes with regard to marking and country-of-origin labeling, for instance, can be avoided with up-front research and consultation with import professionals. Preemptive actions can help ensure a successful application for bonding.

11.7.2 Types of Bonds

Customs bonds are defined by surety companies according to their designated activity codes. Ten different activity codes are used. Most types of bonds are rarely used or seen by importers. Three types of bonds are discussed in this section. It is the responsibility of the importer, working with a customs broker, attorney, or other import professional, to decide on the best method of bonding imported goods.

Activity 1: Bond for an Importer or Broker

These are by far the most frequently used customs bonds. They cover a number of different functions, including temporary importations and entries for immediate delivery. Most consumer products are covered under this type of bond. When goods are entered or removed from bonded warehouses, Activity 1 bonds are used.

There are two basic types of Activity 1 customs bonds:

⊛ Single-entry bonds
⊛ Continuous transaction bonds

Single-entry and continuous bonds are discussed in more detail later in this chapter.

Activity 1A: Bond for Drawback Payment Refunds

Drawback bonds come in two types. Accelerated drawback bonds, for example, allow the importer to collect a refund of customs duties paid before Customs makes an actual determination on the claim.

Under same-condition drawback bonds, importers can claim a refund for duties paid that are eligible for same condition drawback.

See section 10.3 for more information on duty drawback and filing drawback claims.

Activity 2: Custodian of Bonded Merchandise

These bonds cover merchandise that is stored in bonded warehouses and container freight stations. Carriers moving goods within the port district or between cities and states operate under Activity 2 bonds.

Activity 3: International Carrier

International carrier bonds involve clearance or entry of vessels or aircraft arriving from outside the United States.

11.7.3 Single-Entry Bonds

A single-entry bond covers individual import shipments. These bonds are appropriate for small businesses that import inexpensive goods infrequently.

Determining the Single-Entry Bond Amount

The amount that is required to be posted for a single-entry bond depends on the type of merchandise that is imported. See Table 2 for a chart of bond amounts.
Note. Chapter 9 on "Classification and Valuation" covers additional information for determining the value of the imported merchandise.
Once the amount of the bond has been determined, the rate of the bond can be calculated.

Table 2. Bond amounts for single transaction bonds.

Type of Bond Amount Required by U.S. Customs*	
Basic single entry (general goods)	Value + Duty
Entries requiring quota or visa	3% Value
Automobiles (nonconforming)	3% Value**
Entries requiring other federal regulatory compliance	3% Value
Temporary importations	2% Duty
Temporary importations of samples and professional equipment	110% of Duties
Goods unconditionally free of duties	10% of Value
Anti-dumping and countervailing duties	Determined by Customs

*Bond amounts required by U.S. Customs may be subject to change by customs directive or may vary from port to port at the discretion of the district director of customs.
**Bonds for nonconforming automobiles are sometimes valued at amounts other than 3% value. Check with the local Customs district.

Determining Single-Entry Bond Rates

The rate is the amount that the importer is charged by the surety company for the bond. Rates depend largely on the type of merchandise being imported and the amount of the bond.

Bond rates are calculated on a per $1,000 basis. As an example, for a single transaction bond written for an entry of imported, nonrestricted general merchandise, the rate is generally between $1 and $5 per $1,000 of the total bond amount.

EXAMPLE

Consider the following situation: If the bond amount required by Customs equals $45,000, and the rate charged by the bond company is $2.50 per $1,000, then the premium is calculated as follows:

$$\$45,000 \div \$1,000 = 45$$
$$45 \times \$2.50 = \$111.50 \text{ premium}$$

Note. Some goods are considered to be unconditionally free merchandise. In those cases, Customs requires no duty charges under certain conditions, and the single bond amount may be as low as 10 percent of the entered value.

Parties Issuing Single-Entry Bonds

Single-entry bonds are almost exclusively issued through customs brokers on behalf of surety companies. The surety company provides the customs broker with a number of bonds, called U.S. Customs Form 301, for both single entry and continuous bonds. The broker in turn issues the bond to the importer. The broker can issue the bond if the bond does not exceed the broker's own limits of liability. If the shipment is extremely low risk and the broker has a good working relationship with the importer, the broker may in some instances cover the shipment under its own continuous bond.

Some imported goods fall under the purview of other government agencies. For instance, food products imported into the United States are the responsibility of the Food and Drug Administration (FDA) and require at least double the amount required for bonds covering general shipments.

Importers generally do not apply to Customs for single-entry bonds. In addition, many surety companies will not work directly with importers, preferring to work through customs brokers. Therefore, it is imperative that importers have a good working relationship with a reliable and reputable customs broker.

Applying for Single-Entry Bonds

Importers are required to make an application and undergo a credit check by the insurance company issuing the single entry bond. To determine whether an importer qualifies for bonding, the surety company will request to see a financial statement and ask for the year of incorporation of the importing company. It may also ask for:

- A Dun and Bradstreet listing.
- A tax identification number. This number becomes the importer's number of record for Customs purposes. It allows the surety company to verify whether it has had any previous experience with the importer.

In some instances, a broker can issue a bond to an exporter without having to seek specific approval from the surety company. However, if the importer has not previously paid any customs duties or if foreign principals are involved, prior approval from the surety company is required.

Prior approval is also required if there are:

- Bankruptcy or insolvency proceedings involving the importer
- Entries in which the issuing customs broker is not involved
- Bonds covering importations of automobiles
- Antidumping or countervailing duty disputes

11.7.4 *Continuous Bonds*

A continuous bond covers all import transactions made by an importer for a period of one year. All U.S. ports are usually allowed as ports of entry. The bond continues into succeeding years as long as the annual premium is paid.

Determining Continuous Transaction Bond Amounts

A continuous transaction bond is always written for at least $50,000. Continuous transaction bond amounts are generally 10 percent of the annual estimated duties for the next calendar year, rounded up to the nearest $10,000. The figure is often based on actual duties paid for the previous calendar year. If the amount exceeds $1 million, the amount is rounded up to the nearest $100,000.

If the imported goods are conditionally free of duty, the bond amount is calculated at 10 percent of what the duties would have been if the goods were subject to duties.

If the imported goods are unconditionally free of duty, the bond amount is calculated by multiplying the annual estimated import values by 0.5 percent (0.05).

Determining Continuous Transaction Bond Rates

The following is an example of how one surety company determines continuous transaction bond rates. Rates vary between companies, but the formula is the same.

EXAMPLE

If the bond amount required by Customs equals $50,000, and the rate charged by the bond company is $8.00 per $1,000, then:

$$\$50,000 \div \$1,000 = 50$$
$$50 \times \$8.00 = \$400 \text{ premium}$$

Applying for Continuous Transaction Bonds

Continuous transaction bonds are always underwritten by a surety company. It is much harder for an importer to get approval for a continuous transaction bond than for a single-entry bond.

If an importer determines that a continuous bond is the most cost-effective bonding method, based on recommendations from customs brokers and other import professionals, an application letter is sent to the surety company. If the surety company approves the bond, it sends the bond and application letter to Customs. The bond generally becomes effective ten days after receipt by Customs. See Form 11.06 for a sample application for continuous bond.

In addition to an audited financial statement, a surety company typically requests the following information before issuing a continuous bond:

* A credit report
* An interview with a customs attorney working with the importer

The bonding company may also want to see the financial records of the stockholder or stockholders of the importing corporation. In some cases, the importer is required to have personal assets sufficient to cover the obligations under the bond. Cash verifications or collateral may be required when foreign principals or any special risks are involved. Certain classes of goods, such as foreign automobiles not in compliance with U.S. emissions or safety standards, also require collateral prior to entry.

Importers can save money using continuous transaction bonds because the value and number of import transactions increase. For instance, if a machine is imported from Germany at a cost of $50,000 with no special restrictions, and the duty is three percent, the total bond amount would be $51,500. If the single-entry bond rate is $3 per $1,000, the premium for that bond would be $154.50. If the machines are imported at a rate of one per month, the importer would pay $18,000 in duties over the course of the year on $600,000 in value. If each of the shipments were single entry, total bond payments would be $1,854 for the year. If the rate for a continuous transaction bond is $8 per $1,000 on a minimum bond of $50,000 (10 percent of duties paid in calendar year is $1,800), the importer would pay $400 for all twelve importations.

Exporters should note that some of the cost savings attributable to continuous bonds can be outweighed by process and application fees, depending on the complexity and work involved. In addition, it is much easier to bond a shipment under a single-entry bond. Importers should consider their long-range plans and consult with import professionals before deciding which type of bonding to use.

11.7.5 Temporary Import Bonds

Articles imported temporarily for certain purposes may enter the United States duty free under a temporary import bond. Temporary import bonds are discussed in section 10.7.

11.7.6 Customs Bond Violations: Liquidated Damage Claims

If Customs or another regulatory agency determines that an import shipment violates the terms of the entry bond, it issues Customs Form 5955A, Notice of Penalty or Liquidated Damages.

Failure to properly mark the goods is a common reason for issuance of this notice. The importer usually has sixty days to respond to the notice. If the problem is corrected within the sixty-day period, Customs will often reduce or cancel the damage charges. If the problem is not resolved in the sixty-day period, the importer may be placed on sanction, which means that his or her immediate delivery privileges are revoked and that the entry may be rejected.

See Form 11.07 for a sample notice of penalty.

Summary of Key Points Raised in This Chapter

As a general rule, a carrier's liability for damage to shipments is limited; therefore, importers and exporters should insure all shipments.

General average is a maritime law provision under which all parties to an ocean-going shipment share in liability in the event of loss or damage.

There are three basic types of coverage for ocean cargo: all risk, free of particular average (FPA), and with average (WA).

All-risk insurance covers total and partial losses, total and partial damages, and general average perils.

Insured value is determined by adding the invoice value of the goods to freight costs and adding 10 percent. This is known as "CIF plus 10 percent."

There are certain clauses and endorsements that can be used to customize insurance policies and provide additional coverage.

To preserve the right to file an insurance claim, all packages and shipments should be photographed and thoroughly inspected for damage.

A customs bond is a guarantee from a surety company to the U.S. government that an importer agrees to abide by all laws and regulations.

A customs bond (or suitable cash deposit) is required of every import.

Customs bonds are available for individual shipments (single-entry bonds) or for a series of shipments over the course of a year (continuous bonds).

Failure to comply with customs laws is a violation of the terms of an entry bond and can subject the importer to loss of delivery privileges.

For Additional Information

For additional information on topics discussed in this chapter, please refer to the following publications:

Roanoke Companies, *Cargo Insurance Basics for the Transportation Industry* (1993).
Roanoke Companies, *Customs Bond Guide* (1994).
Frank Reynolds, "Marine Cargo Insurance," *Export Observer* (June 1994), pp. 8–9.

Appendix A   Comparison of Partial Losses Recoverable

	Type of Insurance Coverage		
Loss Caused or Resulting From	*FPA*	*With Average*	*All Risks*
Stranding	Yes	Yes	Yes
Sinking	Yes	Yes	Yes
Burning	Yes	Yes	Yes
Collision	Yes	Yes	Yes
Faults or error in management of vessel	Yes	Yes	Yes
Bursting of boilers	Yes	Yes	Yes
Latent defects in hull or machinery	Yes	Yes	Yes
Explosions	Yes	Yes	Yes
Heavy weather	No	Yes	Yes
Seawater as a result of heavy weather	No	Yes	Yes
Jettison	No	Yes	Yes
Freshwater	No	No	Yes
Ship's sweat	No	No	Yes
Condensation	No	No	Yes
Steam	No	No	Yes
Improper stowage by carrier	No	No	Yes
Hook damage, mud, and grease	No	No	Yes
Theft of an entire shipping package	No	No	Yes
Nondelivery of an entire shipping package	No	No	Yes
Pilferage	No	No	Yes
Leakage	No	No	Yes
Breakage	No	No	Yes

Form 11.01   Insured value worksheet (short form).

Insured Value Worksheet for General Merchandise

Invoice Value	_____
Packing	+_____
Consulate and Forwarding Fees	+_____
TOTAL COSTS	_____
Freight	+_____
Subtotal	_____
Policy Advance (10% of subtotal)	+_____
VALUE TO INSURE	_____

Form 11.02   Insured value worksheet (long form).

1. **Calculate Costs and Freight:**

Invoice Value	_____
Packing and Other Costs	+ _____
Total Costs	= _____
Freight	+ _____
Total Costs + Freight	= _____

2. **Add Marine and War Rates:**

Marine Rate	_____
War Rate	+ _____
TOTAL	= _____

Multiply Rate Times Costs:

   _____ × _____ = _____

Add Step 3 Total to Step 1 Total Costs and Freight:

Cost + Freight	_____
Insurance	+ _____
Total CIF	= _____

5. **Multiply CIF Value Times 1.10 to Get CIF + 10%:**

   _____ × _____ = _____

Form 11.03   Certificate of insurance.

CERTIFICATE OF INSURANCE
GUIDE TO COMPLETION

Please Refer to the Form on the Following Page

1. Enter the insured value (C.I.F. + 10%). [See "Determining The Insured Value" for details.]

2. Enter your reference number for billing purposes.

3. Enter today's date or shipping date.

4. Enter your Open Policy number. (Not applicable to Lloyd's form.)

5. Enter the name of your company. (Not applicable to Lloyd's form.)

6. Enter the name of the overseas vessel (or airline) and the voyage number or airway bill number.

7. Enter a description of the merchandise and total number of packages.

8. Enter the name of the place where inland transportation commences. (Example: Chicago via New York.)

9. Enter the name of the place of ultimate destination where consignee takes delivery.

10. Show in script the amount shown in step "1" above.

11. Enter name of person to receive payment in the event of loss. Except in instances where a letter of credit is involved, it will be the shipper or the consignee.

12. Enter the marks that appear on the outside of the package and if each is separately numbered, what they are. In the event of potential claim, this enables the marine surveyor to identify the insured shipment and verify whether all packages have been delivered.

13. Enter any special terms and conditions such as deductibles, exclusions, restricted FPA conditions, required letter of credit wording, etc.

14. Have a responsible person sign the original and the duplicate.

Form 11.04   Letter of claim to carrier.

[Date]

[Name and Address of Carrier]

RE: M/V *[Vessel name]* or Airline
Arrived *[Port and date of arrival]*
[Bill of lading or airway bill number and date]

Gentlemen:

This will notify you that the captioned shipment has been received in the following condition:
[Describe damages, pilferages, shortages, etc.]

We are hereby filing a claim and hold you responsible for this loss and/or damage.

Please acknowledge receipt of this letter and please send us your claim number.

Very truly yours,

Form 11.05 Customs bond.

CHB CODE	PROD ACCT #	RATING CODE		APPROVED THROUGH 1/31/91 OMB No. 1515-0144
JI612	345678	8		

SERIAL #		CHB REF #	DEPARTMENT OF THE TREASURY	BOND NUMBER' (Assigned by Customs)
1039928		FCB90700	UNITED STATES CUSTOMS SERVICE	CUSTOMS USE ONLY FILE REFERENCE
ALL INFORMATION REQUIRED—CHB MUST COMPLETE			**CUSTOMS BOND** 19 CFR Part 113	

In order to secure payment of any duty, tax or charge and compliance with law or regulation as a result of activity covered by any condition referenced below, we, the below named principal(s) and surety(ies), bind ourselves to the United States in the amount or amounts, as set forth below.

Execution Date 3/17/92

SECTION I—Select Single Transaction OR Continuous Bond (not both) and fill in the applicable blank spaces.

	Identification of transaction secured by this bond (e.g., entry no., seizure no., etc.)	Date of transaction	Transaction district & port code
[X] **SINGLE TRANSACTION BOND**	9267254 5	3/17/92	5201
[ ] **CONTINUOUS BOND**	Effective date		

This bond remains in force for one year beginning with the effective date and for each succeeding annual period, or until terminated. This bond constitutes a separate bond for each period in the amounts listed below for liabilities that accrue in each period. The intention to terminate this bond must be conveyed within the time period and manner prescribed in the Customs Regulations.

SECTION II—This bond includes the following agreements. (Check one box only, except that, 1a may be checked independently or with 1, and 3a may be checked independently or with 3. Line out all other parts of this section that are not used.)

Activity Code	Activity Name and Customs Regulations in which conditions codified	Limit of Liability	Activity Code	Activity Name and Customs Regulations in which conditions codified	Limit of Liability
[X] 1	Importer or broker 113.62	$82,400	[ ] 5	~~Public Gauger~~ 113.67	N/A
[ ] 1a	~~Drawback Payment Refunds~~ 113.65		[ ] 6	~~Wool & Fur Products Labeling Acts Importation (Single Entry Only)~~ 113.68	N/A
[ ] 2	~~Custodian of bonded merchandise (includes bonded carriers, freight forwarders, cartmen and lightermen, all classes of warehouses, container station operators)~~	N/A	[ ] 7	~~Bill of Lading (Single Entry Only)~~ 113.69	N/A
			[ ] 8	~~Detention of Copyrighted Material (Single Entry Only)~~ 113.70	N/A
[ ] 3	~~International Carrier~~ 113.64	N/A	[ ] 9	~~Neutrality (Single Entry Only)~~ 113.71	N/A
[ ] 3a	~~Instruments of International Traffic~~ 113.66		[ ] 10	~~Court Costs for Condemned Goods (Single Entry Only)~~ 113.72	N/A
[ ] 4	~~Foreign Trade Zone Operator~~ 113.73	N/A			

SECTION III—List below all tradenames or unincorporated divisions that will be permitted to obligate this bond in the principal's name including their Customs Identification Number(s). (If more space is needed, use Section III (Continuation) on back of form.)

Importer Number	Importer Name	Importer Number	Importer Name
N/A	N/A	N/A	N/A

Total number of importer names listed in Section III: N/A

Principal and surety agree that any charge against the bond under any of the listed names is as though it was made by the principal(s).

Principal and surety agree that they are bound to the same extent as if they executed a separate bond covering each set of conditions incorporated by reference to the Customs Regulations into this bond.

If the surety fails to appoint an agent under Title 6, United States Code, Section 7, surety consents to service on the Clerk of any United States District Court or the U.S. Court of International Trade, where suit is brought on this bond. That clerk is to send notice of the service to the surety at:

Mailing Address Requested by the Surety

WASHINGTON INTERNATIONAL INSURANCE COMPANY
1930 THOREAU DRIVE   SUITE 101
SCHAUMBURG, IL 60173

	Name and Address	Importer No.'	
PRINCIPAL'	Need-It-Today, Inc. 2233 North Elm Street Doohonkus, MO 06444	6501234567	
		SIGNATURE' ABC CUSTOMS BROKERS, Atty in Fact	SEAL
PRINCIPAL'	Name and Address	Importer No.'	
		SIGNATURE'	SEAL
SURETY'·'	Name and Address' WASHINGTON INTERNATIONAL INSURANCE COMPANY (AN ARIZONA CORPORATION) 1930 THOREAU DRIVE SUITE 101 SCHAUMBURG, IL 60173	Surety No.' 891	INCORPORATED SEAL
		SIGNATURE' Attorney-in-Fact	
SURETY'·'	Name and Address'	Surety No.' SIGNATURE'	SEAL
SURETY AGENTS	Name' LEWIS M. DANDY	Identification No.' 345-77-0123 Name'	Identification No.'

Customs Form 301 (111883)

Form 11.06   Application for continuous bond.

APPLICATION TO DISTRICT DIRECTOR U.S. CUSTOMS SERVICE
TO FILE C.F. 301 — CONTINUOUS

Bond Serial No. __034891__   CHB Name __ABC CUSTOMS BROKERS__

Importer Name __NEED-IT-TODAY, INC.__   Importer No. __65-1234567__

Street __2233 North Elm Street__ City __Doohonkus__   State __MO__   Zip __06444__

DESCRIBE MERCHANDISE (Attach additional sheet if necessary)	COUNTRY OF ORIGIN
1. Auto parts	Germahy
2. Industrial Sewing Machines	Japan
3. Machinery Parts for sewing machinery	Brazil
4.	
5.	
6.	

TYPE MERCHANDISE	LAST CALENDAR YEAR			ESTIMATE NEXT CALENDAR YEAR		
	VALUE	EST. DUTIES	NO. ENTRIES	VALUE	EST. DUTIES	NO. ENTRIES
Dutiable	$11,000,000	$55,000	100	$12,000,000	65,000	110
Conditionally Free	2,000,000	$ 8,000	25	$ 2,000,000	8,000	25
Unconditionally Free						
TOTAL	$13,000,000	$63,000	125	$14,000,000	73,000	135

Importer requests that customs approve the filing of C.F. 301
Continuous in an amount determined by customs to be effective on __May 1, 1992__

Activity Code	Activity Name and Customs Regulations in which conditions codified	Amount Required By Customs	Activity Code	Activity Name and Customs Regulations in which conditions codified	Amount Required By Customs
☒ 1	Importer or broker 113 62	$80,000	☐ 3	International Carrier 113 64	
☐ 1a	Drawback Payment Refunds 113 65		☐ 3a	Instruments of International Traffic 113 66	
☐ 2	Custodian of bonded merchandise . . . . 113 63 (includes bonded carriers, freight forwarders, cartmen and lightermen, all classes of warehouses, container station operators)		☐ 4	Foreign Trade Zone Operator 113.73	
			☐ 5	Public Gauger 113 67	

U.S. Customs district where bond is to be filed __4501__
Other districts through which I will import __New York, Los Angeles, Miami, Chicago, Boston__

LIST CURRENT TERM, ANNUAL OR CONTINUOUS BONDS — E.G. 7553,7595,3581, Etc. (Attach additional sheet if necessary)

BOND TYPE	BOND AMOUNT	EFFECTIVE DATE	SURETY	WHERE FILED
1. NONE				
2.				
3.				
4.				
5.				

Local district additional information _____

__25__ Years In Business

☐ Proprietorship
☐ Partnership
☒ Corporation
☐ Individual

CERTIFICATION

I certify that the factual information contained in this application is true and accurate and any information provided which is based upon estimates is based upon the best information available on the date of this application.

BY: __Henry F. Snodgrass__   TITLE __President__   DATE __April 2,__ 199
(Type name)

_____
(Signature)

Form 11.07   Sample notice of penalty.

LIQUIDATED DAMAGE CLAIMS

Key to Understanding Customs Form 5955A

1. CUSTOMS ASSIGNED CASE NUMBER
2. CUSTOMS PORT CODE AND DESCRIPTION
3. NAME AND ADDRESS OF PRINCIPAL
4. FILER REFERENCE NUMBER AND FILER CODE
5. DEMAND AMOUNT
6. CLAIM VIOLATION DESCRIPTION
7. VIOLATED LAW CITATION NUMBER
8. CUSTOMS ASSIGNED BOND NUMBER
9. BOND (PENALTY) AMOUNT
10. BOND EFFECTIVE DATE
11. NAME AND ADDRESS OF PRINCIPAL
12. NAME AND ADDRESS OF SURETY COMPANY
13. SURETY CODE
14. ADDRESS OF ISSUING CUSTOMS OFFICE
15. RESPONSE TIME LIMIT
16. CUSTOMS OFFICER'S SIGNATURE
17. CUSTOMS DEPARTMENT
    F P & F = FINES, PENALTIES & FORFEITURES DEPT.
18. DATE OF NOTICE

DEPARTMENT OF THE TREASURY UNITED STATES CUSTOMS SERVICE	Case Number
	89470124683
	Port Name and Code
NOTICE OF PENALTY OR LIQUIDATED DAMAGES INCURRED AND DEMAND FOR PAYMENT	4701 JFK AIRPORT
	Investigation File No.
	PDJ

FILER REFERENCE NUMBER: 12345

BROKER NUMBER: 987

TO: XYZ IMPORT COMPANY
1234 MAIN STREET
MIAMI, NY 11422
ID: 00123456700

DEMAND IS HEREBY MADE FOR PAYMENT OF $ ___16,616.00___ , representing ☐ Penalties or ☒ Liquidated Damages assessed against you for violation of law or regulation, or breach of bond, as set forth below:

FAILURE TO RE-DELIVER INTO CUSTOMS CUSTODY THE FOLLOWING MERCHANDISE:

ENTRY NUMBER: 567890054321   DATE OF ENTRY: 10/28/88
MERCHANDISE DESCRIPTION: CAR CLEANING LIQUIDS

RE-DELIVERY NOTICE ISSUED: 10/28/88
REQUESTED RE-DELIVERY DATE: 11/28/88

RE-DELIVERY OF THE MERCHANDISE WAS REQUESTED FOR THE FOLLOWING REASONS:
FAILURE TO PROPERLY MARK

SAMPLE

LAW OR REGULATION VIOLATED	BOND BREACHED
19CRF141.113	BASIC IMPORTATION AND ENTRY BOND 108535663

DESCRIPTION OF BOND (if any)	Form Number	Amount	Date
	6732926348	$60,000.	05/21/88

Name and Address of Principal in Bond
XYZ IMPORT COMPANY 1234 MAIN STREET, MIAMI, NY 11422

Name and Address of Surety on Bond WASHINGTON INT'L INS. CO. 1930 THOREAU DRIVE, SUITE 101, SCHAUMBURG, IL 60173	Surety Identification No. 891

If you feel there are extenuating circumstances, you have the right to object to the above action. Your petition should explain why you should not be penalized for the cited violation. Write the petition as a letter or in legal form; submit in (duplicate) (triplicate), addressed to the Commissioner of Customs, and forward to the District Director of Customs at
US CUSTOMS BLDG 178 (FP&F) JFK INT'L AIRPORT MIAMI, NY 11430

Unless the amount herein demanded is paid or a petition for relief is filed with the district director of customs within the indicated time limit, further action will be taken in connection with your bond or the matter will be referred to the United States Attorney.	TIME LIMIT FOR PAYMENT OR FILING PETITION FOR RELIEF ▶ 60 (Days from the date of this Notice)

Signature By 3RD FLOOR	Title ATTN: FP&F	Date 01/19/89

Customs Form 5955A (012386)

12

Trade Barriers and Regulation

What remedies are available when foreign businesses export
goods that infringe U.S. patents, trademarks, copyrights,
or mask works? **12.7**

Introduction

Customs entry procedures are one form of trade regulation. The others are the various kinds of trade barriers—and incentives—that countries use to protect their national interests.

Trade barriers and restrictions exist in many forms. Indeed, there is a subjective aspect to trade regulation: What seems to be a trade regulation to one party is seen as a trade barrier to another. An antidumping duty used to protect a domestic industry is seen by some as an assault on the very notion of free trade.

This chapter deals with regulatory mechanisms—quotas, tariffs, antidumping and countervailing duties, and nontariff trade barriers—designed to restrict the flow of goods, thereby increasing costs to importers. Although multilateral agreements such as GATT and NAFTA seek to reduce trade barriers, countries continue to find ways to protect their interests. Understanding how trade barriers work, and sometimes turning them to an advantage, will be crucial factors to surviving in the global market of the next century.

Note. Tariff preference programs—such as the General System of Preferences (GSP), Caribbean Basin Initiative (CBI), specific GATT and NAFTA provisions, and other programs—are used to ease the flow of imports to the United States by lowering duty and tariff rates. These programs are dealt with in Chapter 10, "Duty Management."

12.1 IMPORT QUOTAS

12.1.1 Introduction

Import quotas are used to establish a limit on the amount or value of a given product that may be imported into the United States. They are generally imposed for a set period of time, often one year.

Quotas are usually established when bilateral and voluntary restraint agreements fail to protect a particular U.S. industry. Like antidumping and countervailing duties (see section 12.5), quotas serve to protect American industries from imports that are being "dumped" at low cost into the U.S. market, or that are being subsidized by the government of the exporting country. A major difference is that quotas are country-specific, whereas countervailing and antidumping duties can apply to individual companies or many countries.

Quotas may be imposed on a particular product, with shares of the quota allocated among many countries. For example, the many apparel and textile goods under quota are supplied by as many as twenty-five countries, each with a percentage of the numerical quota for a given year. Quotas are not an absolute bar to importation, however; goods may be shipped into the United States in excess of a given quota but must be kept in a bonded U.S. Customs warehouse until the next quota period begins.

GATT, NAFTA, and Import Quotas

Multilateral agreements such as the General Agreement on Tariffs and Trade (GATT) and the North American Free Trade Agreement (NAFTA) affect the way quotas are implemented and administered. NAFTA provisions call for the elimination of all quotas between Canada, the United States, and Mexico, except for those that apply to the following industries:

* Agricultural products
* Energy
* Textiles
* Automobiles

While GATT does not eliminate all quotas, it does restrict their use and includes provisions that call for greater "transparency"(i.e., clearer guidelines) in the rules governing quotas. Member countries that administer quotas must publish:

* The overall amount of quotas to be applied by quantity or value
* The opening and closing dates of quotas and any changes to those dates
* Any changes in allocations or shares among supplying countries
* Import license procedures that affect quotas

On January 1, 1995, GATT was replaced by the World Trade Organization (WTO) as the institutional foundation for the world's multilateral trading system. One of the main functions of the WTO is to mediate disputes between nations regarding tariffs, quotas, and other trade barriers. As of December 1996, sixty-two trade disputes had been sent to the WTO for resolution, including an Asian challenge to a U.S. ban on shrimp caught without nets to protect sea turtles; a Japanese tax on vodka from the European Union; and a U.S. quota on underwear produced in Costa Rica. (*The Wall Street Journal,* 12/3/96)

NAFTA has also established a number of panels that mediate and render judgments in trade disputes between member countries.

EXAMPLE

Canadian quotas on poultry, milk, eggs, and other dairy products produced in the U.S. were eliminated under new WTO rules. To protect its domestic industries, Canada then implemented tariffs on those same products ranging as high as 335 percent on American-made butter. The U.S. Dairy Council appealed the tariffs to a five-member NAFTA panel, claiming that the tariffs were in violation of the agreement. In December 1996 the panel ruled in Canada's favor and the tariffs were allowed to stand. (*The Wall Street Journal,* 12/3/96)

12.1.2 *Establishment of Quotas*

Quotas are established through legislation or directives in the U.S. Congress and are administered by the U.S. Customs Service. Multilateral trade agreements and voluntary restraint agreements (VRAs) are also used as a means for implementing quotas, although more often they are used to ease quota restrictions.

In the United States, the process for establishing import quotas is as follows:

1. In general, specific industries apply to Congress, seeking protection in the form of quotas or voluntary restraint agreements.
2. The quota petitions are sponsored by a U.S. government agency.
3. Congress then approves or disapproves of the request.

The United States has implemented several tariffs and quotas to protect its domestic textile and apparel industries. Under GATT, those quotas are supposed to be eliminated by the year 2005. Currently, China, Hong Kong, and Mexico are the top suppliers of imported apparel to the U.S. However, in anticipation of the removal of all quotas, African nations such as Zimbabwe, Kenya, and Mauritius are mobilizing political, diplomatic, and industry resources to be next in line to supply the U.S. market.

Importers and exporters alike should keep abreast of developments regarding tariffs and quotas in emerging economies. The elimination of tariffs on Mexican-made apparel, for example, created trade opportunities not only for U.S. importers but for exporters as well; 70 percent of the fabric and yarn used by the Mexican sewing shops is exported to Mexico by U.S. producers. (*Forbes*, 2/10/97)

Note. To find out if a specific product has quota restrictions, or for a complete list of products under quota, importers can contact the Quota Branch of the U.S. Customs Service in Washington, D.C. (202-927-5850). The National Trade Data Bank also has information on quotas. (See Chapter 1, section 1.3.3.)

EXAMPLE

In 1991, Ukraine, a former Soviet Republic of 52 million people, established a market economy. Apparel factories there began exporting women's woolen coats to the U.S. The garments were of such high quality and low price (retailing in the U.S. for $89 to $139 each) that in the year ending September 1994, 89,000 dozen coats were exported to the United States, a 155 percent increase from the previous year. The Ukraine became the third-largest supplier of woolen coats to the U.S., after the Dominican Republic and Guatemala.

In response, domestic coat manufacturers petitioned the U.S. Commerce Department for protection, and the Ukrainian coats were classified as "disruptive" to the American women's garment manufacturing industry. Quotas were established for 1995 that set the number of imports at roughly 1994 levels.

Note. The woolen textile industry is one of the most protected in the United States. In addition to quotas, the United States maintains a 21 percent tariff on imported woolen coats and has quota agreements with fifteen other countries in Eastern Europe and Central America.

12.1.3 Types of Quotas

There are two types of import quotas: tariff-rate quotas and absolute quotas.

Tariff-Rate Quotas

Under tariff-rate quotas, a product can be entered:

* In specified quantities
* During a given period of time
* At a reduced duty rate

Products covered under tariff-rate quotas can be shipped in unlimited quantities during the quota period. However, quantities in excess of the quota entered during the quota period are subject to higher duty rates.

> EXAMPLE
>
> Imported canned tuna has been under a tariff-rate quota since the 1950s. Tuna imported into the United States prior to the quota being filled is subject to a duty rate of approximately 6 percent. Once the quota is filled, the same tuna is subject to a duty rate of over 12 percent. The 6 percent difference in duty rate has had almost no effect on the amount of imported tuna entering the U.S.

> EXAMPLE
>
> In July 1993, the European Union announced new rules that allowed banana producers from Martinique and Guadeloupe, former European colonies, to export bananas to European countries duty-free and in unlimited quantities. At the same time, a quota was established on bananas grown in the United States and countries with strong U.S. interests such as Colombia, Costa Rica, and Venezuela. The quota called for duty-free imports of up to 2.56 million tons per year, but imposed substantial duties on amounts in excess of that number.
>
> **Note.** In September 1997, the World Trade Organization ordered the European Union to stop giving preferences to select producers in Africa and the Caribbean. The WTO found that the EU's trade policies were costing producers aligned with the U.S. position hundreds of millions of dollars in lost sales. Honduras, for example, said its banana exports to the EU decreased by 90 percent in 1994, the year the discriminatory policies were implemented. (*The Wall Street Journal,* 9/26/97)

The following products are covered under U.S. tariff-rate quotas, as of September 1994:

* Certain types of non-concentrated milk and cream
* Anchovies in oil, in airtight containers

- Tuna fish
- Certain types of olives
- Certain textiles assembled in Guam
- Certain textiles from Canada

Absolute Quotas

Absolute quotas specify a set amount of a product that may be entered during a given quota period. Some absolute quotas are global in nature, while others cover only those goods coming from a certain foreign country. Goods in excess of the quantity specified under the quota may be imported, provided that they are subsequently exported or that they are warehoused for entry during the next quota period.

The following goods are covered under absolute quota restrictions, as of September 1994:

- Condensed or evaporated milk or cream
- Certain types of ethyl alcohol
- Animal feeds containing milk or milk derivatives
- Peanuts
- Certain types of cheddar cheeses
- Cotton fibers processed but not spun
- Textiles and apparel from certain countries

12.1.4 Quotas and World Trade

The right to implement quotas is a major consideration in multilateral treaties such as GATT and NAFTA. In international agreements and trading blocs, most member countries reserve the right to unilaterally impose quotas to protect a domestic industry or as a punitive measure.

In addition to the huge multilateral trade agreements such as GATT and NAFTA, regional trade agreements between two or more nations continue to proliferate. At least twenty-nine such agreements, such as the one concluded in November 1996 between Canada and Chile, have been implemented since 1992. In some cases these agreements duplicate GATT provisions and others conflict with GATT by denying to nonmembers rights negotiated under GATT.

The following are international agreements that use quotas as a regulatory measure.

Long-Term Arrangement Regarding International Trade
in Cotton Textiles

In 1962, the United States negotiated the Long-Term Arrangement Regarding International Trade in Cotton Textiles (LTA), which is now covered under the General Agreement on Tariffs and Trade. The aim of LTA was to protect the U.S. textile and apparel industry from low-cost imports. Thirty-three countries eventually joined LTA and set quotas on textiles from countries not participating in LTA multilateral agreements.

Multifiber Arrangement

In an effort to create a much broader multilateral agreement covering many types of fibers, fifty countries negotiated the Multifiber Arrangement (MFA) in 1973. MFA is also included under the auspices of GATT. The stated goal of MFA was to achieve "orderly marketing" and to avoid market disruptions. Important provisions of the agreement include:

1. The right of importing countries to unilaterally impose quotas when market conditions justify this action
2. A broader definition of acts used to circumvent quotas, including illegal shipments of goods covered under the agreement and false declarations at U.S. Customs.

General Agreement on Tariffs and Trade

The right to establish quotas under GATT is a source of continuing conflict. An international trade war almost started in 1995 when the United States demanded that Japan set numerical quotas for U.S. car imports. The Americans claimed that Japan had trade barriers in place against U.S.-made autos; the United States wanted a commitment that a certain number of American cars would be sold in Japan each year. Several years earlier Japan had agreed to numerical target levels on imported U.S.-made auto parts. The United States set a deadline of June 28 of that year and gave Japan an ultimatum: Either Japan set numerical quotas for U.S. autos or the United States would impose a punitive tariff of 100 percent on thirteen different models of Japanese luxury cars entering U.S. markets. The tariffs were expected to amount to $6.5 billion.

In response to the American threat, the European Union (EU) threatened to sue both countries. The EU claimed that the GATT agreements, signed only months earlier, created a system to settle such disputes through the World Trade Organization.

12.1.5 *Quota Avoidance: Transshipments and Overshipments*

Transshipments and overshipments are two of the ways that countries avoid quotas on goods.

Transshipments involve the shipping of goods, particularly textiles and apparel, destined for the United States to a third country, where they are improperly labeled as having been manufactured in that country. The third countries have no quota agreements or open quota shares with the United States. The United States claims that transshipments involve at least twenty-five countries in Europe, Asia, Africa, and Central and South America. Some of those countries have been accused of allowing China to use their quota shares. The import categories found to account for the largest volume of transshipments were mainly those covering knit shirts, sweaters, underwear, cotton trousers, and shop towels.

Overshipments are shipments that deliberately exceed quota limits specified in a bilateral agreement.

EXAMPLE

> Chinese transshipments and overshipments of textiles to the United States have become a major source of tension between the two countries. For the period 1990 to 1993, the U.S. Customs Service estimates that the value of Chinese textiles and apparel illegally entering the U.S. market totaled about $2 billion annually. The United States claims the shipments are in violation of a bilateral agreement in place controlling the exports of textiles and apparel to the U.S. market. During the same period, annual overshipments occurred in more than 50 percent of the eighty-eight categories subject to limits under the United States–China agreement.
>
> In response the United States imposed additional quotas and tariffs on several Chinese textile imports. China then threatened to impose countersanctions on selected U.S. goods.
>
> On February 2, 1997 the United States and China reached an accord whereby the United States would marginally increase the quotas on Chinese textiles; in turn, China would take steps to end transshipments and the disguising and intentional mislabeling of goods. China also agreed to grant greater market access to a number of U.S. textile products. (*The Wall Street Journal,* 2/3/97)

To deal with persistent transshipment and overshipment problems, the United States is renegotiating its expiring bilateral textile agreements to include language that directly addresses these issues as they relate to particular countries of origin. The new agreements include provisions to:

* Make adjustments in a country's quotas
* Reduce a specific quota by as much as three times the amount transshipped
* Make unannounced visits to a supplying country's textile and apparel factories
* Require the offending country to adopt enforcement procedures that effectively control both transshipments and overshipments

In 1993, the United States concluded bilateral textile agreements incorporating these provisions with sixteen countries.

12.1.6   Quotas and U.S. Importers

It is clear that quotas, especially in the larger context of international trade disputes, can have significant implications for importers. The Customs Modernization Act (see section 8.1.6) shifts more responsibility for determining country of origin to importers and customs brokers; therefore, both need to be alert for goods that are transshipped or mislabeled. Importers shipping goods legally, with all documents in order, may find their goods consigned to a bonded warehouse if the quota is filled by illegal shipments.

12.2 Voluntary Restraint Agreements

Under voluntary restraint agreements (VRAs), exporting countries agree to set export quotas on certain classes of goods destined for the United States. VRAs are used to prevent trade disputes from leading to quotas, tariffs, or all-out trade wars. In the United States, VRAs are often negotiated through the U.S. Trade Representative's Office.

Voluntary restraint agreements most often apply to textiles, steel, automobiles, and machine tools. If a VRA is in place, foreign exporters are required to obtain visas to sell these products to the United States.

Voluntary restraint agreements are not used nearly as much as they have been in the past. When used, they are mostly with nations the United States has targeted for an antidumping or countervailing duty investigation; the VRA, in that case, eliminates the need for imposition of the duty.

Congress renewed its authorization for the use of VRAs in October 1996, but only for a period through May 1997. After that date, the use of voluntary restraint agreements is uncertain.

Note. It is the importer's responsibility to determine whether there are any quotas or foreign government visa restrictions on products before entering into a purchase agreement with a foreign supplier.

Example

In 1986, the United States and Japan signed a five-year VRA on Japanese machine tool exports to the United States. When the agreement expired in 1991, the U.S. machine tool industry had rebounded, with exports increasing by 83 percent during the five years the VRA was in place.

A new agreement was signed in 1992 by the ambassadors of both countries. It eliminates several products from quota restrictions and is designed to allow the U.S. machine tool industry to gradually acclimate to Japanese competition. The VRA applies to four categories of machine tools:

* Numerically controlled (NC) lathes
* Numerically controlled milling machines
* Machining centers
* Numerically controlled punching and shearing machines

Under the agreement, Japanese exports of these products are limited to the specific shares of estimated 1992–1993 U.S. consumption. The VRA also contains mechanisms to ensure that Japanese machine tools not covered by the agreement do not face any barriers in the U.S. market.

12.3 Visas

Visas are used to monitor the status of goods under quota. The government of the exporting country may also require visas to prevent the unauthorized entry of the goods into the importing country. Issuance of visas ensures that both countries count merchandise in the same way in an attempt to avoid overshipments, incorrect quota charges, and embargoes.

Visas appear in two forms:

- As a stamp on an invoice
- As an export control license

Several types of visas are required, depending on the product's classification under the Harmonized Tariff Schedule (HTS) or on the country of origin. The following are the two types of classification visas:

1. *Comprehensive visas.* Comprehensive visas are the most common. They apply to an entire category of goods—for example, all shipments of textiles or textile products made from vegetable fibers, wool, silk blends, and synthetic fibers may be covered under one visa category.

2. *Specific visas.* Specific visas cover particular products in HTS categories. For example, different types of cotton may each require a separate visa.

In addition to visas for specific types of products, the United States has a third visa category: country-specific visas. The United States has entered into visa agreements with a number of countries, covering quota or nonquota merchandise.

While a visa may be a prerequisite to importing into the United States, importers should be aware that issuance of a visa on goods under quota does not guarantee that the goods will enter the United States. In some cases, quota limits are reached between the time the visa is issued and the arrival of the goods. The goods will not be released to the importer until the next quota period.

If a visa contains an incorrect classification category, quantity, or other incorrect or misleading data, the entry is rejected and the merchandise is not released until the importer receives a new visa or visa waiver from the government of the exporting country.

12.4 TARIFFS

A tariff is a duty or collection of duties that must be paid before goods can enter a foreign country. Duty rates are based upon how goods are classified according to the Harmonized Tariff Schedule (see Chapter 9). In practice, as with other forms of trade regulation (e.g., quotas, nontariff trade barriers, and countervailing and antidumping duties), tariffs are themselves often used as trade barriers.

Note. The terms "tariff" and "antidumping duty" are sometimes used interchangeably. Antidumping duties are similar to the punitive tariffs that are imposed in addition to the normal tariff rate on specific imported goods.

In addition to increasing the revenue of an importing country, tariffs can be extremely effective as a means of regulating world trade. For example, when the United States wanted concessions from the Japanese on auto exports, it threatened to impose 100 percent tariffs on Japanese luxury car imports. Similarly, to protect the domestic wool coat industry, the United States imposed a 21 percent tariff on all wool coat imports.

Governments use tariffs as a trade control mechanism for a number of reasons:

- To protect a domestic industry
- As a punitive measure
- For political reasons

Tariffs can be levied on whole classes of goods or individual companies and countries. Following are examples of different ways tariffs can be applied to regulate international trade.

EXAMPLE

In April 1992, a U.S. high-technology firm, Micron Technology, submitted a petition to the U.S. government seeking protection from Korean imports of dynamic random access memory (DRAM) computer chips. In a preliminary ruling, the Commerce Department determined that South Korean manufacturers were in fact selling the chips below cost in the United States. Using a formula designed to estimate by how much the chips were undersold, the Commerce Department imposed tariffs on three South Korean manufacturers. The companies were ordered to pay tariffs equivalent to set percentages of every dollar's worth of goods shipped to the United States. Samsung Electronics Company was ordered to pay 84.7 percent; Goldstar Electronics Company, 52.4 percent; and Hyundai Electronics Company, 5.99 percent.

The tariffs created spot shortages of DRAM chips throughout the world and caused prices to jump by as much as 30 percent. Another effect of the tariffs was to strengthen the position of U.S. market leaders and put additional pressure on smaller manufacturers.

EXAMPLE

In 1992, the U.S. government, in response to a petition from General Motors, Ford, and Chrysler, considered imposing a tariff of between 2.5 percent and 25 percent on Japanese minivan imports. This was to be accomplished by changing the Harmonized Tariff Schedule classification of the vehicles; for tariff purposes, minivans and sport utility vehicles would be classified as trucks, thus subjecting them to higher duty rates.

Note. Tariffs are also influenced by economic conditions. The currency and stock crises that struck world markets in 1997, particularly in Asia and South America, have produced some new tariffs to protect reeling economies. Though at present the new tariffs are limited in scope, they may be harbingers of more protectionist measures to follow and may indicate a slowing of free trade momentum around the world.

In October 1997, Malaysia increased tariffs on construction equipment and other goods while Brazil and Argentina raised tariffs on a number of products. Argentina implemented a 3 percent tariff increase that the World Trade Organization had previously ordered it to eliminate.

At the Asian Pacific Economic Cooperation Summit in Vancouver, British

Columbia, in November 1997, there were indications that Asian nations were slowing down on prior commitments to cut tariffs in the financial services sector. The moves could slow the entry of U.S.-based banks and insurance companies into Asia and Latin America. (*The Wall Street Journal*, 11/24/97)

12.4.1   Tariff Reductions Under GATT

The General Agreement on Tariffs and Trade, which completed its "Uruguay Round" in April 1994, substantially reduced import tariffs in almost all key markets for most sectors of U.S. industry. The following data offers examples of the percentage amount of tariff reductions in major export markets for certain U.S. industry sectors. (The sources for these statistics are: the U.S. Department of Commerce/International Trade Administration, 1994; Office of the U.S. Trade Representative, 1994; *Journal of Consumer Marketing*, Vol. 13, No. 1, 1996.) The tariff reductions are scheduled to be fully implemented by the year 2005.

Computer Equipment

Under GATT, tariffs will be reduced by over 83 percent to the European Union (EU), which buys almost 38 percent of U.S. computer equipment exports. Tariffs will be reduced by 100 percent to Japan and over 36 percent to South Korea.

Household Appliances

Tariffs on household appliances will be reduced by 48 percent in the EU; 83 percent in Japan; and 54 percent in Brazil.

Outdoor and Recreational Equipment

In addition to major tariff reductions in this industry—57 percent for the EU; 74 percent for Japan; an average of 63 percent for all major U.S. export markets—GATT includes provisions that increase penalties for the production and export of counterfeit goods.

Pharmaceuticals

The EU and Japan, which together account for 59 percent of U.S. pharmaceutical exports, have completely eliminated tariffs under GATT. South Korea has reduced tariffs by 52 percent and Brazil by 33 percent.

Miscellaneous Consumer Goods

Tariff reductions to the EU amount to 48 percent; 66 percent to Japan; and 68 percent to South Korea.

Note. Although tariffs on certain products, notably pharmaceuticals, were eliminated immediately upon completion of GATT, most tariffs will be reduced or phased out by the year 2005. However, many exporters need to know the status of tariffs on goods in their target countries right now. Given the volume and complexity of GATT (over 120 nations have signed the accord and 99 percent and 73 percent of product lines, respectively, for developed and developing nations are covered), there is no single source for all GATT-related tariff activity.

The best source to find out the current status of GATT-mandated tariff reductions is the country desks of specific countries at the Department of Commerce. Exporters should be prepared to send, via fax, to the office in question the schedule B Harmonized Tariff Number of the particular product, as well as the address and phone number of the manufacturing facility in the United States. Examples include:

- Brazil office (Telephone: 202-482-3872; Fax: 202-482-4157)
- China office (Telephone: 202-482-3932; Fax: 202-482-4453)

Export professionals such as customs brokers and freight forwarders should also be able to help by checking tariff schedules of particular countries.

Much of the available online information is not current; exporters should never rely on that alone.

12.5 ANTIDUMPING AND COUNTERVAILING DUTIES

12.5.1 Introduction

In addition to normal rates of duty assessed on imported goods, importers may also be required to pay antidumping, countervailing, and other special duties. These duties may be imposed on a foreign country, a specific industry, or an individual firm.

Both countervailing (CV) and antidumping (AD) duties have strong political overtones and are important mechanisms in world trade regulation. As with other forms of trade regulation, CV and AD duties are controversial: Some people regard them as obsolete impediments to international trade, protecting antiquated industries at the expense of free market principles. Others see them as necessary safeguards against unfair competition, low wages. and subsidized industries from abroad.

Rules governing countervailing and antidumping duties are being rewritten worldwide in the context of the GATT accords. Changes to these rules are discussed in Chapter 10, "Duty Management."

12.5.2 Antidumping Duties

The U.S. antidumping laws are contained in Title VII of the Tariff Act of 1930. Under this law, antidumping duties are assessed on imported merchandise when it is sold to buyers in the United States at less than fair market value (LTFV) or when a U.S. industry is injured or threatened by such imports. The duties are intended to offset the margins at which the foreign goods are being sold and thus create a level playing field for domestic goods.

An import is generally considered to be sold at less than fair market value when its U.S. selling price is less than the price of the goods in their home market. The antidumping duty usually amounts to the difference between the U.S. and the foreign market prices. In some cases, higher antidumping duties are assessed as a punitive measure.

Antidumping duties are imposed after an investigation. Most investigations are conducted on the basis of a petition filed with the Commerce Department and the International Trade Administration (ITA) by or on behalf of a U.S. industry.

The Import Administration's Office of Compliance, which is part of the ITA, received twenty-two antidumping and countervailing duty petitions in 1996. Recent petitions include collated roofing nails from Korea, crawfish tail meat from China, and vector supercomputers from Japan.

12.5.3 *Countervailing Duties*

Countervailing duties are assessed by the U.S. government when it has been determined that a foreign company or industry receives a subsidy from its government, giving it an unfair advantage against U.S. products. If the subsidies cause the price of the goods to be artificially low, and "injury" is caused to U.S. manufacturers of similar products, a countervailing duty investigation is initiated. In 1993, eighteen new countervailing duty orders were imposed as a result of Commerce Department investigations.

12.5.4 *Duty Investigations*

Three government agencies are involved in investigation and enforcement of antidumping and countervailing duty regulations: the Department of Commerce, the International Trade Administration, and the U.S. Customs Service.

The Commerce Department is responsible for administering the laws and for investigating allegations of illegal dumping activities and subsidization of imports. If the investigation finds that violations have occurred, specific duty rates are imposed on the imported goods found to be in violation.

The role of the International Trade Administration is to determine whether injury to a U.S. agency has occurred or is likely to occur, or whether an industry may be hindered in start-up efforts as a result of antidumping or countervailing duty violations.

Customs assesses the duties once the duty rates have been established.

An investigation is usually initiated in one of two ways:

1. A domestic industry files a petition with the Commerce Department.
2. An interested party, such as an industry association, claims unfair competition by foreign manufacturers.

Once a case is initiated, the Commerce Department determines the difference between the price at which the imported goods under investigation are being sold in the United States and the actual fair market value of the goods. Duty rates are then set based on those differences. Once rates are set, the Commerce Department directs Customs to enforce the rulings by:

- Requiring cash deposits or bonds on imports of the goods in question
- Refusing to complete and release the entries until it is determined that dumping or subsidization has occurred and until the proper duty margins are established

If the Commerce Department and the ITA determine that subsidization and dumping has actually occurred, Customs is directed to collect cash deposits on the imported goods in question; only cash is accepted—customs bonds are not permitted for antidumping or countervailing duty deposits.

One year from the Commerce Department's final determination of AD and CV cases, an administrative review of the cases must be performed to determine if the rates for the first-year period are fair, provided such a review is requested by interested parties. Parties have thirty days to file for a review. At the one-year anniversary of the ruling, or when the administrative review is completed, the Commerce Department directs Customs to liquidate all entries for the previous yearly period. Customs then reviews the entries and can either refund the deposit to the importer or assess any additional duties that are owed.

Note. Imported goods that are being investigated for antidumping and countervailing duty violations may be in the custody of U.S. Customs for years while the administrative review process is carried out. The duty rates that are ultimately set may be substantially higher than those first established upon completion of the preliminary review. Importers of goods involved in a countervailing or antidumping duty investigation must contend with uncertain duty rates and possible long delays in the liquidation process.

The following is a list of recent antidumping orders:

- Ferrous silicon from Brazil: 35.95 percent
- Circular welded, nonalloy steel pipe from Brazil: 103.38 percent
- Monochrome or color television receivers from Japan: 1.26 percent
- Kiwi fruit from New Zealand: 98.60 percent
- Potassium permanganate from China: 128.94 percent

The following is a list of recent countervailing duty orders:

- Stainless steel cookware from Taiwan: 2.14 percent.
- Brass sheet and strip from France: 7.24 percent.
- Stainless steel cookware from Korea: 0.78 percent.
- Leather riding apparel from Mexico: 13.35 percent.
- Fresh and chilled Atlantic salmon from Norway: 0.71 per kilogram. (This is a specific countervailing duty rate set on a price per pound or unit basis.)
- Cotton yarn from Peru: 1 percent.

Example of a Typical Antidumping Duty Investigation

In June 1992, the Import Administration of the ITA received a petition from major U.S. steel producers, including Bethlehem Steel Corporation, Inland Steel Industries, National Steel Corporation, and LTV Steel Company, alleging that certain types of hot- and cold-rolled steel products were being sold in the United States at less than fair market value. The petitioners claimed that as a result of the alleged dumping, the U.S. steel industry was being materially injured. In addition, the companies stated that the foreign producers were selling the goods in their home markets at prices below the cost of production.

The U.S. companies provided a number of methods for calculating the U.S. price (USP) and fair market value (FMV) of the goods. The ITA used direct price-to-price comparisons based on invoices and price quotations to arrive at a preliminary ruling. In this case, the information provided by the U.S. steel companies was considered the best information available.

In response to the petition, the Commerce Department imposed tariffs averaging 36.5 percent on certain hot- and cold-rolled products from nineteen countries. (The tariffs were later overturned by the International Trade Commission.)

Antidumping duties on steel products are part of a long-standing dispute between major U.S. steel producers, foreign steel companies, U.S. manufacturers, and the U.S. government. Issues surrounding AD duties on imported steel have become the focal point for a larger debate about protectionism and free markets. Steel companies here have been accused of using antidumping petitions to protect themselves from legitimate foreign competition, inefficiencies in the industry, and the emergence of cost-effective minimills.

What is beyond dispute is that antidumping duties on imported steel have tremendous implications for U.S. manufacturers and importers. Supply channels are usually in turmoil and it is difficult to obtain imports. Companies ranging from small machine shops to General Motors bemoan the lack of low-cost steel and metric steel products as a result of antidumping orders.

Example of a Typical Countervailing Duty Investigation

In 1993, the U.S. Wheat Association, an agricultural trade association representing U.S. wheat growers, complained that Canadian wheat growers were being subsidized by the Canadian government under the Western Grain Transportation Act (WGTA). U.S. growers claimed that the transportation subsidies gave Canadian growers an unfair advantage over U.S. producers.

Specifically, they claimed that the subsidies unfairly undercut the prices of U.S. wheat exports to foreign markets. As evidence, U.S. growers pointed out that subsidies paid under the WGTA helped to reduce the U.S. share of the Mexican wheat market from an estimated 75 percent in 1990 to 14 percent in 1992. During that same time, Canada's share of the Mexican market reached 66 percent.

A task force from the U.S. Department of Agriculture (USDA) concluded that the subsidized imports from Canada were "materially interfering" with U.S.

wheat price support programs. They recommended that the International Trade Administration conduct an investigation into Canadian wheat export practices.

12.6   NONTARIFF TRADE BARRIERS

12.6.1   Introduction

Nontariff trade barriers are a major factor in the control and regulation of global trade. As with tariffs, quotas, and antidumping and countervailing duties, nontariff barriers involve both economic and political interests. But nontariff barriers are more subtle, and therefore harder to detect and anticipate, than other trade barriers.

There are many different types of nontariff trade barriers. Some of the most' common are:

- Manufacturing and quality standards
- Shipping and cargo restrictions
- Centralized distribution systems
- Taxes and surcharges
- Import licensing procedures
- Local content and labor laws
- Cartels and business associations
- Payoffs and kickbacks

The net effects of these barriers include the following:

- Certain products are screened out of a market.
- Foreign businesses have difficulty in gaining a market foothold.
- There are negative impacts on pricing of imports.
- Foreign businesses become less competitive.

Nontariff trade barriers are becoming more of a concern to U.S. business. As multilateral treaties such as NAFTA and GATT eliminate or reduce quotas and tariffs, more countries will likely use nontariff barriers to protect their interests. As a result, importers and exporters alike must take into account nontariff barriers when entering the global marketplace.

Note. One of the World Trade Organization's most important and complex mandates is to identify and restrict the use of nontariff trade barriers by member nations.

The WTO made the most controversial decision of its three-year history in December 1997, when it issued a preliminary ruling that rejected a petition from Eastman Kodak Company. Kodak had alleged that Fuji Photo Film Company, Japan's market leader in the $1.8 billion annual film business, conspired with the Japanese government to block Kodak's access to Japan's largest film distributors.

The complaint against Fuji was the first in which the WTO was asked to examine how the functioning of a country's internal markets could create nontariff trade barriers. In past cases the WTO has ruled on tariffs and other easily quantifiable requirements, such as local content rules.

The preliminary ruling prompted analysts to question whether the WTO is capable of dealing with the complex and secretive means by which countries close their markets to foreign competitors. Those same analysts also question whether the WTO sees such issues as beyond its purview, which would weaken the organization's watchdog role as a protector of free markets.

Fallout from the WTO decision could be significant. One possibility is that the U.S. will impose unilateral trade sanctions against Japan. (*Boston Globe,* 12/6/97, *The Wall Street Journal,* 12/4/97)

12.6.2 International Standards

International standards are product and quality guidelines that are intended to create uniformity in international industry. In many cases, however, they can be used as a subtle yet powerful barrier to trade.

International standards generally fall into the following categories:

- Safety standards
- Environmental standards
- Quality standards and inspection requirements

Standards become trade barriers when:

1. A country or major multinational corporation stipulates unusual or particular conformance levels for a given product.
2. The country or multinational requires a supplier to earn certification to an international quality assurance program, such as ISO 9000, with the stipulation that "locally qualified" quality inspectors conduct the final check.
3. Access to the certification process is limited.
4. Standards guidelines are not "transparent" (i.e., clear and comprehensible).
5. The process of standards compliance is inordinately expensive.

Although standards are a serious concern for all companies, they are an even larger issue for smaller importers and exporters. Many smaller firms simply do not have the time, resources, or staffing to comply with a multitude of standards.

International standards are an increasingly prominent trade issue. Some of the world's trading blocs are moving to harmonize products standards among member countries. The following examples provide a look at how standards are applied by two of America's most important trading partners, Japan and the European Union.

Standards in Japan

Product standards in Japan fall into two categories:

* Regulations or mandatory standards
* Voluntary (i.e., not mandatory) standards.

A certification system is used to ensure that products meet regulations and mandatory standards. If a product is found to be in compliance, a certificate or quality mark is granted. Products not certified cannot be sold in Japan, and imported products must be certified in order to clear Japanese customs.

Although some of the standards are termed voluntary, products that do not display the applicable marks may have a hard time gaining acceptance in the Japanese marketplace. Even obtaining the standards is itself a kind of trade barrier, particularly for small companies: Many of the standards are available only in Japan; American companies doing business in Japan need a Japanese agent, distributor, consultant, or lawyer to obtain the right information. Furthermore, there are only a few testing laboratories in the United States that are approved by the Japanese government agencies to test U.S. products for compliance with Japanese standards. Products not eligible for testing in those labs must be tested by Japanese laboratories before the goods can be sold in Japan.

Mandatory standards include:

1. Consumer Product Safety Law (a mandatory S mark is required for some ten categories of products, including baby cribs and baseball helmets)
2. Electrical Appliance and Material Control Law (a mandatory T mark is applied to qualifying products)
3. Measurement Law
4. High Pressure Gas Control Law
5. Gas Utility Industry Law
6. Law Concerning the Examination and Control of Manufacture of Chemical Substances
7. Fertilizer Control Law
8. Road Transportation Law
9. Telecommunications Enterprise Law
10. Radio Law
11. Plant Protection Law
12. Pharmaceutical Affairs Law
13. Food Sanitation Law
14. Industrial Safety and Health Law

So-called voluntary standards include:

1. Japanese Industrial Standards (JIS)
2. Japanese Agricultural Standards (JAS)
3. Electronic Devices Industry Association of Japan (EIAJ) standards

4. Japan Electric Machinery Manufacturers Association (JEM) standards
5. Japan Automobile Technology Association (JASO) standards
6. Japan Iron and Steel Federation (JISF) standards
7. Japan Electronic Parts Dependability Association (RCJS) standards
8. Japan Consumer Product Safety Association (JCPSA) standards (confers the SG mark)
9. Toy Safety Control Administration (confers the ST, or safety toy, mark that is carried on over 85 percent of toys sold in Japan)
10. The ECO mark (used to indicate "environmentally friendly" products)

The Japanese Industrial Standards mark applies to more than 1,000 different industrial products and consists of more than 8,600 individual standards. Companies competing for Japanese government procurement contracts are, practically speaking, required to be JIS-mark certified. Products in compliance with JIS standards are given preferential treatment in procurement decisions under the Industrial Standardization Law.

JIS covers most industrial products (with the exception of goods regulated under other laws or standards); the list of covered products continues to grow. In early 1995, the Japanese Ministry of International Trade (MITI) proposed a "voluntary" system in which independent auditors would certify the production processes of software manufacturers.

Standards in the European Union

Roughly $70 billion of the $100 billion in American exports to Europe are affected by standards, testing, and certification issues. Currently, the European Union is attempting to harmonize all product standards in Europe under the CE mark. On the surface, one set of product standards should make it easier to trade in Europe. However, some American manufacturers fear that under the wrong EU regime, the CE mark could be used as a means of keeping U.S. goods out of Europe. At the very least, a harmonized system such as this potentially closes avenues of trade. For example, it will no longer be possible to avoid Germany's product standards by selling in France or Sweden.

Industries and products most affected by standards requirements include:

- Telecommunications
- Computer equipment
- Medical devices
- Pharmaceuticals
- Electronics

In response to the EU's efforts, the U.S. government wants to ensure that U.S.-based companies have full access to the testing and certification system. There is concern that product or production standards (i.e., ISO 9000), testing, and certification requirements present barriers to trade for U.S. companies. "Transparency," or clarity and consistency, is also a key issue. Transparency in the standards process would greatly benefit small and medium-size firms that cannot afford a battery of international lawyers and engineers to help them wend their way through complex and costly certification procedures.

To address these concerns, the United States and EU are negotiating Mutual Recognition Agreements (MRAs), under which the United States and EU member nations will recognize each other's standards and testing certifications procedures.

12.6.3 *Other Nontariff Trade Barriers*

Standards are not the only kind of nontariff trade barrier. Countries use many mechanisms (some of which were described earlier) to protect internal markets and regulate imports. To varying degrees all countries use them, so exporters can expect to encounter some form of nontariff trade barrier in the course of exporting goods.

Nontariff trade barriers comprise some of the biggest hidden costs of exporting. To the extent that their resources allow, exporters should become familiar with all the regulations, from importing to the actual sale, that affect their goods.

The following examples illustrate some of the types of nontariff trade barriers U.S. businesses may confront.

EXAMPLE

The World Bank estimates that Indonesian nontariff trade barriers, especially in the industrial and agricultural sectors, affect roughly 30–50 percent of production in both industries. The barriers result in high costs and inefficient business processes.

Nontariff trade barriers in Indonesia include:

1. *Import surcharges.* Import surcharges, also called supplemental import duties, apply to 200 Customs tariff lines and range from 5–100 percent.

2. *Taxes.* In addition to a 10 percent value-added tax on all imported goods, a luxury tax of up to 35 percent is imposed on certain goods. A sales tax is also collected at the point of import. The amount of the sales tax is based on the value of the goods, including Indonesian import duties.

3. *Import licenses.* There are four types of import licenses. The least restrictive are importer producer (IP) licenses. These are available to domestic producers using IP items in their production process. Producer importer (PI) licenses are the most restrictive. Items covered under a PI license can only be sold by domestic producers or through a designated sole importer. Products considered PI goods include:

- Milk and milk products
- Wheat, rice, soybeans, flour, and sugar
- Beer, wine, and spirits
- Petroleum products
- Iron and steel and steel products
- Machinery and heavy equipment

1. *Centralized distribution.* The distribution of important commodities such as wheat and sugar is controlled by the state National Logistics

Agency (BULOG). Until recently, state-owned PT Krakatau Steel controlled the import of iron and steel goods. The monopolistic nature of distribution, and much of the domestic economy, makes it difficult for imported goods to gain market access.

2. *Direct foreign involvement ban.* Historically, only companies that were 100 percent Indonesian-owned were allowed to participate in trading activities (defined as the import, export, distribution, and sale of imported and domestic goods and services). Under a 1987 deregulation ruling, a company with at least 51 percent Indonesian ownership, or with 45 percent Indonesian ownership and 20 percent of its stock held through an Indonesian stock exchange, can be considered a domestic company. A company must be designated as "domestic" in order to distribute its own goods without an agent. However, many of these companies still cannot sell at the retail level. They can sell to end users only if their products are raw materials or components.

3. *Local content requirements.* Local content requirements (i.e., regulations that compel foreign manufacturers to use local goods) are in effect for dairy products and soybean cake.

EXAMPLE

In Japan, nontariff trade barriers include:

- Slow customs clearance for air cargo.
- Strict requirements on container sizes. Under these rules, cargo shipped into Japan must be transferred to smaller containers for road travel; this requirement increases costs and delays.
- Laws that significantly restrict the opening of large retail stores by foreign merchandisers. These laws make it difficult for U.S. merchandisers to gain access to the world's second-largest economy.
- A tightly regulated automobile inspection system, which the United States claims creates unfair barriers to U.S. auto parts suppliers.

Note. In March 1995, the Japanese government announced a five-year plan to eliminate a number of these trade barriers.

EXAMPLE

In Switzerland, cartels are tolerated, provided they do not meet the Swiss standard of being "harmful to society." The food industry in Switzerland is controlled by cartels of producers, wholesalers, processors, and retailers. These organizations have succeeded in maintaining nontariff barriers such as an import calendar that is designed to favor domestic production.

EXAMPLE

The government affiliated Korean Broadcasting Advertising Service (KOBACO) has a monopoly on television and radio advertising time. As a result, U.S. firms cannot get prime-time advertising slots. Industrial associations also have substantial regulatory authority in Korea and regularly discriminate against nonmembers and foreign competition. In 1994 an investigation initiated by the Korean government found that forty-eight out of sixty-eight such associations had engaged in unfair or anti-competitive practices.

The government of Ghana allows foreign investment in all economic sectors except for four that are reserved for Ghanaians: petty trading, operation of taxi services, lotteries (excluding football pools), and operation of beauty salons and barber shops.

''Buy Domestic'' Plans

Under ''buy domestic'' plans, a country or company compels its buyers to purchase goods and services from domestic sources only; imports are excluded. Foreign purchases are permitted only if the buyer can demonstrate that no domestic sources exist.

The government of Brazil has a ''buy national'' policy with regard to government procurement. Given the size of the state-controlled sector, the discriminatory policy poses a major barrier to U.S. exports. Under the policy there are specific preferences in place for telecommunications and computer equipment and digital electronics.

On February 15, 1995, the government proposed a package of constitutional amendments that would open state-dominated sectors of the economy to foreign investment and competition. The proposed amendments would eliminate the distinction between foreign and national capital. As a result, companies with production facilities in Brazil, whatever their source of capital would receive ''buy national'' preferential treatment.

Cartels and Business Associations

In October 1997, the U.S. government threatened trade sanctions against Japan because of Japan Harbor Transportation Association (JHTA) rules. All ships from the United States and other nations that enter Tokyo Bay to unload cargo must notify and receive clearance from the JHTA, which has the authority to act as the exclusive agent for all Japanese ports.

In addition, the ships must abide by JHTA rules that restrict the hours when ships can be unloaded. Most ports are closed for up to eight-and-a-half hours per day and are closed on Sunday. There have also been numerous allegations that the JHTA has ties to Japanese organized crime organizations.

The result of JHTA ''prior consultation'' requirements is that costs to U.S. shippers are much higher. The average port-handling cost at docks in Tokyo Bay is around $450 for a forty-foot container, compared with less than $300 for a similar container at ports around Los Angeles. It also takes almost 30 percent longer for a ship to be unloaded in Japan, costing foreign shippers both time and money.

U.S. officials say that the JHTA rules constitute a trade barrier and that dockworkers and unions operating under JHTA rules are in reality a cartel.

In the United States, the large shipping conferences that are empowered to set rates for all ocean-going cargo receive special antitrust immunity from the U.S. government. When exporting goods, U.S. companies cannot negotiate directly with shipping lines; they have to go through the cartels.

The rules prevent shipping lines from developing specialized contracts with large companies for fear that, under Federal Maritime Commission (FMC) rules, the contracts can be viewed and copied by other carriers. Businesses also complain that FMC rules dictate that all contracts must be filed with the commission and are considered public information. Foreign competitors can then use those rates and contract terms to make lower bids and can, in some instances, use the information to deduce the U.S. company's manufacturing costs. (*The Wall Street Journal*, 10/21/97, *Traffic World*, 6/9/97)

Payoffs and Kickbacks

Corruption is pervasive in many parts of the world including India, China, the Middle East, Eastern Europe, and Africa. Providing payoffs and kickbacks in order to facilitate clearance through customs or have projects approved or licensed is a common business practice; in some countries bribes are considered a tax-deductible expense.

Under the 1977 Foreign Corrupt Practices Act, U.S. firms are barred, for any reason, from paying bribes or kickbacks, regardless of what the foreign competition may do. Although small sums may be construed as part of a normal transaction, exporters should be wary of paying suspicious fees that appear to be too large.

The law, which came about after officials of Lockheed Corporation were charged with bribing Japanese politicians, has considerable clout. According to international trade attorneys, the law is vigorously enforced and those found to be in violation can receive hefty fines and prison sentences.

The problem is an especially difficult one for small exporters. Many large multinational corporations have devised methods for "taking care" of foreign officials without violating U.S. law. A major insurance company set up a $1 million educational program at a Chinese University and appointed to the board of directors the very officials who are responsible for granting the company a license. Some offer scholarships to children of foreign officials or pay for expensive junkets to the United States. Others hire agents or "intervening purchasers" (i.e., persons who purchase and then resell contracts to U.S. firms) whose activities are either unknown to the company or difficult to prove.

For small to midsize exporters, gathering as much information as possible about the country or region in question should be a top priority. Exporters are advised to adhere to the letter of U.S. law and, if in doubt, to consult with an attorney experienced in international trade.

12.7 IMPORT RELIEF LAWS

The Trade Act of 1974 established several mechanisms to protect U.S. industries from damage caused by imports. Among them are:

- *The Trade Adjustment Assistance Program.* This program provides monetary support to industries that have been materially harmed from imports.

- *Safeguard actions.* Under Section 201 of the Trade Act, investigations are conducted to ensure that industries are not hurt by imports.

- *Market disruption investigations.* Under Section 406, investigations are used to determine whether imports from a communist country are causing market disruption in a given U.S. industry. ("Market disruption" means that imports of certain goods are causing or threatening injury to an industry.) The U.S. Trade Representative's Office most recently requested a section 406 investigation regarding imports of honey from the People's Republic of China. The investigation concluded that market disruption did exist.

Section 337 Investigations

Section 337 of the Tariff Act of 1930, as amended, authorizes the International Trade Commission, on the basis of a complaint or on its own initiative, to conduct investigations with respect to certain practices in import trade. Section 337 declares unlawful the importation, sale for importation, or sale after importation of articles that infringe a valid and enforceable U.S. patent, registered trademark, registered copyright, or registered mask work for which a domestic industry exists or is in the process of being established. If the Commission determines that a violation exists, it can issue an order excluding the subject imports from entry into the United States, or it can order the violating parties to cease and desist from engaging in the unlawful practices.

Summary of Key Points Raised in This Chapter

Import quotas are used to establish a limit on the amount of a product that may be imported into the United States. Quotas serve to protect U.S. industries from low-cost foreign imports.

Quotas are not absolute bars to importation. Goods in excess of quota levels may be shipped into the United States, but are subject to certain restrictions.

Import quotas are established pursuant to petitions from U.S. industries.

Under a tariff-rate quota, a product can enter the United States in specified quantities, during a given period of time, and at a reduced duty rate. Absolute quotas specify a set amount of a product that may be entered during a given quota period.

Transshipments are a method of quota avoidance, under which goods destined for the United States are shipped to a third country, where they are improperly labeled as having been manufactured in that country.

Under voluntary restraint agreements, exporting countries agree to set quotas on certain classes of goods destined for the United States.

In some cases, import visas are a prerequisite to importing into the United States. However, issuance of a visa does not guarantee that goods will be permitted to enter.

1. Tariffs are duties that must be paid before goods can enter a foreign country.

As trade barriers, tariffs are used to protect domestic industries, as punitive measures, and as a means to further political aims.

2. Antidumping duties are imposed on imported merchandise when it is sold to U.S. buyers at less than fair market value.

3. Countervailing duties are assessed when it has been determined that a foreign company or industry receives a subsidy from its government, giving it unfair advantage over U.S. products.

4. Antidumping and countervailing duties are imposed after investigations by the Commerce Department and the International Trade Commission.

5. Nontariff trade barriers include manufacturing and quality standards, shipping and cargo restrictions, import license procedures, and local content and labor laws.

For Additional Information

For more information on the topics discussed in this chapter, please consult the following publications:

Department of Commerce, *Importing into the U.S.* (1993).
"Report on Current Visa and Exempt Certification Requirements for Textiles" (U.S. Government Printing Office, April 1, 1994).
Department of Commerce, Office of Textile and Apparel, "The MFA and the U.S. Textile Program" (June 1993).
Thomas E. Johnson, *Export/Import Procedures and Documentation*, 2d ed. (New York: AMACOM Books, 1994).
U.S. Customs Service, "Import Quotas" (April 1994).

13

The Entry Process

Key Questions Answered in This Chapter

Introduction

A deal is struck between a U.S.-based importer and a foreign seller for goods, materials, or products that will be imported for sale in the United States. Now the work begins of preparing foreign invoices, securing methods of payment and bonds that will provide surety as the goods travel great distances to market, as well as arranging for shipping and distribution from foreign market to U.S. port and beyond.

This is an exciting time for the importer who anticipates sale of goods or products in the U.S. market. But it is also a precarious time. Importers must beware of rushing the job. As noted in Chapter 5, "International Sales Transactions," and Chapter 11, "Insurance and Bonds," importers must take the time to secure whatever methods of payment and bonds are necessary so they are covered in the event of damage or destruction of property, as well as negligence on the part of a foreign seller.

The next concern should be securing the best possible arrangement for shipping goods from a foreign market to the United States, and then arranging for distribution in this country. It is at this stage that importers, or their assigned parties, deal directly with U.S. Customs, complying with entry procedures and paying duties and tariffs assigned for clearance into the United States.

13.1 MAKING THE SALE

13.1.1 Introduction

Anyone who has purchased items overseas for personal use is familiar with the process of clearing goods through U.S. Customs. Usually, but not always, the tourist is traveling by air. While still airborne, the flight attendants pass out U.S. Customs declaration cards and the tourist, acting on an honor system, must list all goods purchased and their dollar amount. If these purchases exceed the duty-free amount, then the tourist must pay duties on the goods while passing through U.S. Customs at the port of entry.

Purchasing goods for import into the United States is not as simple as buying gifts or items overseas for personal use back home. As will be addressed in the following subsections, the goods, products, and materials must be properly valued and classified, and the sales transaction must be properly documented.

13.1.2 Invoices

Whenever an import transaction takes place, the seller generates an invoice. Customs regulations require invoices to be presented when goods enter the United States. The following are the most common types of invoices required by Customs:

1. *Commercial invoice.* Most commonly, Customs requires the filing of a commercial invoice for all merchandise that does not fall under an exemption. Exemptions include:

- Merchandise valued at $500 or less
- Merchandise not intended for sale or commercial use in its imported condition and for which there will be no commission personally earned from its sale
- Merchandise returned to the United States after being exported for repairs or alterations
- Merchandise returned to the United States because the overseas shipment was aborted
- Merchandise the U.S. government directly imports
- Ballast (not including cargo used for ballast) that is offloaded and delivered for consumption in the United States.

2. *Special summary invoice.* Special summary invoices are required for certain classes of goods under the Harmonized Tariff Schedule. These include:

- Aluminum and alloys
- Certain textiles
- Chemicals

Note. Merchandise requiring a special summary invoice is listed in section 141.89 of the Customs Regulations. Customs offers forms for goods requiring a special summary invoice.

3. *Pro forma invoices.* If a commercial invoice cannot be filed at the time the goods are entered, a pro forma invoice must be filed at the time of entry. A bond is required to ensure that the invoice is filed within 120 days of entry of the goods.

Information to Include on the Invoice

Customs Regulation 141.86 dictates the contents of each invoice. The following information is required:

- The port of entry to which the merchandise is destined.
- The buyer and seller.
- The time and place of sale.
- A detailed description of the merchandise. This description must include the name by which each item is known, the grade or quality, and the marks, numbers, and symbols under which it is sold by the seller or manufacturer to the trade in the country of origin, together with the marks and numbers of the packages in which the merchandise is packed.
- The quantities in weights and measures of the country or place from which the merchandise is packed, or in the weights and measures of the United States.
- The purchase price of each item, in the currency of purchase.
- If merchandise is shipped otherwise than in pursuance of a purchase or agreement to purchase, the value of each item.

● The kind of currency.

● All charges made on the merchandise, itemized by name and amount. This information includes freight, insurance, commission, cases, containers, coverings, and cost of packing, and if not included above, all charges, costs, and expenses incurred in bringing the merchandise from alongside the carrier at the port of exportation in the country of exportation and placing it alongside the carrier at the first U.S. port of entry.

Note. The costs of packing, cases, containers, and inland freight to the port of exportation need not be itemized by amount if included in the invoice price and so identified.

● All rebates, drawbacks, and bounties allowed upon exportation of the merchandise.

● The country of origin of the merchandise.

● All goods or services furnished for production. However, goods and services furnished in the United States are excluded.

Guidance

In practice, invoices are rarely prepared to these exact specifications. Each invoice is different, and it is difficult to get foreign companies, especially ones not used to exporting, to provide all the correct information. Therefore, importers should communicate with sellers to make clear what information is required.

13.1.3 International Payment Methods

No businessperson wants to pay for imports up-front without some assurance that the goods will be delivered as ordered. Within U.S. borders, the law offers certain protections against problems related to payment and delivery. There are far fewer guarantees in the international marketplace. Therefore, importers and exporters rely on several reliable payment methods to cover their expenditures when working internationally.

Cash in Advance

A transaction in which payment is made in cash in advance poses the least risk to the seller, since payment is made prior to shipment of the exported goods. However, this payment method poses great risks to the buyer: Because goods are made available only after payment has been made, the buyer is compelled to rely on the exporter to ship the goods as ordered and has little recourse if the goods do not conform to the order.

Letter of Credit

From the perspective of both the importer and exporter, a letter of credit is one of the safest ways to ensure that the seller is paid and that the buyer receives the goods as ordered. A letter of credit is a contract between the exporter's and importer's banks containing the terms and conditions of the sale. The exporter's risks are minimal, and the buyer is assured of adequate quality and quantity. Goods are available after payment, and payment is made after the appropriate documents are made available at shipment.

The letter of credit process is detailed in Chapter 5, section 5.5.

Sight Draft

A sight draft is similar to a letter of credit in that banks are used to effect payment. Unlike a letter of credit, however, payment is not guaranteed by the buyer's bank. Goods are available after payment, and payment is made when appropriate documents are presented to the importer's bank.

For the buyer, a sight draft is advantageous because it assures him or her that the received goods are adequate in quality and quantity. But the sight draft is somewhat riskier for the seller because if the draft is unpaid, goods must be returned or disposed of, often at a loss. The sight draft payment process is detailed in section 5.6.

Time Draft

A time draft is similar to a sight draft, except that it permits the buyer to make payment within a specified time after receipt of the goods.

For the buyer, this method is advantageous because it allows him or her to check the shipment before payment. There are risks for the seller, though: If the buyer fails to pay, the goods must be returned or disposed of, usually at a loss. The time draft payment process is detailed in section 5.6.

Consignment

In a consignment sale, goods are forwarded to the buyer, but the exporter retains legal title to them. This method presents no risk for the buyer, but substantial risk to the exporter, who is not paid until the consigned goods are sold or used.

Open Account

When the buyer maintains an open account, goods are shipped before payment and the buyer agrees to pay within a certain period of time. The seller bears complete risk in the event that the buyer defaults.

13.2 PACKING, SHIPPING, AND DISTRIBUTION

13.2.1 Packing

One of the best ways to save money in the import process is to expedite the clearance of goods through Customs. Delays in clearance through negligence or omission can mean:

* Fines and penalties
* Lost contracts
* Increased transportation costs
* Spoiled perishables
* Missed marketing opportunities

In addition, a good deal of the importer's own time is spent in trying to untangle any mishaps with U.S. Customs.

There are ways to pack and label imported goods that will save on costs and/ or expedite Customs clearance. For example:

* Invoice goods in a systematic fashion; inconsistent invoices can lead to heightened Customs scrutiny.
* Indicate the exact quantity of each item of goods contained in each box, bale, case, crate, or other form of packing.
* Place marks and numbers on each package.
* Place marks and numbers on each invoice.

Guidance

These packing and labeling guidelines can help importers and exporters avoid a Customs investigation:

* A clearly marked invoice often means there is less chance that U.S. Customs will seek an investigation. This is especially crucial when goods of different types are packaged together or commingled.
* U.S. Customs agents routinely check for narcotics that may be hidden in cargo unbeknownst to the shipper or importer. Narcotics searches often involve complete stripping of a container at added costs, not to mention time lost, to the importer. Importers should anticipate these random searches and pack to speed the process.
* By loading cargo onto pallets (called "palletizing"), importers can expedite U.S. Customs searches of the type described above.
* Another means of expediting Customs investigations is to leave an aisle down the center of a container and enough space at the top to allow a narcotics dog to pass through.

Commingled Goods

Different types of goods that are packed together are considered commingled. Commingling is sometimes the most efficient way to pack and ship imported goods, but it can also mean the highest tariffs. Unless the container is properly marked according to U.S. Customs requirements, Customs agents have the right to assess the entire shipment at the rate that is the highest of all the goods packed together. Importers must decide whether the shipping savings outweigh the potentially higher duties.

Packaging and correct labeling are made much easier when goods of one kind only are packed together, or when goods are imported in packages with uniform values and contents. Packages containing goods of varying kind and value are more likely to be delayed in Customs examinations.

13.2.2 Country-of-Origin Marking

Many importers are unaware that, with few exceptions, merchandise imported into the United States must be marked with its country of origin. Failure to comply with this requirement can result in the delay or detention of merchandise until it is properly marked, as well as the assessment of fines or penalties.

Note. U.S. Customs may seize improperly marked merchandise. Sometimes goods are marked after seizure, but in such cases, importers pay a marking penalty. In other instances, U.S. Customs clears the unmarked goods and then issues a notice for redelivery, which almost always results in a stiff penalty if the importer is not able to redeliver the goods.

The Customs Regulations state that ". . . every article (or its container) of foreign origin imported into the United States shall be marked in a conspicuous place as legibly, indelibly, and permanently as the nature of the article (or its container) will permit, [and] in such manner as to indicate the origin of the article, at the time the importation into the Customs territory of the United States. Containers of articles excepted from marking shall be marked with the name of the country of origin of the article unless the container is also excepted from marking."

For marking purposes, the country of origin is defined as "the country of manufacture, production, or growth of any article of foreign origin entering the United States. Further work or material added to an article in another country must effect a substantial transformation in order to render such other country the country of origin."

U.S. Customs specifies that country-of-origin marking be implemented as follows:

- Imported merchandise must be clearly and conspicuously marked in a permanent manner with the English name of the foreign country of origin.
- Generally, the outermost container that will go to the end user must be marked.

Note. Some product and industry groups have specific country-of-origin markings.

Guidance

Importers should consult the country-of-origin regulations before purchasing foreign products. If possible, foreign manufacturers should be advised to mark the country of origin on goods during the manufacturing process. But in many cases, foreign goods cannot be marked during manufacture; sometimes off-the-shelf inventory cannot be modified after manufacture to comply with U.S. standards.

Identifying the Ultimate Purchaser

Part of the country-of-origin marking procedure involves indicating the "ultimate purchaser" of the goods in the United States. The ultimate purchaser is defined as the last person in the United States who will receive the imported goods. The following are some guidelines for determining the ultimate purchaser:

- In the event goods are imported for use in manufacturing, the U.S.-based manufacturer may be the ultimate purchaser, provided the goods are markedly transformed during manufacture (even though the process may not result in the creation of a new or different article).
- If the goods go through minor transformation during the manufacturing process and are substantially the same as when imported, the consumer is the ultimate purchaser.
- If the goods are imported for immediate retail sale, the retailer is the ultimate purchaser.
- If the imported article is distributed as a gift, then the recipient is the ultimate purchaser.

13.2.3 *Special Government Agency Regulations Affecting Shipping and Packing*

Several U.S. government agencies maintain strict requirements on imports for health and safety reasons. These requirements may affect shipping and packaging. If the products in question contain a variety of ingredients, then there are strict requirements for listing of ingredients and their printed appearance on the outside of a package.

Several main categories of products are regulated by other agencies.

Agricultural Commodities

The following goods are regulated by the Food and Drug Administration and/or the Department of Agriculture:

- Cheese, milk, and dairy products may be subject to quotas and require special import licenses.
- Fruits, vegetables, and nuts must meet requirements pertaining to size, grade, quality, and maturity. The Department of Agriculture is the regulatory agency.
- Live insects are prohibited except for scientific purposes. The Department of Agriculture is the relevant regulatory agency.
- Meat and meat product imports are inspected by the Department of Agriculture before entry into the United States.

EXAMPLE

Company X imports cereal from the Netherlands. Entry is made and the company's customs broker forwards the notice of importation to the local FDA office. The merchandise clears U.S. Customs. However, the FDA requests a sample of the cereal to determine admissibility. The FDA samples the shipment and finds it contains unacceptable levels of insect filth. The FDA notifies Company X that it must export the goods or destroy them under U.S. Customs supervision.

Food, Drugs, and Cosmetics

The Food and Drug Administration enforces the Food, Drug, and Cosmetics Act by prohibiting entry of articles that are adulterated, mislabeled, or misbranded. Shipments that do not comply with FDA regulations are detained until brought into compliance, destroyed, or re-exported. The FDA supervises any sorting, reprocessing, or relabeling at the expense of the importer.

Textiles, Wool, and Fur Products

These products are regulated by the Federal Trade Commission:

* *Textile products.* Under the Textile Fiber Identification Act, all textiles imported into the United States must identify a number of characteristics, from the types of fibers to the identity of the manufacturer.
* *Wool.* Any product containing woolen fiber—with the exception of carpets, rugs, mats, upholsteries, and articles made twenty years before importation—must be tagged, labeled, or clearly marked according to the Wool Products Labeling Act of 1939.
* *Fur.* In accordance with the Fur Products Labeling Act, any piece of apparel made in whole or in part with fur or used fur must be tagged, labeled, or clearly marked.

13.2.4 Distribution: From Foreign Market to U.S. Port

Goods purchased from an overseas seller must be transported to market in the United States. This process is multilayered. Importers must make arrangements for:

* Overseas shipment, whether by ocean or air
* Transport from the seller to the port or airfield
* Clearance through U.S. Customs at the port of destination
* Transport to the final destination

Until recently, different professionals handled each leg of the shipping and distribution process.

As discussed in Chapter 7, the terms of sale arranged between importer and foreign seller specify the level of responsibility the importer bears during the shipping and delivery process.

Depending on that negotiated arrangement, the importer uses whatever outside assistance he or she deems necessary to successfully complete shipment. Importers might handle everything, from overseas transport to the dock to U.S. distribution, or work with import/export and transport specialists.

As mentioned in Chapter 6, "Export Shipping and Distribution," many international transport companies are offering door-to-door service throughout the developed world. Importers who qualify for these services place much of the burden for their international shipment in the hands of one company.

Note. Although small shipments are accepted, many transport companies would prefer to handle large shipments.

EXAMPLE

A coalition of U.S. auto manufacturers decides to import metric-produced tooling steel from Germany. The steel shipment travels from the supplier near Frankfurt to the Port of Hamburg and then on to New York. Frans Maas in the Netherlands and Yellow Freight in the United States, two companies that have formed a shipping alliance, handle the shipment as follows:

⊛ *From the overseas market.* A coalition representative contacts Yellow Freight in the United States to initiate the import from Germany to a Michigan warehouse. Yellow Freight informs Frans Maas of the import request and a company representative reaches the importer's representative to make suitable arrangements. (If the shipment is routine, all arrangements may be made electronically through the Frans Maas sales communication system.) Pickup is arranged through the Frans Maas terminal closest to the seller in Germany. In the meantime, Frans Maas arranges a steamship line and informs the import coalition of a transatlantic shipping time of twenty-eight days. A delivery date is set.

⊛ *At the port of entry and beyond.* The freight arrives in New York. The importer's customs broker clears the shipment. The broker pays duties on behalf of the consignee under a credit arrangement. The broker arranges inland transport to Detroit or Ann Arbor.

Note. Companies such as Yellow Freight handle all of the above work upon the customer's request. Major corporations often have their own customs professionals on staff, as well as their own transport departments.

EXAMPLE

In another scenario, one of the importer's German subsidiaries plans to ship steel auto parts to the United States. Once again, the shipment travels through the Port of Rotterdam to New York. The importer's representative contacts the U.S. office of CaroTrans, an international shipper, who then alerts the CaroTrans Rotterdam office of the order. The CaroTrans Rotterdam office contacts its German agent to arrange for a consolidated shipment and to arrange for the sailing out of Rotterdam. In this case, the German agent also arranges for a customs broker in the United States to clear U.S. Customs.

The consolidated shipment arrives in New York and the goods are trucked to the CaroTrans bonded warehouse in New Jersey. Once at the New Jersey terminal, the containers are stripped and deconsolidated for trucking anywhere in the United States. CaroTrans arranges for direct delivery to Flint, Michigan. The company has the option of either using CaroTrans trucks or what's called a "basket" of carriers (i.e., other companies) to cover the short haul.

13.3 THE CUSTOMS ENTRY PROCESS

When a shipment reaches the United States, the importer of record must file entry documents with the district or port director at the port of entry. The importer of record may be:

- The owner
- Purchaser
- Licensed customs broker
- Consignee

Imported goods are not legally entered until after the shipment has arrived within the port of entry, U.S. Customs has authorized delivery of the merchandise, and estimated duties are paid. It is the importer's responsibility (with the help, if desired, of customs professionals) to arrange for examination and release of the goods.

Note. It cannot be stressed enough that a customs broker bears responsibility along with the importer for false declarations or any other breach of the law. As a result, importers may find customs brokers more cautious in all aspects of the entry process, especially in the country-of-origin identification of product parts in areas that may be considered questionable in the eyes of U.S. Customs and other U.S. government agencies.

13.3.1 Evidence Required to Make Entry

In most cases, the owner of the goods, the purchaser, or a licensed customs broker facilitates entry into the United States. The owner may be the actual party that owns the property or someone authorized to act in the owner's behalf. Here are the steps of entry for an average shipment:

1. When the goods are consigned to order, the bill of lading may serve as evidence of the right to make entry. An airway bill may be used for air shipments.

Note. A bill of lading is only considered official when the consignee properly endorses it.

2. Whoever is charged with making official entry on behalf of the owner is considered the carrier of a "carrier's certificate." This party may also carry a duplicate bill of lading or a shipping receipt.

3. Actual entry is a two-part process that involves:

- Filing the documents necessary to determine whether merchandise may be released from U.S. Customs custody

* Filing the documents which contain information for duty assessment and statistical purposes

Note. An average shipment that does not require special licenses can be entered via the Automated Broker Interface program of the Automated Commercial System (ACS).

13.3.2   Entry Documents

The following entry documents must be filed within five working days after a shipment arrives at a U.S. port:

1. Entry Manifest (Customs Form 7533,) or Application and Special Permit for Immediate Delivery Customs Form 3461, or any other form of merchandise release the district director may require. (See the sample Form 13.01 included in this chapter.)
2. Evidence of the right to make entry.
3. Commercial invoice, or a pro forma invoice when the commercial invoice cannot be produced.
4. Packing lists, if appropriate.
5. Other documents that may be necessary to determine the admissibility of merchandise.
6. Evidence that a bond is posted with U.S. Customs to cover any potential duties, taxes, or penalties that may accrue.

Once goods are released from U.S. Customs, the owner files an entry summary for consumption and estimated duties must be deposited at the port of entry within ten working days of the time the goods are entered and released. The following entry summary documents are presented to U.S. Customs at this time:

* Entry summary or Customs Form 7501 (a sample entry summary is included in this chapter as Form 13.02)
* Other invoices and documents necessary for the assessment of duties, collection of statistics, or proof that all import requirements are satisfied

13.3.3   Immediate Release Into the U.S.

Besides taking advantage of automated entry systems such as ACS, importers can also apply to U.S. Customs for a Special Permit for Immediate Delivery on Customs Form 3461 (see the sample Form 13.01 at the end of this chapter). Application may be made before the arrival of the merchandise. Carriers participating in the Automated Manifest System (AMS) can receive conditional release authorizations after the goods leave the foreign country, up to five days before the shipment arrives in the United States. Approval means far speedier entry and release into the States. The entry summary procedure is then followed.

Company X imports footwear from Hong Kong. The customs broker prepares Customs Form 3461 for electronic submission to U.S. Customs in the Port of Boston. After determining through electronic selectivity that no physical inspection is required and that the requisite Customs bond is in place, the U.S. Customs Service conditionally releases the shipment under the immediate delivery procedure. Customs duties are payable within ten working days from the date of release of the shipment.

Release under Customs Form 3461 is limited to the following merchandise:

- Goods arriving from Canada or Mexico, if the district director approves the shipment and an appropriate bond is filed.
- Fresh fruits and vegetables arriving from Canada and Mexico that are removed immediately from the area contiguous to the border to the importer's facilities.
- U.S. government imports.
- Goods or products designated for use at a trade fair.
- Tariff-rate quota merchandise and, under some circumstances, merchandise subject to an absolute quota. (Absolute quota merchandise requires a formal entry at all times.)
- Merchandise for consumption that is released from a warehouse within ten working days under a "warehouse withdrawal for consumption" stipulation.
- Merchandise U.S. Customs headquarters has assigned immediate release status.

Note. Quota merchandise that is perishable may, at the U.S. Customs' district director's discretion, be entered under the immediate delivery procedure. Given the nature of the goods, the date of presentation is a major determining factor in terms of acceptability.

13.3.4 Entering a Warehouse

Sometimes it is desirable, or even necessary, to postpone the release of goods into the United States. Under these circumstances, goods are placed in a U.S. Customs bonded warehouse under a special warehouse entry document. The following goods, however, are not allowed into a bonded warehouse:

- Perishables
- Explosive substances
- Prohibited importations

Goods may remain in a bonded warehouse up to five years from the date of importation. Throughout this period goods may be re-exported without payment of duty or withdrawn for consumption into the United States. Duties are paid at that time at the duty rate in effect on the date of withdrawal. No duties are assessed if the goods are somehow damaged or destroyed while under U.S. Customs protection. Goods may be cleaned, sorted, repacked, and moved while in the warehouse.

EXAMPLE

An importer purchases 300 cases of 100 percent cotton unnapped embroidered sheets from the United Kingdom. The duty rate is 23.5 percent under Harmonized Tariff Schedule (HTS) No. 6302.31.5020.

The importer could move into a bonded warehouse and pay U.S. Customs duties only in amounts withdrawn for consumption as needed. This approach delays duty liability. It is up to the importer to weigh the duty deferment advantages against the costs of bonded storage.

For more information on bonded warehouses, see section 10.5.

13.3.5   Mail Entries

For goods valued at $1,250 or less, it is often possible to import goods into the United States via the mail system. Usually, duty is collected at the time of delivery and no customs broker is involved.

For mail importation valued above $1,250, a notice is sent to the importer advising that formal entry is required. The importer then contacts a customs professional to facilitate entry through the Postal Service.

13.3.6   Entry Mishaps

Goods may end up in a general order warehouse, or even be sold at public auction, under the following conditions:

1. If the owner fails to file an entry for the goods at the port of entry or port of destination for inbound shipments within five working days after arrival.
2. If goods are not entered within one year from the date of importation.
3. If the goods are perishables, liable to depreciation, or explosive substances that U.S. Customs has seized. Such goods may be sold sooner.
4. Where the documentation does not clearly identify the consignee/customs broker. In this case the transport line does not know whom to contact to advise of arrival in the United States.
5. Where the documentation is inaccurate.

Note. If the goods remain at the terminal for a period of time and the importer does not take steps to move the goods into a bonded warehouse, then they will go into "general order." U.S. Customs assesses importers charges for storage, sales expenses, IRS taxes, duties, and other fees when goods are seized, stored, and then resold. Any surplus, post sale, is usually paid to the official holder of the bill of lading that covers the goods. Goods may be destroyed if the cost of sale exceeds the amount that would be received at public auction.

EXAMPLE

> Foreign Company X returns a shipment of PC boards to U.S. Company Y. The U.S. firm did not authorize the return and requests its broker not to make entry on the goods. Foreign Company X does not want the goods returned. The terminal operator eventually moves the goods to a general order warehouse. If the goods go unclaimed, U.S. Customs will auction off the merchandise.

Summary of Key Points Raised in This Chapter

Customs regulations require importers to provide detailed commercial invoices when goods enter the United States.

Some goods do not require an invoice. These include merchandise valued at $500 or less, merchandise not intended for sale, merchandise returned after being exported for repair or alteration, and rejected merchandise.

Certain international payment methods protect the importer when goods do not conform to the sales contract. These methods include letters of credit, sight drafts, and time drafts.

Customs agents routinely check for narcotics that may be hidden in cargo unbeknownst to the shipper or importer.

Commingling (i.e., packing different types of goods together) is an efficient way to ship imported goods, but it can also mean higher tariffs.

With few exceptions, merchandise imported into the United States must be marked with its country of origin and the identity of the ultimate purchaser.

When transporting goods purchased from an overseas seller, importers must arrange for overseas transport, transport from the seller to the foreign port or airfield, clearance through Customs at the port of destination, and transport to the final destination.

1. When a shipment reaches the United States, importers of record must file entry documents with the district or port director at the port of entry.

2. Imported goods are not legally entered until U.S. Customs has authorized delivery and estimated duties are paid.

3. Entry documents must be filed within five working days after a shipment arrives in a U.S. port. Documents required include an entry manifest, evidence of the right to make entry, a packing list, and evidence of the posting of a customs bond.

4. Importers can use a Special Permit for Immediate Release to expedite delivery of shipments.

5. Goods valued at $1,250 or less may be imported by mail.

For Additional Information

For more information on topics discussed in this chapter, please refer to the following publications:

Thomas E. Johnson, *Export/Import Procedures and Documentation*, 2d. ed. (New York: AMACOM, 1994).

U.S. Customs Service, *Importing into the U.S.* (1994).

Form 13.01 Entry/immediate delivery form (Customs form 3461).

TABS: ▼ ▼ ▼ ▼ ▼ ▼

DEPARTMENT OF THE TREASURY
UNITED STATES CUSTOMS SERVICE

Form Approved
OMB No. 1515-0069

ENTRY/IMMEDIATE DELIVERY

19 CFR 142.3, 142.16, 142.22, 142.24

1. ARRIVAL DATE	2. ELECTED ENTRY DATE	3. ENTRY TYPE CODE/NAME	4. ENTRY NUMBER

5. PORT	6. SINGLE TRANS. BOND	7. BROKER/IMPORTER FILE NUMBER	
	8. CONSIGNEE NUMBER		9. IMPORTER NUMBER

10. ULTIMATE CONSIGNEE NAME	11. IMPORTER OF RECORD NAME

12. CARRIER CODE	13. VOYAGE/FLIGHT/TRIP	14. LOCATION OF GOODS—CODE(S)/NAME(S)

15. VESSEL CODE/NAME	
16. U.S. PORT OF UNLADING	17. MANIFEST NUMBER	18. G.O. NUMBER	19. TOTAL VALUE

20. DESCRIPTION OF MERCHANDISE

21. TL/AWB CODE	22. IT/BL/AWB NO.	23. MANIFEST QUANTITY	24. TSUSA NUMBER	25. COUNTRY OF ORIGIN	26. MANUFACTURER ID.

27. CERTIFICATION	28. CUSTOMS USE ONLY

27. CERTIFICATION

I hereby make application for entry/immediate delivery. I certify that the above information is accurate, the bond is sufficient, valid, and current, and that all requirements of 19 CFR Part 142 have been met.

SIGNATURE OF APPLICANT

X

PHONE NO.	DATE

29. BROKER OR OTHER GOVT. AGENCY USE

28. CUSTOMS USE ONLY

☐ OTHER AGENCY ACTION REQUIRED, NAMELY:

☐ CUSTOMS EXAMINATION REQUIRED.

☐ ENTRY REJECTED, BECAUSE:

DELIVERY AUTHORIZED	SIGNATURE	DATE

Paperwork Reduction Act Notice: This information is needed to determine the admissibility of imports into the United States and to provide the necessary information for the examination of the cargo and to establish the liability for payment of duties and taxes. Your response is necessary.

Customs Form 3461 (112085)

Form 13.02   Entry summary (Customs form 7501).

DEPARTMENT OF THE TREASURY
UNITED STATES CUSTOMS SERVICE

ENTRY SUMMARY

1. Entry No. | 2. Entry Type Code | 3. Entry Summary Date

4. Entry Date | 5. Port Code

6. Bond No. | 7. Bond Type Code | 8. Broker/Importer File No.

9. Ultimate Consignee Name and Address | 10. Consignee No. | 11. Importer of Record Name and Address | 12. Importer No.

13. Exporting Country | 14. Export Date

15. Country of Origin | 16. Missing Documents

State

17. I.T. No. | 18. I.T. Date

19. B L or AWB No. | 20. Mode of Transportation | 21. Manufacturer I.D. | 22. Reference No.

23. Importing Carrier | 24. Foreign Port of Lading | 25. Location of Goods/G.O. No.

26. U.S. Port of Unlading | 27. Import Date

28. Line No.	29. Description of Merchandise 30. (A) T.S.U.S.A. No. (B) ADA CVD Case No.	31. (A) Gross Weight (B) Manifest Qty.	32. Net Quantity in T.S.U.S.A. Units	33. (A) Entered Value (B) CHGS (C) Relationship	34. (A) T.S.U.S.A. Rate (B) ADA/CVD Rate (C) I.R.C. Rate (D) Visa No.	35. Duty and I.R. Tax Dollars	Cents

36. Declaration of Importer of Record (Owner or Purchaser) or Authorized Agent

I declare that I am the

☐ importer of record and that the actual owner, purchaser, or consignee for customs purposes is as shown above.

OR ☐ owner or purchaser or agent thereof.

I further declare that the merchandise

☐ was obtained pursuant to a purchase or agreement to purchase and that the prices set forth in the invoice are true.

OR ☐ was not obtained pursuant to a purchase or agreement to purchase and the statements in the invoice as to value or price are true to the best of my knowledge and belief.

I also declare that the statements in the documents herein filed fully disclose to the best of my knowledge and belief the true prices, values, quantities, rebates, drawbacks, fees, commissions, and royalties and are true and correct, and that all goods or services provided to the seller of the merchandise either free or at reduced cost are fully disclosed. I will immediately furnish to the appropriate customs officer any information showing a different state of facts.

Notice required by Paperwork Reduction Act of 1980. This information is needed to ensure that importers/exporters are complying with U.S. Customs laws, to allow us to compute and collect the right amount of money, to enforce other agency requirements, and to collect accurate statistical information on imports. Your response is mandatory.

U.S. CUSTOMS USE

A. Liq. Code | B. Ascertained Duty

C. Ascertained Tax

D. Ascertained Other

E. Ascertained Total

41. Signature of Declarant, Title, and Date

TOTALS

37. Duty

38. Tax

39. Other

40. Total

RECORD

Customs Form 7501 (030984)

Index